The Pill, Pygmy Chimps, and Degas' Horse

The
Autobiography
of
Carl Djerassi

THE PILL, PYGMY CHIMPS, AND DEGAS' HORSE

BasicBooks
A Division of HarperCollins*Publishers*

BY THE SAME AUTHOR

FICTION

The Futurist and Other Stories
Cantor's Dilemma

POETRY

The Clock Runs Backward

NONFICTION

The Politics of Contraception
Steroids Made It Possible

Excerpts of several chapters appeared first in modified or abbreviated form in the following magazines:

Exquisite Corps: "Kinshasa to Brussels" (an excerpt from "Pygmy Chimps") and "Wien, Wien, nur du allein . . ."
Grand Street: "The Quest for Alfred E. Neuman"
The Hudson Review: "Dear Mrs. Roosevelt," "My Very First Divorce" (an excerpt from "Like Father, Like Son"), "The Big Drop," and "A Scattering of Ashes"
Michigan Quarterly Review: "Cleansing My Doors of Perception" (an excerpt from "What Kind of Chemist Are You?")
Negative Capability: "White House Enemy" (an excerpt from "Like Father, Like Son")
New Letters: "Degas' Horse"
The Southern Review: "Freud and I"

Sections of "Birth of the Pill" first appeared in *The Politics of Contraception* (New York: W. W. Norton, 1979).

The poems "The Twins," "Godfather," and "I Have Nothing Left to Say" were first published in *The Wallace Stevens Journal, New Letters*, and *Negative Capability*, respectively.

Library of Congress Cataloging-in-Publication Data
Djerassi, Carl.
 The pill, pygmy chimps, and Degas' horse: the
autobiography of Carl Djerassi.
  p. cm.
  Includes index.
  ISBN 0–465–05759–4
  1. Djerassi, Carl. 2. Chemists—United States—Biography.
3. Oral contraceptives. 4. Steroids. I. Title
QD22.D63A3 1992
540'.92—dc20
[B]   91–58542
                                               CIP

For Dale and Alexander Djerassi
For Gordon Harvey
And, as always, for Diane and Leah Middlebrook

Contents

Introduction

IN THE AUTUMN of 1981, I spent some weeks trekking in western Bhutan near the Tibetan border. As we crossed ever higher passes on the way to Chomo Lhari, Bhutan's highest and holiest Himalayan peak, I experienced an unforeseen clearing of my mind. For many hours, I walked in total solitude in a majestic and humbling setting. The only man-made sound was my labored breathing and the crunch of my boots against the loose rock. For once in my life, I had time for day-long reflections, from which chemistry had virtually vanished. This experience was so powerful that four years later I was ready to embark on another period of physical exertion and psychic housecleaning, this time to cross from Tibet into Nepal. But on the day of my intended departure for Asia, I was hospitalized for cancer surgery. Instead of waking up on a Himalayan mountain, I found myself coming out of anesthesia with tubes in my nose, arms, and belly. The weeks in the hospital provided another type of journey—one of onco-prompted self-exploration—which, though originating in the depth of depression, caused me to write some memoirs that eventually grew into a full-fledged autobiography.

What sparked this public disclosure? In most people there's probably something of both exhibitionist and voyeur. In literature, exhibitionism is often manifest as autobiography which, depending on contents and treatment, can attract a range of voyeurs. Considering how compulsively private, even secretive, I was in the past, does the publication of this volume suggest a sudden burst of exhibitionism? If it does, I am likely to be the last to recognize such open display. The pedagogue in me is pursuing another question: Is there something useful to be learned from my life as a scientist?

I believe there is on two grounds: First, my working style for decades was rather different from that of the majority of my scientific peers. Second, through luck and right timing, I was involved from the beginning with one of the most important technosocial achievements of the postwar years: the Pill.

The first synthesis of a steroid oral contraceptive—now known generically all over the world as the Pill—is by no means my most significant *scientific* accomplishment. Nor is the synthesis of cortisone from a plant raw material, although in the early 1950s this was considered a chemical *tour de force*. As indicated already by the title, this volume is not a conventional scientific autobiography, since the science I did over nearly five decades occupies only a few chapters, albeit long ones. But from a *societal* perspective, the creation of the Pill had an impact that will persist well into the next century for reasons that the public and our government—at their peril—generally ignore. Just as the first explosion of an atomic bomb indelibly marked many physicists—overnight converting ivory-tower academics into persons tainted by the societal impact of their research—so the chemical birth of the Pill on 15 October 1951 in our laboratory in Mexico City has caused me to become progressively more occupied with the social ramifications of such scientific inquiry. In chapters 9 and 15—"The Pill at Twenty" and "The Pill at Forty"—I record how my thoughts and attitudes as well as those of society have changed over the last forty years.

My scientific work and interest were not limited to human birth control. Controlling insect reproduction in novel ways—in fact, in ways that conceptually resemble human contraception—has been a topic of my life as an industrial entrepreneur. Among the many kudos I have received over the years as a scientist, I am particularly pleased that two presidential recognitions at the White House dealt with birth control: the National Medal of Science in 1973 for advancing birth control in humans, and the National Medal of Technology in 1991 for paying attention to novel approaches in insect control. In this age of chemophobia, these offer balm to my bruised chemical ego.

How has a person, who considers himself intellectually a basic scientist, been able to accomplish significant applied results? I have always displayed a tendency for intellectual bigamy, indeed polygamy; and much of what I write in this volume can be construed as an ode in praise of such polygamous behavior. That this is not necessarily a prescription for unqualified happiness will be obvious to every reader; still, I hope that the excitement and diversity of such a life comes across on these pages.

Like any chef wishing to present a tempting, but also full banquet, I have inserted items to cool the palate and allow for periods of digestion after some particularly heavy course. In this autobiography, some of these interludes serve the purpose of demonstrating that I do not take myself too seriously. If I did, why would I disclose my mishaps in movieland or the preening of my peacock feathers? On the heavy side of the menu, I have even tried a daring experiment: to describe the scientific high points of cortisone and the Pill in two chapters with the aid of chemical structures of steroids, presented so as to require no chemical knowledge whatsoever on the part of the reader.

Finally, with this autobiography I want to make a point that is particularly relevant in these days of scientific illiteracy and anti-intellectualism: scientists are not necessarily narrow specialists, communicating in an incomprehensible language and dealing in the cloistered ambiance of their laboratories with subjects far removed from everyday concerns. They can be as widely curious, and as self-centeredly imperfect, as scholars and thinkers in any intellectual endeavor and, at the same time, involve themselves with burning social issues. This latter concern led to my gradual transition from a typically "hard" scientist to one with substantial "soft" overtones—a transformation I try to trace in this autobiographical record through my shifting attitude toward birth control in general and the Pill in particular.

CHAPTER 1

Freud and I

I T IS 3 JULY 1988 when I arrive at Vienna's Schwechat airport from San Francisco. Although I am fogged by jet lag, the date hits me as I fill out the car rental agreement: tomorrow will be the fiftieth anniversary of my departure from Hitler's Vienna. Of course, then the fourth of July figured to me, a European Jew, as the day my mother and I left that city to escape the Nazis. But today, as I arrive in Vienna, an American, the emotional resonances are complicated, my psychic response a mixture of pride and nasty fault searching, covered with a *Schlag* of nostalgia.

It starts with passport control. During our stopover in Hamburg, my passport had been examined with Teutonic thoroughness, every page turned, my bearded face scrutinized and compared with my picture. At the Vienna airport, I see the passengers ahead of me flashing their travel documents at the bored official behind the glass partition, who simply waves them on. "*Schlamperei*" (an untranslatable Austrian version of "sloppiness"), I want to say, but I am also touched by the man's trust in this age of kidnapers and bomb throwers. With my third wife—a native Westerner, born in Idaho, educated in Washington State, and now a Californian—I drive to the village of Kirchberg am Wechsel. The signs on the *Autobahn* begin to fire off neurons in my brain: Favoriten, Wiener Neustadt, Bucklige Welt, Aspang . . . places I hiked on Sundays and holidays during the 1930s.

Arriving at our *Gasthof*, we sit down for lunch. The choices in our small inn are limited to various *Schnitzel*. At the sight of my *Naturschnitzel mit Champignons*, drowned in cream sauce, the Viennese in me salivates, even as the weight-conscious, lipophobic Californian draws back in horror. I assuage my calorie guilt complex by deciding to behave abstemiously at dinner. After a few hours of deep sleep, we stroll to the restaurant where the other visiting academics are assembled, to face the second Austrian menu of the day. "No main dish," I proclaim to my wife in a voice full of virtuousness, "just soup and a modest dessert." I should have known better, but I had not been back to Austria for a long time: "just" and "modest"—at least in matters culinary—have a very different meaning in this country. The soup is *Leberknödel Suppe*, which I, born with a soupspoon in my mouth, have not tasted for decades. Attacking the huge liver dumpling, I rediscover Archimedes' principle: I have consumed hardly half the *Knödel* when I find the remaining broth barely covering the bottom of the soup plate. Culinary symmetry and gustatory nostalgia lead me to choose *Germknödel* for dessert. *Knödel*, the German word for "dumpling," has no plural, like *sheep* in English. Since my departure from Vienna in 1938, I have tasted on occasion *Marillenknödel* or *Zwetschkenknödel*—small dessert dumplings stuffed with apricots or plums; but my last *Germknödel* dates back to the pre-Anschluss days. I have forgotten that this comes as one giant *Knödel*, squatting over the entire plate, generously freckled with poppy seeds, drenched in butter, and, most delectable, stuffed with *Powidl*, the Austrian plum jam. In California, I would have gone on a four-day fast to make up for this megacaloric sin, but here, in Kirchberg am Wechsel, instead of sinking like a stone to the bottom of my stomach, the first bite of the *Germknödel* immediately penetrates my blood-brain barrier. Like a crack smoker after the first puff, I experience an instant high.

Next day, 4 July, in self-defense against the guilt-inducing starch and protein diet of our Austrian country fare, I shop for fresh fruit at the only grocery in town. As I pay for the cherries with a fifty-schilling note, a familiar face passes through my hands. On the sidewalk outside, I take out my billfold to look at the Austrian banknotes. The twenty-schilling note bears the face of Carl Ritter v. Ghega, a name totally meaningless to me, as is Eugen Bohm v. Bawerk on the hundred-schilling note. Both men are bearded, as am I, and as is the man on the fifty-schilling note, Sigmund Freud, whose face pulls the memory trigger and holds it. Last night my wife, who has brought along Peter Gay's biography of him, showed me a reference to Freud's school in the Zweite Bezirk, the second district, also known as Leopoldstadt—the predominantly Jewish quarter of pre-Anschluss Vienna. Freud went to the Leopoldstädter Communal-Real-und-Obergymnasium in Taborstrasse 24, which subsequently moved around the corner to the Sperlgasse. (After the First World War and the departure of the Hapsburgs, it was commonly called the Sperlrealgymnasium: a *Gymnasium* requires both Latin and Greek; a *Realgymnasium* substitutes a modern language for Greek.) I entered that same school at age ten, when, as in Freud's days, three quarters of the Sperlrealgymnasium's student body was Jewish. Freud graduated from "our" school at age seventeen and had invariably received the grade of *musterhaft* ("exceptional") in *Betragen* ("behavior"—the first entry in our report card); I left Vienna in 1938, not yet fifteen, never having achieved better than a *befriedigend* ("satisfactory") in *Betragen*. I had not thought about the Sperlrealgymnasium for years until the *Freudlichkeit* of Kirchberg started to radiate through me. And I recall another vicarious connection with Freud: my father, even into his nineties, would tell me of going, as a Bulgarian medical student at the University of Vienna, to some of Freud's lectures.

Now I am sitting in another school, the Volksschule ("elementary school") in Kirchberg am Wechsel, where the Fifth European-American Conference on Literature and Psychoanalysis is about to begin. As a chemist, I am here as consort to my new wife, who is to read a paper. I am rather pleased at this role reversal, with me serving as academic impedimenta. In the middle of the first lecture, on the function of language in psychoanalysis, I tiptoe out in search of privacy, to put on paper in my own language some record of the associations pressing on my mind. I find a young woman making preparations for the coffee break: a *Jause* composed of open-faced sandwiches covered with *Liptauer* and other cheeses, two kinds of cake, and lots of *Schlagobers*, the whipped-cream signature of Austrian desserts. "I can let you into this classroom," she says, unlocking a door, then laughs apologetically. "The pupils' desks are too low for you, but you can use the teacher's table."

Left alone, I think of another Viennese of Jewish descent, Ludwig Wittgenstein, and his "lost years" from 1919 to 1926, when he temporarily dropped philosophy after completing his *Tractatus logico-philosophicus* to serve as a *Volksschule* teacher in this very area of Kirchberg. Through the window I see the sunlight reflecting from the copper steeple of St. Wolfgang's church in the woods. The trees are taller, and occasional motor vehicles now interrupt the twittering of the birds; but otherwise, Wittgenstein must have seen exactly the same view in the early 1920s. All local public school teachers were summoned to this school in Kirchberg by the new Social Democratic authorities to discuss the postwar educational re-

forms. (Wittgenstein, I learn today from a local philosopher at the Wittgenstein Museum, opposed them strongly.)

I think of teachers from my time and cannot remember a single name.
I recall the geographer who terrified us with his jailer's voice, only to end
up himself in a jail and then in a gas oven. And our spindly home-room
cum Latin teacher, with his bobbing Adam's apple, high voice, and panicky
look, who kept recording my misbehavior in the class record book. A
mother's visit was required after three such entries. But my mother was no
hausfrau; she was a physician turned dentist; she did not appreciate sum-
monses from her son's teacher, and let me know it. I went to heroic lengths
to pay my teacher back for these domestic problems. Though not yet in my
teens, for example, I learned shorthand in order to insert hieroglyphic
translations of the Latin texts between the lines of my book—my private
way of thumbing my nose as well as a bit of brinkmanship. What if he also
knew shorthand? One of the few volumes that has accompanied me from
the Vienna of my boyhood to California via Bulgaria, New Jersey, Missouri, Ohio, Wisconsin, Mexico, and Michigan—is a tattered, paperback
Metamorphoses, of which we had to learn entire sections by heart, and scan
their prosody. I still hear the beat of the opening lines, *In nova fert animus
mutatas dicere formas*, but am unable to decipher a single word of the
German shorthand penciled above it.

An even more elaborate revenge was the way in which I communicated
sub rosa with one of my friends. By the time we were twelve or thirteen,
our teachers took it for granted that everyone would cheat during examinations; it was standard practice to give different questions to alternate rows
of students so that no neighbor would be faced with the same questions. But
there was really no scholastic reason for me to cheat; I did so as a matter
of principle: distrust elicits cunning. In Boy Scouts, I had earned a merit
badge for "Communications," which required competence in semaphore
and Morse code. I used these skills, learned under the readily accepted and
rigid honor code of the Scouts, to be an academic Robin Hood. During
exams I would fold my hands in front of me, thumbs parallel, ostensibly
deep in thought. In reality I was checking to see whether the teacher noticed
my furtive dactylic movements: two raised thumbs were a dash; one elevated thumb was a dot. Two rows away and one seat behind, my friend and
fellow Boy Scout read me with ease. The moment the roving teacher's
searchlight eyes swept past my hands, they froze into immobility, one or
both thumbs pointing toward the ceiling. On 4 July 1988 in Kirchberg am
Wechsel, as these childhood scenes flash by, I wonder what mischief Freud
performed in "our" *Realgymnasium*. His biographer Peter Gay does not
refer to any; there is no entry for *Morse* in his index. The photographic

documentation of the Sigmund Freud Museum in Berggasse 19 in Vienna, though vast, is reverential, showing only Freud's superb grades in his report card from his last year in "our" school. Were we two different versions of "Mama's boy"—Freud nice, and I naughty?

With what picosecond ease I leaped that five-decade gulf! Wichtenstein's school district, Freud's *Realgymnasium*, Morse code, the Boy Scouts—all are signposts of my mental flittering. The Wechsel, where I stand now, and the nearby Schneeberg and Rax, were the mountains where our Scout troop camped in the summer and skied in the winter. Our troop leader was eighteen-year-old Kurt, an opera lover. He managed to attend free the Vienna Staatsoper by joining a claque—a chorus of groupies paid by an opera star, whom they greeted with a standing ovation and screams of *Bravo!* or *Brava!* as the star's gender demanded. Kurt was a Viennese, but his hero was Wagner, not Mozart. I do not know what other Austrian Scouts sang at night around their camp fires, but I got my first introduction to *Tristan und Isolde* in the woods near Kirchberg am Wechsel. This may even be the site of the only photograph I have from my Boy Scout days. It shows me in uniform proudly smiling, right hand lifted in the Scout salute, index and middle finger touching the pancake-brim hat.

I rise from the teacher's chair to scrutinize the desks. Still in 1988 each has an inkwell, like my desk in the Sperlrealgymnasium of the 1930s. The graffiti on the desktops are illegible after the summer cleaning, but a few initials and two full names, Maria and Martin, are still decipherable. The coupling of these two names reminds me of my first conscious pubertal stirrings. I was approaching my teens when my mother sent me for a few weeks to a summer camp near Kirchberg. The names and even the faces of some of my lovers from the intervening five decades have sunk in the depths of memory, but the name of the first woman who made my mouth dry and my hands moist still floats on the surface. Manya Brazlawska, dark-eyed and light-skinned, exuded the incomparable assurance of the older woman. She was, after all, one or possibly even two years older than I—an insurmountable age gap for a twelve-year-old youth feeling the first flush of testosterone. The provocative and forbidding laugh she gave me was a terrifying challenge. There were times when I was certain she would let me kiss her, but nothing happened. The afternoon of my scheduled return to Vienna, during the camp's compulsory rest time, I approached Manya's open ground-floor window with jackhammer heart and dry mouth. She was lying on her stomach, chin propped up by her hands, reading a book. As I appeared at the window with a look that must have been drenched with shameful longing, she rose and tiptoed to the window. "I'm leaving," I stuttered. "I came to . . . " "Yes?" she prompted, the width of the windowsill separating my parched mouth from her moist lips. On 4 July 1988, I am cocksure she was about to kiss me; but in 1935, I simply blushed. "I came to say goodbye," I finally mumbled, reaching out my hand through the open window. "Goodbye," she said and shook my hand. We never met again.

My thoughts turn, as Freud would have predicted, to my mother, who has virtually disappeared from my daily memory since her death over a dozen years ago. My parents, who divorced when I was six, managed to hide that fact from me until my early teens; and there are puzzling lacunae in my knowledge of both of them. My mother was the more mysterious, even though during my childhood and early teenage years I saw a great deal more of her than of my father, who lived in Bulgaria, where I spent my summers between the ages of six and fourteen. I always had an enjoyable time with my Bulgarian cousins, uncles, and aunts, even though Ladino, the language they used among themselves, was *lingua incognita* to me.

The routine of my family life ended with the Anschluss in 1938, when everybody in Vienna started to wear insignia: swastikas for the Nazis and the gentile cowards, the Star of David for the Jews, and various national emblems for the lucky foreigners. After a few months, my mother and I joined that élite when my father arrived in Vienna, remarried my mother long enough to provide her and me with Bulgarian passports, and then took us to Sofia; there my parents promptly terminated the marriage. My mother, who had always displayed contemptuous antipathy for Bulgaria (or any place but Vienna, which she felt to be—as in the song *"Wien, Wien, nur du allein . . ."*—the only place for her), did not change her view of the Balkans. She departed for England to wait for our American visas, while I stayed in the American boarding school in Sofia and relished on weekends and holidays my new status as "Papa's boy." At age sixteen, a few months after the outbreak of the war in September 1939, I again switched parents when I left Europe with my mother.

I do not know the year of my mother's birth. She was the oldest of three daughters and one son of Karl and Sophie Friedmann—a Jewish, middle-class, Viennese family. Somehow, she managed to keep the year a secret from my father—indeed, from all men. One day in America, I came across her M.D. diploma and noticed the date. When I started to calculate the years between her graduation from medical school and her supposed birth-date, I realized that there were at least seven missing years. Otherwise, she would have been the youngest M.D. in the history of the University of Vienna. For the first half-century of her life, my mother did in fact look much younger than her age. A photograph I have depicts her in her late twenties (probably): a smallish woman with a beautiful face and an abundant head of hair; a mysterious look of haughtiness and melancholy in her eyes, which are topped by strongly marked eyebrows. None of the pictures shows her laughing.

My maternal grandfather, for whom I was named, died when I was an infant, and I never met, nor knew the name of, my mother's brother. In fact, I was unaware of my uncle's existence until my father mentioned him once in passing. Some sense of filial delicacy—or was it foreboding?—kept me from raising the subject with my mother. Now I wish I had been more curious.

My grandmother, who died in her sleep when I was eleven, was a warm, silver-haired matriarch, who never raised her voice, never cried, and, in direct contrast to my mother, never complained. The most memorable years of my childhood—from age six on—were spent in *Omama*'s home in Vienna, to which my mother had returned from Sofia after divorcing my father. The huge apartment (which also housed my mother's dental office) consisted of a dozen or more rooms, most of them with such high ceilings that, in spite of the double windows and upholstered bolsters to keep out drafts, it was not feasible in the absence of central heating to keep all of the rooms warm in the winter. Since cold bedrooms were supposed to be healthy, we used thick comforters and hot-water bottles to keep us warm in bed.

Our second-floor apartment had a long balcony overlooking the Donau Kanal, a branch of the Danube separating the fashionable first *Bezirk* from the largely Jewish second one. The day after the Anschluss, I crouched behind the balcony's balustrade to watch the Brown Shirts with the swastika armbands pour across the bridge. In retrospect, it seems strange that I had no foreboding of Hitler's takeover of Austria. Was it the naïveté of life in a household full of apolitical women, or was this another instance of a maternal security blanket thrown over the only child? In pre-Nazi days, my mother had used the balcony as an occasional observation post to watch me prance away from the police in the park across the Donau Kanal. Soccer was *verboten* on the park lawns—a preposterous ban in soccer-mad Austria; and as soon as a player yelled "*Polizei!*," we grabbed the ball and ran. Soccer in that park ended abruptly with the Anschluss, when the mere thought of a Jewish child in the hands of the police caused nightmares. At a recent exhibition of Viennese *fin de siècle* art at the Museum of Modern Art in New York, our corner at Aspernbrückengasse 5 and our illegal soccer field across the Donau Kanal were prominently featured in a drawing by Otto Wagner, Vienna's most famous architect. Overwhelmed by nostalgia, I bought from the museum store a huge supply of postcards bearing a reproduction of that drawing.

The rest of this day—for the first time in decades—I reach back to other members of my mother's family. To my aunt Muschi, a small, clever, and sarcastic woman, who had no children, hardly ever visited my grandmother's home, for some undisclosed reason never spoke to my mother, and only barely re-established contact after her emigration to America following the Anschluss. My favorite aunt was my youngest, Tante Grete. Unmarried and childless, she lived part of the time in my grandmother's apartment and committed suicide in London in her middle thirties. A stunning beauty, European fencing champion, and aspiring actress of unconsummated ambition, she was passionately in love with one of Central Europe's most famous actors, whose death mask eventually lay on the grand piano in our living room in Vienna. I still have a photograph of Tante Grete in her fencing costume, hands resting on her fencing mask, the foil, ready to pierce my heart, under her left arm.

Both my parents were Jewish—my mother arrogantly Ashkenazi, my father aggressively Sephardic. The arrogance and aggressiveness reflected each spouse's opinion of the other's origin. But my home life was virtually nonreligious with two exceptions, one public and the other private. In the Viennese public schools, religious instruction was obligatory. Three times weekly, the Jews were separated from the Catholics, and each group drilled in matters religious. At home, each evening, my mother came to my bed to listen to my recital of a prayer ("*Müde bin ich, geh zur Ruh . . .*"), a German version of the child's prayer "Now I lay me down to sleep. . . ." It almost seemed that the occupant of the other apartment on our floor, Herr Hassan, an elder in Vienna's only Sephardic synagogue (the Türkische Tempel), had sensed this evidence of assimilation, so typical of the Austrian Ashkenazi Jews, and decided to put a stop to it. As I approached my Jewish manhood, my thirteenth birthday, Herr Hassan proposed to my mother that I have a *real* bar mitzvah; all arrangements could safely be left in his hands. My mother, who did not catch the significance of *real*, did not say no, and that was how I ended up with a super bar mitzvah: for one day, I became the central character of the entire service in the "Turkish" synagogue. (Even the term *Turkish*—this generic oversimplification for Sephardic—was an indication of Ashkenazi disdain.) After I had spent weeks learning the Hebrew prayers and melodies for a particular day of the Jewish calendar, a telegram arrived from my father in Sofia, informing my mother that my rite of passage had to be postponed a week because he had a new syphilitic patient. My father's specialty was venereal diseases, and in those prepenicillin days, a new and affluent syphilitic guaranteed a doctor's income for at least three years. As a result, I had to take crash lessons to prepare myself for an entirely new service for another day, the rabbi singing to me and I singing back until everything had sunk in, including the look heavenward at every mention of God. When the lessons were finally over, the rabbi asked what I would wear. I had never worn long trousers; *Lederhosen* was the usual garb, and knickerbockers the longest pants in my possession. When the most religious day of my life arrived, I effectively entered manhood, I remember, in new knickers and a man's hat. A few years later, the Nazis burned the "Turkish" temple to the ground, and there have not been enough Sephardim in Vienna since to build a new one.

My mother indulged me, perhaps to prevent any longing on my part for siblings. In this respect, she succeeded totally: I never regretted being an only child. In Vienna, I was surrounded by classmates playing soccer and field hockey in the spring and autumn, skating and skiing in the winter, and most surprising (considering our age), playing vicious poker in the late afternoons before dinner. By the time we left Austria, I was something of a cardsharp. Once in America, I became a Puritan: I judged, and still judge, playing cards to be a waste of time—in marked contrast to Herr Professor Freud's lifelong addiction to cards.

On this fourth of July in Kirchberg am Wechsel, there are no fireworks—hardly a man-made sound. In bed in our small *Gasthof* in the woods, I am kept awake by the sound of a rushing stream below the window. My childhood memory has become a dusty lens, the focus poor, the picture patchy. Finally, the rigors of the twenty-hour journey from San Francisco to Kirchberg, and then of the fifty years back in time, put me to sleep. By the time I wake up, it is 5 July 1988—another anniversary, this time sharply focused: ten years have passed since my first child, and only daughter, killed herself.

CHAPTER 2

"Dear Mrs. Roosevelt"

T HAT'S HOW I FINALLY STARTED the letter, after rejecting several more flowery salutations. "Your Excellency" was the one I'd considered most seriously. After all, to me, sixteen years old, a refugee from Hitler, just arrived on these shores, President Roosevelt's wife was clearly queen of America, the woman who could make things happen with the mere wave of her wand. But her shy smile and buckteeth—I'd studied them in countless newspaper photographs—convinced me that such a populist queen would be most comfortable with a simple, everyday sort of address. "Dear Mrs. Roosevelt," I wrote in early 1940, in a letter that, improbably enough, would launch me on the lecture circuit in the Corn Belt.

I

In early September 1939, just after the German army had marched into Poland, my mother had written from London that our American immigration visas had been granted: it was time to leave Europe. I seemed to accept that news with considerable equanimity, the Bulgarian interlude having been a soothing balm to the traumatic disruption of my Viennese childhood. Bulgaria was my father's country—the Djerassis having lived there for hundreds of years since their emigration from Spain during the Inquisition; and I was immediately accepted into my paternal family with true Balkan warmth. But that did not make me a Bulgarian patriot, in spite of my valuable Bulgarian passport. Except for the early, and largely forgotten, years of my infancy in Sofia (I was two months old when I left Vienna the first time), Bulgaria had turned into a synonym for summer vacations. Now it became a remarkably effective preparation for American life, my father having enrolled me in the American College, a private boarding school on the outskirts of Sofia, where I was tutored in a *mélange* of languages that left a permanent imprint on me. (I dream in unaccented English, but when others hear it, they always ask, "Where are you from?") The bulk of the instruction was in English, taught by Yanks, Brits, and Bulgars; but some of the classes were given in Bulgarian (notably mathematics, since American high school texts were not up to local *Gymnasium* standards) and in French—all of them foreign languages to my Viennese ears and tongue. That multilingual sophomore year of my Sofia high school education also introduced me to American literature. For some reason, American history was taught in a later year, but by that time I had already arrived in the country where the fourth of July carried a very different meaning from that embedded in my personal history.

My experience with the Bulgarian language is curious: I must be one of the rare persons who have twice forgotten the same language. While the first five years of my life, shortly after my Viennese birth, were spent in Sofia, we spoke German at home rather than Bulgarian, because my mother never learned that language. My own Bulgarian prattle was carried on largely with our maid and cook, so that I used female endings when referring to myself, and forgot most of it once I was again settled in Vienna and entering elementary school. (The female aspect of my Viennese youth started on a spectacular scale: The schools were not yet coeducational, and boys and girls went to separate schools in adjacent buildings in the Czerningasse. Since I had arrived from Sofia after the start of the Viennese school year and the boy's school was already full, I, together with three other male latecomers, was put among the girls. Sigmund Freud would doubtless have considered that nugget of information a bonanza.) During my 1938–39 residence in Sofia, I learned teenage Bulgarian from my classmates at the American College, but that second exposure was too feeble to withstand my subsequent, decades-long immersion in American lingo once I had crossed the Atlantic.

When the time came for our departure for America, my father accompanied my mother and me on the train journey to Genoa. I remember him waving his hat from the pier as my mother and I boarded the Italian liner *Rex*, soon to be sunk in the war. There were several reasons my father did not join us. He had a highly successful medical practice in Sofia, and led an intensive and extensive social life (some of which I only discovered shortly before his death) in his native country, where he felt deeply at home. He spoke no English and would have had to start from scratch, living alone in America, since he and my mother would certainly not have lived together. Even if he had wanted to come with us, it would have been impossible, because American immigration quotas were based on place of birth, rather than on citizenship. As my mother and I were born in Vienna, we fell into the Austrian quota, which was enormous compared with the minute Bulgarian one with its ten-year waiting list. Besides, my father did not believe that Bulgaria would be involved in the war, and hence felt neither threatened nor inclined to assume that it would last long. We did not meet again for ten years, by which time I had passed into adulthood and marriage.

My mother and I arrived penniless in New York City in December after a crossing so stormy that our huge ship was delayed more than a day. All that remains in my memory of our steerage accommodations is that I was seasick throughout most of the transatlantic passage. We were not totally penniless when we descended the gangplank—we actually had twenty dollars in precious American currency which had been difficult to secure in Bulgaria; but in less than an hour, we lost that little hoard to the taxi driver, who took us from the pier to the Washington Heights apartment of my mother's Viennese cousins (who had arrived a few months earlier) and knew greenhorns when he saw them.

Within a few days, the Jewish refugee aid organization HIAS (Hebrew Sheltering and Immigrant Aid Society) had found us a studio apartment in a brownstone on West 68th Street in Manhattan and provided us with funds for day-to-day survival until we got something more permanent. My mother, who had no license to practice medicine in the United States, was hired by an Austrian physician, who had arrived the preceding year and already passed the board examinations. He had settled as a country doctor in a small hamlet, Ellenburg Center, near the Canadian border in upstate New York, and my mother served as his assistant and housekeeper. I was luckier.

In terms of grades, I had been only an average student at the *Realgymnasium* in Vienna, sacrificing a good part of scholarship to sports and poker. But I changed dramatically before my fifteenth birthday, when I began my sophomore year at the American College in Sofia. Knowing that it was a steppingstone to my eventual education in America, where grades were bound to count, I became a star student during the two and one-half semesters I spent in Bulgaria, waiting for the magic visa.

Within days of my arrival in Manhattan, clutching my A-studded certificate from Bulgaria, written in plain English—so different from school certificates carried by most other refugees of those days—I visited a faculty member at New York University. He was a friend of one of my former American teachers, who had told me to get advice on where to complete high school. Apparently he paid no attention to my age for, upon learning that I had been at a "college" in Bulgaria, he informed me that though it was too late in the year to apply to New York University, he could probably arrange for the now-defunct Newark Junior College in Newark, New Jersey, to accept me at the start of the January semester. I didn't correct his misapprehension, figuring—correctly—that once I transferred from the junior college to a four-year institution, no one would look again at my high school record and notice that I had missed two years.

While my mother headed for upstate New York, HIAS placed me into the Newark home of an extraordinarily generous family. My relatively painless adjustment to America was helped along by Frank Meier, an inorganic chemist working at Engelhardt Industries; his wife, Clara, a local high school teacher; and their two high school-age sons, August (now a history professor at Kent State University) and Paul (professor of statistics at the University of Chicago). They did not treat me as surrogate parents, but in retrospect their family life was an example of everything good and decent in America: liberal, generous, caring.

In my mind, and most likely also in that of my mother and father (although I recall no concrete conversations on the topic), the tacit assumption was that I would eventually follow in my physician-parents' steps, but no seed of inspiration had yet been sown. Given my fairly logical frame of mind and argumentative nature, I might have turned to law; when I reflect on the ancient-history books I devoured in Europe, and the pleasure I derived in subsequent years from exploring Mayan, Inca, Khmer, and many other sites of early civilizations, I can imagine a career in archeology. As it happened, the person who sowed and sprinkled one of the first chemical seeds was Nathan Washton, the inspiring freshman chemistry teacher at Newark Junior College, where I started with the standard premedical course requirements of chemistry and biology.

It did not take me long to realize that Newark Junior College, aside from providing an effective laundry for my missing years of high school, could serve only as an early launching pad. The following year I would have to find a four-year institution to complete my college education. Rather than waiting until I had exhausted the resources of Newark Junior College, I turned to Eleanor Roosevelt.

II

"I am writing already now because next year I must have a scholarship to continue my schooling." Decades later, my spoken and written English is still sprinkled with "already now" (*schon jetzt*)—a verbal wart from a German-speaking childhood. Never mind the touch of redundancy, the idiomatic flavor. When I make reservations "already now" for next winter's holiday, I do so because my "now" feels naked and incomplete without the security of "already."

Grudgingly I accepted the fact that pressing affairs of state might prevent my letter from rising instantaneously to the top of Mrs. Roosevelt's pile of correspondence. Still, I had to admit to a touch of disappointment when a brief reply finally arrived from the Institute for International Education to which she had forwarded my request. Only in the autumn was my faith in the limitless power of that most democratic of all queens restored in the form of a postcard from an officer of the institute: "I have some good news for you. You have been awarded a scholarship for the next semester at Tarkio College in Tarkio, Missouri."

Now I had been first exposed to spoken English by a teacher in Vienna who had mispronounced American place names with a certain savoir-faire. His careful enunciation of "Seekaygo, Illinoa" made an indelible impression on me. To this day, I get a jolt whenever I fly to O'Hare Airport and hear the captain announce over the intercom our impending landing in "Sheekahgo." No wonder I managed to give "Meezooree" a Viennese ring when I announced to my mother that in January 1941 I was heading west to a town I couldn't find on any map then at my disposal. Even the Greyhound ticket office in New York had some difficulty discovering that the northwestern corner of Missouri was my ultimate destination. St. Joseph ("Saint Jo, Masura," to many natives) was the city where Greyhound deposited me after changes in Pittsburgh and Kansas City, and where I transferred to a local bus, which eventually passed the sign "Welcome to Tarkio, Queen of the Corn Belt." In that town I launched my career as a public speaker at the age of seventeen.

Within hours of my registration at Tarkio College—a Presbyterian school where a God-fearing student body of one hundred forty was guided by a faculty of twenty (including the business manager, a house mother, and the superintendent of grounds)*—I learned a piece of historical lore that seemed a superb omen to a budding chemistry major like myself: Tarkio's most illustrious alumnus was none other than Wallace Carothers, the inventor of Nylon. (No one mentioned that he'd committed suicide just a few years after making his discovery.)

At the end of my first week, the program chairman of the Tarkio Rotary Club invited me to address its membership on the "Current Situation in Europe." He informed me that I was scheduled to address the local members who had contributed to my scholarship and wanted to inspect the recipient of their largesse. I was too nervous and too innocent of public speaking even to imagine the many pitfalls a teenage, city-bred kid might face in front of an audience of middle-aged farmers and businessmen. I was not, however, too innocent to plagiarize ruthlessly John Gunther's *Inside Europe*. His reference to the Balkans—"Must every little language have a country all its own?"—still sticks in my mind.

My peculiar accent gave the speech an air of authenticity that no one—even one who knew the facts—could possibly resist. Its Viennese base from my "Seekaygo, Illinoa" days had been contaminated by my exposure to Bulgarian-speaking classmates at the American College, whose Slavic assaults on the English language had yielded little to the faculty's British and American accents. Already in sophisticated New York City, I'd learned that to the incessant inquiry "Where're you from?" the single word "Bulgaria" was a much more distinctive answer than "Vienna."

At the end of my Rotary debut, the minister of the local Presbyterian church congratulated me on my performance and proposed that I give a similar talk to his congregation after his Sunday sermon. In order not to repeat myself, I rushed back to my source—*Inside Europe* was not only up to date but also full of entertaining tidbits—and shamelessly borrowed new material, which I dressed up in my Viennese-Bulgarian-British accent. This second talk propelled me almost overnight from amateur to professional. In the minister's office that Sunday, with an apologetic reference to the size of the offering, my pleased host shoved toward me the contents of the collection plate—nickels, dimes, and occasional quarters. It was my first lecture honorarium.

The ministerial grapevine apparently crossed denominational boundaries. From that Sunday on, I received almost weekly invitations to address various church groups in northwestern Missouri and southwestern Iowa

---

*One would never have guessed that almost exactly fifty years to the day after my arrival, this once conservatively managed college would go bankrupt following major financial shenanigans that propelled it, probably for the first time in its history, onto the front page of the *New York Times*.

about the "European Situation." My plagiarism of Gunther became more sophisticated. I mixed his journalistic wisecracks, such as his definitions of *Balkan Peace* ("a period of cheating between two periods of fighting") or *Balkan Revolutions* ("abrupt changes in the form of misgovernment"), with my personal reminiscences of life in prewar Bulgaria. Pre- or post-Anschluss Vienna became *verboten* territory in my speeches. By focusing on Bulgaria, I was unlikely to encounter contradiction from my rural audiences, most of whom probably could not even have named the four countries bordering on Bulgaria. At the same time, I was eliminating potential questions about Viennese experiences I wished to bury rather than resurrect. Just as Tarkio bragged about its basketball team, I boasted about the amazing quality of the Sofia opera, the fact that Bulgaria was the source of most of the world's attar of roses, and that all male students in public schools had to shave their heads. Although long hair was hardly the vogue in the early 1940s in Missouri, my audiences reacted sympathetically when I described the luxurious hair of some of my classmates at the private American College, which did not require such draconian preventive measures against hair lice.

As the weeks passed, the collection plates became the chief source of my pocket money. Instead of waiting on tables or performing other plebeian part-time work, I pontificated to ladies' auxiliaries, church congregations, and even an eighth-grade commencement ceremony with the self-assurance of a so-far-undetected plagiarist. My talks followed the church services, which I always attended because a member of the congregation was usually my host and source of transportation. I found that the small format of the *Reader's Digest* discreetly fit within the covers of all bibles or hymn books. While others lustily sang Christian hymns, I devoured what at that time passed for *au courant* literature and clever humor. The *Reader's Digest* provided a virtuous camouflage which certainly seasoned its otherwise bland contents. But I had an unconscious reason for reading secular literature while others prayed and sang: I was exercising my agnostic Jewishness among the *goyim*.

One Sunday I answered the call of the First Methodist Church of Shenandoah, Iowa. Five decades later, as I review the scene through the double lens of nostalgia and dimming memory, I can still see the collection plate attached to a long handle move slowly in my direction; with a little effort, I can still capture the tinny sound of dimes hitting other dimes or nickels. The fingers in my pocket were already clutching my usual five-cent offering when a daring thought occurred to me: Why not deposit a fifty-cent piece? After all, it would be back in my needy pocket within a couple of hours at the latest. Perhaps it might shame other parishioners into more generous contributions. It's probably my imagination when I now remember that the majestic bong of my half-dollar piece crashing onto the puny pile of small coins startled the neighbor on my right into contributing a quarter. I made a mental note to carry henceforth a half-dollar coin to all my future speaking engagements. To this day, I have the definite impression that on that Sunday in Shenandoah, Iowa, my talk about Bulgaria was particularly polished, my accent unusually mysterious, my anecdotes only faintly schmaltzy. I felt that my prospective honorarium, suitably weighed down by huge half-dollar coins and possibly even blanketed by an unprecedented dollar bill, merited that extra effort.

When the Reverend J. Richard Sneed shook my hand, I felt a particularly firm grasp. His voice seemed almost tremulous as he thanked me. His hope that I should return in the not-too-distant future appeared to emanate straight from his heart. With his hand on my shoulder, he walked me toward the waiting car of the farmer who had offered to drive me back to Tarkio. Only as he removed his hand and gave me an ever so subtle shove toward the vehicle did the infamy of the First Methodist Church of Shenandoah descend on me: I'd paid the outrageous sum of fifty cents—scandalous in those days of nickel Cokes and subway tokens—to listen to myself talk.

"Dear Mrs. Roosevelt," I wanted to write, "warn the President not to trust the Methodists"—but, of course, I did nothing of the sort. By then I was savvy enough to realize that notes from a teenager—even one on the Corn Belt lecture circuit—were unlikely to be read by the President's wife. Besides, it would have been extraordinarily boorish of me to blame the minister of a God-fearing and, on the whole, extraordinarily hospitable congregation for my yearning for a more substantial lecture fee. In any event, this Methodist fiasco was one of my last church appearances before I headed east to spend the summer with my mother in upstate New York. Although I never returned to the northwestern corner of Missouri, I received there an introduction to the heartland of America experienced by relatively few refugee students of my generation, most of whom seldom got beyond the East Coast or were drafted, whereas a knee injury kept me out of the military. Thus, I was able to board a civilian express train that bore me, with one brief, but highly productive stop in industry, straight toward a Ph.D. and a research career in organic chemistry.

CHAPTER 3

The Quest for
Alfred E. Neuman

I

It seemed at times as though some American Protestant fairy had taken this
Jewish refugee from Europe under its wings—first the Presbyterians from
Tarkio, and then the Episcopalians at Kenyon. For on my way from Missouri to upstate New York, I stopped in Gambier, Ohio, where the latter
is located, and immediately fell in love with that charming small men's
college. When I applied for admission, I was offered a room, board, and
tuition scholarship.

By American standards, Kenyon had an old tradition: it was the first
men's college west of the Alleghenies, and its lovely Oxbridge architecture
made it seem transplanted from England. Although its church affiliation
was even stronger than Tarkio's—the college prided itself on its Episcopalian seminary, Bexley Hall—church attendance was relatively liberal and
obligatory only on Sundays, in contrast to the daily chapel services in the
Cornbelt. Far different from the predominantly rural student body of
Tarkio, the three hundred Kenyon males came mostly from affluent subur-

Myself with my father and an unidentified man in Sofia, *c*.1926.

My mother, Alice Friedmann, when at medical school at the University of Vienna.

Myself, at 18 months, in Bulgarian national dress.

The *Donau Kanal* and *Aspernbrücke (center)*. My mother's family lived on the second floor of the building at the extreme right. The park in the lower left was the site of my illegal soccer field.

Myself and my mother (Alice Friedmann Djerassi), *c.*1928.

Myself as an Austrian Boy Scout, *c.*1935.

Myself, a few months after arriving in the United States, in the home of Frank and Clara Meier, Newark, New Jersey, 1940.

Sure - I'm for Roosevelt

If you are opposed to the Third Term send these to your friends.
15 cards for 25c. Send coin or stamps. Low, quantity prices
on request. Send to Bob Howdale, Box 625, Oak Park, Ill.

The infamous predecessor of the Alfred E. Neuman figure in *MAD* magazine.

ban families ranging west to Illinois and east to New York. Many of them had cars, the majority were fraternity jocks, and virtually all of them drank. I was an exception: I had neither money nor car, lived in Douglass House—a modest, college-owned, clapboard structure in Gambier, inhabited by a few maverick literati and disciples of John Crowe Ransom, the famous editor of the *Kenyon Review*—and didn't touch alcohol. The instruction was superb; and while there were five times as many faculty members in English, Kenyon's most distinguished department, than in chemistry, it was here that I became a chemist.

I was not yet eighteen when I entered Kenyon as a junior in the fall of 1941 and set out to get my bachelor's degree within a year. Operationally, this was not as difficult as it sounds: I took heavy course loads during the next two semesters and then stayed on during the summer, taking some expedited programs that had been instituted because of the war. Aside from wishing to earn a living, I was in a hurry because, after my eighteenth birthday, I would be eligible for the draft; I thought that as a college graduate, I would stand a better chance of ending up in officer's training.

The semester in Missouri had barely served to moisten the chemical seeds sowed at Newark Junior College. The most memorable course at Tarkio was taught by a disciple of the parapsychologist Joseph B. Rhine; though it was ostensibly a class in gestalt psychology, he spent most of the time trying to convince us that extrasensory perception (ESP) has a scientific basis. But the two-man Kenyon College chemistry department provided really fertile ground for my chemical flowering in classes that were virtual tutorials, since only a handful of students took them: Walter H. Coolidge introduced me to organic chemistry; Bayes M. Norton taught me physical chemistry and was also the person with whom I did my first research on a project in photochemistry. By the time I graduated summa cum laude from Kenyon, a few months before my nineteenth birthday, with a Phi Beta Kappa key dangling from my tie clasp, I was ready to decide on a profession. It was simplified by an accident, earlier in my life, in Bulgaria.

An avid skier in Austria, I had continued skiing in Bulgaria in the foothills of Mount Vitosha where the American College was situated. In those days, skis were wooden, and the bindings primitive and not self-releasing. I was practicing on a slalom course when I injured my left knee. A few days of rest with a tight bandage and a diagnosis of "water on the knee" persuaded me that nothing serious had happened. But even though I continued with sports such as soccer, swimming, and tennis, by the time I was at Kenyon my knee was permanently swollen and warm to the touch. When I was called up for my draft physical examination, the army doctor classified me as 4-F, because of my inability to perform deep kneebends.

(Three years later, just when I received my American naturalization papers in Madison, Wisconsin, a biopsy of my knee indicated that I had probably developed a chronic infection of my knee joint as the aftermath of a tubercular episode from my Viennese childhood; eventually my knee had to be fused permanently.) Thus, while most other refugee students were going off to fight in the war that had driven me to the States, I had the luxury of pursuing my professional ambitions.

Although my doctor parents had probably drawn me toward medicine, it was my reading in Newark of Paul de Kruif's *Microbe Hunters* that deeply glamorized medical research in my mind. My financial situation, however, totally precluded the possibility of my going to medical school; before worrying about further schooling, I had to earn some money. On a visit to my mother in Ellenburg Center, who at that time was living with the physician for whom she also served as professional assistant, I browsed through the fancy brochures and other promotional material that lay scattered in the doctor's office. Suddenly I realized that the majority of pharmaceutical companies were located in New Jersey within commuting distance of Newark, my emotional American home. I proceeded to send letters of application to every New Jersey address I could locate. Most did not reply; but one of them, the American branch of the huge Swiss pharmaceutical company CIBA, made me an offer. It was in Summit, New Jersey, that I crossed my Rubicon into organic chemistry.

As luck would have it, I was assigned as a junior chemist to the laboratory of Charles Huttrer, another refugee from Hitler's Vienna, who, though twenty or more years older than I, treated me like an equal. In less than one year, we discovered one of the first antihistamines—Pyribenzamine (tripelennamine)—by synthesizing a class of compounds, called "ethylenediamines," which were screened pharmacologically by another European refugee, Rudolf L. Mayer, who had brought the concept of histamine's role in allergic reactions to the CIBA management's attention. I appeared on the list of inventors of what proved to be my first patent, and was also one of the co-authors of the eventual scientific publication in the *Journal of the American Chemical Society*—all heady stuff for a budding chemist in the last year of his teens. The rapidity with which Pyribenzamine became the drug of choice for hundreds of thousands, if not millions, of allergy sufferers spoiled me for a long time; I became an inveterate optimist as far as scientific success was concerned.

The Swiss parent of CIBA in Basel was one of the original powerhouses in steroid chemistry and medicine. Thus, even though my first year at CIBA was dedicated exclusively to antihistamines, I was exposed to steroids through contacts with some of my older laboratory colleagues. I also read the first edition of a technical treatise, *Natural Products Related to Phenan-threne* by Harvard's Louis F. Fieser, at that time one of the best-known American organic chemists. More than any other factor, this highly read-able book got me permanently hooked on steroids.

My year in Summit, spent with joyful independence in a genteel room-inghouse (where women guests were not allowed beyond the front parlor), was exciting. I had discovered American girls in Newark, Tarkio, and Ohio (where from all-male Kenyon I had to hitchhike for female companionship to the myriad small coeducational Ohio colleges within a couple of hours of Gambier), and continued on this passionate, but virginal course of discovery in Summit. Since my amorous explorations were restricted by the fact that I neither owned a car nor knew how to drive one, I lacked the key to the all-American bedroom. But instead of getting a driver's license, I took up cello lessons as well as a couple of graduate chemistry night classes, first at New York University, and then at the Brooklyn Polytechnic Institute.

It didn't take me long to realize that this was no way to get a Ph.D., at least not for someone with my sense of urgency: working a full day at CIBA and then gulping down a dinner snack on the Lackawanna Railroad, fol-lowed by a ferry trip from Hoboken to Manhattan, and a subway ride to the university. The clincher was when an organic chemistry professor at the university canceled half his classes because of alcohol problems—an unfor-givable sin in the eyes of a young teetotaler. But the canceled classes did have two beneficial consequences: they convinced me that I should start full-time graduate work, and taught me, even years later, never to cancel a class of my own.

After a year at CIBA, I applied for and received a Wisconsin Alumni Research Foundation fellowship, which allowed me to pursue graduate research without additional teaching duties at the University of Wisconsin in Madison. In the fall of 1943, the Wisconsin chemistry department had two young assistant professors, Alfred L. Wilds and William S. Johnson, who were about to undertake ambitious projects dealing with the total synthesis of steroids. At that time, only one steroid hormone had ever been synthesized totally: equilenin, an estrogenic hormone found in horse urine and of somewhat simpler chemical structure than the human estrogens. Wilds had, along with Werner E. Bachmann and Wayne Cole, been one of the members of the famous team responsible for that feat at the University of Michigan, and I chose him as my Ph.D. advisor. My doctoral thesis project was a compromise between Wilds's interests in total synthesis and my budding one (based on the Fieser book and CIBA lore) in chemical transformations of intact steroids—specifically, the transformation of the male sex hormone testosterone into a human estrogen. This choice had amazingly long-term consequences for me, as did my acquaintance with William Johnson, who ultimately was the person responsible for my move to Stanford University.

I startled Wilds by announcing right at the beginning that I planned to get my Ph.D. in two years. This statement may have been prompted by my overinflated opinion of the chemical prowess I had acquired at CIBA—an extra year of sophisticated laboratory work not shared by many beginning graduate students. I pointed to the University of Wisconsin catalogue, which specified six semesters as the minimum requirement for a Ph.D.; by spending both summers in Madison, I proposed to satisfy these residency requirements. "Spending six semesters in Madison is necessary, but not sufficient," my prospective mentor warned. "A successful piece of research is even more important, and that requires perseverance and luck."

I had both. By the fall of 1945, an American citizen with a Ph.D. degree and a wife, I returned to CIBA (the firm had supported me at Wisconsin with a supplementary stipend) for another four years, to resume work on antihistamines and other medicinal compounds. Since we were permitted to spend about 20 percent of our time on independent research, I was able to continue developing my steroid interests on the side. In fact, in spite of the industrial setting, I managed to publish a fair amount on my own in the scientific literature. I considered such publications crucial, because I had hoped to establish a sufficient reputation in organic chemistry to permit me entry into academia at some advanced level.

This plan turned out to be somewhat naïve. At that time moving from industry to a university position was mostly a one-way street going in the wrong direction, although a few chemists had shown that it was not impossible. At the ripe age of twenty-five and a half, I had accumulated nearly five years of industrial experience and concluded that I was ready for an academic career. Even now, after having worn a professorial hat for nearly four decades, I am still not certain what fueled this academic ambition other than the conventional snobbery picked up in graduate school that the academic ladder leads to more challenging and nobler intellectual heights. But since I had absolutely no luck—very few interviews and no academic offers—I searched for challenges on my own industrial turf.

The late 1940s were exciting days in steroid chemistry, especially since the anti-arthritic properties of cortisone had just been discovered. I was anxious to work on an improved synthesis of cortisone at CIBA. Fortunately, permission was not granted, most of that work being conducted at CIBA in Switzerland. Thus, when a chemist friend, Martin Rubin from Schering, who was aware of my restlessness at CIBA, proposed me for an opening as associate director of research at Syntex in Mexico City, I did not reject the possibility—crazy as it sounded—completely out of hand. Not only had I never heard of Syntex, but at that time the idea of doing any chemical research in Mexico seemed preposterous: "serious" chemistry supposedly stopped at the Rio Grande. When, however, I received an invitation to visit Syntex in Mexico City with all expenses paid and no other advance commitment, I accepted. I had never been to Mexico and as a bonus decided to include a visit to Havana in my tourist itinerary. George Rosenkranz, the thirty-two-year-old technical director of Syntex and another refugee from Hitler's Europe, absolutely charmed me personally and professionally.

Rosenkranz, a first-class steroid chemist of Hungarian descent, made me a tempting offer. I, who had always worked alone or with one or two technicians, was suddenly presented with the chance to head a research group that would attempt a practical synthesis of cortisone and work on other aspects of steroid chemistry that might interest me—and to do this in surprisingly well-equipped laboratories. Learning another language seemed like an additional bonus. Nevertheless, when I returned to the States and told my friends at the University of Wisconsin and Harvard of the reasons for my decision, they thought I could not be serious.

I was convinced that the best route to the academic job still eluding me was to establish a scientific reputation in the literature. Even though my friends thought me mad for trying to do this in Mexico, I felt intuitively that this was the right place. Syntex had the same objective I did: to establish a scientific reputation. Our common goal—a new and more productive synthesis of cortisone from plant raw material—was one of the hottest scientific topics in organic chemistry at that time. I was young and willing to gamble on a few years in Mexico—partly because living in another country and learning another language appealed to me, but also because I thought that any scientific achievement from a laboratory in Mexico was likely, upon publication, to make a much bigger impression on academia than one coming from the usual laboratories in North America or Europe.

Consequently, I really had only one requirement before I accepted the Syntex job offer, and that was to publish any scientific discoveries promptly in the chemical journals. Syntex agreed to this and stuck to its bargain, and I certainly had my own personal incentive to make good on it. From my previous industrial experience, I fully understood that discoveries have to be patented by the firm in whose laboratory the work is performed before they are written up for publication. But instead of having patent attorneys run the show in terms of deciding whether and when to publish, Syntex operated in the reverse manner: here Rosenkranz and I called the shots—extraordinary for a pharmaceutical company.

As a result of this policy, during my first two years at Syntex we published more rapidly in the chemical literature than did any other pharmaceutical company or even many university laboratories. Long before Syntex sold drugs under its own name in the open market (in order to become known to the medical profession), its international scientific reputation in chemistry was well established. (Ten years later, in 1959, Professor Louis F. Fieser of Harvard reported at an international steroid conference his analysis of the references in the latest [1959] edition of his text *Steroids*. He had broken down the several thousand references by origin into those from academia and those from industry and then analyzed them even further by institutional origin. Even though the survey was made only ten years after the founding of Syntex's research department, no laboratory in the world—academic or industrial—had published as much in the steroid field during that period. Chemistry south of the Rio Grande had finally made the grade.)

II

The first decade of my life in America was a period of seemingly total assimilation (except for not losing my accent) and of nearly total immersion into chemistry. But I was not just a chemist; I was a Jewish chemist. At that time, I would have made that pronouncement with much hesitation, because advertising (as distinguished from admitting) my Jewish origin was the last thing I was prepared to do. In the 1940s, many chemistry departments of major American universities had not a single Jewish faculty member, a fact I was ready to ascribe to active discrimination. To this day, I know several Jewish colleagues of my generation—faculty members in some of our most distinguished universities—who refuse to broach the subject of their Jewish origin.

For years on end, I lived with the self-imposed, but rarely admitted, burden of wondering how to dodge the question "Are you Jewish?" without lying; of anticipating that question with typical Jewish paranoia, and attempting to change the direction of the conversation, when the other person may never have even thought about the topic; and yet on numerous occasions displaying the same inquisitiveness, "Is *he* Jewish?" I never seemed to ask whether *she* was Jewish, because my psyche recognized only male anti-Semites. (No wonder all three of my wives were gentiles.) While I have not stopped wondering about other people's Jewishness, I find that nowadays, among professional peers, I practically flaunt my own. Is it because I have finally turned impervious to overt anti-Semitism, or because of the recognition that I would not have become a chemist if I hadn't been born a Jew in Vienna? I didn't have any childhood chemistry sets; I never blew up our basement; prior to my sixteenth birthday, I never had any chemistry nor did I have a single chemical "hero," not even Madame Curie. If I hadn't been born a Jew, I wouldn't have left Vienna and would doubtless have ended up as an Austrian physician—possibly even one voting for Kurt Waldheim. But I am a Jew—and never forget it. My acute awareness in those years of possible anti-Semitism involved me in a curious obsession, even though the Americans who eased my path in those early years couldn't have been more benevolent.

Although half a century has passed, I still remember every detail: the big ears projecting straight out like a wary deer's; the tooth missing just above the thick lower lip, its gross thickness accentuated by the virtual absence of its upper partner; the eyes, big yet hooded; the tousled black hair; the grin moronic but also devious; and finally the nose—after the ears, the boy's most prominent feature.

His image occupied the center of a filthy poster plastered on the walls in our neighborhood in Vienna, just after the Nazis had taken over in 1938. The head was attached to a gangly neck, protruding from an absurdly adult suit, its black vest buttoned almost to the sternum, leaving visible only the knot of a black tie. In a remarkably succinct way, his attire managed to stigmatize the boy as a sly street peddler. The poster's brutal message consisted of just three words: *Tod den Juden*—Death to the Jews!

I encountered the face the second time in a newsvendor's stall in the Midwest during the early 1940s. Still extraordinarily sensitive to every real or imaginary anti-Semitic innuendo, I did not touch the picture. I knew exactly what it stood for. And in my state of shock, I overlooked the fact that this grinning boy's nose was somewhere between triangular and bulbous, rather than sharply Semitic.

At the time, I did not tell anyone what I had seen, just as I hardly disclosed anything about my past life. It was my way of attempting to "pass," which even without my accent would not have been easy in this small midwestern town where I was the only Hitler refugee; many of the locals had never even met a Jew.

"Where're you from?" they'd ask as soon as I'd finished a sentence or two.

"My mother lives in upstate New York," I'd reply, sometimes mentioning the hamlet near the Canadian border where she worked.

"Yes, but where're you *from*?" they'd insist. "What kind of an accent is that?"

"Bulgaria," I'd lie, hoping the remoteness of that country would deflect the inquisition.

Of course, some of my inquisitors were more persistent. (Was it my paternal Sephardic background that invariably made me attribute to innocent midwestern curiosity fifteenth-century Spanish inquisitorial motives?) "Why didn't you stay in Bulgaria?" ("Idiot," I wanted to retort but didn't, because that would have taken explanations incompatible with "passing"). "Were you born there?" Once I owned up to having been born in Vienna, the questions tended to become more precise and, worst of all, more intrusive. Still, I equivocated. Only when asked pointblank, "Are you Jewish?" did I acknowledge the fact, and then I promptly changed the subject.

Some years later in the 1950s—probably in Michigan where I taught and where rabid anti-Semites like Gerald L. K. Smith and Father Coughlin operated—I again came upon that face: on the cover of a publication with the implausible title of *MAD*. But having by this time become an American citizen, I felt more secure. I picked up the magazine and flipped it open. I was stunned to find it filled with comics—an American infatuation to which, along with football and peanut butter, I had never succumbed.

I was too preoccupied with other matters, and also too impatient, to delve into the contents of *MAD*, but I did make some discreet inquiries about the nature of its cover picture. To my surprise, virtually every person I asked knew the identity of that boy: Alfred E. Neuman.

"Where does he come from?" It was my turn to ask that pointed question, only to be told that nobody knew or even cared. He had just existed as long as my informants could remember.

"N,E,W,M,A,N?" I spelled the name.

"No," I was corrected. "N,E,U,M,A,N."

"Aha!" I cried out triumphantly. "I knew it! It isn't 'Nooman.' It's 'Noyman.' German, of course."

Decades passed, and the boy's face receded again from my conscious memory. Then one day, on a visit to Yad Vashem, the Holocaust memorial in Jerusalem, as I stared at some of the enlarged photographs from that most despicable and horrible period in European history, Alfred E. Neuman's face seemed to surface here and there. I decided that the time had come to uncover the origin of the face whose memory had never quite left me.

As soon as I returned to California, I went to a local news agent. "Do you carry *MAD*?" I inquired, not even knowing whether the magazine still existed. "Over there," the man pointed. I turned and saw a grinning Alfred E. Neuman dressed in a snow rabbit's outfit stepping out of a chimney, holiday cheer practically oozing from the January 1988 cover of the latest *MAD*. I handed over $1.35 and walked to a corner of the store, where for the first time in my life, I read a comic book from cover to cover. In spite of my ingrained suspicion, it became clear to me that no Nazi had ever had his hands on that issue. In fact, it was not even obvious to me why kids would read it: the political cartoon on the last page featuring Gary Hart and Ronald Reagan was clever and biting. I would not have been surprised to find it on the cover of a magazine like *Mother Jones*.

I was puzzled: How could I reconcile my memory of that taunting face of nearly fifty years before with this benign comic? My first American vision of Alfred E. Neuman's face had been around 1942, give or take a few months. Yet on telephoning the editorial office of *MAD* to inquire when the first issue had appeared and how I could secure a copy, I received a preposterous reply: number 1 of *MAD* had hit the newsstands only in October 1952. Even more absurd was the claim that Alfred E. Neuman—face as well as name—had not graced the cover of *MAD* until 1956. Had the Nazis sold the original magazine to some innocent purchaser with the proviso that the origin of the publication be disguised? Everyone knows of notorious examples of the falsification of historical facts. If *MAD* was just another such victim, it was time for me to correct the record—if not for the public's sake, then at least for mine. Two weeks later, I flew to New York and headed for 485 Madison Avenue, the current perch of *MAD*.

The bemused tolerance with which the small editorial staff received me was reflected in the genial disarray of their offices, in which, after a short search, they located the bound volumes of the magazine starting with the first issue. Its cover featured a terrified family, the man yelping, "That thing! That slithering blob coming toward us!"; the woman screaming, "What is it?"; and the small child at their feet exclaiming, "It's Melvin!" Melvin Coznowski, I was told, was Alfred E. Neuman's predecessor.

The face I'd remembered—the face that had remained with me for decades and brought me to *MAD*'s New York office—first surfaced in *MAD* in November 1955. It appeared above the masthead in number 26 (surrounded by Socrates, Napoleon, Freud, and Marilyn Monroe), but so small that it occupied less than half the space of the central letter *A* in the title. The next issue, number 27 of April 1956, had a somewhat larger boy crouching at General Eisenhower's feet amid a bewildering crowd of at least sixty characters ranging from Thomas E. Dewey, Adlai Stevenson, and Richard Nixon to Churchill, King Farouk, and Khrushchev. Not until the December 1956 issue did the likeness of Alfred E. Neuman—the famous Norman Mingo portrait apparently familiar to all Americans but me—fill the cover in lonely splendor. He was featured as a write-in candidate for president under the slogan "What—Me Worry?"

I was totally perplexed by the discrepancy between these facts and my memory until I read an early Letters to the Editor section, where an amusing collection of feisty and succinct missives presented no fewer than eleven different images of Alfred alias who-knows-who, sent in by readers claiming to have known the Ur-Alfred. In three pictures, the hair was actually slicked down; he could have been a neighborhood schoolkid. In the three craziest ones, he wore various kinds of hat. The other five approached my image from Nazi days.

These letters and many other fascinating exhibits were in a huge binder containing background material from a copyright suit that had been filed against MAD in the 1950s. I found myself rooting for MAD—my belated and, by now, favorite introduction to American comics. I was relieved to find that the magazine had won by demonstrating an abundance of prior art with that face and with legends such as "Me worry?" or "Da-a-h . . . Me worry?" There were references to a publication of that face by Gertrude Breton Park of Los Angeles around 1914; to a 1936 advertisement from Brotman Dental Lab in Winnipeg; to a somewhat corny book, Hall of Fame, published in 1943 in Toronto by one J. J. Carrick. There was no question that, at least in terms of chronology, that face existed when I was a teenager in the Midwest.

I had almost forgotten my role as a Nazi hunter, but then I got warmer. Not hot, not quite there, but warm enough: a postcard with the Nazi version of the face, except for the hooked nose, and the legend "Sure—I'm for Roosevelt." The reverse side read: "If you are opposed to the Third Term send these to your friends. 15 cards for 25c. Send coin or stamps. Low, quantity prices on request. Send to Bob Howdale, Box 625, Oak Park, Ill."

I suppose I could have flown to Chicago, searched the old phone books, and tracked down Bob Howdale. Maybe he was one of Father Coughlin's followers. But I had lost my taste for chasing down the real Alfred E. Neuman. I was certain that neither MAD nor Bob Howdale could make me forget the specters of my youth. As to my own memory of Alfred's face, a line in a poem by Bruce Bawer says it all: "The past cannot move into the present uncorrupted."

CHAPTER 4

"No Depression"

THE TELEGRAM, DATED 8 JUNE 1951, bore the name of Tadeus Reichstein, who the year before had shared the Nobel Prize in medicine for his isolation and structural elucidation of cortisone. The telegram—sent from Basel to Mexico City, then the site of tiny Syntex, S.A. (*Sociedad Anónima*, "anonymous company" at that time an apposite description)— said only, "No depression." It signified that the melting point of the authentic steroid, isolated by Reichstein from adrenal glands, was not depressed when mixed with the synthetic specimen we had dispatched to Switzerland. (In 1951, a "mixed melting point" was one of the standard ways of establishing identity between two crystalline chemicals. A grammarian might well ask how a melting point can possibly be mixed; and "mixture melting point" might be more precise, but was not part of accepted chemical jargon.) Thus, our unknown research group—the oldest member of which, was, at age thirty-four, seven years my senior—won the race described in *Harper's Magazine* that year in one breathless sentence: "The new ways of producing cortisone come as the climax to an unrestrained, dramatic race involving a dozen of the largest American drug houses, several leading foreign pharmaceutical manufacturers, three governments, and more research personnel than have worked on any medical problem since penicillin."

Those were the days of unrestrained optimism, when cortisone was believed to be a wonder drug for treating arthritis and other inflammatory diseases. Philip Hench, one of Reichstein's fellow Nobel Prize winners from the Mayo Clinic, had shown movies in 1949 of helpless arthritics receiving cortisone and then, in days, getting up to dance. The only problem was that cortisone cost nearly $200 per gram, and depended on not readily available starting material: slaughterhouse animals. In 1944, it had taken Lewis H. Sarett of Merck & Company in Rahway, New Jersey, thirty-six chemical steps to synthesize cortisone from cattle bile. Thus, a potentially unlimited source for cortisone was needed: if not through *total synthesis*—building from scratch from air, coal or petroleum, and water—then through *partial synthesis*, starting with a naturally occurring steroid and transforming it chemically into cortisone. Sarett had prepared the first few grams of cortisone by such a partial synthesis—somewhat akin to the conversion of a barn into a villa, the bile acid being his barn, cortisone his villa. To understand why an "anonymous company" in Mexico would have the temerity even to enter the scientific competition, let alone "win" it in the face of much larger international rivals, academic and industrial, one needs to understand the rudiments of the chemist's steroid language. Here I shall try to emulate Einstein's dictum: "We should make things as simple as possible, but not simpler."

I

Steroid is derived from the Greek, meaning "like a sterol." Sterols, in turn, are solid alcohols that occur widely in plants and animals—the best known being cholesterol, the most abundant sterol in humans and other vertebrates. Contrary to popular assumption, *steroid* is a purely chemical definition with no biological connotation: all steroids (and all sterols) are substances based on the chemical skeleton pictured in figure 4.1, which consists of carbon and hydrogen atoms arranged in four fused rings and known generically as perhydrocyclopentanophenanthrene. Steroid chemists—who require paper and pencil, or blackboard and chalk, when communicating on their subject among themselves—have simplified this cumbersome diagram by both dropping the symbols for carbon (C) and hydrogen (H) and assuming that carbon is tetravalent (four bonds are connected to each carbon). The shorthand representation in figure 4.2 shows clearly the three six-membered rings (A, B, C) and one five-mem-

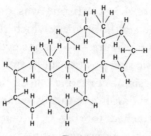

Fig. 4.1
Steroid skeleton
(perhydrocyclopentanophenanthrene)

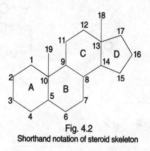

Fig. 4.2
Shorthand notation of steroid skeleton

bered ring (D) that define a steroid. In this notation, every corner of each ring is assumed to be a carbon atom, whose tetravalency is assumed to be satisfied by hydrogen atoms, which are not written. The carbon atoms are numbered from 1 to 19; atoms 18 and 19 are not part of a ring but are attached as methyl groups (CH_3 in figure 4.1).

Thousands upon thousands of synthetic, and many hundreds of natural, compounds are based on this simple steroid skeleton, all differing minutely in chemical structure. The minute variations, however, not only alter the chemical constitution of the molecule; they can also produce dramatically different biological results. Many of the most important biologically active molecules in nature, indeed, represent slight variations on the steroid skeleton: the male and female sex hormones, bile acids, cholesterol, vitamin D, the cardiac-active constituents of digitalis, the adrenal cortical hormones (related to cortisone and usually referred to generically as "corticosteroids"). The wide-ranging biological activity of steroids—for instance, the fact that one is responsible for male and another for female secondary sexual characteristics—is, in part, associated with the introduction of a third atom, oxygen (O), located in special positions of the steroid skeleton. In a way, one can consider the entire steroid bible as a text written in a three-letter alphabet (C, H, and O), the location of O being used predominantly to express the type of biological activity.

The structure of the adrenal hormone cortisone, with its five oxygen atoms, is shown in figure 4.3. Cortisone was difficult to synthesize be-cause—in contrast to the sex hormones, which possess only two oxygen atoms (such as progesterone, figure 4.4)—it has five. Of these, one is located in a chemically inaccessible site: position 11 of ring C. That was why Sarett, in his 1944 *partial* synthesis of cortisone, chose the bile acid, deoxycholic acid, as his starting material: it is a naturally occurring steroid that at least has an oxygen atom attached to ring C, albeit in the wrong position (number 12, figure 4.5). First, Sarett set out to move the oxygen atom from position 12 to 11. Then he converted the five-carbon "side chain" attached

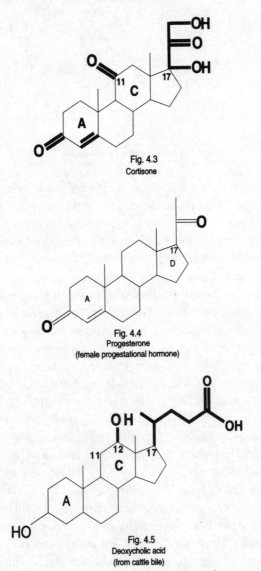

Fig. 4.3
Cortisone

Fig. 4.4
Progesterone
(female progestational hormone)

Fig. 4.5
Deoxycholic acid
(from cattle bile)

to position 17 of deoxycholic acid (top right of figure 4.5) into the two-carbon chain of cortisone with its three oxygens (top right of figure 4.3); finally, he generated the latter's characteristic ring-A substitution pattern. Altogether, it took nearly forty steps to accomplish that feat—at that time the longest organic chemical synthesis ever performed on an industrial scale.

The starting material our Syntex team chose, as a more widely available alternative to Sarett's bile acid, was diosgenin. At first glance, the choice seems to make neither chemical nor geographical sense. While its chemical structure (figure 4.6) does contain the four rings typical of steroids (see figure 4.2), diosgenin is burdened by extraneous chemical appendixes, encompassed by two more rings—E and F in figure 4.6—attached to positions 16 and 17. Diosgenin, however, had been the raison d'être for Syntex's formation just a few years earlier. In the late 1930s and early 1940s, Russell E. Marker, a brilliant but unorthodox chemistry professor at Pennsylvania State University, conducted research on a group of steroids called "sapogenins," compounds of plant origin so-called because their chemical combination with sugars (termed "saponins") display soaplike qualities in aqueous suspension. Natives of Mexico and Central America, where saponin-containing plants occur wildly and in abundance, had long used them for doing laundry and to kill fish. Marker concentrated on the chemistry of the steroid sapogenin diosgenin, which was present in certain types of inedible yams growing wild in Mexico. He discovered an exceedingly simple process whereby the two complex E and F rings (for us, molecular garbage) could be degraded to a substance then easily transformed chemically into the female sex hormone progesterone. In 1944, unable to convince any American pharmaceutical firm of the commercial potential of diosgenin, Marker formed a small Mexican company named Syntex (from *Synt*hesis and *Mex*-

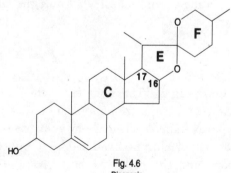

Fig. 4.6
Diosgenin
(from Mexican yams)

ico) with Emeric Somlo and Federico Lehmann, two European immigrant owners of a local pharmaceutical company, Laboratorios Hormona, which was in the business of selling glandular extracts of hormones such as progesterone. A few months later, Syntex started to sell to other pharmaceutical companies pure, crystalline progesterone prepared from diosgenin by *partial synthesis* in five steps.

Within a year the partners had a disagreement, and Marker left the company. Early in his academic career, however, while still at Pennsylvania State University, he had published a scientific description of his chemical processes in the *Journal of the American Chemical Society*; and since no one had taken out patents in Mexico for his discoveries, the commercial production of progesterone from diosgenin was up for grabs in that country. Somlo and Lehmann, looking for another chemist who could re-establish the manufacture of progesterone from diosgenin at Syntex, recruited Dr. George Rosenkranz from Havana. A Hungarian like Somlo, Rosenkranz had immigrated to Cuba a few years earlier from Switzerland, where he had received his doctorate under the Nobel laureate Leopold Ruzicka (one of the giants of early steroid chemistry) and read Marker's publications. Within two years, Rosenkranz had not only reinstituted at Syntex the large-scale manufacture of progesterone from diosgenin but, even more important, had achieved the large-scale synthesis, from these same Mexican yams, of the commercially more valuable male sex hormone testosterone. Both syntheses were so much simpler than the methods used by the European pharmaceutical companies—such as CIBA, then dominating the steroid hormone field—that in a short while tiny Syntex broke the international hormone cartel. As a result, prices were lowered considerably, and these hormones became much more available. In the late 1940s, Syntex served as bulk supplier to pharmaceutical companies throughout the world, but few people outside these firms even knew of the existence of this small chemical manufacturing operation in Mexico City, which was soon to revolutionize steroid chemistry and the steroid industry all over the world.

II

In the eyes of our European and U.S. competitors in the race to reach that Everest of synthetic chemists, cortisone, our crew was a motley lot. Our chemical base camp was staffed exclusively by young Mexican women who had, at best, a grade school education and had been trained in the manufacture of progesterone and the male sex hormone testosterone, first by Marker and then by Rosenkranz. Although when I had arrived as a gringo a year and a half earlier to assume the position of associate director of chemical research, I had been dismayed by the limited academic background of these workers, I soon learned to appreciate their advantages over the high school or college-trained laboratory assistants found in the United States. By a combination of mimicry and osmosis, our Mexican technicians had learned the necessary chemical operations and, that knowledge acquired, always produced the required chemical goods on time. Their occasional improvisations were refreshingly original. Thus, one woman, Teodora (whose surname, like that of the saints, was never known to me), who had been assigned certain chemical steps in the synthesis of an important intermediate, somehow managed to get precisely the same yield—say, 82 percent—every time she performed the reaction. Even the most experienced synthetic chemist expects to encounter variations from experiment to experiment; a range of 77 percent to 85 percent is considered acceptable. It took us months to discover Teodora's secret: when she obtained an 85-percent yield in a reaction, she kept the extra 3 percent in a secret cache in her drawer. When in a later repetition, she ended up with only 80 percent of the expected yield, she would add the missing 2 percent from her hoard.

The sherpas moving supplies to the more advanced camps were again mostly women: undergraduate students of the huge National University of Mexico, where the chemical instruction at that time was poor. What the students lacked in formal preparation, however, they made up in innate intelligence and desire to succeed. As part of their graduation requirements, they had to present a thesis and were permitted to perform thesis research at Syntex—under conditions far superior to what was then available in Mexican academic laboratories. These were probably the first undergraduate theses from Mexican university students to be published in the international chemical literature, such as the *Journal of the American Chemical Society* or the *Journal of Organic Chemistry*.

Our fellow climbers for the final assault were all men. Octavio Mancera, the only Mexican Ph.D. in organic chemistry of his generation, had received his degree at Oxford University under one of the greatest organic chemists of all times, Sir Robert Robinson. A second Mexican, the late Jesús Romo, eventually became one of the top professors in the Instituto de Química of the university. Juan Pataki, a Hungarian refugee like Rosenkranz, had been trained in Switzerland.

Rosenkranz and I, the expedition leaders, made occasional exploratory forays to find the shortest chemical route to the top. Nearly forty years after the event, we still smile proudly whenever we recall that Sunday morning when the two of us entered the empty laboratories to try for the first time a reaction that began our attempt to generate ring A of cortisone (see lower left of figure 4.3). Even the tortilla stand across the street, usually thronged with employees during weekday lunches, was closed.

This was the first component of our three-pronged attack. The second—degradation of the two extra E and F rings (see figure 4.6) of diosgenin and construction of the two-carbon–three-oxygen side chain attached to position 17 (see figure 4.3) of cortisone—was tricky and replete with obstacles. Nevertheless, there was precedent in the chemical literature for the various individual steps, and the completion of that sequence was accomplished in good time by the group under Pataki's command. The real *terra incognita* was the introduction of an oxygen atom into position 11 of ring C of diosgenin. A few years earlier, Sarett had accomplished a similar feat by a lateral move: in about half a dozen chemical steps, he had managed to shift the oxygen atom from position 12 of his bile acid (figure 4.5) to the neighboring center at number 11. We had set a much more ambitious goal, similar to that of groups in Europe and America: to introduce an oxygen atom into ring C of a precursor that possessed no oxygen atom whatsoever in that ring. Diosgenin from Mexican yams was so abundant, its cost so low, and the ease of degradation of the side chain to a useful steroid hormone intermediate so great, that we gambled and put most of our intellectual and physical resources on that portion of the problem.

This was the area in which I personally spent the most time, and in which we could count on our only assistance from north of the Rio Grande: Gilbert Stork, like Rosenkranz and myself an immigrant from Europe, who had been my graduate school classmate at the University of Wisconsin and then had become assistant professor at Harvard. I considered him one of the brightest American organic chemists and had persuaded Syntex to hire him as our consultant shortly after my own move to Mexico City. Stork flew down for a few days every three or four months and thus became our intelligence service to the outside world. It is probably difficult to imagine nowadays the scientific loneliness of Mexico in the early 1950s, or how long it took scientific journals to reach us. Long-distance telephone conversations between Mexico City and Cambridge, Massachusetts—with static, crackling, and sudden total silences—resembled radiotelephone communications in the Himalayas. Often, after a particularly exciting phone exchange about chemistry, my throat was hoarse from shouting and my ears aching—one from the pressure of the earpiece, the other from the pressure of my right index finger boring into my other ear, in a vain attempt to exclude extraneous sounds.

As we got closer to the summit, as the chemical obstacles—including the effect of Mexico City's rarefied altitude on the course of certain chemical reactions—were overcome and we got ready for the final push, we switched to a two-shift operation. This is common enough in chemical factories, but research phrases like "refluxing overnight," "stirring for twenty-four hours," or "extracting for forty-eight hours" usually indicate that the laboratory chemist sleeps at night or may have taken off for a Sunday or an entire weekend. During that period in early 1951, however, we persuaded our team to undergo mitosis into one group working from 8:00 A.M. to 5:00 P.M. and another from 4:00 P.M. to midnight. The one-hour overlap was needed for the first group to hand over the day's protocol and for the second to plan how to continue reactions without the conventional "overnight" recipes.

Gilbert Stork not only helped plan chemical strategy but also telephoned about relevant scientific articles that had arrived in the current periodicals section of the Harvard library long before they had reached Mexico. He was also instrumental in recruiting a sympathetic informant (nicknamed "Flash"), who was a Harvard graduate student engaged to a beautiful Mexican chemist. Like the *Washington Post*'s Woodward and Bernstein, we had our "mole," except that our White House was Harvard and our Nixon was not engaged in nefarious activities. He was Robert Burns Woodward, then professor of organic chemistry at Harvard and now considered the leading American synthetic chemist of this century. Neither was there anything nefarious about our desire for information. We were working on a totally different chemical approach from Woodward's. We wanted only to know how close his group was to reaching their goal. The same was true of our interest in the team of Louis Fieser, another Harvard professor, which was also striving to introduce an oxygen atom into the elusive 11-position of a "naked" steroid precursor.

Our participation in the cortisone competition was no secret. We had announced that we were contenders through the standard scientific equivalent of an expedition communiqué, a "Communication to the Editor," in the *Journal of the American Chemical Society*. Generally known as *JACS*, this most prestigious of chemical journals accepts two types of publication. Conventional papers, replete with experimental details and having no page limit, are subjected to the criticism of at least two, and sometimes as many as four, anonymous referees selected by the editor of the journal. In the early 1950s, it took over half a year from date of submission for the average article to satisfy its referees and editors and reach publication; periods in excess of one year were not uncommon. A second and particularly prestigious form of publication is the "Communication to the Editor." Limited to one thousand words or their equivalent in tables and formulas, its subject matter must be important, timely, and novel. Experimental details can hardly be accommodated within such a space constraint, but even a "Communication" must provide enough information for an expert to be capable of evaluating the experiment. Refereeing is particularly strict—at best, one out of four submitted "Communications" appears in print; but the entire publication process is greatly expedited.

The real reason for "Communications" is establishment of priority, beating the competition to the draw; but in our case, announcing partial advances toward cortisone on several chemical fronts was also a way to establish scientific credibility. Except for Marker's work—which was not really credited to Mexico or Mexicans—no organic chemical research of any significance performed in Mexico had ever appeared in the international chemical literature.

By the spring of 1951, however, everyone was taking at least one Mexican coup seriously. By then our Syntex team had published a "Communication" in the *JACS* describing an original way—defined as "performic acid oxidation of 7,9(11)-dienes followed by base isomerization of the resulting epoxyketones" in the precise, though generally incomprehensible language of the steroid chemist—of introducing the elusive oxygen function into position 11 of a "naked" ring C. Another "Communication" recorded our discovery of a novel path to the characteristic ring-A structure of cortisone or of other hormones, such as progesterone, from an intermediate that was particularly suitable to steroidal sapogenin precursors such as diosgenin (figure 4.6). In the terms of my initial metaphor: we had announced in public that we knew how to install modern heating and plumbing in a barn without destroying floors or walls; we had shown how to add balconies to any type of barn, to transform hay storage areas into bedrooms, to create a new roof without dismantling the beams and rafters. And we were ready to apply this knowledge to our specific barn and to so transform it into that gorgeous villa depicted in the architect's drawings that the original structure would no longer be recognizable—even though it provides the principal support and frame of the new edifice.

At this point, we moved into the two-shift mode, which led to the synthetic crystals that were shipped to Reichstein in Switzerland. Within hours of the arrival of the "no depression" telegram, I wrote the first draft of our "Communication" entitled "Synthesis of Cortisone." After Rosenkranz and Pataki had added their comments, we sent it off to the University of Rochester where the new editorial offices of the *JACS* had been established recently. Overnight deliveries did not then exist; and, though propeller-driven airmail from Mexico was not reliable, registered mail took an extra few days, so we gambled on the former. Now we could do nothing but wait. Rosenkranz and his wife took off for Texas to an international bridge tournament (eventually he would become a master of Olympic status and author of eight books on bridge); my wife and I departed for Chiapas in order to explore the pre-Columbian ruins at Palenque, one of the most exquisite of classical Mayan sites and at that time not easily accessible.

A few days after our return, before we even had received an acknowledgment from Rochester about the fate of our "Communication," a worrisome telegram arrived at my home from our Harvard mole. The stamped date and hour of its arrival—8 July at 7:41 A.M.—are still clearly visible on my copy:

> Woodward finished cortisone Thursday. Writing note title Total Synthesis of Cortisone. Leaving nothing to imagination or intelligence of reader. Observed on his desk note quote tell Bliss, Gates says hold journal day or two unquote. Don't know importance of this. Arranged with Fieser publish same time. Suggest change your title. Flash.

Now we knew that our duo of Harvard competitors—Woodward and Fieser—had reached the goal just a few weeks after us. The second and third sentences of the telegram referred mostly to one-upmanship. Woodward's group had not really accomplished a *total synthesis* of cortisone; they had not really built a villa from scratch. They had only completed a *formal total synthesis*—construction of a cortisone precursor, a barn, which had been transformed by Fieser into another intermediate (say, a barely livable house) and, finally, by other workers into the cortisone villa itself. In the *formal* sense, Woodward's group had indeed accomplished the total synthesis of cortisone; and I, for one, was not blaming them for wanting to get maximum publicity for this achievement. (Woodward frequently quoted the saying "No publicity is bad publicity!")

More disturbing was the sentence, "Tell Bliss, Gates says hold journal day or two." We, who had sent in our "Communication" a couple of weeks earlier, did not know whether our manuscript had been accepted; Woodward and Fieser, who were still writing their papers, had already arranged to have them appear in an issue of the *JACS* that was being held up for them. It was clear that the Harvard papers would not be subjected to the standard refereeing process, and that the Harvard group had learned of our own manuscript submission. It was impossible not to brood on the overpowering, quasi-incestuous influence the Harvard chemical establishment had on *JACS*. The preceding editor, Arthur Lamb, had been professor of chemistry at Harvard; when he retired, the assistant editorship for organic chemistry passed to Marshall Gates at the University of Rochester. Gates was a Harvard alumnus who had received his Ph.D. degree under Louis Fieser, one of the Harvard participants in the cortisone race—but Lamb's managing editor, Allen Bliss, remained at Harvard. Robert Burns Woodward, our most powerful academic competitor, was a Harvard professor; Max Tishler, Merck's research vice president and leader of the Merck cortisone team, was himself a Harvard product and had close relations with Fieser. For a few days, a wave of paranoia overwhelmed us. Though a gringo chemist, I suddenly felt like a native Mexican—misused and discriminated against by the Yankees up north. Even now, four decades after the event, I can still feel my adrenals respond.

In the end, no fewer than four "Communications to the Editor," dealing with different synthetic approaches to cortisone, appeared in the August 1951 issue of *JACS*. Ours had been received on 22 June (every *JACS* article contains the actual date of receipt of the manuscript); Woodward's and Fieser's on 9 July; and the Merck group's on 13 July. In spite of their undeniable excellence and expertise, we felt that the Merck team had gotten away with murder. The last two steps of their cortisone synthesis involved "a procedure to be described later." Obviously, no chemist could evaluate or repeat such a statement; it simply had to be taken on faith—something that under ordinary circumstances would be inadmissible under the publication practices of the *JACS*.

I cite these publication minutiae to illustrate the sensitivity of a small research group working in the chemical wilderness of Mexico, who felt that such privileges would never have been extended to them: *quod licet iovi non licet bovi* ("what is allowed to God is not permitted to the oxen"). Yet struggling in a scientific backwater had its compensation, since it drew particular attention to our achievement.

Life magazine featured us in a huge picture—Rosenkranz, Stork, and I in coat and tie, the rest of our team (Octavio Mancera, Jesús Romo, Juan Pataki, Juan Berlin, Rosa Yashin, Mercedes Velasco, Alexander Nussbaum, and Enrique Batres) in immaculate white lab coats, grouped around a gleaming glass table and apparently mesmerized by an enormous yam root, which overwhelms the molecular model of cortisone lying next to it. Rosenkranz is holding a test tube, filled almost to the brim with white crystals—the chemist's equivalent of the climber's flag on top of Mt. Everest. For the photographer's benefit, the tube had been filled with sodium chloride, because at that time we had synthesized only milligram quantities of cortisone. *Life*'s headline above the picture read, "CORTISONE FROM GIANT YAM," with the subsidiary headline "Scientists with average age of 27 find big supply in Mexican root." *Newsweek* had actually beaten *Life* by a week. (Do I attribute priority mania to the media to show that we scientists are not the only ones so driven?) Its headline read: "SYNTHETIC CORTISONE—AND FROM YAMS," followed by more balm for our rapidly healing wounds of Yankee-induced paranoia: "Unexpectedly the cortisone race was won by Syntex, Inc., of Mexico City." But the quotation that probably made our entire team feel best appreciated—one last blast of the bellows on the flickering flame of our pride—appeared in the September issue of *Harper's Magazine*:

> As perhaps no other recent development, it [cortisone] . . . also under-
> scores a point often overlooked in a big-money age. Big minds rather than
> big research budgets lead to big discoveries. . . . Last but not least, it
> should be noted that the leader in the race was a chemical manufacturer
> in presumably backward Mexico.

III

Although my story thus far would seem to illustrate the competitive aspects of scientific research, it does not disclose the collegiality and mutual esteem that even bitter competitors, like athletes or mountain climbers, display after an event. The following summer, a Gordon Conference focusing exclusively on steroid chemistry was held in New Hampton, a hamlet in central New Hampshire. Gordon Conferences are high-prestige, five-day research retreats in specialized disciplines, limited to fewer than a hundred participants, who live together while talking, breathing, and dreaming science. The mornings and evenings at Gordon Conferences are dedicated to competition and peacockery: to the presentation of one's latest scientific achievements before a passel of peers who dispense approbation and skepticism in various degrees. Even the adjectives employed to describe one's competitors' work are carefully chosen: "sound" is meant pejoratively, while "useful" is damning; "brilliant" is standard approval; it takes combinations like "rapierlike" to make one sit up. The afternoons, usually spent on the shores of Lake Winnipesaukee, are dedicated to collegial exchanges. Many a scientific collaboration has first been spawned while the chemists swat mosquitoes by that lake.

All the cortisone competitors—the four who had already reached the summit, and the others who were still climbing toward that goal—were present at the conference, along with other chemists and biochemists actively pursuing steroid research. One afternoon, the leaders of the various cortisone teams were reminiscing about the events of the past year. Our competitiveness and paranoia had been forgotten. By then, after all, the Syntex group had joined the exclusive club: a second "Communication" of ours, dealing with the synthesis of cortisone from hecogenin (another steroid sapogenin which Marker had isolated years before from the waste juice of sisal production) had breezed through the editorial machinery of the *JACS* without any referees. Its structure (figure 4.7) was quite different from that of diosgenin (figure 4.6)—being more like that of the bile acids (figure 4.5)—because of the presence of oxygen in ring C. We had succeeded in devising a partial synthesis of cortisone from that commercial waste product, a process that the British pharmaceutical giant Glaxo subsequently used for many years (under license from Syntex), using sisal wastes from East African plantations.

It may have been Woodward, or maybe Gilbert Stork, who mused, "I bet all it takes these days is the title 'Synthesis of Cortisone' and a reasonable address for a 'Communication' to appear in the next issue of the *JACS*." Two days later, Stork, Woodward, Sarett (the Merck chemist who had accomplished the Ur-synthesis of cortisone), and I had concocted a manuscript of fewer than a thousand words entitled "Partial Synthesis of Cortisone from Neohamptogenin." The supposed authors were F. Nathaniel Greene and Alvina Turnbull; the address, the most prestigious of them all: Converse Memorial Laboratory, Harvard University, Cambridge, Massachusetts. Drs. Greene and Turnbull, our collective nom de plume, had made the sensational discovery that New Hampshire maple syrup represented a potentially inexhaustible source of a new steroid, now named "neohamptogenin." This steroid from the WASPish jungles of New England already possessed the crucial oxygen atom in position 11 of ring C—the structural feature of cortisone (figure 4.3) which had presented the greatest obstacle to the Syntex-Harvard-Merck groups—as well as the two-carbon–three-oxygen side chain of cortisone. What neohamptogenin (figure 4.8) lacked was an oxygen atom at position 3 of ring A, in which all conventional steroids are oxygenated. Greene and Turnbull were faced

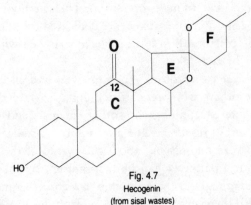

Fig. 4.7
Hecogenin
(from sisal wastes)

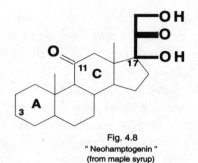

Fig. 4.8
" Neohamptogenin "
(from maple syrup)

with the task—unprecedented in steroid chemistry in the 1950s (or even in the 1990s)—of having to introduce an oxygen atom into a "naked" ring A from a precursor that already had the crucial cortisone oxygen atom in ring C. The "Communication" consisted of a description, with faked literature citations, of how this was accomplished. Subtly interwoven was a version of the Merck group's August "Communication," in which we used the "take it on faith—we'll tell you later" dodge for the key step.

On the last evening of the conference, Woodward announced that he had been asked by two Harvard colleagues to present a preliminary announcement. He had a remarkable ability to maintain a deadpan mien and was a consummate speaker, notorious for his insistence on using chalk (two colors at a minimum) and blackboard, rather than slides, the better to display his virtuosity in drawing chemical structures. Slowly he led the assembled audience through the step-by-step transformation of "neohamptogenin" into cortisone. Halfway through his lecture, while pontificating on Greene and Turnbull's discovery of a new chemical reaction, he was interrupted by a well-known Swiss steroid chemist, a still-climbing cortisone competitor, who proclaimed that his group had also performed this reaction. Woodward threw one of his fishlike, nonblinking stares into the audience; Stork, Sarett, and I were convulsed at this display of priority-manship, oblivious of the fact that all of us were infected by that same ubiquitous virus. Only as Woodward approached the end of his talk, and explained that purification of the penultimate synthetic intermediate had been accomplished by passage through a column of Milorganite (a commercial fertilizer) supplied by the New Hampshire Maple Syrup Producers Association, did shoulders in the audience begin to shake.

Upon his return to Harvard, Woodward presented at one of his evening seminars—famous for their rigor even then, years before he won his Nobel Prize—the latest news from the Gordon Conference, including the putative cortisone synthesis from neohamptogenin. I was already back in Mexico

47

City, but both our agent Stork and our mole "Flash" reported what transpired. Woodward presented the work so forcefully that the assembled graduate students and research fellows left with the firm conviction that they had heard of exciting new research. Irritated at the gullibility of Woodward's audience, Stork later approached a group of students to debunk the tale, but was totally unsuccessful. Not one of the students was prepared to accept that neohamptogenin was phony. This event more than any other persuaded us not to submit our bogus "Communication" to the editor of the *JACS*. What if he so greased the editorial trail that the manuscript appeared in print before we even had time to admit that it was a hoax? The *JACS* was not known for its humor, and none of us was willing to have our *real* papers ostracized in the future.

In the end, none of the cortisone syntheses that appeared in the August 1951 issue contributed to the treatment of a single arthritic patient. A few months later, Syntex's management received an inquiry from the Upjohn Company of Kalamazoo, asking whether we could supply them with *ten tons* of the female sex hormone progesterone. Since the world's entire annual production at that time was probably less than a hundredth that amount, such a request seemed outlandish. No one in our group could conceive of a medical application of progesterone that would require tons of a steroid hormone. We concluded that Upjohn was planning to use progesterone as a chemical intermediate rather than as a therapeutic hormone. Our conclusion proved correct when, a few weeks later, we learned through a patent issued to Upjohn in South Africa (where patents are granted much more rapidly than in the United States) that two of its scientists, Durey H. Peterson and Herbert C. Murray, had made a sensational discovery: fermentation of progesterone with certain microorganisms resulting in a one-step, high-yield introduction of oxygen into the desired 11-position of ring C. What we chemists in Mexico City, Cambridge, and Rahway had accomplished laboriously through a series of complicated chemical transformations, Upjohn's microorganism did in a single step in a few hours.

Still, our successful synthesis of cortisone from diosgenin had permanently placed Mexico on the map of steroid research. It was, moreover, Upjohn's requirements for tons of progesterone—a quantity that at that time could be satisfied only from diosgenin—that started Syntex on the way to becoming a pharmaceutical giant. The process was accelerated by our synthesis—a few months later, again in Mexico City—of the first oral contraceptive. Reichstein's telegram, "No depression," of just a few months earlier applied to cortisone, but not to us. We were elated: *Que viva México!!*

CHAPTER 5

Birth of the Pill

F OR A TIME AFTER A CANCER OPERATION, the patient is allowed morphine almost *ad libitum*. The effect of my last injection had worn off, and I had rung for the nurse to give me another one. I focused on the chocolate-colored, Teflon-smooth skin of the nurse's upper arm, and lightly touched it. "How did you end up with such superb muscles?" I asked. "I'm a bodybuilder," she replied, and continued, "Are you really the father of the Pill?"

I am often asked the question in this phallocentric way; if I had been a woman, would she have asked, "Are you the mother of the Pill?" Usually I respond in the same vein, pointing out that for a new drug to be born there is needed also a mother and frequently also a midwife or an obstetrician. The organic chemist must first produce the substance; the biologist must then demonstrate its activity in animals; only then can the clinician administer the material to humans. I led the small chemical team at Syntex in Mexico City, which accomplished the first synthesis of a steroid oral contraceptive on 15 October 1951. Gregory Pincus of the Worcester Foundation for Experimental Biology in Shrewsbury, Massachusetts, headed the biological group that first reported the ovulation-inhibiting properties of these steroids in animals. The Harvard gynecologist John Rock and his colleagues performed the clinical studies to demonstrate contraceptive efficacy in humans. If I am the father, Pincus must be the mother, or is it vice versa? At least there is no doubt about the part John Rock played in this birth.

But to be accurate, one needs to retrace its genealogy at least down to the grandparents and a few uncles. By definition, every synthetic drug originates in a chemist's laboratory; what happens to this chemical entity after it has been synthesized, however, how it ultimately becomes a drug that reaches the consumer, depends very much on circumstance. Frequently, a substance synthesized in connection with some specific chemical problem is only as an afterthought, sometimes even years later, submitted for wide pharmacological screening in the hope that some useful activity will be noted as an extra bonus. The insecticidal activity of DDT was discovered through such screening decades after the substance was first synthesized in a German university laboratory. Alternatively, a substance may be synthesized for a specific biological purpose, found to be inactive in that regard, and then exposed to wider pharmacological scrutiny in the hope that something might be salvaged. The literature of medicinal chemistry is replete with instances in which such random screening uncovered unexpected biological activity that provided the impetus for further chemical, pharmacological, and clinical work.

It is hardly surprising that the modern medicinal chemist is unhappy with this state of affairs, as predictability rather than serendipity is the essence of science, and especially of chemistry. Chemists since Paul Ehrlich, who founded modern chemotherapy in the early part of this century, have attempted to establish relationships between chemical structure and biological activity that lead to the a-priori prediction of a potentially useful drug. To a considerable extent, the development of steroid oral contraceptives represents a successful instance of this predictive approach, in which we deliberately set out to synthesize a substance that might mimic the biological action of the female sex hormone progesterone when administered orally, since progesterone itself is essentially inactive by this route unless given in huge doses.

I

By the middle of this century, the multiple biological functions of the female sex hormone progesterone were well known: among them, maintenance during pregnancy of the proper uterine environment and inhibition of further ovulation (so a pregnant woman cannot be fertilized during pregnancy). Accordingly, progesterone could be considered "nature's contraceptive," and suggestions had appeared in the literature of the preceding three decades—notably by the Austrian endocrinologist Ludwig Haberlandt—that progesterone (secreted by the woman's corpus luteum) might be useful in fertility control. So infatuated had he become with the contraceptive potential of the corpus luteum hormone that during one carnival celebration in the 1920s, Haberlandt's students hung a banner by his home in Innsbruck with the ditty, "*Verdirb nicht Deines Vaters Ruhm mit Deinem Corpus Luteum*" ("Don't mar your father's renown with your corpus luteum"). Were it not for the fact that the natural hormone displays only weak activity when given by mouth and requires daily injections for sustained activity, progesterone might have found practical application as a contraceptive, rather than just in the treatment of various menstrual disorders and as an occasional palliative for certain types of miscarriage.

Until the late 1940s, the dogma was that progestational activity was extremely structure-specific, to use the terminology of steroid chemistry introduced in chapter 4, and limited to progesterone itself and some analogs with an additional carbon-carbon bond between the 6–7 or 11–12 positions (see figure 5.1). This supposed structure specificity was supported by the observation of Swiss investigators that even stereoisomers of progesterone displayed no progestational activity.

(This statement requires one more detour into an aspect of the steroid chemist's language not broached in the preceding chapter. The two-dimensional drawing in figure 5.1 implies nothing about the *stereochemistry* of progesterone—that is, about the position of the individual atoms in space. But, in fact, one should visualize the ring carbons as located in the plane of the paper and all other connecting substituents [for instance, the hydrogen atoms] as projecting either above or below that plane. With a more refined steroid shorthand that takes account of stereochemistry, the structure of progesterone can be rewritten as depicted in figure 5.2 by indicating this planar location only for those atoms to which one wants to call attention: the conventional shorthand notation employs a solid line [also called β] for bonds above the plane [for example, carbon atoms 18 and 19, and the hydrogen atom at position 8] and a dotted line [also called α]

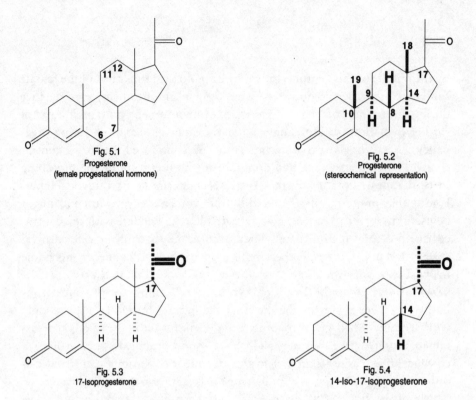

Fig. 5.1
Progesterone
(female progestational hormone)

Fig. 5.2
Progesterone
(stereochemical representation)

Fig. 5.3
17-Isoprogesterone

Fig. 5.4
14-Iso-17-isoprogesterone

for substituents below the plane of the paper [for example, hydrogen atoms attached to positions 9 and 14].)

The Swiss scientists noted that neither 17-isoprogesterone (figure 5.3) nor 14-iso-17-isoprogesterone (figure 5.4)—which differ from the natural hormone (figure 5.2) only in the *spatial* orientation of the 17-, or 14- and 17-substituents, respectively—exhibited any discernible progestational activity.

It was for this reason that I was so impressed as a graduate student when Maximilian Ehrenstein of the University of Pennsylvania reported in 1944 the multistage chemical transformation of the cardiac stimulant strophanthidin, another type of naturally occurring steroid (figure 5.5), into an oily "19-norprogesterone" (figure 5.6)—so called because it lacked the methyl carbon atom number 19, *nor* meaning "less." Ehrenstein's synthetic substance differed from the natural hormone progesterone (figure 5.2) in two important respects:

1. It had the *wrong* orientation at positions 14 and 17—stereochemical changes (see figures 5.3 and 5.4) that in the natural hormone destroyed progestational activity.
2. Even more important, there was a *structural* difference in that the carbon atom number 19 attached to position 10 in the natural hormone progesterone (figure 5.2) was now replaced by a hydrogen atom (see position 10 in figure 5.6).

Ehrenstein's minute amount of oily product (more precisely called 14-iso-17-iso-19-norprogesterone) was sufficient to be tested for biological activity only in two rabbits, but it exhibited a high progestational effect in one of them. In ordinary circumstances, doing such an experiment with only two rabbits would be totally unacceptable, but that is all the material that was available. Strophanthidin, isolated from foxglove, proved to be hopeless as a starting material because its chemical structure (figure 5.5) is so different from that (figure 5.2) of progesterone or even 14-iso-17-iso-19-norprogesterone (figure 5.6) that it took Ehrenstein a full ten years to repeat even the synthesis he had achieved in 1944. Thus in 1951 the question remained: Was the high progestational activity that had been observed in one rabbit in 1944 a fluke, or was it real? If real, retention of biological activity in spite of extensive changes (structural *and* stereochemical) clearly upset the then-prevailing assumption that any chemical alteration in the structure of progesterone would lower or abolish its biological activity.

This apparent contradiction of a generally held dogma had intrigued me as a graduate student when I first encountered Ehrenstein's paper. Yet,

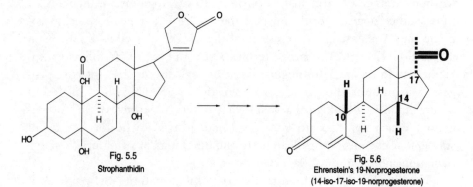

Fig. 5.5
Strophanthidin

Fig. 5.6
Ehrenstein's 19-Norprogesterone
(14-iso-17-iso-19-norprogesterone)

as happens so often in science, many other things suddenly fell into place. It was almost as if my earlier training and personal ambitions had been deliberately assembled to allow me to capitalize, in Mexico City, on the seemingly disparate observations I have just cited. For the first time in my career, I had ample laboratory manpower at my disposal, even though most of it consisted of locally trained technicians rather than professionals. This enabled me, together with George Rosenkranz, to institute other projects in the steroid field in addition to cortisone synthesis. For instance, I was able to pursue my first love in the steroid field (and the chief topic of my Ph.D. dissertation at the University of Wisconsin): the possibility of chemically producing the estrogenic hormones from the much more readily available male sex hormone testosterone (figure 5.7). In contrast to the latter, which was produced in Europe on an industrial scale from cholesterol (and at Syntex from diosgenin), the female sex hormone estradiol (figure 5.8), used for clinical purposes, had to be isolated from huge volumes of pregnant mares' urine because of the great difficulty of synthesizing it chemically from accessible steroid raw materials.

At the start of the Second World War, Hans H. Inhoffen at Schering in Germany had discovered a chemical method to accomplish this goal, and Syntex was interested in having an alternative procedure at its disposal. One of our first publications in 1950, in fact, dealt with an innovative solution to the problem of the chemical synthesis of the estrogenic hormones from the more readily available testosterone. In the technical jargon, what we had accomplished was the *aromatization* of ring A of testosterone (figure 5.7) into the *aromatic* benzene ring A of estradiol (figure 5.8): that is, we discovered a way of selectively expelling the methyl group (carbon number 19) attached at position 10 of testosterone, which was nature's barrier to the simple transformation of the male into the female sex hormone. Using that same procedure, we decided to remove the methyl group (carbon number 19) attached to position 10 of progesterone (figure 5.2), thus synthesizing a hybrid molecule (figure 5.10) that possessed the aromatic ring A characteristic of estradiol (figure 5.8) as well as a side chain at position 17 typical of progesterone. Our hope was that this chemical Siamese twin (figure 5.10) might exhibit biological properties of both progesterone and estradiol; as it turned out, this synthetic hybrid was devoid of any interesting biological activity whatsoever. Nevertheless, this investigation, which appeared to be a dead end, proved to be the key to all subsequent chemical work leading to the development of an orally active ovulation inhibitor.

The likelihood that Ehrenstein's *structural* alteration—the removal of the angular methyl group (carbon atom 19 in figure 5.2) of progesterone—

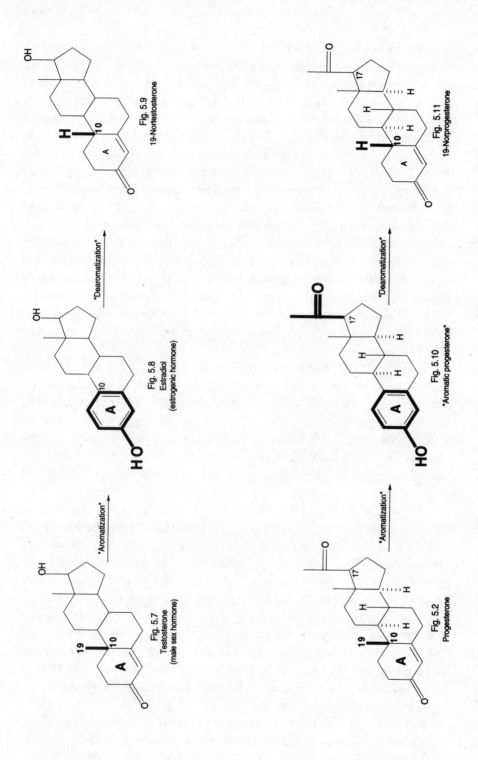

Fig. 5.7
Testosterone
(male sex hormone)

"Aromatization"

Fig. 5.8
Estradiol
(estrogenic hormone)

"Dearomatization"

Fig. 5.9
19-Nortestosterone

Fig. 5.2
Progesterone

"Aromatization"

Fig. 5.10
"Aromatic progesterone"

"Dearomatization"

Fig. 5.11
19-Norprogesterone

55

was responsible for the high biological activity of his "19-norprogesterone" (figure 5.6) suddenly seemed more remote when, in 1950, the Australian chemist Arthur J. Birch described the synthesis of 19-nortestosterone (figure 5.9). This was a substance identical in every stereochemical detail with the natural male sex hormone testosterone (figure 5.7), but lacking its angular methyl group attached to C-10. Birch had achieved that feat by a *dearomatization* process from the estrogenic hormone estradiol (figure 5.8). According to Birch, such removal (figure 5.9) of the 19-angular methyl group of testosterone (figure 5.7) resulted in a marked *reduction* in androgenic activity compared with the parent male sex hormone. Nevertheless, since we had available a substantial quantity of the synthetic Siamese twin of progesterone and estradiol, the "aromatic" progesterone (figure 5.10), we decided to apply Birch's dearomatization process to it, and obtained for the first time crystalline, pure 19-norprogesterone (figure 5.11), which—in contrast to Ehrenstein's oily 14-iso-17-iso-19-norprogesterone (figure 5.6)—was identical in all stereochemical respects to the natural hormone progesterone, except that it had a hydrogen atom rather than a methyl group attached to position 10.

Since in 1951 we had no facilities at Syntex in Mexico City to examine the biological activity of our new steroid, we mailed it immediately to a commercial laboratory in Madison, Wisconsin, with the request that it be tested for progestational activity. The compound proved to be highly active, thus confirming Ehrenstein's observation seven years earlier that the removal of carbon atom 19 from progesterone not only did *not* diminish biological activity, as might have been expected from prior work, *but in fact augmented it.*

We also sent some of our synthetic crystalline 19-norprogesterone to Dr. Roy Hertz of the National Cancer Institute in Bethesda, Maryland, because of his interest at that time in the possible treatment of cervical cancer through local injections of high doses of progesterone. This was a painful procedure, and it was clearly desirable to consider a more potent progestational compound. Hertz confirmed the progestational activity of our substance: in fact, he showed that when *given by injection*, it was four to eight times as active as the natural hormone, thus making it the most powerful progestational agent known at that time. We submitted our work for publication to the *Journal of the American Chemical Society* on 21 May 1951, and immediately set out to develop an approach to synthesize an *orally effective* progestational analog.

Here again, a lead from the scientific literature expedited our work; in science one invariably builds on the work of predecessors. Over a dozen years earlier, just before the outbreak of the Second World War, Inhoffen and his colleagues in the Berlin laboratories of Schering had introduced acetylene (two carbon atoms connected by a triple bond, written as HC≡CH) into position 17 of the estrogenic hormone estradiol and the male sex hormone testosterone. The resulting product in the estrogenic series, called 17α-ethynylestradiol (figure 5.12), surprisingly showed increased oral estrogenic activity. (Twenty-five years later this was to become one of the estrogenic components of the combination oral contraceptive pill.) The product resulting from the addition of acetylene into position 17 of the male sex hormone testosterone, 17α-ethynyltestosterone (figure 5.13), displayed totally unanticipated properties.

Not only was this synthetic steroid orally active; but, according to the German investigators, it also exhibited perceptible *progestational* (female sex hormone) characteristics, rather than the expected androgenic (male sex hormone) activity. This was the first observation that an orally effective, progestational compound could be synthesized; and though this synthetic steroid (figure 5.13), also known generically as *ethisterone*, never found great utility in medicine, it was precisely the hint we needed in the summer of 1951.

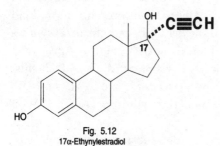

Fig. 5.12
17α-Ethynylestradiol

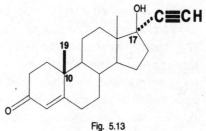

Fig. 5.13
17α-Ethynyltestosterone;
ethisterone

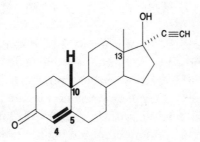

Fig. 5.14
Norethisterone or norethindrone
(19-nor-17α-ethynyltestosterone)

Having found that the removal of the 19-methyl group of progesterone (figure 5.2), leading to 19-norprogesterone (figure 5.11), greatly increased progestational activity when injected, we did not take long to predict that removal of the 19-methyl group of orally active ethisterone would increase its progestational activity while (we hoped) retaining its oral efficacy. Using the chemical methodology developed in synthesizing 19-norprogesterone (figure 5.11), Luis Miramontes, a Mexican chemistry student carrying out his bachelor thesis in the Syntex laboratories under the direction of George Rosenkranz and myself, succeeded, on 15 October 1951, in synthesizing 19-nor-17α-ethynyltestosterone (figure 5.14), generically known as "norethisterone" or "norethindrone." Not in our wildest dreams did we imagine that this substance would eventually become the active progestational ingredient of nearly half the oral contraceptives used worldwide.

We immediately submitted the compound to our favorite commercial testing laboratory in Wisconsin for biological evaluation and gloated happily when the report came back that it was more active as an oral progestational hormone than any other steroid known at that time. In less than six months, we had accomplished our goal of synthesizing a superpotent, orally active progestational agent.

We filed our patent application for norethindrone on 22 November 1951 (it is the first patent for a drug listed in the National Inventors Hall of Fame in Akron, Ohio), and I reported the details of our chemical synthesis, together with the substance's biological activity, at the April 1952 meeting of the American Chemical Society's Division of Medicinal Chemistry in Milwaukee. The abstract of this report was published in March 1952, and the full article with complete experimental details appeared in 1954 in the *Journal of the American Chemical Society*.

A few weeks after having synthesized the substance, we sent it to various endocrinologists and clinicians: first to Roy Hertz at the National Cancer Institute and Alexander Lipschutz in Chile; later to Gregory Pincus at the Worcester Foundation in Shrewsbury, Massachusetts, to Robert Greenblatt in Georgia, and to Edward Tyler of the Los Angeles Planned Parenthood Center. In fact, it was Dr. Tyler who in November 1954 presented the first clinical results of using norethindrone for the treatment of various menstrual disorders and fertility problems.

On 31 August 1953, well over a year after my first public report on norethindrone, Frank D. Colton of Searle filed a patent for the synthesis of a closely related compound (figure 5.15), generically known as "norethynodrel," which differed from norethindrone (figure 5.14) only in having the double bond between positions 5 and 10, rather than between positions 4 and 5. Mild treatment of Colton's norethynodrel with hydrochloric acid or,

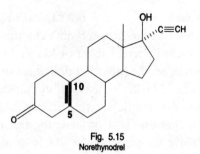

Fig. 5.15
Norethynodrel

in fact, even so weak an acid as human gastric juice converts it to a large extent into norethindrone.

II

The Syntex and Searle compounds, together with many other steroids, were tested for ovulation inhibition during 1953–54 by Gregory Pincus and his collaborators at the Worcester Foundation. Pincus and Dr. John Rock, the Harvard clinician, were interested in ovulation inhibitors as possible agents for contraception (eventually turning into a reality Haberlandt's prediction, made thirty years earlier, that a substance with the biological properties of progesterone might be a useful contraceptive) and found that Syntex's norethindrone and Searle's norethynodrel were the two most active steroids in that respect.

Pincus, a consultant for Searle, understandably picked the Searle compound for use in his further biological and clinical studies. In the meanwhile, Syntex—a minute company compared with other pharmaceutical enterprises, and having neither biological laboratories nor marketing force—went its own way in trying to convert this laboratory discovery into its first proprietary commercial product. We were able to handle the lack of biological laboratories by sending the synthetic steroids we developed to outside investigators. Our lack of a marketing organization, however, required that we collaborate with another pharmaceutical company. For a strange historical reason, we chose Parke-Davis.

No great affection existed between the two companies during the late 1940s through the mid-1950s, primarily because Parke-Davis, one of the most conservative of all pharmaceutical companies in the United States, had totally missed out in the steroid field by not capitalizing on Marker's steroid work in Mexico (as described in the preceding chapter), even though Parke-Davis had been the chief financial backer of Marker's academic research at Penn State. Tiny Syntex, on the other hand, had followed through with the industrial exploitation of Marker's observation that steroidal sapogenins of plant origin constituted versatile starting materials for steroid hormone manufacture. We felt that one way of lessening this resentment of Syntex was to offer an exclusive license to Parke-Davis to market norethindrone. After intense negotiations, an agreement was reached in 1956. Parke-Davis received an exclusive license to market norethindrone, in return for purchasing it from Syntex at a price that bore a fixed relationship to Parke-Davis's final sales price. Syntex thus had a major financial stake in Parke-Davis's commercial success.

I participated in these negotiations because, although I had left Syntex in 1952 to teach at Wayne State University in Detroit (next door to Parke-Davis), I had retained a close relationship as a consultant to the Mexican company. We provided Parke-Davis with all the laboratory and preliminary clinical data we had accumulated through our outside investigators; and after doing some additional required toxicology and monkey experiments, Parke-Davis received Food and Drug Administration approval for norethindrone in 1957—at the same time as did Searle for its compound—for the treatment of menstrual disorders and for certain conditions of infertility. Thus, both norethindrone and norethynodrel went on the market independently in the same year.

We at Syntex had filed a patent application on norethindrone in November 1951 and published the results the following year; Searle did not submit its patent application on norethynodrel until August 1953. To what extent their work was prompted simply by a wish to circumvent our patent priority will probably never be known, because Searle never chose to publish any of Colton's chemical research in the scientific literature, although Searle scientists were otherwise well known for publishing their results widely. But the fact that their norethynodrel (figure 5.15), which was not covered by Syntex's patent, is transformed into our patented norethindrone (figure 5.14) by gastric acid after ingestion, raised an interesting legal question: Is synthesis of a patented compound in the stomach an infringement of an issued patent? I urged that we push this issue to a legal resolution, but Parke-Davis did not concur. Searle was selling an important antimotion sickness drug, Dramamine, which contained Parke-Davis's antihistamine Benadryl, and our norethindrone seemed in 1957 small potatoes over which it was not worth fighting with a valued customer.

Preliminary clinical experiments by Pincus, Rock, and their associates in Puerto Rico had demonstrated that the ovulation-inhibiting properties of these substances could be employed for contraception as well as for menstrual regulation. Pincus, a remarkable entrepreneur, convinced Searle that the commercial potential of an oral contraceptive warranted some risk taking. He deserves a great deal of credit for persuading that firm to proceed, ignoring fears of a potential consumer boycott of other Searle drugs as a result of the Catholic Church's opposition to birth control. (In certain countries, such as Spain or Italy, where contraceptive use of these steroids was not approved for many years because of religious opposition, the euphemism *menstrual regulation*—for which these compounds had been approved in the United States in 1957—served to hide their much wider contraceptive usage. In Japan, such a subterfuge persisted for over thirty years.) Syntex, of course, had no such problem, since it had no other drugs on the market that could be the object of any real or imagined boycott. We had a much bigger problem—no marketing organization; but we did not lack entrepreneurs.

Syntex's entrepreneurial counterpart to Pincus was Dr. Alejandro Zaffaroni, who had joined the firm in 1951, shortly after receiving his Ph.D. from the University of Rochester, to head at age twenty-eight a newly formed biochemical department. A native of Uruguay, Zaffaroni had demonstrated in graduate school the applicability of a new separation technique, paper chromatography, to steroids—a feat that promptly earned him an international reputation. Though he was not involved with the original scientific work on oral progestational steroids, Zaffaroni was the driving force behind parallel clinical experiments conducted on behalf of Syntex by clinicians in Mexico City, San Antonio, and Los Angeles in order to accumulate the necessary human data for FDA approval of norethindrone as a contraceptive agent.

The geographical locations of these early clinical trials merit a detour into a question of medical ethics. From time to time, criticism has been expressed, notably by relatively affluent women in America, that the first clinical studies of the Pill in the 1950s were performed by Searle with Puerto Rican women, and by Syntex with Mexican ones—in each instance, from the poor strata of those societies—without the type of "informed consent" forms now used routinely in all clinical experiments with new drugs. Was this just another manifestation of exploitation of the poor?

Even though this question is usually posed by persons looking through today's glasses at yesterday's problems, the answer is still unsatisfactory: yes and no. Yes, the poor are frequently the human guinea pigs in drug trials, just as they play such roles for young dentists, surgeons, or barbers honing their skills. How realistic is it to expect wealthy suburbanites to volunteer for such functions? But the situation becomes even more complicated in respect to contraception, especially for women who often desperately desire to avoid unwanted pregnancies, but have no access to birth control. If the clinical work is done carefully and under appropriate supervision, is it unethical to use poor volunteers and in the process offer them their first opportunity for personal control over their fertility? And is it then surprising that some clinical side effects are first detected with poorer clinical subjects, when incidents such as nausea and bleeding irregularities, or effects on libido can *only* be discovered through clinical experimentation? Where again is that long line of affluent matrons volunteering for clinical studies with some new experimental contraceptive? The question to what extent such work with predominantly Hispanic poor women represented gross exploitation of the disadvantaged is further addressed in chapters 9 and 15, where I deal with the question of the Pill's side effects.

But to address an even more complicated issue: several women's groups in the United States, such as the sophisticated Boston Women's Health Book Collective, vigorously opposed the use of certain injectable steroid contraceptives, leading to the battle cry, "Ban the Jab!" Yet the health authorities of a number of poorer countries, such as Thailand or Mexico, demanded such injectable preparations for their country on quite pragmatic grounds, such as ease of distribution and more general acceptance of injectable drugs as compared with the American preference for oral ingestion, and conducted clinical trials among rural population groups under World Health Organization auspices. Do comparatively wealthy Americans have the right to call such clinical studies in Thailand or Mexico "exploitation of the poor"? And are "informed consent" forms for college-educated Bostonians appropriate for illiterate peasants, who, nevertheless, deserve access to modern contraception? These problems, which are still not resolved in the 1990s, were even more difficult in the 1950s, when abortion was illegal, and when comparatively high dosages of the first steroid contraceptives were employed so as to avoid the risk of method failure with the first groups of women volunteers to whom otherwise nothing but an unwanted pregnancy could be offered as an alternative.

But to return to the history of the late 1950s. Just as it became obvious that oral contraception was about to be converted into practical reality, Parke-Davis got cold feet and refused even to consider marketing norethindrone as an oral contraceptive. Thus, while Searle was proceeding full steam ahead toward FDA approval, Syntex suddenly had to find an alternative marketing outlet or be deprived of any financial benefit from a field in which, relatively speaking, it had committed a larger proportion of its resources than had anybody else. Parke-Davis's apprehension about a possible Catholic-inspired boycott of some of its other products was perhaps not unreasonable, but such a consumer backlash never developed. Actually, three years earlier, Charles Pfizer & Company had an option from Syntex to market norethindrone, an option Pfizer had not exercised because its president, an active Roman Catholic layperson, felt that Pfizer should not touch any agent even potentially related to birth control.

Thus, it was up to Zaffaroni to start almost from scratch to find another marketing candidate. He made a brilliant choice by negotiating a favorable contract with the Ortho Division of Johnson & Johnson, probably the most effective and important marketer of contraceptive hardware devices at that time. But a monumental snag was about to occur: Parke-Davis refused to release to Ortho the monkey studies it had completed on norethindrone. I can only speculate on the reason for this refusal: "If I dare not taste this tempting cake, why should I help someone else do so? What's more, though the cook offered it to me first, I still don't like him."

As a result, Ortho had to repeat a number of studies that had already been carried out; and thus was unable to receive FDA approval to market Syntex's norethindrone for contraceptive use until 1962 (under the trade name Ortho-Novum), two years after Searle first hit the market with its oral contraceptive norethynodrel (under the trade name Enovid). In 1964, Parke-Davis finally woke up to the facts of life and decided to enter the contraceptive market after all. After obtaining a license from Syntex for a derivative of norethindrone—norethindrone acetate—the company received FDA approval to market the compound as an oral contraceptive. Thus, though initially Searle had the oral contraceptive market to itself, by the mid-1960s Syntex—through its two licensees, Ortho and Parke-Davis, and through its own sales force established in 1964 by the initiative and under the direct supervision of Zaffaroni—had gained the major share of the U.S. oral contraceptive market.

III

Starting in the 1960s, I was often asked, "How do you feel about the social outcome of this work?" Depending on the circumstances, I may have grinned affectionately, shrugged my shoulders modestly, or even answered seriously that if I had to do things over again, there is little I, *as a chemist*, could or would have changed. Perhaps more relevant is the feeling that had I been a woman scientist, I would have been unashamedly proud to have been associated with the creation of oral contraception. I have no regrets that the Pill has contributed to the sexual revolution of our time and perhaps expedited it, because most of those changes in sexual mores would have happened anyway. Still, as this question continued to be posed in the 1970s and 1980s, my answer became progressively more complicated. As I shall recount in chapters 9 and 15, those last two decades were an important transition period for society and for me, during which I turned from a "hard" physical scientist to a much "softer" chemist concerned with the deeper social ramifications of my work.

But there is one question, frequently just implied or transmitted through look or voice inflection, that turns me irritably defensive. It deals with the questioner's perception of the mint of money that supposedly ended up in my pocket as a result of my name appearing first on the list of inventors of U.S. Patent No. 2,744,122. I can give two answers.

One is short and devoid of humor or even suspense. As a full-time employee of Syntex, my employment agreement contained the standard clause that every chemist working for a pharmaceutical company affirms: for $1.00 and/or "other valuable considerations," the inventor agrees to sign all patent applications and to assign to the company all rights to any issued patent. "Other valuable considerations" refers to the security of one's employment, the salary one receives, and possibly even a bonus or stock option, but never to a royalty based on a percentage of eventual sales. That would be reserved to outside inventors or other third parties.

I prefer, however, to answer the question by recounting my tussle with the *Berkeley Barb*, an acerbic muckraking tabloid which bit the dust in 1980. Three years prior to its demise, the paper published a long article criticizing the financial gains that had accrued to various university professors as a result of their association with the many biotechnology firms that had started to flourish in the San Francisco Bay area and around Boston in the shadows of Harvard and MIT. Even though my own scientific research had never impinged on the biotechnology revolution, the reporter quoted an apparently uncontaminated Berkeley professor to the effect that my academic position "hadn't kept Stanford chemist Carl Djerassi from privately patenting birth control steroids he discovered under his own name for profit, even though he had discovered them while doing NIH [National Institutes of Health]-funded research. Perhaps significantly, Djerassi . . . used his own company to market such steroids."

I was not a reader of the *Berkeley Barb*, but several copies of this particular issue promptly landed on my desk. Since their allegation, that I used government funds to feather my personal nest or that of my industrial employer, could and should have had a major impact on my academic career and on any further government funding of my academic research, I responded immediately. I pointed to the public record, showing that the patent application on the oral contraceptive was filed in November 1951, that the patent was assigned to my then-employer Syntex, that my Stanford University affiliation had started only in 1959, and that I had not filed a single patent application since that time. (While there is nothing illegal or even improper, especially under current government regulations, in filing personal patents for inventions made with governmental subsidies in universities, I have never chosen to follow that practice.) I also added that I had never received any royalties for my work on oral contraceptives or for any of the other one-hundred-odd patents of which I was an inventor while employed full-time by industry. Though the *Berkeley Barb* was not known as a paper likely to print retractions, in this instance they published a full-page palinode.

My reason for telling this story is that while the reporter printed an unequivocal *mea culpa* for not having checked the public record or interviewed me, he did insist that he had both quoted the Berkeley professor correctly and been given the impression "that Dr. Djerassi's alleged private patents on birth control drugs were common knowledge in the scientific community." In that respect, I believe the reporter to have been dead right. There is little I can do about that perception, which is caused by a mixture of academic naïveté and wishful thinking, often also tainted by professional jealousy. Perhaps I should have told the *Berkeley Barb* that the continuing acceptance of the Pill by millions of women all over the world is the most "valuable consideration," worth all the gold in Fort Knox.

CHAPTER 6

Like Father, Like Son

IN 1953, I WAS TEACHING at Wayne State University in Detroit while consulting for Syntex in Mexico City. On one of my many flights between those places, as I was engrossed in the *Journal of the American Chemical Society*, the shadow of a passing passenger momentarily darkened my page. I glanced up to catch the fleeting image of my first wife making her way down the center aisle to the lounge at the back of the DC-6. She was talking to a dark-haired man. Although I hadn't seen her in over three years, I knew that she had married a Mexican and might still be living somewhere south of the border. I waited, with some effort, to surprise her until we landed. Finally, as the line of passengers pushed by me, I rose to face her at eye level, to catch the first expression as her gaze fell unprepared upon her first husband. Somehow I thought that such a naked glance would tell me how she felt about me after three years. She couldn't have been more than three feet away when she noticed my look. She stopped, puzzled, but said nothing. "Virginia?" I started. Something seemed out of focus: I realized I'd made a mistake. I mumbled, "I'm sorry," and then let her pass on without explaining my error.

If you asked most of my current friends, they'd say I had been married twice; in fact, I have had three wives. I married Virginia before I reached the age of twenty. "I see," you might nod, jumping to the obvious conclusion, but you'd be wrong. I married, not because my bride was pregnant, but because I thought I was old enough to marry, even though—or especially because—I was still a virgin. I had already graduated from college (where I had met Virginia on a blind date at a neighboring college) and had worked for a year as a research chemist at CIBA in Summit, New Jersey. On my way to start a doctoral program at the University of Wisconsin in Madison, I stopped in Dayton for the wedding at my twenty-four-year-old bride's home. Our bridal night was spent on the train in a Pullman compartment—a locale quite in keeping with fantasies I'd had as a teenager traveling on the glamorous Orient Express between Vienna and Sofia on my annual summer visits to my father.

Six years later, still childless, my wife and I moved to Mexico City, where I had accepted the position with Syntex as associate director of chemical research. Early in 1950, I asked Virginia for a divorce to marry the woman who was pregnant with my first child. My wife could have been nasty or at least recalcitrant, but she was neither. Since there was no argument about money—apart from my salary we didn't own much—we decided to retain one lawyer for both of us and to get the quickest Mexican divorce possible. The drive to Cuernavaca (where Mexican residents could be divorced in one day) and our *déjeuner à trois* were so civil, that our *licenciado* asked whether we were really certain about a divorce; he had never encountered a more *simpático* couple who were about to get unmarried. But two hours later, I was an ex-husband and, within weeks, a first-time father with a new wife. Soon thereafter, Virginia also married someone in Mexico and promptly became a mother. My relief on hearing that news was, of course, partly attributable to its dilution of residual guilt about my extramarital affair; now, I felt, our respective family portraits were being drawn on similar canvases.

When I was asked to fill out a biographical inquiry for *Who's Who in America* or some such compendium, I listed my second spouse in response to the question "Name of Wife." "Date of Marriage," I left blank. These were not lies, but once I'd denied the existence of my first wife in print, it wasn't easy to resurrect her, even for those close to me. Should I have announced, as soon as my two children were old enough to understand, "By the way, I've been married once before"? It seemed cavalier, in the absence of a good reason, to bring up the topic, which their mother and I never discussed. During one of our wedding anniversaries, when my nine-year-old daughter asked, "Papa, when were you and Mom married?" I fudged and moved the date back a year.

Although it took me years to see the parallel, my own parents divorced when I was six years old and kept the fact from me until I was nearly fourteen. People to whom I tell this are usually shocked. How come I didn't notice? And, more to the point of my own history, why did my parents keep it a secret?

I

My mother and my father had met when both were attending medical school at the University of Vienna; after graduation they had settled in a house on Ulitza Marin Drinov in Sofia. Eight months pregnant, my mother returned to the Viennese hospital where she had trained and which, in her opinion, was the only institution suitable for delivery of her first child. Two months after my birth on 29 October 1923, we arrived in Sofia, on a day so cold that all water pipes had frozen. It was not a good omen for my mother, who disliked living in Sofia, never really learned Bulgarian, and, not surprisingly, found it difficult to establish a practice there. Besides, to any sophisticated Viennese, Sofia was the backwater of Europe and no place for the education of an only son. Thus, when I was old enough to enter school, my mother and I moved back to Vienna; and thereafter it didn't seem odd to me to see my father only when he visited us on holidays or during the summers when I traveled to Sofia. I suppose I was simply too young and generally too happy to wonder that my parents didn't live together.

The extreme possessiveness of my mother for her only son—a comfort during my childhood, but an ever-growing discomfort in my late teens and early twenties—finally resulted in a complete break between us by the time of my real manhood. Attempting to maintain her place as the dominant woman in my life, she behaved toward my first wife with increasing intrusiveness. Repeated threats of suicide, coupled with the presence of bottles full of pills—both before and after my marriage—became nerve-wracking. Even though Virginia was remarkably tolerant, my mother was clearly a contributing factor to the failure of that marriage, which ended when I was twenty-six. Adjustment to the new Mexican environment, to a second wife, to my first child, and nearly total commitment to exciting research left me with a low tolerance for maternal pressure. At the first suicide threat during my second marriage, I said, "Enough!" and asked my mother to leave me alone. Only then did she resume medical practice as an attending physician in a New York hospital. Except for rare letters, and my financial support during her last years, our rupture was complete. When I encountered my mother again, she was suffering from advanced Alzheimer's disease and did not recognize me.

My father, however, gave me a glimpse of his private life the summer I was thirteen. His specialty was, as I have said, venereal disease. In those days, before penicillin, syphilitic patients had to be treated with arsenicals for several years. They were, moreover, embarrassed to be seen in such a specialist's waiting rooms, and appointments had to be scheduled so that patients wouldn't meet. I hardly ever encountered any of my father's patients, even though his office and living quarters were in the same apartment. One day, however, I saw a handsome woman reading on the sofa, who not only wasn't embarrassed but greeted me by name. The following Sunday, she joined my father and me on our weekly hike to the Vitosha mountain, at whose foot Sofia was located. When we got home that evening, my father—whom I recognized even then as a dashingly confident and eloquent man—become tongue-tied. At last, he stammered that my mother and he had been divorced, but that the time had come for me to understand why there was a woman friend—"not a patient," he hastened to add. To his apparent surprise, the revelation of my parents' divorce made no particular impression on me. I had just fallen in love for the first time and was wondering when and where I'd get my first kiss. Somehow, the fact that my father also had a girlfriend just made everything more intriguing.

Years later, when my own daughter had reached about the same age, she walked into my study after dinner and sat on my desk. A contented look on her face, she mentioned that one of her classmates, already living with a third father, had complimented her that morning in school on the evident stability of our domestic life. On the spur of the moment, I decided to bite the bullet. "Actually, I've been married once before," I announced in an offhand sort of way, as if I had just remembered that fact, and quickly went on, "but not your mother. It's her only marriage."

Like my father, I ended up surprised. "Papa, you too?" she exclaimed, breaking into giggles, rather than being shocked. "Tell me more." It didn't take long for my daughter to get the whole story: my first wife's name, the circumstances of our meeting, what she looked like, and the absurdly young age at which I married. I even had to produce the group of pictures from my former connubial life which I'd so carefully guarded from everyone among my chemical files. After studying them, she asked, "How long were you married?"

"Six years," I replied. Then I asked, "How should we tell this to your brother? How about you telling him?"

My daughter looked at me distantly, saying nothing. I was about to repeat my request, when she stopped me. "Six years? But I was born—"

When I had finally confessed it all—I, a synthesizer of the first oral contraceptive—she broke into a whoop. "Wait till I tell Dale!" she exclaimed, and ran out to look for her brother.

My father, whom I saw little of in the two decades after 1939, never knew about that episode with my daughter. Perhaps I should have told him. For there was also at least one tale he should have told me.

My father was dashing and unconventional for prewar Bulgaria—his predilection for women extending even to occasional flaunting of mistresses. (*Concubinage* he used to call it, pronouncing the word in the French manner.) But he faced a real dilemma: he did believe in the institution of marriage, and no one in his large family or wide social circle had ever been divorced. His only son, he thought, would be embarrassed to be the child of divorced parents. And when I asked him why he had kept his divorce from me for so long, he always answered, "We did it for your sake." Only when he arrived in America, nearly sixty years old, did he remarry, and he remained married to my marvelous stepmother, Sarina, who was two decades younger, for the rest of his life.

Since he came to the United States only in 1949, the very year I moved to Mexico City for a two-year stint, it was not until I was in my forties that we met with any frequency. But from then, until his death at ninety-six, we occupied neighboring seats at the San Francisco Opera. It was, after all, my father who had taken me at age four to my first opera in Sofia. Many a time in San Francisco he leaned over and whispered *sotto voce*, "Not bad, but you should have heard Caruso" or Chaliapin or Gigli or Christov or whatever legendary operatic figure had reigned in that role in Europe.

Until the age of ninety-five, my father was judged by most persons to be, mentally and physically, twenty years younger. He took up skiing at fifty, when other men become cautious and stick to golf; he learned to drive in his sixties, and continued to do so until he was nearly ninety-five. Although he had been afraid of water most of his life, shortly after his eighty-fifth birthday he somehow learned to swim the backstroke. After that, forty minutes a day in the pool became one of his routines until the last year of his life, when he broke his hip stepping off the scale in the exercise room.

On the last day of his life, he lay unconscious in the hospital, all life-support systems disconnected. I sat by his bed holding his hand. My son, Dale, and his cousin, Ilan, from the paternal side of the family were close by. Suddenly my son's whisper startled me. "Papa, why didn't you tell me Grandpa was married before?" "Before?" I echoed stupidly, thinking he was referring to my mother. "Yes, in Bulgaria. Before he came to this country." He motioned toward his cousin. "Ilan just told me. His mother knew her in Bulgaria." I looked at my father, wanting to beg "Papa, please don't die yet. Who was she? Why didn't you tell me?" But it was too late. He was no longer breathing.

II

More than a quarter of a century since the day I thought I had seen Virginia on a plane to Mexico City, and years after telling my children about her, I still had not acknowledged her existence to anyone else in my second married life. Then one day, after my second divorce, I received out of the blue a letter from her, sent from her home in the Midwest. She had seen me on a television program and, in spite of my silver hair and the partial mask of a beard, recognized me immediately. She asked whether we could meet again, since she was about to visit California on a vacation. I agreed to meet, though wondering whether I would recognize her, considering how poorly I had done just three years after our divorce.

One's imaginings about long-delayed disclosures usually prove to be exaggerated. I recognized Virginia right away. The bare outlines of our separate lives we told each other in just a few hours. Yet how does one reconstitute a quarter-century of absence? She could not know, nor I tell, that I had denied the existence of our marriage—all six years of it. A Stalin of the emotions, I had erased from public record a segment of our joint history. If she guessed, she was discreet about it, as she had been discreet during so much of our married life.

After her return to her home, she sent me a thank-you note together with a gift, whose box indicated that it was an electric yogurt maker. It was the last thing I needed. Modern laboratory chemist that I am, I make my yogurt in the old-fashioned, large-scale Bulgarian way: I bring the milk to a boil, let it cool until I can dip my finger in it without discomfort, stir in a couple of spoonfuls of yogurt, and keep the mixture overnight in a wide-mouthed thermos. I thanked Virginia for her gift and then, without unpacking it, put it away and forgot it. Several months later, I had occasion to move the box. Hearing something rattling, I thought the yogurt maker had probably broken and that it served me right for being so thoughtless. I ripped open the box, only to discover inside thirty daffodil bulbs—one for each of the years since our divorce.

According to the accompanying note, Virginia had dug them up in her own garden and intended them for my ranch house in northern California. I planted them within the week; and the following spring, all thirty bloomed.

III

When on 10 October 1973—the very day Vice President Spiro Agnew resigned—President Richard Nixon presented the National Medal of Science* to eleven men in the East Room of the White House, I was one of the recipients. My citation read, "In recognition of his major contributions to . . . steroid hormones and to [their] application to medicinal chemistry and population control by means of oral contraceptives." At this festive occasion, attended by the First Lady and cabinet officials as well as by the medalists, their wives, and other members of their families, I had a special distinction about which I learned only two months later when the *San Francisco Examiner* published an article with the headline "NIXON GAVE MEDAL TO SCIENTIST ON WHITE HOUSE 'ENEMIES' LIST."

I was not at all dismayed to find that I had made the White House "enemies" list (of Watergate fame) because both of my involvement in Senator George McGovern's presidential campaign, including serving as a delegate for him at the Miami Democratic convention in 1972, and of my open opposition to our Vietnam policy. When I was informed that Nixon would present me with the National Medal of Science, I determined not to be caught smiling at him when our picture was taken. But I underestimated the inanity of the brief tête-à-tête that would take place as Nixon shook my hand and presented me with the medal.

"How's Stanford going to make out against Cal?" he asked. Perhaps divining from my hem-and-haw that he was speaking to one of the few peculiar Stanford professors who'd never attended a "Big Game," he switched topics: "You know, I never took chemistry at Whittier," he confided. "I got an A in high school, but I never understood it." Then the flashbulbs popped. Thus it is that every one of the 8-by-10 color photographs the White House mailed to me, including the one inscribed "To Carl Djerassi with best wishes, Richard M. Nixon," has me laughing and beaming at the President as if I'd been the winning quarterback at the Big Game, and he the coach. The framed one now hanging on the wall of my office is accompanied by an explanation written in beautiful calligraphy by one of my students: "Support Your Local Enemy."

*During his second term, President Nixon showed his discomfort with scientists by abolishing the President's Science Advisory Committee (PSAC) and downgrading the White House Science Advisor's office. There was even a two-year hiatus in the award of the National Medal of Science, which, together with PSAC, had been initiated during the Eisenhower period. Cynics saw the 1973 event as a pure public relations gesture, prompted by the increasing threat of the Watergate affair, rather than as indicating any impending presidential embrace of domestic détente in science.

I had another distinction, however, among the medalists: I was the only one to attend the award ceremony alone. To the repeated "Where's your wife?" I offered innocuous excuses. How could I tell them that Norma had *never* been present at any occasion when I received an award for my scientific work? At such ceremonies I always thought back to other events she'd missed.

After returning from Kenyon College, where I got an honorary doctorate in 1958 together with the poet Robert Lowell and the Episcopalian bishop of Southern Ohio, I told her that the student marshal of the procession had solemnly said to me, "Bishop Blanchard, would you please follow me?" She laughed. But didn't say, "I wish I'd been there." Even during the twilight of our marriage, our overt relationship was civil enough for her to have attended the Columbia graduation that sunny day in May 1975. After Arthur Rubinstein received an honorary doctorate, the entire audience rose in a standing ovation as if he'd just hit the last note at a concert in Carnegie Hall. I was next in line. When the president of Columbia University said that my oral contraceptive research had made its most significant impact on the emancipation of women, the graduating seniors of Barnard, the women's college, jumped up and cheered, followed by a second cresting human wave. "Yeh!" the seniors of all-male Columbia College thundered, right fists thrust in the air. (The interruption was duly noted in the *New York Times* and eventually also in Rubinstein's autobiography.) I don't think I even bothered to tell my wife about that student response, which had pleased me so much. However delicious a meal is, it doesn't taste the same reheated.

Perhaps she would not have enjoyed the early, purely scientific events, like the American Chemical Society's Award in Pure Chemistry given annually to a person under thirty-five, where only chemists and their ilk paraded. But there were commencements Norma might have enjoyed. For years, we went to the theater and opera together; yet when in 1974 I shared a podium with the actress Julie Harris, or in 1978 with Sherill Milnes, the operatic baritone, I traveled alone.

The week after I was served my divorce papers in 1976, Norma and I had a marathon duel of words—perhaps the longest in our life together, and surely the most frank. Tight-shut doors were unlocked, a quarter-century of wounds ripped open. Finally, we fell silent, exhausted from the brutal catharsis. But as I checked once more my list of grievances—shorter than my wife's, but still substantial—I found one more, perhaps the most deeply buried.

"Not once did you see fit to come to an event that honored me," I began, "not once in all those years."

"That's not true," she said quietly. And then reminded me of a single occasion, twenty years ago to the day, that I'd forgotten and she'd remembered. She recalled that for it I'd bought my first tuxedo, the optimist in me having calculated that with just four more black-tie awards I'd recapture the investment. The tone of her reply, tinged with sadness, stopped me from pursuing the topic. I said, "I guess it doesn't matter any more."

But, clearly, Norma had known all along that it did matter; yet neither one of us had broached the subject over the years, just as there were many other topics we hadn't raised. Playing the role of faculty wife was bad enough, in the 1950s and 1960s, for an intelligent and highly educated woman, accustomed to independence in her premarital life. Living with a scientist, whose everyday life was conducted in an incomprehensible language, whose workdays lasted sixteen hours, and who brought his mistress home every night, must have been hardly bearable. That the mistress wasn't a real woman, but an intellectual obsession with chemistry, didn't make it any easier to tolerate. No wonder that the husband in tuxedo, receiving an award for work she didn't share and resented, yet certainly had made easier, was all my wife remembered. Was it really reasonable to expect her to participate in events that publicly honored her husband's way of life? Although it had barely dawned on me in our last exchange, Norma's silent boycott now seems almost a civilized response to protracted grievance. Yet in those years few people would have accepted that state of affairs as legitimate cause for complaint. "What's she bitching about?" they'd have asked. "He comes home every evening. He doesn't drink. He's a good provider. He doesn't run around with other women." ("Are they so sure about that?" she probably thought, but didn't say.)

Although I had forgotten the tuxedo, I remembered another aspect of that ceremony. As usual, I was expected to deliver a lecture on the work being honored by the award. Chemists are congenitally unable to do so without some visual aids in order to present the complex two- and three-dimensional structural formulae of organic molecules, such as the steroids about which I was talking. At that time, most chemists used large 3-by-4-inch glass slides, but I had decided to be modern: I had brought a light, all-plastic version of such diapositives. Partway through my lecture, I noticed the projectionist gesturing as if he wanted me to hurry up. The room was dim, but his face was illuminated by the light of the projector, and I could see his wide eyes, his finger pointing at the screen, his mouth silently enunciating something over and over. When I finally turned to the screen, I saw a huge amoeba developing around the images of the chemical structures. Within seconds, the structures had entirely disappeared, leaving only the quivering, virtually transparent amoeba. The projectionist removed the slide, his hands signaling knockout: the light of the projector had obviously been too hot for my plastic slides. My lecture became a symphony in timing, the projectionist my Toscanini, his raised hand moving in an ever-increasing tempo to a crescendo, then instantly dropping. Every few sentences, I turned to look at the images behind me; as soon as I saw the edges begin to quiver, forecasting imminent meltdown, I remarked nonchalantly, "Next slide, please."

When I went to retrieve my slides, I found the projectionist drenched in sweat, pointing to the detritus of my lecture: a pile of slide frames with blobs of molten plastic draped around them. This is the image that came to mind as I thought of the one award ceremony Norma had attended. Did she, too, remember that incident with the slides? Had she recognized, even then, the analogy to our lives? The beautifully drawn structural formulae, with which I wanted to impress the audience, had served their purpose, but only once and for a strictly limited time. Since I had no manuscript and the talk was not recorded, all that remained was what the listeners remembered. I didn't ask her; it seemed years too late.

CHAPTER 7

"What Kind of Chemist Are You?"

I

When—during the first decade of my professional life, after I had received my Ph.D. from the University of Wisconsin in 1945—people asked me what kind of chemist I was, I would say "a medicinal chemist." They understood that this meant I was working on antihistamines, antispasmodics, corticosteroids, oral contraceptives, anabolics, and other steroid hormone analogs, and approved. Later, I'd say, "I'm an organic chemist"; but since the 1960s, an ever-increasing chemophobia and "organic" hype has led the general public to equate organic chemistry (the study of carbon compounds) with synthetic chemicals—a definition burdened with distinct pejorative overtones.

The most common offenders are the owners and suppliers of "organic" food stores and many of their customers. Even though I frequent such stores on occasion, I do so for the quality of the produce and not for their claimed organic virginity. "Grown totally organic" or some such hyperbole is a manifestation of ignorance, of linguistic slovenliness, or of deliberate imprecision. How does one grow any plant without inorganic components: fertilizers, trace metal constituents, and the like? Furthermore, let those who inevitably equate synthetic organic chemicals with toxicity remember that some of the most powerful and lethal poisons are naturally occurring, "organic" substances. In fact, in recent years, the distinguished University of California biochemist Bruce Ames, once the darling of all "organic" chemophobes because of his development of the simple "Ames Test" for detecting presumed carcinogenicity, has now become their bête noire, owing to his subsequent recognition that the danger of cancer associated with "natural" foods may be much higher than any risk posed by pesticides synthesized by organic chemists.

Although, as I shall demonstrate in chapter 11, I have been an active and highly visible proponent of better alternatives to conventional pesticides, I still feel that even in that area of organic chemistry, some clarity is sorely needed with respect to the nuances of *organic* and *synthetic* or even of *chemical* and *biological*. Environmentalists believing in *biological* insect control, for instance, use traps equipped with some adhesive and baited with the sex attractant pheromone secreted by the female of a specific insect pest. But such biological insect control uses pheromones, synthesized by a chemist in a laboratory, that have a chemical structure identical to the natural substance. This is much more practical than collecting virgin females, placing them in cages in such traps, and having them synthesize minute quantities of the same sex attractant. In light of the facts that pheromones are organic chemicals, and that the entomologists employ synthetic material in the field, such a biological approach to pest control could just as well be categorized as a "synthetic chemical" one.

Since this may be dismissed as semantic nitpicking, let me place some other aspects of the synthetic pesticide problem into proper perspective. I have selected synthetic pesticides, rather than other organic chemicals, because a recent (1990) survey has shown that on a graph plotting the public's familiarity with and favorable acceptance of different industries, only nuclear power received a lower rating than agrochemicals. Bruce Ames's fall from grace among conventional chemophobes rests on his recent debunking of several popularly held misconceptions, such as the following:

1. Other than lung cancer, the age-adjusted mortality rate for all cancers has been declining since 1950 (except for people above the age of eighty-five), implying that in general, life in the modern industrial world has not contributed to increased death from cancer.

2. According to Ames, 99.9 percent of all pesticides consumed by humans are derived not from synthetics but rather from the plants themselves, which produce such toxins to protect themselves against natural predators (insects, fungi, animals). He estimates that Americans consume daily ten thousand times more of natural pesticides than of synthetic pesticide residues, and concludes that almost every plant product in an "organic" food store contains natural carcinogens. He makes the point that while the overwhelming proportion of our food consumption consists of "natural" chemicals, few of them—in contrast to *all* synthetic pesticides—have so far been subjected to systematic toxicological scrutiny. Thus at normal exposure levels, the cancer risk to humans from synthetic pesticides is likely to be minimal compared with the background hazards of natural plant pesticides. This finding does not, of course, justify increasing the chemical load of the environment through indiscriminate additions of synthetic chemicals—notably when the consumer has no choice; nor does it imply that safety standards for agricultural workers be relaxed; but it does show that popular fear and media hype have left reason far behind.

Like most literate consumers, I am in favor of more informative labeling of packaged food, but how should we do this with fresh vegetables or fruit if Ames's findings are valid? Take, for example, residues of synthetic chemical additives, as when in 1989 minute residues of the fruit ripener Alar were found in some apples. We should look at this incidence not only through the eyes of Meryl Streep—a distinguished actress, though hardly a chemist—who was a key factor in the media blitz that caused the removal of apples from school cafeterias (and subsequently the voluntary withdrawal of Alar from the market by its producer), but also through the very different glasses of two distinguished chemists, each of whom discussed this incidence during his acceptance speech for the Priestley Medal, the American Chemical Society's highest honor.

George Pimentel of the University of California lambasted Streep and the media on the basis of the facts: even if one accepts Streep's and other opponents' worst-case extrapolations that the presence of Alar in apples may cause 5,000 children annually to develop cancer in their old age, this is a barely noticeable addition—0.025 percent—to the 5.5 million of our 22 million preschool children who will get cancer anyway as adults. Even more to the point, only 5 percent of apple growers sprayed their produce with Alar.

On the other hand, an equally distinguished chemist, the Nobelist Roald Hoffmann from Cornell University commented:

> I didn't know Alar existed. To be sure, I knew apples were treated in various ways. . . . But I didn't know, or maybe I didn't want to know, what found its way inside. . . . I didn't like the feeling of ignorance. Here I was a Columbia B.A., a Harvard Ph.D., supposedly a good chemist. . . . And even when I heard what was there—Alar, daminozide—I didn't know what these were. I was not happy with myself for not knowing; I was not happy with the apple producers for putting those chemicals in and not letting me know about it. I was not happy with my education for withholding this information.

Like Roald Hoffmann, I, and most likely also 99.9 percent of all chemists, did not know the chemical structure of Alar or its biological properties or that it was added to apples. But I can conceive of no simple solution—through improved education or labeling—to resolve an issue such as Alar in apples, except to trust the legislative regulatory mechanism and the sophistication (rather than public relations extravaganzas) of watchful and *informed* gadflies. I would not include many actresses or actors among the latter.

Now, having relieved myself of all my accumulated defensiveness as an organic chemist, I turn to ways of subdividing the field of organic chemistry itself in a manner less liable to distortion, and one that at the same time describes my own chemical persona. The broadest differentiation is between theoretical and experimental organic chemistry, the latter being my discipline. Of its various subdivisions, I shall consider only two: synthesis and structure determination. All of my industrial research, first at CIBA and later at Syntex, was in synthetic organic chemistry; whereas the overwhelming part of my academic research, starting with my first cactus studies in 1952, was in one way or another related to the elucidation of the chemical structures of natural products.

In January 1952, I packed our belongings into our Chevy and drove with my second wife, Norma, and two-year old daughter, Pamela, from Mexico City, through miles of cactus landscapes, to Michigan. I had finally been offered an academic post, a tenured associate professorship at Wayne University, with the promise of a full professorship within a couple of years. Again, I was proceeding against the advice of my friends and colleagues up north. Two and a half years earlier, they had advised me not to go to Mexico for chemical research. Now they thought I was crazy to leave a well-paying and productive research career at Syntex in sunny Mexico to go to cold and slushy Detroit. Wayne was not exactly on the top of the academic totem pole: in fact, as far as graduate programs were concerned, it was then fairly close to the bottom—a city university with a primarily blue-collar constituency. But it was the only academic offer I had received; and, at age twenty-eight, I thought it was time to find out whether the dreamed-for academic career was indeed what I wanted.

When I arrived in Detroit, Wayne had not yet become Wayne State University. Except for one new science building, most of the classrooms, offices, and laboratories were located in Old Main, a huge, nineteenth-century building that was formerly a high school, and in an assembly of private houses that had been taken over by the university as the urban slum enveloped the campus. Since there was not room in the new science edifice for all faculty members, I, as the newest arrival, ended up in Old Main. I have not visited all American university chemical laboratories, but I have seen my share of them, and Old Main was clearly the dingiest. Moreover, it had a distinction that must be unmatched in American university circles: the stockroom, from which all necessary chemicals, glassware, and other instrumentation had to be secured, was in the new science building; to reach it, my students had to make many daily trips across one of the busiest, four-lane streets of Detroit, irrespective of rain, snow, slush, and speeding traffic. My first Chinese postdoctorate fellow, Liang Liu (now Huang Liang and a director of the Institute of Materia Medica of the Chinese Academy of Medical Sciences in Beijing), was once followed into the lab by a police-man after she had dashed across in a heavy downpour while the traffic light was still red. She may be the only chemist in America to have received a jay-walking ticket while doing research.

Fortunately, the stockroom was generously stocked, the instrumenta-tion more than adequate, and the chemistry library superb. Old Main was hot in the summer and overheated in the winter, but it did not leak; the water and electrical supply worked; and while the lab benches were old, they were serviceable. And the graduate students were hard working: the work ethic of Detroit in the 1950s could be felt in the students, who went to Wayne to get an education, not to play around. I managed to secure research support from organizations like the National Institutes of Health, the American Heart Association, the National Science Foundation, the American Cancer Society, and various pharmaceutical companies, such as Merck and Schering. Within a couple of years, I had over a dozen graduate students and postdoctorate fellows in my research group.

In my wanderings around Mexico, visiting the pre-Columbian ruins in Yucatán, Chiapas, Oaxaca, and other regions, I had become intrigued by the Mexican flora, especially the yuccas, agaves, and giant cacti. I was acquainted with the chemistry of yuccas and agaves; many steroidal sapogenins are isolated from them, and one of them, hecogenin, which is abundant in the industrial wastes of sisal processing from *Agave sisalana*, served as the starting material for one of the cortisone syntheses we had completed in 1951. On a few occasions while traveling, I had cut off small pieces of cactus and shaken them vigorously in a test tube filled with water, a simple test for saponins (a water-soluble, sugar-containing form of the steroid sapogenins with which we had been working). Many of the cacti had produced soaplike foams when shaken in water—an effect that had stuck in my mind.

As soon as I arrived at Wayne, I looked through the literature and discovered that virtually nothing was known about the chemical constituents of giant cacti. Through a botanist in Arizona, I secured a few specimens and persuaded a couple of new graduate students and a Swiss postdoctorate fellow to start on the only two leads I had at that time. One was my simple test-tube observation that these cacti seemed to be rich in saponins; the other, that the hallucinogenic alkaloid mescaline and some of its congeners existed in Mexican peyote, a cactus belonging to the genus *Lophophora*. We were lucky right from the beginning: some of the giant cacti contained new alkaloids, while the majority were rich in saponins. The saponins turned out not to be steroids; they belonged to a class of natural products, the pentacyclic triterpenes, which were then being studied extensively in Europe. These plant products bore some structural resemblance to the steroids—we now know that they have a common biogenetic precursor—but were based on a five- rather than four-ring chemical skeleton. Although these cactus triterpenes displayed no interesting biological properties, they had a great impact on the direction, or rather the two directions, of my budding academic research. They were my first serious involvement in structure elucidation and thus indirectly got me interested in the development of physical methods; the latter turned into a long-term, intellectual infatuation of mine about which I tell more in this chapter.

II

The best synthetic chemists are both architects and builders, and in the scientific literature often anoint their work with terms like *beautiful*, *elegant*, or *dazzling*. As architect, the chemist designs a strategy for synthesizing a complex molecule which may involve permutations of dozens upon dozens of separate chemical steps. As builder-engineer, the chemist devises new chemical reactions and discovers new synthetic reagents. Both architect and builder know precisely what the edifice should ultimately look like.

The structural elucidation of a new natural product, however, entails elements of secrecy and suspense that are absent in synthesis. When I first entered the field of structure determination, it was a chemical variant of the game "Twenty Questions." Although the questions do not mean much to a nonchemist (Does the substance contain only carbon and hydrogen? Does it contain oxygen atoms? How many? Does it contain nitrogen? Any other heteroatoms? Is it saturated or unsaturated?), they make for a winnowing process through which one can eventually create a picture of a substance's chemical constitution. Perhaps a more useful metaphor for the process is that of entering a pitch-dark room with the aim of ultimately determining its contents, the precise location of the furniture, the color and composition of each item. Some people might enter brusquely, bumping into a chair or a table, which they would then touch in order to derive some idea of its dimensions and composition—wood, plastic, upholstered material. Others might be more cautious and systematic: they would start by feeling their way around the wall, perhaps counting the steps so as to determine the overall dimensions of the space, crossing the room at fixed intervals to determine the rough location of certain objects before focusing on them one at a time. Someone may come equipped with a penlight capable of illuminating only small areas; or with a powerful flashlight to get a quick picture of the whole room and its contents. Or somebody with a flash camera and a wide-angle lens may with one picture record the contents of the entire room—even its colors if the camera is loaded with color film.

Organic chemistry started in the nineteenth century as an attempt to determine the structures of chemical substances that, isolated from plant and animal sources, had interesting biological properties; only when this was accomplished could the synthetic chemist, the architect-builder, enter the field. The early methods of structure elucidation, the feeling and stumbling process in the dark room, could deal only with relatively simple chemical structures. But as more refined penlights and then flashlights became available, ever more complicated chemical structure problems could be solved in less and less time. The great age of natural products chemistry was the period from 1930 to 1960, when all the important steroid hormones, vitamins, and antibiotics, along with a host of other biologically significant molecules, were isolated and their structures established. The main techniques—the ever more powerful flashlights—were ultraviolet and infrared spectroscopy, nuclear magnetic resonance spectroscopy, and mass spectrometry. The principles behind these techniques were discovered by physicists, who also developed the first instruments to detect them. But it was the chemist interested in structure elucidation, rather than in synthesis, who first applied these new physical tools to the solution of organic chemical problems. The reason is obvious: the architect-builder already knows what the room should look like. Only a person entering a dark chamber is interested in flashlights.

Ultraviolet spectroscopy is not exactly analogous to an ordinary flashlight. It illuminates only certain structural features, known in chemical jargon as "double bonds" (to differentiate them from the conventional single chemical bond connecting any two atoms), which are present in many "unsaturated" organic molecules (substances lacking double bonds are considered "saturated"). Thus, ultraviolet spectroscopy is equivalent to a flashlight that illuminates only wood or cloth or metal in a dark room, or—to use a human analogy—to a method of scanning that responds solely to hair, but not to skin, bones, or flesh. By such a method, no picture would be obtained from a totally hairless individual, whereas large segments of body outline would appear for a very hirsute man. Organic chemists studying carotenoids in the 1930s were among the first to take advantage of ultraviolet spectroscopy, since these substances (related to vitamin A) are indeed, in terms of my hair analogy, the chemical equivalents of hirsute men. Steroids, whose degree of "unsaturation" more closely resembles the relatively limited hair distribution in women, were studied next by that technique, which called attention to select portions (analogous to the hairy regions of a woman's head, armpit, and groin) of their chemical nucleus.

Infrared spectroscopy is, in reflecting the vibrational movements of chemical bonds, a more powerful flashlight: such vibrations are displayed by all bonds in an organic molecule, not just by "unsaturated" components. Advances in instrumentation in the late 1940s made it possible to measure quickly the infrared spectrum of an organic molecule; and shortly thereafter, steroid chemists derived a set of empirical generalizations that permitted them to deduce many structural features from one such spectrum.

The third spectroscopic technique, nuclear magnetic resonance, was first used in the 1950s. NMR is perhaps the most powerful flashlight of all, because it sheds light on the interconnection of individual carbon and hydrogen atoms, which are present in all organic compounds. Starting with one hydrogen atom, one can frequently follow its connectivity neighbor by neighbor through long stretches of a molecule. A quarter of a century later, NMR has also turned into a powerful flashlight in medicine by establishing itself as an essential imaging technique for uncovering abnormalities in the human body that are frequently undetectable by X rays.

Mass spectrometry, though known for several decades, only entered the general organic chemistry laboratory in the early 1960s. A mass spectrometer shoots a stream of high-energy electrons at the organic molecule in question, which, upon impact, fragments into many components that can be separated in a magnetic field. If there are too many fragments, the method is useless; one is left only with debris. But frequently there are produced only a limited number of such components, which can offer a great deal of information about the structure of the parent molecule—much as an archaeologist, finding fragments of an arm and a foot, can conclude that these are the remnants of a human figure—except that the mass spectrometer requires an amount of material that may not be visible to the naked eye.

Structure elucidation became less of an exciting intellectual exercise in the late 1950s and early 1960s with the introduction of X-ray diffraction, the equivalent of a flash camera. The technique is only applicable to perfect crystals (many organic compounds are not crystals at all, and others crystallize in forms unsuitable for this technique), and it was not applicable to complicated molecules because of the enormously time-consuming computations involved. Improvements in instrumentation, however, and especially the advent of powerful computers, have made possible the acquisition of precise pictures of even exceedingly large molecules such as proteins or nucleic acids. (Francis Crick and James Watson's double-helix model of DNA, for instance, was largely based on information derived from X-ray crystallographic analyses; and more Nobel prizes have been awarded over the years for various aspects of X-ray crystallography than for any other technique.) When applicable, this "flash camera" has thus eliminated the function of the chemist interested in structure elucidation, who is reduced to growing the crystal and pushing the camera's button.

III

At the time my Wayne students and I started our research on the chemical constituents of giant cacti, not much was known about cactus chemistry in general, with one notorious exception: the chemically simple, but biologically complicated alkaloid, mescaline, from the peyote cactus—not a giant, but rather a radish-sized member of the genus *Lophophora*. Our own studies with the genus *Lophocereus* had, in fact, turned up much more complicated alkaloids. Chemical complexity does not necessarily imply high biological activity, however; and in any event we had not as yet isolated enough material for biological scrutiny. But I had read a great deal about the hallucinogenic properties of mescaline—especially its use in Native American religious ceremonies—and had become intrigued by an article that Dr. Marinesco, a Romanian physician, had published in 1933 in *La Presse Médicale*, replete with color reproductions. In it, he recorded the effect of subcutaneously injected mescaline on the artistic output of two painters, whose work was lushly colorful but a bit busy for my taste. Since no pre-mescaline paintings were shown, the real contribution of the alkaloid was not clear to me. Still, the article set me wondering: if I were a painter, would I take mescaline?

What at last persuaded me, however, was not those frenetic reproductions but the prose of Aldous Huxley. During my younger days, Huxley had been one of my favorite writers. When his little book *The Doors of Perception* appeared in 1954, its description of how "one bright May morning, I swallowed four-tenths of a gram of mescalin [*sic*] dissolved in half a glass of water and sat down to wait for the results," fascinated me in a way the painters had not. The skeptic scientist in me discounted Huxley's claim that mescaline "changes the quality of consciousness more profoundly than any other substance": after all, how many others had he tried? Rather, what attracted me to Huxley was his emphasis on perception, an approach to which I have always been susceptible. For me, the enthralling passages of *The Doors of Perception* were those describing its author's responses to a favorite rose, a composer, a painter.

I found Huxley the Aesthete so compelling that I was willing to forgive Huxley the Mystic, who was given to pursuing questions that struck me as gibberish: "And how can a man at the extreme limits of ectomorphy and cerebrotonia ever put himself in the place of one at the limits of endomorphy and viscerotonia, or, except within certain circumscribed areas, share the feelings of one who stands at the limits of mesomorphy and somatotonia?" I was indeed looking for a scientific rationale for pursuing my own experiments with mescaline, but I was sure that this was not the question I needed to answer. Rather, I thought that I, as one of the few persons in the world working on new cactus alkaloids, should experience personally the biological effects of mescaline in an individual previously uncontaminated by exogenous behavioral modifiers.

Huxley's basic message was that mescaline ought to become the opium of the intelligentsia; at my next research seminar, I announced that this thesis would be tested experimentally the following Sunday afternoon at a picnic in my backyard. Were there any volunteers? To my surprise, only two offered to join me: one, Sandy Figdor, was a postdoctorate research fellow; the other, Mickey Gorman, a graduate student, who eventually rose high in the management of one of the largest American pharmaceutical companies. Even now, several decades after the event, the decision to ingest mescaline seems surprising for a puritan like me: I have never smoked, and alcohol did not cross my lips (unless one counts rum-filled chocolates) until I was in my late forties, when I spent a week in the central Congo, where the drinking water was the color of urine and no microscope was needed to determine what was floating in it. With lukewarm beer the only bottled beverage available, in just seven hot, humid days I made up for decades of abstinence. I may also be one of the few inhabitants of northern California who has never smoked marijuana. Even though I have invented several drugs that are still being taken by millions of people, in my own life I shun the psychoactive molecule—even sleeping pills. I like my pleasures *au naturel*. Still, if some righteous senator were to look me in the eye and ask, "And now, Professor, would you please tell this committee whether you've ever partaken of illegal substances," I could only clear my throat and mumble that what I did in 1955 was not then against the law.

Obtaining a supply of mescaline presented no problem. I was not going to fool with mescal buttons, the raw material Indians use in their religious ceremonies. Work by the Austrian chemist Ernst Späth had shown this source to contain many other alkaloids in addition to mescaline. If I was going to submit to some chemically induced experiences—especially sublime ones—I at least wanted the causative agent to be untainted. Besides, I happened to have enough pure mescaline sulfate in my lab to treat a herd of elephants. The problem was the correct dosage. Dr. Marinesco had administered the drug subcutaneously to his Bucharest painters; we, of course, were going to take it by mouth, like the Indians and Huxley, whose experiences we wanted to replicate. But when we went back to *The Doors of Perception*, we found that Huxley had neglected to state whether he had taken free mescaline or a salt, like our sulfate. Since mescaline itself has a rather low molecular weight, it makes a considerable difference in terms of active ingredient whether one ingests mescaline or mescaline sulfate. In spite of Huxley's doctorly assurance about the safety of mescaline ("less toxic than any other substance in the pharmacologist's repertory . . . leaving no hangover and consequently no craving for a renewal of the dose"), we decided to play it safe. We looked up the acute toxicity of mescaline in mice, corrected for the difference in body weight between mouse and man, and took one tenth of that dose in the form of the sulfate.

The menu for the Sunday picnic was pizza for the students and spouses, pizza-*cum*-mescaline sulfate for the three experimentalists. At least, that was our plan. In fact, the mescaline sulfate was so extremely bitter that we took it with orange juice. I felt sufficiently squeamish to skip the pizza. Instead, I lay down in the grass to wait for my experiences. Relaxing was not easy, since at least twenty pizza eaters were looking out of the corner of their eyes at me and my two fellow guinea pigs.

Huxley's *The Doors of Perception* and all other reports cite hallucinations of color as the most prominent effect of mescaline. I stared at the flowers in our garden, periodically closing my eyes and trying to retain the image of the flower I had last possessed visually. I had no luck. The flowers did not look any different, with eyes closed or open, nor were the colors any more intense than in my previous, drugless life. True, we did not have any roses, but surely that could not have mattered. Was there anything wrong with my sensibility? I was too embarrassed to pose any horticultural questions to my two colleagues, who were hovering suspiciously close to the patch of geraniums by the house.

The previous day, I had reread the section on mescaline in the 1953 edition of *The Alkaloids: Chemistry and Physiology*. That otherwise dry compendium raved about the effects of mescaline in words rarely found in chemical treatises: "ordinary objects appear to be marvelous . . . sounds and music are 'seen' in color . . . color symphonies and new, unknown colors of unimaginable beauty and brilliancy are perceived." I turned on the record player on the porch. Mozart's C-minor Piano Concerto—the piece Huxley had mentioned—was waiting for the needle. While Mozart resounded in the garden, I felt only the nausea that crested in my stomach every time one of my pepperoni-smelling students asked, "What's it like?" Somewhere between two and three hours passed, without any further effects becoming noticeable to this colloid of young chemists, who kept throwing me sidelong glances.

And then, as the first few students started to depart, I rose to accompany them to the gate—and the first effect hit me. With each step I seemed to be floating, weightlessly, toward the street. Pretending uncharacteristic chumminess, I put my arms around the shoulders of two students as they walked to their car. They did not know I needed their ballast to prevent me from sailing up into the sky.

I floated back to the garden, my nausea all but gone. I headed for the fence, mouthing with anticipation the words "deep smoky raspberry, dusky plum, gold bronze, shell pinks. . . ." I looked across the bushes at our neighbor's roses, close enough to catch a whiff of their fragrance, but I saw only roses. To hell with roses, I thought, be grateful for weightlessness.

After a while, only six of us were left: three mescalinized men, who for some reason had not talked to each other until that moment, and three sober and somewhat worried wives. As we started to compare notes, we realized that embarrassment had kept us apart. Each had been afraid to learn from the others that he was the sole mescaline failure. The resulting cacophony of laughter manifested not solely relief, but also our delayed response to mescaline. We were not only floating, we were boisterously merry. A gaggle of Falstaffs, we demanded food. "Not just pizza," I told my wife, "let's have ham and pickles and chutney and pie." Neither my behavior nor the choice of food were typical of me (tongue, pumpernickel, Bulgarian feta, dolmades—perhaps baklava for dessert—would have been more my style), yet our guide Aldous could have reassured our spouses. Though rarely stumped for nouns or adjectives, he could say only this of mescaline and food: "A meal had been prepared. Somebody, who was not yet identical with myself, fell to with ravenous appetite."

Toward the end of the evening, another wave of the mescaline experience descended upon me. The "real" me seemed to be sitting in one corner of the room observing, coolly, the spectacle of the other me acting without inhibition. I remembered that Huxley and most clinical investigators had pointed to this as the great advantage of mescaline over all other recreational drugs—the ability to recall and to record one's experiences while under its influence. I began to contemplate trying mescaline again, some three or four hours prior to one of my chemistry lectures. Would my graduate students notice any difference? But what would I do if they complimented me upon my new professorial style? While still under the influence of my first mescaline experience, I dropped the idea of repeating it.

Even from a scientific standpoint, this was probably just as well. For although my personality alteration lasted for well over ten hours, with one exception only trivial memories—like my giggling at my reflection in the mirror while brushing my teeth—stick in my mind. Was the experience so unworthy that my memory erased that storage bank to make room for less flippant inputs? Or did the "real" me, thirty-five years ago, simply prevent the other me from letting go at a serious level? Was I a puritan even when dosed with mescaline?

Yet the one event remaining with me does seem significant. Usually I speak rapidly—much too fast, I have been told. That night, in bed, I spoke so slowly that even my curious, "real" me became impatient and hastened me on. Ponderously, I announced to my wife that with mescaline I seemed to be shedding one protective layer of my personality after another. It was like peeling off the layers of an onion, I added, thinking the simile brilliant. Soon, I declared, I would arrive at my ultimate truth. Some three decades after the event, I ascribe Norma's reply to her weariness with my verbal pomposity rather than to some Zenlike insight. "You've obviously never peeled an onion. There's nothing left when you've finished peeling." Some years later, we were divorced.

IV

My encounter with cacti and their five-ringed triterpenes, during my early years at Wayne, encouraged me to enter the huge edifice of terpenoid chemistry with its many dark rooms. The terpenoids ("like a terpene") encompass a wide group of natural products, encountered especially in essential oils and plant resins. Quite soon, my research group was active in the structure elucidation of all types. Chemically, terpenes are derived from five-carbon units, called "isoprene," which are also building blocks in the biological synthesis of the steroids—hence, the close biosynthetic relationship between steroids and terpenoids. Substances made from two such isoprene units (such as camphor, pinene, and many essential oils) are "monoterpenes"; from three units, "sesquiterpenes"; from four, "diterpenes." The triterpenes, like those we isolated from giant cacti, are made up of six isoprene units and thus contain thirty carbons as their chemical skeletal backbone.

One curious result of my efforts to study these substances was an excursion into coffee chemistry. Except for an occasional cup of sweet Turkish coffee, a gustatory gesture toward my partial Balkan background, I did not drink coffee until 1977, when I met my third wife, Diane Middlebrook, who can metabolize amazing quantities of French roast. So it was not the taste of coffee that led me to persuade two Israeli postdoctorate fellows—first the late Hillel Bendas and then Michael Cais, now professor at the Technion in Haifa—to start work on the chemical structure elucidation of cafestol, an important constituent of coffee oil. Rather, it was cafestol's intriguing history. Karl Slotta, the German chemist who first isolated the female sex hormone progesterone in the early 1930s and then fled Hitler's Germany for Brazil, isolated a substance named "cafestol" from coffee oil and reported that it exhibited estrogenic properties. This finding caused quite a stir among the various pharmaceutical firms active in the steroid sex hormone field. The possibility of isolating an estrogenic substance from coffee—a potentially inexhaustible starting material—was sufficiently challenging that researchers at CIBA in Switzerland set out to repeat Slotta's work. They found the report of estrogenic activity to be erroneous, and performed chemical studies that convinced them that cafestol was not a steroid. The intervention of the Second World War led them to drop this work. In 1951, while we at Syntex and many other investigators were racing to develop a practical synthesis of cortisone, an Italian investigator aptly named Ferrari roared out of nowhere to claim that cafestol not only was a steroid but, moreover, mimicked the therapeutic properties of cortisone; and an Italian firm even started to market cafestol suppositories. But by 1955 we had demonstrated at Wayne that Ferrari's lead was a dud. We established the complete structure of cafestol, which was that of an unusual diterpene (four isoprene units, strung together in a unique five-ring assembly) rather than of a steroid; and the Italian company soon withdrew its product from the market.

This was not the end of my involvement with coffee. To isolate sufficient cafestol for our chemical studies, we required significant quantities of coffee oil, which is obtained by continuous solvent extraction of green coffee beans. General Foods, then in Hoboken, New Jersey, was the largest American coffee producer and provided us with generous quantities of such oil. General Foods had at that time started research on other constituents of coffee, primarily volatile ones associated with aroma and taste, and invited me (probably the only American academic organic chemist then studying coffee chemistry) to serve as a consultant for a couple of years. These volatile constituents, though much simpler in structure than our cafestol, were an extraordinarily complicated mixture; at least three hundred of them had then been isolated from coffee (many of them by the steroid chemist Tadeus Reichstein, the discoverer of cortisone), and the number nearly doubled over the years as the separation and detection methods—notably gas chromatography and mass spectrometry—became ever more refined. The naïve hope that one might prepare a completely synthetic coffee substitute could never be realized; to this day, I smell and taste with humble admiration a well-brewed cup of coffee. (I shudder to think of the effect on the economies of at least half a dozen countries in Latin America and Africa if acceptable synthetic coffee had come out of that research.)

In the end, the major beneficiary of my consultancy with General Foods proved to be my son. Dale's grade school in Portola Valley (an affluent suburb inhabited by Stanford professors, Silicon Valley engineers, and executives of corporations in the Bay Area) held an annual science fair, which seemed more a reflection of the competitive spirit of the fathers than of the scientific ingenuity of the students. I decided to help Dale with an experiment that might interest nonscientists: a simple demonstration, using coffee as an example, that something capable of being smelled has to be volatile. I lent him a distillation apparatus and an electric heating mantle, his mother brewed him some strong coffee, and I then showed him how to distill the coffee and catch the colorless distillate in an ice-cold container so as not to lose any volatile constituents into the atmosphere. After Dale had distilled a couple of cups, I asked him to smell the colorless condensate in the ice-cold container and then the black fluid remaining in the distillation flask. The latter, though looking like coffee, had no perceptible smell; the colorless liquid had the aroma of a passable cup of coffee. At the school competition, Dale offered cups of colorless liquid to the judges and asked whether they wanted it with sugar and cream. We won second prize.

V

Just as my interest in cactus saponins led us from triterpenes to the much wider area of terpenoid chemistry, so our initial examination of cactus alkaloids (which turned out to be much more complicated, structurally, than mescaline, though devoid of hallucinogenic properties) prompted me to look into the field of alkaloid chemistry. In the early 1950s, a Swiss chemist at CIBA, Emil Schlittler, established the chemical structure of reserpine, an alkaloid from an Indian *Rauwolfia* species that found wide application in medicine as a tranquilizer and sedative. I persuaded two of my graduate students to see whether this medicinally important substance could also be found in Mexican *Rauwolfias*. In the process, we encountered not only reserpine but other alkaloids of unknown constitution with the same "indole" building block (a benzene ring connected to a five-membered ring incorporating a nitrogen atom) present in reserpine and many psyche-delic alkaloids, like LSD or psilocybin (from hallucinogenic Mexican mush-rooms). Over a period of twenty years, a portion of my research group isolated and established the structures of close to one hundred such indole alkaloids, with particular emphasis on plants from the Brazilian side of the Amazon basin.

I had by then attracted a passel of postdoctorate fellows as diverse and exotic in background as the plants we analyzed. Chemists from England, Switzerland, Japan, Italy, India, China, Mexico, Israel, New Zealand, Aus-tralia, Costa Rica, and Brazil worked together in one huge lab and variously assaulted the English language. Shortly before the arrival of my first Italian and Japanese postdoctorate fellows, Riccardo Villotti from Rome and Tatsuhiko Nakano from Kyoto, Jim Gray from Glasgow had entered my laboratory. He had a Scottish burr that, in terms of intensity and purity, bordered even to Americans on incomprehensibility. Villotti and Nakano had hardly ever been exposed to spoken English. The three shared a lab bay, and for many weeks most of their interchange was restricted to sign language or written communication. When Villotti finally gained sufficient confidence in spoken English, he inquired hesitatingly of Gray, "Jim, your native language, it is what?"

My first Brazilian postdoctorate fellow was Walter Mors, who was fluent in English. Before returning to the Instituto de Química Agricola (located in the Rio de Janeiro botanical garden), he asked whether we could possibly start a U.S.-Brazil cooperative venture similar to what I had then under way between my group at Wayne and the Instituto de Química of the National University of Mexico. While directing Syntex's chemical research in Mexico City, I had had several Mexican university chemistry students doing thesis work with me (one of them, Luis Miramontes, synthesized the first few milligrams of norethindrone, the progestationally active ingredient of the Pill [see chapter 5]). A number of these Mexican chemists then formed the nucleus of a small research institute, the Instituto de Química, which was established on the university campus and partly funded by Syntex. When I left for Detroit, I maintained a collaborative program with that group; I felt that the best way to establish an academic research center in Mexico was for the chemists to work on local problems. The academic counterpart to the industrial example of Syntex, with its production of steroid hormones from Mexican yams, became the structure elucidation of natural products from a variety of Mexican plants, especially those that had a history of indigenous medicinal use, and from cacti. I asked my first British postdoctorate fellow at Wayne, Alan Lemin from Manchester, to spend a year at the University of Mexico training a group of young Mexican chemists in the techniques and methodologies we had just developed at Wayne. I was able to provide guidance for this program during my frequent Syntex consulting trips to Mexico. Just as explorers or astronomers have the privilege of naming newly discovered territory, chemists can do so likewise with newly isolated natural products. Prompted by some form of linguistic masochism developed during those Mexican days, I introduced into the chemical literature some real tongue twisters such as *tlatlancuayin* and *cuauchichicine*, based on the Aztec names of their plant progenitors.

During the 1950s, the Rockefeller Foundation supported our Wayne-Mexico collaboration. As a result, the American chemical journals suddenly found themselves publishing Mexico-originated research not only from Syntex, but also from the Universidad Nacional Autónoma de México. (My very first honorary doctorate came from that university. At every Stanford commencement when I wear the black hexagonal hat, crowned with a blue powder puff and tassels hanging down on all sides, I think of the time my Columbia University friend Gilbert Stork tried to photograph the occasion, and the flashbulb exploded in his hand as the rector of the university was placing that silly-looking hat on my head. Owing to recent bombings in Mexico City, everybody responded with panic—as the newspapers later reported—as if this were another terrorist attack. On seeing my friend's look of utter shock, I found myself incapable of saying a word, not even *"Muchas gracias,"* and just sat down, wiping tears of hysteria from my cheeks.)

The Rockefeller Foundation generously supported the cost both of the frequent trips I began taking to Brazil, and of the annual residencies of the postdoctorate fellows from Detroit who performed joint research with Walter Mors's group in the Rio botanical garden. The first such scientific ambassador, Ben Gilbert, met his future wife in Mors's lab and remained in Brazil, where he heads an important effort to make Brazil less dependent on imported drugs. We decided to concentrate on alkaloids from the rich Amazonian flora, notably on indole alkaloids, which were known to display a variety of pharmacological effects on the central nervous system. The productivity of this collaboration, which continued for over a decade, even after I had moved from Wayne via Mexico to Stanford, was impressive in terms of both chemical accomplishments and human intangibles. In the late 1960s, when I chaired the Latin America Science Board of the National Academy of Sciences, I proposed the formation of a U.S.-Brazil chemistry program—modeled after our more modest natural products collaboration—in which half a dozen major professors from Stanford, Caltech, the University of Michigan, and the University of Indiana participated. Programs in synthetic organic chemistry, inorganic chemistry, physical chemistry, and polymer chemistry were instituted at the universities of São Paulo and Rio, and involved over a dozen young American postdoctorate fellows. Chairing this program over a period of years has remained one of my most joyful memories of how science transcends geographic and political boundaries. This pleasure was marred in the 1970s when Brazil, which had received and benefited from so many scientist refugees from Hitler, voted with Cuba at the United Nations in favor of the notorious resolution equating Zionism with racism. Having heard no outcry from Brazilian scientists, I resigned from membership in the Brazilian Academy of Sciences.

VI

So far, I have dealt with the "dark rooms," the natural products of Mexican cacti, coffee, and Brazilian plants; but what about the "flashlights" my research group started to develop concurrently? Just as my interest in natural products chemistry was piqued by Mexican flora, so my two-year Mexican stint at Syntex in 1950 and 1951 was indirectly responsible for my first academic foray into research on physical methods.

Many natural products, and *all* naturally occurring steroids, are "optically active," or capable of existing in mirror-image forms. If light is passed through a solution of such an optically active molecule, the plane of polarized light will be rotated either to the left ("levo-rotatory") or to the right ("dextro-rotatory"). Only one of these mirror-image forms retains the biological activity: for instance, naturally occurring dextro-rotatory-testosterone is responsible for all the androgenic properties of this male sex hormone, whereas the levo-rotatory antipode (available by synthesis) is biologically inactive. At the time I worked in Mexico, individual steroids were characterized by various physical parameters, among them the melting point and the "optical rotation." The conventional way of accomplishing this latter measurement was to determine the extent to which the angle of polarized yellow sodium light is rotated upon passage through a solution of the substance in question. I wondered about the possibility of defining the optical rotation of a steroid not just at this single (visible) wavelength—the yellow sodium line frequently seen in fog lights—but at many different wavelengths down into the ultraviolet range of the spectrum. The resulting plot of wavelength versus angle of rotation is called an "optical rotatory dispersion" curve.

When I started my new academic position at Wayne, one of the first research proposals I submitted to the National Science Foundation was for funds to construct a "spectropolarimeter," which would allow us to carry out such measurements on steroids. Their overall chemical structure is based on a single template, the tetracyclic steroid skeleton, which I have illustrated in chapters 4 and 5 dealing with cortisone and steroid contraceptives. The individual steroids, therefore, differ only in a fairly subtle way, notably the place where certain oxygen atoms are attached with double chemical bonds, known as "ketones." In the event, after measuring the optical rotatory dispersion curves of many steroid ketones in the ultraviolet region, we observed that the shape and sign of these curves ("positive" or "negative," depending on whether the curves went above or below the zero-degree line) related to important structural and stereochemical parameters. In a series of investigations, which involved many graduate students and many Ph.D. man-years, we were able to convert this method—which by then had entered chemical jargon under the acronym ORD—into a powerful flashlight. In the end, ORD proved useful not only for steroids but also for the exploration of many other classes of natural products. One of the most important applications was the "establishment of the absolute configuration" of optically active molecules, the specific determination of the mirror-image formulation of a given substance. (That work was the principal reason I received in 1958 the American Chemical Society's Award in Pure Chemistry.) For the first few years, it took us at least three hours to measure one ORD curve. Toward the end of that decade, we secured an instrument that recorded these measurements automatically, thus reducing the time of measurement to a few minutes.

But if this period at Wayne State University had many peaks of intellectual joy, it also had ever deeper and wider valleys of physical pain. My knee was by then so painful, especially in the Michigan winters, that I consumed daily at least two dozen aspirins. Finally, a biopsy reaffirmed an earlier suspicion that I suffered from a tubercular infection in my knee joint. When I learned that henceforth I would have to use a brace and crutches, I decided to have the joint removed and my left leg fused, and to have that operation in Mexico City during a two-year leave of absence from Wayne while serving as vice president in charge of a greatly expanded research department at Syntex. (The company had just been acquired from its Mexican owners by Allen & Company, a New York investment banking firm, and "taken public." Over the next fifteen years, Syntex's stock, though traveling somewhat on a roller coaster, was one of the great success stories on Wall Street.) I took with me to Mexico a group of postdoctorate fellows from Wayne to start what eventually became the first industrial postdoctoral fellowship program in a pharmaceutical company. Several of them stayed at Syntex—first in Mexico, and later transferring to Palo Alto as the company followed me to California—and became department heads, vice presidents, and in the case of the late Albert Bowers, the eventual chief executive officer of the company.

My initial two-year leave of absence from Wayne State University became a three-year stint at Syntex, which never brought me back to Detroit except for a personally moving honorary degree ceremony in 1974. The reason I did not return to Detroit was not dissatisfaction with Wayne—the university that had launched me on my academic career. Rather, toward the end of my second year in Mexico City, by which time I was pain-free and about as mobile as one can be with a fused knee, a professor from my graduate school days at the University of Wisconsin, William S. Johnson, was offered the chemistry department chairmanship at Stanford. Would I be interested in joining him? he asked one day over the crackling long-distance telephone. By 1959, I had published a great deal, had won my share of awards and honors, was a full professor though on leave, and hence could negotiate from a position of strength. So I flew to San Francisco, drove down the Peninsula to Palo Alto, and met the legendary Frederick Terman, then Stanford's provost and the man generally recognized as the creator of the Stanford Industrial Park and of Silicon Valley. While many academics over the years had been suspicious of my bigamous professional life, Terman was not. Just two years earlier, Stanford's medical school had moved from San Francisco to the Palo Alto campus, with a dramatic shift in emphasis toward the basic medical sciences and research rather than just focusing on health care delivery. Terman felt that the presence of a first-rate medical school and an upgraded chemistry department would encourage biomedically or chemically oriented industrial enterprises to join the electronic and computer companies in the Stanford Industrial Park. In his eyes, my industrial connection with Syntex made me attractive, not suspect.

Johnson and I decided that we would come either as a pair or not at all. Terman liked that, and was only temporarily taken aback when we refused even to consider moving into space that would be renovated for us in the existing chemistry building. To me, this structure, which had survived the 1906 earthquake, ominously resembled Wayne's Old Main. I felt that I didn't have to demonstrate again that exciting and productive research can be performed in an ancient building, and was ready to show that new, up-to-date facilities wouldn't be a hindrance either. In no more than eight weeks, Terman found a donor in the person of the chemical industrialist John Stauffer, who, together with his niece, agreed to fund the building that would be the bait to bring Johnson and me to Stanford.

I well recall the lunch at the Faculty Club when Terman and I agreed on the terms. As we sat, I mentioned a book on the Russian revolution, by the Australian journalist Alan Moorehead, that I had read on the plane trip from Mexico City. I remarked how well Moorehead had drawn the figure of Kerensky, and how the course of history would have changed if that moderate Russian revolutionary had just made a couple of different decisions, which might well have kept the Bolsheviks from assuming power. Terman's eyes twinkled as he leaned across the table. "Tell this to Kerensky. He's sitting right behind you." I had assumed that Aleksandr Feodorovich Kerensky was dead; now I found that the little old man eating by himself was a research fellow at Stanford's Hoover Institution. I pondered the contrast between his fate and that of his fellow revolutionary Leon Trotsky (whose grandson was then working with me at Syntex) whom Stalin's henchmen followed to Mexico and, in spite of high walls and bodyguards, assassinated.

Since it would take nearly a year to build the new Stauffer Organic Chemistry building, I decided to sit out the building phase in Mexico City by extending my Syntex stay. During this time, Syntex generated a flow of new drugs that pharmaceutical companies many times our size could not match. (Our greatest coup, and indirectly the most meaningful accolade extended to us, was when Eli Lilly, then one of the two biggest American pharmaceutical companies, committed itself to fund for a five-year period

50 percent of our research, with the choice of research topics and ownership of patents remaining with Syntex, provided Lilly would get co-marketing rights for any inventions.) During those three years, in addition to laying most of the clinical groundwork for our norethindrone Pill, we also created a second progestational agent (chlormadinone, which Lilly eventually marketed as an estrogen-free contraceptive), the powerful anabolic oxymetholone, the best-selling topical corticosteroid Synalar, a systemic corticosteroid related to prednisone, and finally dromastonolone propionate, a steroidal breast cancer palliative, which Lilly brought to the U.S. market in the early 1960s.

Concurrently I directed my academic research group in Detroit in various structure-elucidation projects in the field of antibiotics (which led to the first complete structure determination of a macrolide antibiotic, methymycin, to which clinically important compounds like erythromycin belong), alkaloids, terpenoids, and, most important, optical rotatory dispersion. During that third year in Mexico City, in addition to writing a lot of articles, I even managed to complete my first book, *Optical Rotatory Dispersion: Applications to Organic Chemistry*. This wasn't the tour de force it might seem: the bulk of the contents dealt with our own research; the entire literature was at my fingertips. Furthermore, by then I had stopped doing laboratory research. Like virtually all scientists who wish to climb rapidly up the academic ladder or, for that matter, head into the higher echelons of corporate management, I was directing a large group of researchers, which made it virtually impossible to continue working or even dabbling on the bench. The choice is usually clear-cut: to work personally in the lab, one has to do it alone or with a small team. If a large group is needed—because one is in a hurry or wishes to attack various problems concurrently—one should stay in the office or the library. For me, the choice was never in doubt: not only did I always put a great value on time, but invariably I wanted to work simultaneously on a variety of projects and do so, furthermore, side by side in two worlds, the academic and the industrial. Since 1952, my lab coat, figuratively and literally, never got dirty again.

One aspect of my publishing contract with McGraw-Hill was unusual. When the publisher invited me to prepare this first monograph dealing with organic chemical applications of optical rotatory dispersion, I insisted on a penalty clause, whereby my royalties would escalate by 1 percent for each week the book's appearance might be delayed beyond my six-month deadline, but as a quid pro quo I offered a similar royalty reduction for each week's advance appearance prior to my requested publication date. To everyone's surprise, the McGraw-Hill lawyers accepted my proposal, provided I agreed to return the corrected page proofs from Mexico City within twenty-four hours of their receipt. This was supposed to prevent a horror scenario, whereby my royalties might escalate to unprecedented heights were I simply to sit on the page proofs. As a final compromise, the publisher set each chapter in print as it was received, rather than waiting for the entire manuscript. I managed to finish the book in time by sticking to a rigid Monday-Wednesday-Friday writing schedule, and McGraw-Hill was equally diligent. The royalties from the book eventually paid for a swimming pool at my new house in California, whose steps were set in Mexican tiles reading "built by optical rotatory dispersion."

That house did not come into being quite as easily as the new chemistry building. In Detroit we "owned" (the quotation marks indicate the size of my mortgage) a small two-bedroom tract house in a suburb north of the city, built right after the war and indistinguishable from its neighbors. When Dale was born in 1953, we finished the micro-attic so that my daughter, Pamela, would have her own room. Now, seven years later, as Syntex's stock started its first climb, I could afford a bigger mortgage and a house built to fit our needs and tastes. My wife Norma and I found an ideal spot in Portola Valley, a fifteen-minute drive from the campus. The lot of less than two acres was located in a hilly and heavily wooded area, the live oak, madrone, pine, and eucalyptus trees shielding us on three sides from neighbors and yet providing a superb view of the Santa Cruz mountains in the distance. Norma remembered the former wife of one of my Wayne chemistry department colleagues, who had moved to Taliesin West to study architecture under Frank Lloyd Wright, married another Wright disciple, and settled on the other side of San Francisco Bay in Sausalito. When we visited them to get architectural advice, they offered "as friends, with no further commitment," to provide us not only with a design but also with a model. So we took them to our dream lot and outlined our desiderata: decks on three sides of the house, whose floor plan should resemble that of a cross, thus providing four separate areas, and lots of wall space for pictures and books. "Forget family and dining rooms," I emphasized. "Three large bedrooms, a study, and a large living room is what we want." As I read these words now through my self-analytical glasses, I wonder whether "cross-shaped" and "forget family room" were not unconsciously precise formulations of my view of a suitable life style for an academic paterfamilias.

Six weeks later, in October 1959, we returned to San Francisco and drove in great anticipation across the Golden Gate to Sausalito. When we entered our architect's living room, there was our model covered by a white cloth. With a flourish, he whisked off the cover to display the carefully constructed model. But where were the decks I'd been dreaming about all these weeks? I turned to my wife and saw stony New England disapproval. The architect mistook my desperate expression for timid admiration. "Lift off the roof," he encouraged me, "and look at the inside." It was lovingly constructed, like a doll house, but all wrong. I hardly knew where to start. "Are the bookshelves adjustable?" I finally stammered, picking something simple but to me, the stickler for details, important.

"Of course not." He looked startled, as if I had asked an inane question. "That would look messy."

"But I told you I wanted adjustable shelves," I almost whined. "We have lots of art books."

"You can always stack them horizontally." His tone was that of an adult instructing a child how to stow a tricycle.

"There is hardly space for any pictures," I observed, pointing at the Lilliputian living room. "I told you—"

My complaint was stopped with a policeman's raised hand. "Look," he pointed to a spot near the mini-fireplace, "this is the display area. It will take a good-sized picture."

"Picture?" I practically levitated from my sofa seat. "I said we needed space for pictures." I hissed the *s* as if there were several attached to the word. "Lots of them."

"No problem," the architect smiled. "It's all taken care of. Here is a storage area for the art. You display one item at a time, while you store the others. You'll like this rotation."

I wondered how the director of the Guggenheim Museum felt when Frank Lloyd Wright first described the curved walls and slanted floors in his plans for the projected building. Let the curators worry about trivia like hanging large canvases on curved walls! But this was not Frank Lloyd Wright, I reminded myself, nor was our future home a public edifice. I was being talked down to by one of his many apprentices, who had all too well learned the master's manners. By now, I didn't even worry about the absence of the decks—"too fussy," I was told later; I knew the project was beyond repair, and that I should have known better than to mix business with friendship.

The next evening, dining at the home of Joshua Lederberg (chairman of Stanford's new genetics department) and lamenting the time we had lost in planning our house, we were given the name of his architect, whom he much admired. Two days later, back in Mexico City, I called William Hempel to ask whether he had ever been to Mexico. Hearing he hadn't, I invited him to spend three days in our house to learn how we lived and to see what we wanted in our California home. Within one month, Hempel had shipped to us three different drawings of cross-shaped houses surrounded with outdoor decks and replete with display space for art. Adjustable bookshelves, I decided, would be mentioned later. In January 1960, we flew once more to California to approve the final plans. The architect and the Finnish builder-carpenter were nonplused that we were ready to make all detailed decisions right there and then, down to doorknobs and bathroom fixtures.

"The house has to be ready on September eighth in the evening," I announced, "because we are flying up from Mexico City in time for our children's school opening. We want to sleep here the very first night." Using my McGraw-Hill book contract as a model, I demanded a penalty payment for every day the house was late, but offered incentive payment for more rapid conclusion. We did indeed sleep there that night, and the house thereafter proved an unmitigated joy. I was deeply saddened to leave it sixteen years later, when my wife retained it as part of our divorce settlement.

VII

My research at Stanford took off with a flying start. My entire Detroit research staff of seventeen graduate students and postdoctorate fellows had moved to California and established itself within a week in a long laboratory constructed to my specifications. Johnson, who occupied the second floor, favored four five-man labs. I had asked for one lab with twenty benches, twenty sinks, and twenty desks, because I wanted no barriers: everyone should know what everybody else was doing; equipment should be shared; cooperation should flourish. I had visions of a quasi-socialist, intellectual enterprise, presided over by a benevolent dictator. One of my Brazilian graduate students, Hugo Monteiro, later chairman of the chemistry department of the Federal University of Brasilia, put me in my place by consistently referring to me with an impertinent grin as *El Supremo*. He also bilked me of one hundred dollars by calling my bluff when I aggressively bet him that a certain experiment could not be completed by week's end. He even had the gall to request the canceled check from me after confessing that he had won the bet by subcontracting the work to three other graduate students, with whom he split the money.

Our research on Brazilian indole alkaloids was then proceeding at full steam. It had achieved sufficient notoriety that, one day, on one of my frequent trips to Mexico, Timothy Leary (then a psychology lecturer at Harvard) visited my office to proposition me, in a disarmingly naïve manner, about supplying him with a large amount of LSD. Within a couple of years, Leary became the guru of an LSD cult with the motto "tune in, turn on, and drop out"—but he didn't get the hallucinogen from me.

Our concurrent research on two distinct types of natural products, steroids and alkaloids, offered another illustration of the virtue of working side by side on several topics—like throwing several pebbles into a pond to produce more ripples. Our steroid work had pointed me toward optical rotatory dispersion; our alkaloid studies prompted me to examine another flashlight, mass spectrometry. Among many other applications, this method—which makes possible the identification of impurities on the order of one part per billion—is currently the method of choice in monitoring atmospheric pollution and in detecting toxic contaminants in vegetables or fruit. Originally, mass spectrometry had been used primarily by petroleum chemists for specialized analyses of hydrocarbons; but in the late 1950s, groups in Sweden and Scotland, and at MIT, had started to employ it in investigating more complex molecules such as lipids and alkaloids. As soon as I arrived in Palo Alto, I applied to the National Institutes of Health for financial support in buying a mass spectrometer in order to conduct a systematic study of the technique, using steroids as initial model substrates before applying it to the, structurally, much more diverse group of alkaloids. We wanted to determine whether special rules of fragmentation and reassembly could be developed (were certain areas of the molecule broken preferentially?) which would make this method of more general utility. Using steroids as substrates, we set out to "mark" certain portions of the molecule with stable, nonradioactive isotopes of hydrogen and carbon to facilitate the reassembly of the broken pieces. Eventually we used the marking technique, which on its own involved many man-years of synthetic effort, to establish the rules of mass spectrometric decomposition for a wide variety of molecules, such as steroids, triterpenes, and alkaloids. Four monographs and well over two hundred publications later, our group has contributed in a major way to making mass spectrometry one of the most powerful and generally useful techniques in organic chemistry.

We were well advanced in our mass spectrometry research when, one day in the mid-1960s, Joshua Lederberg approached me with a proposal for collaboration. His interest in exobiology (evidence for life in outer space) had prompted him to establish an instrumentation facility in the genetics department of Stanford's school of medicine, in preparation for an eventual unmanned mission to Mars. Like other investigators in the field, he felt that placing a rugged mass spectrometer with a remote-control sampling device on the space vehicle might be the most effective method for screening molecules indicative of organic life, such as amino acids, the building blocks for proteins, and porphyrins, which are substances related to chlorophyll. Would I join him and Edward Feigenbaum, a professor in the computer science department and one of the pioneers of artificial intelligence, in determining whether AI could be used to derive chemical structures from a single mass spectrum sent back from outer space by telemetry? Over a dozen years, our three research groups collaborated to lay some of the cornerstones for the imposing edifice that computer-aided knowledge engineering now represents in chemistry. As Lederberg put it in an interview, "We are trying to teach a computer how Djerassi thinks about mass spectrometry."

Two other types of flashlight were studied intensively in my laboratory during the decades of the 1960s and 1970s. One was the spectroscopic extension of optical rotatory dispersion, known as "circular dichroism." It provides the same information as optical rotatory dispersion, but more conveniently, by measuring the preferential absorption of polarized light by a left-handed or right-handed organic molecule. Such chirality (handedness) obtains only in "optically active" molecules, which encompass virtually all biologically active substances in nature but exclude the vast majority of organic substances—millions of synthetic, and also many naturally occurring, products. As Michael Faraday had noted in the nineteenth century, however, "optical activity" can be *induced* in any molecule when it is exposed to a magnetic field, the induced rotation being directly proportional to the strength of the magnetic field. This phenomenon, named the "Faraday effect," seemed to me worth studying, especially now that high magnetic fields could be generated readily (using superconducting magnets and liquid helium) in the laboratory. I persuaded the Japan Spectroscopic Company to construct a prototype instrument that would permit us to measure the circular dichroism of organic molecules under such conditions. We pursued our research on magnetic circular dichroism (MCD) for well over a decade. In the process, we developed a variety of useful applications ranging from the detection of lead poisoning in urine to the detection of subtle structural changes in biologically important molecules of the porphyrin type, present in chlorophyll and in many enzymes.

VIII

Our increasingly sophisticated knowledge of the mass spectrometric behavior of steroids led me to my last area of research, the structure and biosynthesis of unusual marine sterols, which ultimately involved my group in the use of another kind of flashlight and, oddly enough, completed a circle leading back to our work of the very early 1950s on the active ingredient of the Pill. As a bonus, this research also introduced me to the joys of scuba diving and to the magic underwater world in Papua New Guinea, Hawaii, the Indian Ocean, and the Caribbean.

Until 1969, we had carried out only one investigation on a natural product of marine origin. I had read reports that sea cucumber toxins appeared to be steroidal in nature, and suggested to Ben Tursch, a Belgian postdoctorate fellow of mine, then a member of the Stanford team in Brazil, that he collect some. Tursch, who spent his childhood in the Congo, is a superb diver and the most adventurous chemist I ever met. (In the 1970s, he located an idyllic uninhabited island off the north coast of Papua New Guinea, where, in Robinson Crusoe style, he established a small marine biology laboratory and gave me my first scuba lesson.) Tursch located an abundant source of sea cucumbers in northeastern Brazil; but since we wanted fresh material, and in large quantities, we had to find a way of transporting them to Rio without decomposition in that tropical climate. Tursch's ingenuity was memorialized by an acknowledgment in our publication in the chemical journal *Tetrahedron*: "We gratefully acknowledge the help of the Brazilian air force which provided us with various aircraft, ranging from small planes for exploratory trips, to a B-25 bomber and its crew when rich collecting grounds were located." As Ben told the story, he managed to persuade a Brazilian bomber pilot to fly his old plane to an abandoned airstrip near the beach. The crew lolled around in the sand while Ben did his collecting. On the return flight, the bomb bay was filled with sea cucumbers; Tursch occupied the rear gunner's seat all the way to Rio. I have always considered this use of the Brazilian air force as a modern variant of beating swords into plowshares.

In 1969, Paul Scheuer, one of America's pioneers in marine natural products chemistry, sent me from Hawaii a sample of a sterol that he assumed was pure; he had isolated it during an investigation of marine toxins. On subjecting his sample to mass spectrometric analysis, we found it to consist of at least three sterols: two conventional ones of the cholesterol type, and a third one with a seemingly unprecedented number of carbon atoms. I encouraged Scheuer to isolate more of that "impurity," which we then subjected at Stanford to some of our flashlights such as nuclear magnetic resonance and mass spectrometry. In a joint communication with Scheuer, we published the structure of "gorgosterol," which has the same tetracyclic steroid nucleus as cholesterol, but an extremely unusual "side chain"—an assembly of eleven carbon atoms attached to position 17 of the steroid skeleton.

We determined the complete structure of gorgosterol only by means of

X-ray crystallography—the physical technique corresponding to the flash camera in my "dark room"—and promptly got hooked on a research line my group pursued for the next twenty years. By 1970, when we deduced the structure of gorgosterol, the structures of most significant animal and plant sterols had long been established, and a great deal was known about both their biogenesis (how the organism actually synthesizes them and what chemical building blocks it uses) and their biological significance. We know that cholesterol, to take as just one example the principal sterol of all higher animals and humans, serves two functions: it is the starting material from which all steroid hormones (male and female sex hormones as well as corticosteroids secreted by the adrenal gland) are generated; and it is a key ingredient of all cell membranes. Given our extensive knowledge of sterol chemistry and biology, it seemed extraordinary to encounter a sterol from a marine source with an unprecedented side chain attached to the conventional steroid nucleus. We set out to examine the sterol composition of a wide variety of marine organisms, notably sponges, from tropical and semitropical waters all over the world. Since a few other groups—in Canada, Japan, and Italy—also became intrigued by this subject, during the 1970s and early 1980s well over one hundred new sterols were isolated, possessing structures that in many instances had no precedent among terrestrial plants and animals. Whereas the early studies on natural products involved a great deal of laborious chemical degradative work, often consuming years for just one substance, the postwar physical methods—notably nuclear magnetic resonance and mass spectrometry—and the newly developed separation techniques now permit the solution of many of these structural problems in a few weeks and with minute amounts of material. But if eliminating the need for "wet chemistry" (the laboratory equivalent of "Twenty Questions") saves a lot of time and material, it also makes structure elucidation a more mechanical endeavor. Ironically, much of our own research into better flashlights has made obsolete the traditional and often intellectually exciting ways of exploring dark rooms.

In recent years, therefore, the focus in natural products chemistry has shifted from structure to biosynthesis and biological function. Now that chemists can establish rather quickly the contents of a room, they are more interested *how* the various objects in it were manufactured and what their purpose is. These are the questions we asked of sterols from marine sponges—the lowest members of the animal kingdom but the richest sources of unique sterols. We did not believe for a moment that they were there only to titillate a chemist's curiosity. Through laborious and sophisticated separation techniques, we sorted out the individual sponge cell types and fractionated them further into pure cell-membrane fractions, which were shown still to contain unique marine sterols. It is likely, therefore, that these replace the cholesterol of higher animals in some process related to membrane integrity or function. In addition to the sterols, we also examined the other lipid component of the sponge's cell membrane, the so-called phospholipids, and found that class of marine natural products also to differ uniquely from the phospholipids of higher animals. Perhaps it is not surprising that sessile, filter-feeding animals possess cell membranes of an unusual kind to permit ready passage of nutrients from their surroundings, when this process is so different from how we feed ourselves. Furthermore, their environment differs in temperature, salinity, and pressure from that of terrestrial organisms. These leads are thus worth pursuing; they are likely to shed light on the manner in which living organisms modulate the structural integrity of their cell membranes. Without a membrane, there can be no cell; without a cell, there can be no life.

Even more interesting to us was the question of how the sponge synthesizes such sterols. Since they are filter-feeders, securing all of their nutrients from the aqueous environment, they may not synthesize them at all but acquire them through their diet. We tested this possibility by setting up near the sponge's natural habitat, generally at depths of 40 to 80 feet, underwater laboratories consisting of metal grids to which sponge samples were attached, and which were protected by chicken wire to prevent grazing by predators. A diving chemist, equipped with scuba gear, can spend up to one hour performing relevant experiments, which involve feeding the sponge radioactively labeled starting materials (synthesized in the laboratory) to see whether these will be further utilized by the sponge and converted to the final sterol that has earlier been identified. Such "feeding" is not easy. It cannot be done by underwater injection with a syringe, because the material would immediately be diluted beyond all recognition by the mass of surrounding ocean water; and only in some cases can the sponge be brought to the surface and maintained alive in aquariums equipped with circulating sea water. Often we had to conduct these experiments in the sponge's natural environment for several weeks after having "fed" it, before the samples could be harvested in a form useful for eventual chemical analysis in the laboratory and for counting of radioactivity (still another of our flashlights). Sometimes we used small osmotic pumps, connected to the sponge, which slowly administered a solution of the precursor over a very long time. Sometimes we performed quick underwater surgery, excising a small piece of sponge, inserting a gelatin capsule containing the radioactive precursor, and plugging up the hole with the excised piece of sponge. In this manner we established the operation of at least three different biosynthetic pathways: many sponges synthesize their sterols de novo from acetic acid, like terrestrial animals or plants; others derive them from their environment and then perform certain clever enzymatic steps to generate the unique structural features encountered among marine sterols; at times, they are lazy and simply use dietary sterols in unaltered form.

One boon to these experiments, unusual in standard chemical research, is the pleasure of experiencing the extraordinarily beautiful, womblike underwater environment of the tropics. None of my students and associates ever complained about her or his professional travel to the Australian Great Barrier Reef, Papua New Guinea, and Hawaii, to the Caribbean and the Mediterranean. But there were also disappointments: before we introduced the protective cover of chicken wire, a chemist might return after a few weeks to the underwater platform to find that some predator (fish? turtle?) had consumed our precious samples. The most costly incident occurred when one of my students made a special trip to Naples to set up over thirty incorporation experiments, involving precursors that several members of my research team had synthesized laboriously over a period of months. Even though the metal grid was located at a depth of 80 feet, a major autumn storm produced such underwater turbulence that divers, returning to collect the specimens for us, found nothing. This single storm set us back for well over one year.

Auditors of grant-giving institutions might question why we have to do some of our experiments near Capri in the Mediterranean, rather than one hour away from Stanford on the California coast. I offer as justification only a single example, which will also illustrate the completion of a major circle for me. A pair of Italian chemists in Naples, Luigi Minale and Guido Sodano, made the remarkable observation that a sponge species indigenous to that area contained a group of sterols that did *not* differ in the nature of the side chain from the sterols of terrestrial animals, but differed rather in terms of the nucleus. They found that all of the sterols in that particular sponge contained the "19-norsteroid" nucleus. In my description of the birth of the Pill (see chapter 5), I emphasized that this structural feature, which we introduced *synthetically* in 1951, was responsible for the powerful progestational activity of the Pill's key ingredient. In fact, all oral contraceptives currently on the market are 19-norsteroids and are prepared by total synthesis, since no naturally occurring starting material has been available with that nucleus. And suddenly there appears a potential source of such starting material in the form of a single species, belonging to the lowest form of animal life and living deep in the ocean! It should not come as a surprise that we actively worked on providing answers to two fascinating questions: What are these 19-norsterols doing there, and how does the sponge synthesize them? One also wonders how oral contraceptives would now be produced had this sponge research been performed a quarter of a century earlier.

IX

"What kind of chemist are you?" is basically a tourist's question. No wonder I gave a guide's reply: descriptive, anecdotal, at times metaphoric, on occasion historical. But if one is to gain insight into the intellectual persona, one needs to pose different questions:

"Why did you become a scientist?" "Serendipity," would be not only the shortest, but also the most honest reply.

"Why did you remain one for so long?" would probably be countered with "Excitement, curiosity, and ambition."

"Do you plan to die in your lab coat?" My answer to the last question is no. I stayed with chemistry for all my adult life because satisfying my curiosity gave me a great deal of pleasure: each question answered raised another. And I could live simultaneously in a world of research, with no ostensible utility, and of practical projects potentially benefiting millions of people. So why am I taking off my lab coat?

Cynthia Ozick, in an interview in the *Paris Review*, likened poets and prose writers to amphoras, waiting to be filled with wine or water. Scientists, I observe, do not wait for their amphoras to be filled; they search for faucets producing spurts of liquid. Only the passage of time tells whether ambrosia or vinegar has issued. The search for the faucet is what counts. As I note in the concluding chapter, instead of turning on more faucets I am now examining the contents of my own literary amphora by writing fiction. Not only does this genre offer me the opportunity of moving from the exclusively monologuist written discourse of the scientist to the dialogic style of the novelist, but, for once, it also gives me full rein to let my imagination roam over autobiographical as well as imaginary terrain without the slightest hindrance imposed by embarrassment or shame. For a scientist, being able to say, "It's just fiction," is a startlingly refreshing luxury.

CHAPTER 8

Interlude: The Big Drop

A TACITURN MAN I DIDN'T KNOW sat between me and Sheldon Glashow, the Nobel Prize physicist from Harvard, who had predicted the existence of charmed hadrons. We were on the dais at the Banquet of the Golden Plate, an award ceremony arranged by an entrepreneurial organization self-anointed the American Academy of Achievement. A bevy of "Captains of Achievement" faced a raft of high-school superachievers: National Merit Scholars, All-American halfbacks, star farmers of America, patriotic-art competition winners, America's Junior Miss (sponsored by Coca-Cola), the National Spelling Bee champion, and a twelve-year-old named David Glassner who, according to the illustrated program, had scored a perfect 800 in math on the college entrance exams, wore braces on his teeth, owned a Norwegian elkhound named King, and, of course, ran a paper route. The names of my fellow captains were mostly unknown to me: Ed Asner, Cicely Tyson, Darrell Griffith, Henry Winkler were only some of the names whose identity I learned later. I hardly watch TV (and didn't own a set until 1985), never go to basketball games, and only occasionally put on earphones when movies are shown on airplanes. I do so much long-distance traveling that I relish the opportunity for uninterrupted reading or writing. Looking up occasionally at the screen more than satisfies my curiosity; as a consequence, though I see a fair number of films in that manner, I don't remember their titles or the names of the actors.

I was eager to converse with the few other scientists on the program. But who was this man next to me, the focus of a stream of starry-eyed students, who kept pressing him to sign their programs? Why didn't they ask for our autographs, Glashow's or mine? "Do you live here?" I asked him. For a moment, he seemed startled, his eyes following my hand as I gestured around the banquet hall, until he realized that I meant Los Angeles. "Yeah," he said, staring at me suspiciously. He had hard eyes, a sharp, well-shaped nose, thick sideburns, and a high forehead—not intellectually so, but indicative of incipient balding, which was offset by the dark hair spilling over the back of his collar and part of his ears. The creases on his cheeks looked like the dueling scars of a Prussian officer. He seemed wary, watching my mouth. "Do you work here?" I asked, feeling embarrassed. "Yeah," he nodded, his eyes again narrowing. "What *do* you do?" Glashow asked, the ever-curious physicist. After signing a couple of programs with great flourish and a loud scraping of the pen, the man turned to Glashow: "I work in Hollywood." "You mean the movie industry?" I intervened, trying to be helpful. "Yeah," he admitted, and took a long time signing the next program, as if wondering what to write. "But *what* do you do?" persisted Glashow. "Are you a director?" I added; he certainly didn't seem dashing enough for an actor. "Yeah," he admitted, "I do some directing."

I was ready to give up, but Glashow persisted: "What kind of movies?" Our neighbor replied, "*Play Misty for Me*," and then turned to me, "*Breezy* and *Bronco Billy*." "I see," I said, having heard of none of these films, but nevertheless impressed. "What did you say your name was?" Glashow asked, saving us from trying to shuffle unobtrusively through the 128 pages of our program. A truly pregnant pause intervened before the man responded: "Eastwood." "How do you do?" said Glashow, proffering his hand, "I'm Shelly Glashow." To this day, I don't know whether "Eastwood" signified anything to Glashow, but to me the simple name meant only that the man didn't have to spell it every time he telephoned for a restaurant reservation, in marked contrast to my own experience. "And I'm Carl Djerassi," I added, and went on sociably: "Tell me, Mr. Eastwood, why are all these people asking for your autograph?" This brought the first laugh to Clint Eastwood's stern face. "Are you for real?" he challenged me.

Such was my ignorance that, had there been time, I would have told Mr. Eastwood about my own experience as a movie tycoon. For that misadventure the huge, garish slush-metal medallion dangling from the red, white, and blue ribbon draped around the neck of each Captain of Achievement was the perfect award. So was the accompanying gilt-edged plate with my name embossed in the center—a suitable vehicle for serving crow.

I

In 1957, I spent four weeks in the American-British-Cowdray hospital in Mexico City, following the knee fusion operation that promised to relieve the ever-increasing pain I had been suffering for years. Most knee fusions at that time required that one be encased for many months in a body cast. But Dr. Juan Farill of Mexico City—who performed in a week more knee fusions than most American surgeons did in a couple of months, and himself had a fused knee—rather inserted two metal pins into the tibia and femur and clamped them together on the outside, where they penetrated the skin. Immobilized in this manner for about a month, I would require only a walking cast for the remaining period until the knee fusion had healed completely. (The operation proved so successful that within a couple of years, after a skiless interval of two decades, I resumed skiing, albeit with a peculiar stiff-legged technique and a specially designed left boot.)

In the month I spent in the hospital, I made friends with the American supervisor of the nursing staff. During her visits to me, Betty told me about her husband, Mike, who was active on the budding Mexican TV scene but really wanted to write, direct, and produce a movie. A few weeks later, when I was out of the hospital, I met Mike, and he told me about Mexico's film industry. It was extensive, he said, with all the requisite infrastructure: studios, technicians, cameramen, gaffers, best boys—the lot. Making movies in Mexico cost only a fraction of what it did in Hollywood, the usual supplier of B movies for double features at drive-in theaters and provincial emporia, where people went to neck rather than to watch. If a film consisted primarily of sex and suspense, even those few who did watch it would be satisfied. Enough S&S would also eliminate the need for expensive color film. According to Mike, even the cheapest B movie in Hollywood then cost several hundred thousand dollars, whereas a full-fledged film in Mexico could be produced within a middle-sized, five-figure budget. Indeed, if one operated outside the union, and offered financial participation in the profits to the chief actors and staff, thirty thousand dollars would provide a satisfying morsel for the gringos' insatiable appetite.

"So why don't they do it?" I asked, not realizing that I was already nibbling on the bait.

"Because the local movie industry only makes Spanish movies for the

Latino market: Mexico, Latino centers across the border (like in Los Angeles or San Antonio), and other Latin American countries." He looked at me sideways. "The real market ought to be the English-speaking one, but the only films made in Mexico for that audience are location blockbusters with stars like Elizabeth Taylor. So . . . " he said slowly.

"So?" I echoed.

"What's needed are scripts in English with Mexican locations; very few studio shots, which also eliminate most of the union problems; just a couple of key characters who are Americans, with the subsidiary roles written in such a way that they can logically be Mexicans speaking accented English . . . black and white . . . sex and suspense . . . save money and dub . . . hummable music. . . ."

By then, only key phrases were registering; I already had visions of a mini-Metro Goldwyn Mayer enterprise for B movies, all based on that first thirty-thousand-dollar investment. "Yes, of course," I murmured, "but how does one get such a script?"

"Oh, that? Simple. I have one."

Eventually I read Mike's script and, incomprehensible as this now sounds to me, liked it. I had never perused a film script, but the very first lines sounded like the real stuff: "WILLIE has just taken out a handkerchief. He begins to wipe his mouth. Looking up, he reacts to something o.s. The CAMERA DOLLIES in to a CU. A smirk appears on WILLIE'S face as he slowly, deliberately. . . ."

Mike needed only part of the money to begin. Within a couple of weeks, I'd persuaded three friends to join in this guaranteed bonanza. The easiest to convince was my oldest friend, Gilbert Stork, then professor of chemistry at Columbia University, who knew as little about movies as I; the other two were my Syntex colleagues, George Rosenkranz and Alejandro Zaffaroni, whom I had joined on a two-year leave of absence from my professorship at Wayne State University to serve as Syntex's vice president for research. Alex even had the foresight to organize a Panamanian holding company called SOXA. "Who knows," he mused, "if this is an *espectacular* success"—he always added the Spanish *e* as in *estupido*—"we might as well shelter the profits in a tax haven to fund the next film." We may not have known much about the movie business, but we had learned how to synthesize cortisone and the first steroid oral contraceptive; surely movie production would be a snap.

Reading a film script is like reviewing an architect's rough plans and visualizing the final house. Or what's even more difficult, guessing how it would feel to live in it. Mike's script was called (ominously, in retrospect) *The Big Drop*. The story was simple—at that time, convincingly so. An

American gangster, Willie, with the help of an American cop turned venal, misappropriates a bundle of money belonging to the mob. In a manner not clarified in the script (or eventually to the viewing public), this money is to be "dropped" in Mexico City, where Willie and his police bodyguard will retrieve it. Matters go awry when the protagonists arrive by train in Mexico, chased by hitmen sent down by the Mafia. In spite of the gangster's honest and stupid younger brother, a charming Mexican whore, and the policeman's new Mexican girlfriend, a series of complications prevent recovery of the money until the final "big drop," which occurs on the very top of Mexico City's ten-story Monumento a la Revolución. The gangster falls over the parapet at the top of the monument and is smashed on the pavement below.

Unfortunately, things went nearly as bad for the movie's makers. *Item:* Mike's script required two American principals, the gangster and the cop, and a few minor American characters—the pursuing mobsters, the young brother. All other actors could be local Mexicans with a minimal command of English. In the event, the Mexican actors spoke better English than the two "American" principals, whom Mike located after a long search. Both were French. Marc, the cop, spoke passable though heavily accented English. At least, his lips moved authentically and thus lent themselves to direct dubbing. But Willie, the gangster, supposedly from Jersey City, was played by a short, hirsute Frenchman who didn't speak a word of English. His classically Gallic hand gestures and facial expressions might have suited a *Mafioso* from Marseilles, but not one from Jersey City. "Don't worry," Mike assured us. "We are dubbing everything to save money. We'll write a special French dialogue for Julien, so his lip movements coincide with the English text." The result was hilarious: English snarls of the "I'll knock your head off" variety were mouthed as *"je t'aime beaucoup"* or some such affectionate labial equivalent.

Item: Two days into the projected forty-day shooting schedule, while the crew was on location in Morelia, the camera was stolen. Imaginative people can improvise around unexpected disasters, but this camera was the prize possession of the only non-union cameraman in Mexico willing to work for a percentage of future profits. Purchasing a replacement would have blown our entire production budget. After letting us stew for a couple of days, the police chief of Morelia let it be known that for an immodest, but not preposterous sum he could recover the equipment. He could recover it, of course, since the camera had been stolen by local police.

Item: The initial shooting didn't take forty days; it spread over more than eight months. Some of the actors, such as the woman playing the cop's girlfriend, had to find alternative employment during this frequently interrupted marathon. In one scene, the blonde woman kissed her man good-bye. A scene occurring ten minutes later was shot after four months had passed, during which she had dyed her hair black to satisfy the demands of a more lucrative acting assignment that had come her way in the interim. Thus for the second scene she had to wear a kerchief—so tight and all-encompassing that not a single black strand showed. Even the Ayatollah would have approved.

Item: The final and most gory scene, in which the gangster's body comes hurtling down from the sky to crash onto the stony ground, had to be reshot. Watching the rushes of that climax, we couldn't believe our eyes. There, in one corner of the picture—admittedly some forty or fifty feet from the fallen body—sat a worker calmly munching a rolled-up tortilla. "Mike," I whispered in the darkness, "maybe he didn't *see* the body falling, but surely he would've *heard* it."

Item: Had the shooting been completed in forty or even eighty days, there would have been no problem with the union. We didn't use a studio, the crew was small, and the incentive great for keeping the operation secret. But some time during the eight months of shooting, the union had learned about *The Big Drop* and arranged for an export embargo, though not for confiscation—on the correct assumption that there was no market for our masterpiece inside Mexico. Thus we had to resort to illegal means. Whenever any of us flew to the States, we stuck a film can or two into our luggage with our shirts and underwear. After several months of such smuggling by driblets, we still had sixteen cans in Mexico City. Gilbert Stork was due for one of his scientific consulting visits from New York, and since he traveled on a Mexican tourist card, there was little risk of his baggage being inspected at the Mexico City airport upon his departure. We packed an entire suitcase with the remaining cans, taking care to label each with the legend "Professor Gilbert Stork, Department of Chemistry, Columbia University."

"Is this an educational film?" the inspector at New York's Idlewild Airport asked deferentially, upon reading the labels.

"Not exactly," replied Gilbert.

"Is it pornographic material?"

"I wish it were," said Gilbert, grinning.

"Are you going to make any money out of it?" persisted the inspector.

Gilbert's sincere "I doubt it" carried the day.

"Next!" the agent barked and waved *The Big Drop* on its way.

Item: One working print was made in New York, and somehow Mike found a few distributors willing to look at our long epic. "What do you think this is—*Gone with the Wind*?" was the most charitable comment. It soon became clear to us that the film had to be cut drastically to satisfy the

B market—or any market, for that matter—and that the cost of such cutting would be prohibitive in the States. We had to smuggle all thirty-odd film cans back into Mexico. In case there is no statute of limitations for such smuggling offenses, I shall skip the details of that operation.

Item: When the cans arrived back in Mexico City, together with the request for an additional infusion of capital to pay for the cutting, Alex Zaffaroni, demonstrating his business acumen, announced that his stake in *The Big Drop* investment and all corresponding Panamanian SOXA shares were up for sale. No reasonable offers would be refused. Using the same charm I employ when describing potential Ph.D. thesis problems to new graduate students, I contacted another friend about this fantastic opportunity. Elkan Blout, the former research vice president of Polaroid, had just accepted a professorship in biological chemistry at Harvard. I suspected that his prior experience with Polaroid would make him receptive to a venture dealing with film. Elkan accepted but decided to spread the risk. Would we mind if he took only half of Zaffaroni's equity and brought his brother-in-law, Jack Dreyfus, as another partner to our group? Why not? I thought. Although Dreyfus didn't have a Ph.D., he had founded the Dreyfus Fund and certainly added panache to our group of backers. So *The Big Drop* was edited down to a seventy-five-minute film, and some original music inserted in the sound track. This latest decision delayed completion by over a year, but even now I still consider the music the best part. I have long forgotten the name of the composer, who was freelancing after having supposedly written the music for a Frank Sinatra film, *The Man with the Golden Arm.*

By the time *The Big Drop* had acquired its final gestalt, over four years had elapsed and I was back in the States teaching chemistry at Stanford University. Our new eastern partners, Blout and Dreyfus, had good connections. The new *Big Drop* was spirited to New York and promptly seen by Warner Brothers, Columbia, and lesser establishments. My inner defenses let me remember only two of the kinder pronouncements: "This is too arty for a B movie," and, "This is too B-ish for an art movie." (I have a feeling that these messages were first transmitted to Jack Dreyfus, whom the studios did not wish to antagonize.) So we lowered our sights and eventually uncovered a minor film distributor in Georgia, who supplied the rural drive-in theaters. With northern arrogance, we assumed that the racy *Big Drop* would be a hit among the redneck audiences south of the Mason-Dixon Line, and that the money would come rolling in.

We waited for a couple of years. We got nothing; we heard nothing; we couldn't even locate our print. The Georgia distributor had simply evaporated with the film. Around that time, a faculty member from Emory

University in Atlanta was spending his sabbatical leave in my laboratory at Stanford. Did he know of an attorney (*cheap*, I emphasized) able to help us track down this movie peculator who had absconded with our *Big Drop*? He knew a divorce lawyer, who agreed to take our case and in the end managed to locate the culprit (appropriately named E. M. Creamer). Our attorney's pithy message ("This is a rural Georgia county, and although Mr. Creamer is not a native, we could have a difficult time there if forced to trial") concluded with the recommendation that we abandon the suit in return for the film and reimbursement of court costs. Creamer was lucky: the Carroll County Superior Court demanded the princely sum of $14.50 (*anno Domini* 1965). So we dropped the idea of litigation to pick up *The Big Drop*. By then, our Atlanta divorce lawyer was himself bitten by the movie bug: for a modest participation in the future profits, would we let him locate a bona-fide distributor in the South? We gave him that option, but all it accomplished was to satisfy the curiosity of the lawyer. He and his potential distributor concluded that *The Big Drop* was not for Georgia. "Too sophisticated," he pronounced.

Nine years had passed from the time I left my hospital bed in Mexico City until finally, in Palo Alto, California, I lifted the heavy canister containing all film cans of the only print of *The Big Drop*. By that time, all I wanted was to see the complete opus. I'd watched innumerable rushes without sound, some sections with a separate ill-matched sound track, but never the complete Ur-version or its finely honed offspring. I felt goose pimples, like a miner sure that the glittering rock in his hands contains gold.

I discovered that one could not easily rent a 35-millimeter film projector for one's home; one had to rent a movie house. My secretary came up with an irresistible bargain: as a faculty member, I could use Stanford's Memorial Auditorium during the Christmas recess at no charge, provided I paid the six-dollar hourly fee for the student projectionist. For the puny sum of twelve dollars, my wife and my two children, who had crossed from childhood into adolescence during *The Big Drop*'s interminable gestation, would see it in the lonely splendor of an eight-hundred-seat auditorium. To make the splendor a little less lonely, I invited some company. Before the week had ended, over five hundred invitations were mailed through the Stanford interdepartmental mail or posted on bulletin boards: "Carl Djerassi invites you to the world premiere of THE BIG DROP at 8 P.M. in Memorial Auditorium."

My Walter Mitty vision now came to fruition. Over four hundred people showed up: deans, professors, graduate students, friends, friends of friends, the odd passerby. As I stood in front of the huge screen and described to the hushed audience that they were about to see a film whose odyssey to Palo Alto eclipsed the *Perils of Pauline*; as I, the experienced professor, usually attuned to every glazed look and hidden yawn, sensed their rapt attention, I had a glimpse of what an Oscar presentation in Hollywood might be like. This was the high point of my movie fantasizing. I concluded my tale and deposited myself next to my son, just in front of the dean of our medical school and his physician wife. At a wave of my hand, the trumpet sounds of a mariachi band resounded, and the opening scene of *The Big Drop* lit the screen.

As the movie progressed, I found myself sliding forward until my head had virtually disappeared behind the back of my seat. It wasn't the dean's desperate question to his wife, "Helen, what the hell is going on here?" Long before then, I was asking myself the same question. There was no way to ascribe the disaster unfolding before us to incompetent cutting or to the outmoded fashion of the automobiles or the actors' clothes. In fact, the decade-long hiatus from conception to début had given the film whatever traces of charm it possessed. One could only conclude that the original product had been hopeless, that the four Ph.D.s and the banker had been blinded by avarice. How could one claim suspense when the audience hadn't the foggiest notion what was going on before their very eyes? And how could one talk of sex, when the most erotic scene consisted of the Mexican whore standing primly in front of a four-poster bed, her modest nightgown descending below her knees and displaying just the faintest trace of a cleavage between her ample, but suitably covered breasts? All she did was lick her lips and run her hands slowly up and down one of the bed posts. ("Get it?" Mike had grinned salaciously when we watched the rushes.) But in the intervening decade, the sexual revolution had taken over—influenced in part by the oral contraceptive some of the movie backers had themselves developed; and what might have been sexy in the 1950s produced only yawns in the 1960s.

As I left the auditorium, I pretended not to see anyone. I focused on my grinning son, who has not often seen his father fail so dismally. "Wasn't the music good?" I kept asking. At least my colleagues and friends had a rare experience, seeing both the very first and the very last screening of a movie in the same night.

II

I could have regaled Clint Eastwood with my story, but maybe an Academy of Achievement banquet wasn't the right venue. In any event, this was not the end of my affair with the movie industry. If there was a lesson in *The Big Drop*, my son has ignored it. Dale has become a professional filmmaker and with his former wife co-produced a feature film, *'68*, which was released in early 1988. The film deals with the events of 1968 seen through the eyes of a Hungarian immigrant family. All of it was filmed in 1987 on location in San Francisco. At one point Dale needed some extras for a restaurant scene, where a Hungarian birthday party was being held. So I came, together with Alex Zaffaroni (who had moved to Palo Alto, where he founded his own pharmaceutical firm, ALZA). We are both silver-haired, look reasonably distinguished, and still own some clothes from the late 1960s. For three hours, we sat in a fake restaurant, playing fake chess, while we reminisced about our adventures in Mexico. I knew this was no star role, but I became convinced of the seriousness of my cameo appearance when one of the assistants interrupted the filming to ask me to remove my digital wristwatch. "Not in 1968!" she reminded me.

Dale's film opened at a benefit at the Palace of Fine Arts in San Francisco before an audience of over a thousand. The first scene of *'68* appeared on the screen: newsreel excerpts of Russian tanks rolling into Budapest in 1956, followed by a view down a hilly street of San Francisco, and the movie was under way. I barely noticed the contortions and fine balancing act of the naked pair copulating on a motorcycle seat. I drummed my fingers nervously with the vintage 1960s music while the hippies caroused during a rock concert in Golden Gate Park; I knew that we would see shots of Martin Luther King and Robert Kennedy's assassinations in 1968. But where was the climax? Finally, the restaurant scene came into view, full of boisterous Hungarians, their sing-song accents filling my ears. I spied the director's little daughter near one table. "Shameless nepotism," I thought. As the birthday party started to wind down, as the last guest departed from the restaurant, it dawned on me that no one would ever see the elegant movement of my Seiko-less wrist as I lifted my pawn to capture Alex's queen. Where were those marvelous character shots, which needed no explication in either Magyar or English to make their impact on the audience? On the floor of the cutting room, I was finally told, that's where I had been dropped.

CHAPTER 9

The Pill at Twenty

I HAVE ALWAYS IMAGINED that it was a macho journalist in the late 1950s—sleeves rolled up, eyes squinting through the smoke of the cigarette dangling from the corner of his mouth, two index fingers producing a machine gun rattle on the Remington—who, while writing some pithy piece on oral contraceptives, decided to capitalize the word *pill* and thus inadvertently converted this pedestrian generic term into a powerful four-letter word. Since then, the Pill has been equated to everything from a woman's panacea to her poison.

The Pill was born at the best possible time—15 October 1951—and matured at the worst. It was synthesized in the heyday of new drugs. Pharmaceutical companies, the media, and the public proclaimed and accepted the benefits of the postwar chemotherapeutic revolution with barely a reservation. Every problem, be it a medical one or a social one such as the population explosion, seemed capable of a technological fix. An example of the disarmingly naïve faith in the power of technology is the following citation from a *New York Times* editorial of the 1960s: "if significant reductions in population growth are to be achieved there must be a techno-

Myself on crutches in Detroit, 1956, the year before my permanent knee fusion.

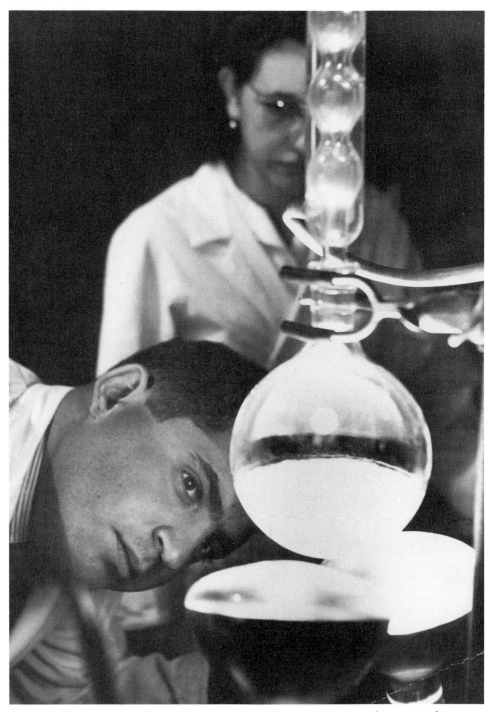

Myself at Syntex, Mexico City, 1951, with my assistant Arelina Gonzalez, working on synthesis of progestational component of the Pill.

The press conference announcing the first synthesis of cortisone from a plant source at Syntex in Mexico City, 1951. Standing, left to right: A. L. Nussbaum (subsequently, one of my first Ph.D. students at Wayne), Mercedes Velasco, Gilbert Stork (then at Harvard and serving as consultant to Syntex), Juan Berlin, and Octavio Mancera. Seated, left to right: Juan Pataki, George Rosenkranz, Enrique Batres, myself, Rosa Yashin, and Jesus Romo.

Myself with Alejandro Zaffaroni pointing at the key chemical feature of all steroid oral contraceptives in Syntex conference room, Mexico City, 1958.

President Richard Nixon presenting me with the National Medal of Science for the first synthesis of a steroid oral contraceptive, 1973.

The picture that did not make it into the 1979 Annual Report of Occidental
Petroleum Corporation.

In Stanford University research laboratory with my doctoral student Barbara Grant, 1974.

King Carl XVI Gustaf of Sweden eyeing two immobilized cockroaches held by Zoecon's director of biological research, Gerardus Staal, 1984. Between the king and me (wearing one of Tegen Greene's jackets) is Karl-Erik Sahlberg (president of Perstorp AB); at the extreme right is Bengt Modeer of the Royal Swedish Academy of Engineering Sciences.

Evidence of successful knee fusion operation: on skis, showing off my stiff leg near Mt. Rose, Nevada, 1990.

logical breakthrough in contraception similar to that in food production."

In the late 1950s, the search for new approaches to contraception—dramatized by the meteoric appearance of the steroid Pill—had become a glamorous and exciting field promising to change at one fell swoop the course of family planning and birth control. In the late 1960s, thirteen major pharmaceutical companies—nine of them American—were still active in research and development of new birth control approaches. The topic itself was hot, with a high priority among academic and industrial scientists. But shortly thereafter, the action started to move from the scientific main stage to ever smaller, provincial theaters, with the Pill still reigning as star. By the early 1980s, only four large pharmaceutical companies remained, one of them American, that could be considered to have any sort of R&D commitment to this field. A 1988 survey of research priorities of the international pharmaceutical industry showed that the search for new human fertility control methods is not even among the top thirty-five priority topics. I consider this market judgment tragic, because history demonstrates, in capitalist as well as in socialist countries, that no major advance in drug innovation can occur without the active participation of the pharmaceutical industry—in production, distribution, development, and even research. The causes of this deplorable situation go back to the early years of the Pill, just a few years after its FDA-approved introduction into medical practice.

I

In contrast to the preceding decade, when the active steroid ingredients of the Pill were synthesized and their biological properties defined, the 1960s—the period of ever-increasing clinical use of the Pill—proved to be the worst of times. The changed climate was triggered by the thalidomide tragedy, which resulted (primarily in Europe, where the drug was widely used) in the birth of hundreds of children with serious limb deformities to mothers who had taken that highly effective sedative in early pregnancy when the embryo is at greatest risk. In the late 1950s, the Democratic Senator Estes Kefauver of Tennessee had chaired a series of highly publicized congressional hearings which were critical of the pharmaceutical industry and of the FDA. His legislative proposals, opposed by the medical community as well as by industry, seemed at first to stand little chance of realization; then the thalidomide bomb exploded, ensuring passage of his bill and leading to the 1962 amendments of the Federal Food, Drug, and Cosmetic Act, commonly known as the Kefauver-Harris Amendments. The thalidomide disaster raised everyone's consciousness to the importance of prior teratological studies in suitable animal models before introducing a drug that pregnant women might consume. While demonstration of safety was always the core of FDA requirements, the Kefauver Amendments now stipulated explicitly that efficacy also had to be demonstrated—a requirement that had hitherto been only implicit in the FDA's mandate.

In principle, all of these changes made sense, but the FDA was totally unprepared for these new responsibilities. In the words of Peter B. Hutt, the former counsel of the FDA, "For roughly the first ten years under that statute [the Kefauver Amendments of 1962], FDA basically was playing catch-up ball . . . a simple reflection of the fact that FDA did not have the resources when the statute was enacted, and was not given the resources following enactment . . . and there was no time whatever to think through the issues before decisions had to be made." Hutt also admitted that "FDA employees have been praised only for refusing to approve a new drug, not for making a courageous judgment to approve a new drug that has in fact helped patients and advanced the public health." An example of these attitudes is the fact that for a ten-year period, the FDA refused to approve any new cardiovascular agent, because some agency personnel insisted that reducing hypertension would not necessarily reduce heart attacks, stroke, and kidney disease. Such drugs were introduced in Europe years before they finally reached American consumers; some critics of the FDA claimed that the delay had caused at least fifty thousand unnecessary deaths and crippled over two hundred thousand people annually. No wonder that such a regulatory climate seriously inhibited the introduction of new contraceptives: contraception is generally considered to be the practice of a healthy person, whom regulatory agencies (and society, for that matter) are not prepared to expose to potential risks that might be tolerated in respect to an individual suffering from a disease. Most societies do not yet equate an unwanted pregnancy with a disease.

The issue of a new drug's deleterious side effects came to preoccupy the American public owing to a pervasive misunderstanding about the real meaning of safety in medicine. A brief extract from an exchange between Wisconsin's Democratic Senator Gaylord Nelson and FDA Commissioner Charles C. Edwards during a congressional hearing on 4 March 1970 illustrates this point:

> *Senator Nelson:* On the use of the word "safe" in respect to the oral contraceptives, I think that there is considerable confusion within the medical profession and the public alike as to how the word "safe" was being used.

Commissioner Edwards: In categorizing this drug as safe, I do not want to imply, by any stretch of the imagination, that this is an innocuous drug. ... There are certain dangers in taking any drug, and they have to be taken under the conditions which are stated very clearly in the labeling.

Senator Nelson: The use in this context, then, was not in the ordinary dictionary use of the word?

Commissioner Edwards: It certainly was not. It was a Food and Drug Administration description of the word "safe," which really is "safe under the conditions of labeling. . . ."

Lengthier FDA requirements for all prescription drugs, and the continuing debate about the definition and ambiguity of the word *safe*, have led, since the late 1960s, to a marked slowing in the rate and number of new pharmaceuticals, and especially contraceptives. But does it follow, especially in the field of birth control, that the primary dictum in medicine— *primum non noceri* ("above all, do no harm")—automatically leads to *primum bonum faceri* ("above all, do good")?

Of course, the sexual revolution had its own intimate cause-and-effect relationship to the Pill; but during the 1960s, contraceptive advances were even more affected by the flowering of three of contemporary society's most beneficial movements: the women's movement, environmental protectionism, and consumer advocacy. All three were intrinsically suspicious of technology and even science, and all three depended largely on the uniquely American litigation system to further their aims. While successful in many important respects, this litigious approach also caused unintended damage, most notably in ultimately reducing the future contraceptive choices open to women and men. To comprehend this unexpected outcome, we need to turn to the first ten years of the clinical life of the Pill, which started with the marketing of Enovid—G. D. Searle's trade name for norethynodrel (see chapter 5)—when the firm received FDA approval for limited use (initially, one year) of this drug in contraception.

By the end of 1961, nearly half a million American women used a contraceptive Pill consisting of 10 milligrams of Searle's norethynodrel (to inhibit ovulation) and 0.15 milligrams of the estrogen mestranol (to reduce the incidence of spotting and bleeding when a pure progestational agent is used alone). The number of women users doubled within a year and then rose precipitately (2.2 million in 1963, 4.0 million in 1964, 5.0 million in 1965, and nearly 9.0 million by 1970) when in 1962 the FDA extended permission to Ortho, and in 1964 to Parke-Davis and Syntex, to market

Syntex's norethindrone (combined with mestranol) as an oral contraceptive under various trade names such as Ortho-Novum, Norlestrin, and Norinyl. By that time, the FDA's one-year restriction for contraceptive use had been lifted and the dosage of the progestational steroid reduced from 10 milligrams to 2.0 milligrams. Further lowering of the progestational content to 1.0 milligram, and of the estrogenic component to 0.05 milligram, occurred during the second half of the 1960s, with more substantial reductions to come in later years.

The initial clinical studies in Puerto Rico, Mexico, and Los Angeles (see chapter 5) and the subsequent media and public attention focused first on efficacy and obvious, short-term side effects (among them nausea, weight gain, bleeding irregularities) and then on the question of restored fertility after discontinuance of the Pill; only later did attention shift to the problem of long-term safety when the unexpectedly rapid and wide acceptance of the Pill raised the specter of basically healthy individuals consuming a potent hormone for years. George Bernard Shaw might well have been prophesying about the Pill when he said, "Science is always wrong: it never solves a problem without creating ten more."

By the summer of 1962, various anecdotal reports started to appear claiming serious incidents and even fatalities due to pulmonary embolisms, clotting, and vein inflammation in women who had been on the 10-milligram dose of Enovid. The FDA appointed a special committee to investigate this issue, but its August 1963 report, though acknowledging 272 cases of serious blood clots and thirty deaths among the 1.5 million to 2 million Pill users, concluded that the Pill did not result in an increased risk of thromboembolic disease. Among the reasons for this apparent exoneration of the Pill were the scant epidemiological data on the occurrence of serious thromboembolic episodes among young American non-users of the Pill. John Rock, who had carried out the first clinical experiments with Enovid, called the new critics of the Pill "irresponsible and uninformed." Gregory Pincus, who had led the initial biological investigations at the Worcester Foundation for Experimental Biology, went much further in a 1963 article in the *Ladies' Home Journal*: "When subjected to careful scrutiny, all of these conditions have been found to be unrelated to the use of the contraceptive."

The debate whether serious side effects occurred in a small number of Pill users did not rest there. Because of the existence of the National Health Service, Britain's epidemiological data were qualitatively and quantitatively superior to those then existing in the United States. In 1967, a well-documented report by a British Medical Research Council task force stated, "The sum of evidence . . . is so strong that there can be no reasonable doubt that some types of thromboembolic disorder are demonstrated with the use of oral contraceptives." This judgment was supported in 1969 by the FDA's Advisory Committee on Obstetrics and Gynecology; according to congressional testimony by the commissioner of the FDA, in the United States blood clots could be expected in one out of two thousand Pill users. Furthermore, thirty out of each one million women on the Pill would die from such complications compared to only five fatal clots per one million non-users of the Pill in that same age group. In other words, the increased risk *with Pill dosages of the 1960s* was sixfold, but the absolute number of deaths was still smaller than would occur in childbirth. In heavy smokers, notably in Pill users beyond the age of thirty-five, the risks are much higher—a finding that has led to the generally accepted recommendation that heavy smokers in their thirties should use other forms of contraception. As I shall note in chapter 15, the cardiovascular risks of *today's* Pill are now greatly reduced, primarily because these large-scale studies with *yesterday's* Pill implicated the estrogenic component of the Pill as the principal culprit. As a result, there have been substantial reductions in the dosage of the estrogen and even in its composition: mestranol, chemically the methyl ether of 17α-ethynylestradiol, has now been replaced by 17α-ethynylestradiol itself.

I am citing this convoluted history of one of the most serious of perceived side effects of the Pill to illustrate how such a low incidence could never be uncovered in initial clinical studies with a few hundred women (the FDA required preclinical studies with two hundred women volunteers prior to marketing approval). The safety of a new drug is hardly ever determined with any degree of assurance until after it has been marketed—especially when so heterogeneous a population is exposed to it, as happened with the Pill. This causes me to return to an issue I have already raised briefly in chapter 5, where I described the site and characteristics of the earliest clinical studies: Puerto Rico, Mexico City, and Los Angeles. Is this indeed another example of the exploitation of the poor, who were to serve as human guinea pigs and thus suffered most from unanticipated side effects? The answer is largely no.

The purpose of these early and relatively short-term clinical explorations in the middle and late 1950s was to determine the appropriate dosage, to demonstrate efficacy, and to uncover acute side effects in humans that were unlikely or impossible to be detected in the type of animal toxicology *then* customary in all new drug research. Questions of long-term safety—whether some people might suffer serious morbidity- or mortality-causing effects, or develop tumors, years later—can be studied only through epidemiological surveys on huge groups available once a drug is on the market. In the case of oral contraceptives, the economic as well as educational level of the first couple of million American consumers of the Pill was far above average. In other words, the women serving as human guinea pigs for the evaluation of long-term safety were predominantly affluent WASPs rather than impoverished minorities.

II

In the 1960s, for obvious and deserved reasons, initially having nothing to do with the Pill, women became increasingly vocal and also heard more widely. The early influential books of the modern feminist movement emphasized the urgent need for improved *female* contraception. Simone de Beauvoir's *The Second Sex* stated explicitly, and Betty Friedan's *The Feminine Mystique* implicitly, that a liberated woman must be in control of her own fertility. Probably most women will agree that the Pill, more than any other single factor, contributed to that aim. But an informed and highly motivated minority of women—primarily North American and, by world standards, exceedingly affluent—not only expressed their rage and abhorrence at male domination, but also vented their frustration with the Pill—and, in so doing, frequently claimed to speak (as Germaine Greer does in her *Sex & Destiny*) for women all over the world. As usual, the rich were oblivious of the real problems of the poor: the contraceptive counterpart to the "let them eat cake" became "let them use a diaphragm," in facile disregard of the fact that millions of poor women in the third world lack even a place to store a diaphragm, in addition to facing cultural barriers that sophisticated American or European women never experience.

It angered those eloquent women that virtually all the original chemical, biological, and clinical work on the Pill had been conducted by men. And rather than seeing this situation as yet another instance of the exclusion of women from many areas of science and medicine, they saw a sexual conspiracy focused on an intimate aspect of their own sexuality. When the first large-scale, postmarketing, epidemiological studies documented some of the Pill's less obvious deleterious side effects, women who earlier had objected to being used as human guinea pigs asked, "Why wasn't the Pill tested more thoroughly?" The fact that in the final analysis a female contraceptive must be tested in women and not just animals, and that most experimenters at that time were men, only exacerbated women's feelings of being helpless and exploited.

An undercurrent of such feelings persists. Even the authors of the latest edition (1984) of *Our Bodies, Ourselves*, produced by the Boston Women's

Health Book Collective, stated that "the Food and Drug Administration approved the Pill for marketing in 1960 without adequate testing or study. . . . The Pill became a gigantic experiment: within two years about 1.2 million American women used it." In their annoyance, these authors forget that such large-scale, postmarketing "experiments" are the rule rather than the exception in respect to every vaccine and every drug to which a person is exposed for long periods.

Until the introduction of the Pill in the early 1960s, abortion (then illegal in all but a handful of countries) was the only method of birth control separated from coitus. In my opinion, it was this separation, and the privacy the Pill offered a woman, rather than its efficacy, that made its initial acceptance so rapid. By the end of that decade, the cumulative decisions of nearly ten million American women, and probably double that number abroad, had made the Pill the most popular method of birth control.

Yet some women became even more suspicious when the subsequent avalanche of clinical studies made the Pill the most intensely examined drug in modern medicine, but did not provide unambiguous answers. Did women feel more comforted upon reading the report of a Swiss clinical trial in 1969 in which various oral contraceptive preparations were tested for presumed psychosomatic effects, by changing the women subjects' contraceptive Pills every six months? To quote the Swiss researchers:

> The importance of the psychic influence [on the perception of side effects] is shown by the fact that the incidence of nausea is increased every sixth cycle, when the woman is transferred to another preparation and then obviously loses confidence in the Pill and/or her doctor. Libido changes are following a similar pattern: whenever the preparation is changed, more women show an increase in libido, fewer women a decrease.

Women were neither impressed nor amused to learn about esoterica such as decreased ear-wax production in Pill users; they wanted a yes or no about whether the Pill caused cancer. They would have shouted down Dr. Alexander M. Schmidt, commissioner of the FDA in the mid-1970s, had they known of his judgment that this was largely a political question:

> What science can do is tell us that under a certain set of carefully controlled conditions, a substance probably will cause cancer, that at certain dose ranges over the lifetime of a number of mice, a few mice, perhaps a number significantly greater than the control group, developed liver cancer. Thus far, science can take us, but no further than that. Whether and

how to apply those mouse studies to human conditions and then in yet
another step to decide whether to permit human exposure to that substance, that, in my view, goes beyond the realm of science into the setting
of public policy, into politics.

Some women's outrage knew no bounds when segments of the press, who
first promulgated the virtues of the Pill with extraordinary naïveté, began
to sensationalize every new side effect with headlines like "Pill Kills!" At a
time when congressional committees blamed the FDA for every real and
imagined oversight, women considered themselves the victims of a sinister
cabal of avaricious drug companies and incompetent bureaucrats, whose
technological output was peddled by members of what was then the most
patriarchal medical specialty of them all: gynecology. On occasion, these
feelings were expressed in vituperative language, as in the December 1970
issue of *Science for the People*:

> How is birth control practiced in our society? . . . We go to a doctor and
> lowering our eyes, embarrassed at our dependency, with a mixture of fear
> and anger we stumble through that horrible sentence, "What do I do not
> to get pregnant?" Remember, we are asking this of a male doctor, behind
> whom stands the whole power-penis-potency complex (PPP). What do
> you think he's going to tell us? Right! "Get high on our latest special, the
> PPP's Pill." Great new wonder drug! It launches frontal attack on the
> pituitary gland and "saves us from pregnancy" in exchange for a two-page
> long list of side effects . . . which our male pharmacist or male doctor
> threw in the waste basket, and which we will never see. What we do see
> are little booklets from the drug companies decorated with roses, tulips,
> and peach blossoms full of reassuring babbling.

Such outcries and the drug industry's poor press came together in the late
1960s to culminate, between January and March of 1970, in hearings before
the Senate Subcommittee on Monopoly of the Select Committee on Small
Business, mercifully abbreviated as the "Nelson hearings" after the subcommittee's chairman, Senator Gaylord Nelson—at that time considered
by the American pharmaceutical industry a Torquemada, by the public a
Robin Hood. I am convinced that these hearings would never have been
held had it not been for the concerns—many of them legitimate, especially
when examined through 1991 spectacles—raised by the women of the
1960s, who played the same catalytic role thalidomide had performed in the
context of the Kefauver Amendments of 1962. In spite of the circus and
klieg-light atmosphere, the Nelson hearings doubtlessly illuminated many
little-understood aspects of Pill use and distribution, including many topics

related to contraception. Hardly anyone at that time, however, predicted that this senatorial inquisition—now barely recalled—would become the pivotal event to push contraceptive research permanently into the minor leagues.

III

The Nelson hearings accomplished some good, notably in pressuring the FDA to demand that written information, with emphasis on potential side effects, be inserted into every oral contraceptive package. Unfortunately, such requirement has been fought by the medical profession and by pharmacists, who consider such inserts a usurpation of their professional function and have so far managed to keep them out of virtually all drug packages other than oral contraceptives. The pharmacists compound the problem through their perpetuation of an archaic and predominantly American practice: they open the manufacturer's sealed bottle or box, properly labeled with respect to *recommended price*, contents, and warnings, and transfer the material into an anonymous brown container, which generally has only the name of patient, physician, and pharmacist, followed by the incomprehensible trade name of the medication and some simple statement such as "take three times per day." (Once so camouflaged, the price of the prescription becomes the pharmacist's decision.)

As a result, once the industry's lawyers started working on the text of the insert, it turned into a densely printed, three-page document which practically required a college degree in both English legalese and biology to be fully comprehensible. I had always been in favor of package inserts for *all* drugs, from over-the-counter items like aspirin to prescription drugs. Nevertheless, I seriously questioned whether the legalistic manner in which the negative side effects, however rare, of the Pill were described in order to protect the manufacturer against possible liability suits was the most helpful way of conveying important information. Such overkill package inserts can be frightening to the nonspecialist, if not overwhelming. For instance, would not one view with caution, even suspicion, a pill reported as having the following list of side effects: asthma, allergies, hives, edema, nausea, vomiting, disturbances of hearing and vision, anemia, mental confusion, sweating, thirst, diarrhea, and gastrointestinal bleeding? Yet these are the reported side effects of an aspirin pill, not of the contraceptive Pill. (As far as the latter is concerned, not until early 1991 was any effort made to improve the obligatory patient package inserts of oral contraceptives. The FDA's Fertility and Maternal Health Drugs Advisory Committee recommended unanimously that the instructions should be written at a fifth-grade reading level, using large print and easily understood phrases, with emphasis on how to follow directions and what to do when one inadvertently misses a pill. Both experts and manufacturers now agree that the wording of the patient package inserts needs to be simplified, but have so far reached no consensus about standardization of instructions for manufacturers.)

Hysteria surrounded the Nelson hearings, as witness after witness was produced to illuminate the potential dangers of the Pill. Most of the vocal Pill antagonists were scheduled to testify during the earlier part of the hearings, which received maximum newspaper publicity. Though Nelson stated that the witness stand was open to any representative from any pharmaceutical company, not one testified—in my opinion, an important tactical mistake, but one that reflected the industry's paranoid perception of both the hearings and the Senator as adversarial.

One source of hysteria was the testimony on 22 January 1970 of one Herbert Ratner, a public health official, in response to questions from Kansas's Republican Senator Robert Dole:

> **Dr. Ratner:** Incidentally, leaving the pill out in the open so as not to forget it has led to numerous child poisonings.
>
> **Senator Dole:** Do we have some evidence on how many cases you know of?
>
> **Dr. Ratner:** Of accidental poisoning, child poisoning, it was the number two cause two years ago in Missouri, and it has a high incidence in the United States.
>
> **Senator Dole:** Not to hold you up, but have there been numerous child poisonings because of the pill? If you will just insert some evidence on that, it would be helpful.

Some time later, Dr. Ratner supplied the following documentation: "Contraceptive pills have become a major . . . source of childhood poisoning, the Public Health Service reports. There were 962 reported childhood poisonings due to the Pill during 1962–1965, according to Mr. Henry L. Verhulst, chief of the Poison Control Branch of the P.H.S. *Modern Medicine*, May 9, 1966, p. 28."

Ratner's testimony caused fireworks in the press. Jack Anderson's nationally syndicated column "Merry-Go-Round" headlined the story "New Frightening Dangers of 'The Pill' " and proceeded in the following vein:

> For the 8 million American women taking birth control pills, who already face an increased risk of heart attack and blood clots, this column has uncovered a new and frightening danger. . . . In most instances, the youngsters took their mother's pills thinking they were candy. . . . All too typically, most drug companies are more interested in profits than in protecting children.

Such child poisoning was totally new to me, and I decided to follow up Ratner's allegations—as any responsible reporter could have done in the few minutes it took me to uncover the real facts. In the original reference in *Modern Medicine*, I found that, in accusing the Pill of being a "major . . . source of childhood poisoning," Ratner had used ellipses to skip over the following key words: "although relatively benign." But there was more. *Modern Medicine* had carried only a news comment on the original article by H. L. Verhulst and J. J. Crotty in a 1967 issue of the *Journal of Clinical Pharmacology*. In commenting on accidental ingestion of oral contraceptives by children, these authors wrote: "A recent analysis of oral contraceptive reports showed that where the symptoms were indicated on the form, 99 percent of the ingestions had checked signs and symptoms—none."

Another source of panic involved cancer, which, as expected, was treated extensively during the hearings. The question of potential tumor production, of course, was and still is foremost in people's minds, as it should be whenever a drug is to be consumed over long periods. (Only medicines used to treat acute conditions and employed over short intervals can be effectively screened for most side effects during the premarketing, clinical test phase.) Even now, three decades after the Pill's introduction into open medical practice, epidemiological reports debate whether its prolonged use increases the risk of breast cancer. Many women will be discouraged to learn that a conclusive answer cannot be available before the turn of this century, because the dosages of both the progestational and the estrogenic components of the Pill have been progressively lowered since the middle 1970s, whereas induction times for tumor appearance are measured in years and decades. The long-term studies are only telling us about the potential effects of *yesterday's* Pills. The same reservation applies to some of the beneficial, *noncontraceptive* effects of the Pill, such as protection against benign breast tumors and against ovarian and endometrial cancers, which were first noted in the mid-1970s. Whether the protection will persist for women taking the lower-dosage steroid regimens, will not be known for one or two decades.

Around the time of the Nelson hearings, careful epidemiological studies in many thousands of Pill consumers had established that a minute group of young women—3 per 100,000—would come down with liver cancer. This is an extremely rare and usually fatal condition—a terrible tragedy for three such women and their families. The headline "Pill Kills!" was factually correct, but was it warranted from society's standpoint? Penicillin kills many more than 3 per 100,000, but nobody would suggest that it be removed from the market as several witnesses implicitly recommended with reference to the Pill during the Nelson hearings.

If in 1980—the Nelson hearings then long forgotten—a group of women had been asked to cite the most negative development in female birth control, I suspect that the overwhelming majority, including strong opponents of the Pill, would have offered the "Dalkon shield." This defective IUD design harmed thousands of women and resulted in multibillion-dollar lawsuits which led the manufacturer into bankruptcy. The inventor of the Dalkon shield, Dr. Hugh J. Davis, then at Johns Hopkins University, had been one of Nelson's early star witnesses and received ample press billing. At the outset, in response to questioning by New Hampshire's Republican Senator Thomas J. McIntyre, he made it plain where he stood with respect to steroid oral contraceptives:

> *Dr. Davis:* I think it can be stated fairly that never in history have so many individuals taken such potent drugs with so little information available as to actual and potential hazards. The synthetic chemicals in the pill are quite unnatural with respect to their manufacture and with respect to their behavior once they are introduced into the human body. In using these agents, we are in fact embarked on a massive endocrinologic experiment with millions of healthy women.

> *Senator McIntyre:* Lastly, Doctor, does the fact that many of the dangers of the pill which you have described here this morning just now coming to light, some ten years after they were approved for the market, indicate to you that they were not properly tested before they were allowed to market?

> *Dr. Davis:* Well, I am not Solomon, but I think there are many things that we would not do today that were being done in 1959 and 1960. The experience with a few hundred women in Puerto Rico prior to the approval of the pill, was certainly very limited.

Davis was, of course, correct in stating that with hindsight one nearly always can improve on actions performed ten years earlier. But then the good doctor suggested out of all the wisdom hindsight had brought him,

"In our experience, some modern intrauterine devices [IUDs] provide a 99-percent protection against pregnancy and can be successfully worn by 94 percent of women, to cite but one alternative." Here, without so stating, he was referring to his own invention—the Dalkon shield. Furthermore, he did not volunteer the information that IUDs are rarely recommended for use by nulliparous women. Senator McIntyre and the minority (Republican) counsel, James J. Duffy III, had to extract this information through further questioning:

> **Senator McIntyre:** Doctor, one of the arguments frequently used against the intrauterine device is that it is not suitable for women who have never had a child. How would you reconcile this with your statement that such devices can be successfully used by 94 percent of the women?
>
> **Dr. Davis:** . . . In Baltimore, we have a series [of women] now that exceeds some 300 women who have never borne children, who have been quite successfully fitted with intrauterine devices.

In other words, Davis, having damned the initial clinical work on the Pill for having rested on "a few hundred women in Puerto Rico," was perfectly willing, *ten years later*, to recommend that the Dalkon shield be substituted for the Pill, based on experience with "some 300 women" in Baltimore! Somehow, Senator Nelson and the press ignored this monumental gaffe. Davis's bias and financial interest became obvious after the following two questions:

> **Senator McIntyre:** I understand that you yourself have devised an intrauterine device [the Dalkon shield] that is extremely good?
>
> **Mr. Duffy:** Doctor, while we are on the subject of intrauterine devices, in our preparation for these hearings we became aware of the report that indicated that you had recently patented such a device. Is there any truth or substance to that report?

Two months earlier, at the opening of the hearings, Senator Nelson had sounded positively inspiring:

> I hope that these hearings will be regarded as a major incentive to the researchers, physicians, biologists, chemists, drug companies, and government agencies to find answers to the many questions which have been and are being raised by oral and other contraceptives. It is urgently necessary

that solutions be found as quickly as possible which are compatible with the health, welfare, and the dignity of human beings here and throughout the world.

But, in the end, the combination of anti-Pill women activists and this politically liberal Democrat, who had shown compassion and concern for public welfare, including increased and improved family planning in America and abroad, inadvertently caused the startling deterioration in contraceptive development which began around 1970. These critics indulged not only in bitter condemnation of the pharmaceutical industry which had invented and promoted the Pill, but also in incessant rebukes of the most underfunded regulatory agency of them all, the FDA, and in the process terrified it. The FDA's predictable response of hypercaution had long-lasting consequences, the most important of which was the beagle story, another tale now largely forgotten, though not by me. Perhaps this is the reason that since the early 1970s I have not owned a dog.

IV

In the development of new medicines, the unsolved dilemma faced by both manufacturers and regulatory agencies is the public's demand to have all possible untoward effects anticipated and documented, and yet to do so with a minimum of clinical experimentation. The term *human guinea pig* bothers everyone: experimenter, experimental subject, and public. This dilemma is most pronounced in the cancer field, and is the reason toxicity experiments are initially performed on animals. But one still-unanswered question is the extent to which animal data can be extrapolated to human experience. Although every agent causing cancer in humans also does so in *some* other animal species, the converse has not been demonstrated. Since testing for potential carcinogenicity is an urgent issue, much effort has gone into developing quick, short-cut screening methods (for instance, by testing for mutagenic effects in bacteria) that frequently uncover some potential carcinogenicity of a given agent before animal experiments are begun. Unfortunately, steroids do not respond to such simple and rapid bacterial assays.

This brings me to the single biggest bottleneck in fertility-control research: the lack of a satisfactory test animal, other than the human, for evaluating contraceptive efficacy and safety. Because of the widely divergent effects of steroid sex hormones on different species, and the extreme species-specific nature of the reproductive process itself, it is exceptionally difficult to extrapolate to humans data gained from administering steroid drugs to experimental animals. Despite this uncertainty, shortly before the Nelson hearings, the FDA imposed an unprecedented, multitier requirement for animal testing of female contraceptive agents (requirements that had never before been considered for any other drug): two-year, multidose toxicity studies in rats, dogs, and monkeys, before substantial human clinical experiments can be performed, followed by *seven-year* toxicity studies at *2, 10, and 25 times the human dose* (on a scale of milligram of steroid per kilogram of body weight) in beagle dogs, and *ten-year* studies at *2, 10, and 50 times the human equivalent* in monkeys. (It was this monkey requirement that got me interested in the pygmy chimpanzees of Africa and their endocrinological and reproductive behavior, as I discuss in chapter 14.)

The motivation for the unprecedented length of these toxicology studies, which enormously increased the development time for any new contraceptive pill (be it for women or men), was understandable on humane and political grounds. After all, these drugs may be consumed for prolonged periods by millions of healthy women, and should therefore carry minimal risks. Imposing such strict requirements was the FDA's understandable response to the pressures exerted by women, politicians, and, indeed, the public at large. Nevertheless, while the FDA's *motivation* was understandable, the *scientific rationale* behind the agency's selection of these specific animal species was highly debatable.

The FDA selected monkeys because of their presumed close evolutionary connection to humans. While there is no doubt that the higher primates are the closest animal relatives available, the broad description *monkey* may be virtually meaningless in respect to the characteristics of a particular monkey species. It should be obvious that for such studies to yield the most useful information they should be based on an animal model that most closely resembles humans in its metabolic handling of the particular drug in question. In 1970, I summarized a study in *Science*, in which the excretion pattern and plasma half-life (the time during which 50 percent of the administered drug is still present in circulating blood) for a new drug was compared in humans and seven animal species; the finding was that the differences between rhesus and capuchin monkeys are far greater than those between any other animal species in the study, including a comparison between man and rats! If Gertrude Stein had said, "a monkey is a monkey is a monkey," she would have been dead wrong from a metabolic standpoint.

The FDA's choice of dogs (beagles) was based on their decades-long use as the subject of pharmacological and toxicological scrutiny; hence, a great deal was known about their response to various drugs. However, it was also known that the bitch is enormously sensitive to female sex hormones, and that her *semiannual* heat cycle bears little resemblance to a woman's *monthly* menstrual period. Such differences allow hardly any meaningful extrapolation from dogs to women.

Thus, although there was no real argument about the necessity for strict animal toxicology, the FDA's immovable position on the use of beagles turned into an unmitigated disaster. Although all important European regulatory agencies soon dropped the beagle requirement, and the World Health Organization had convened a special scientific advisory group on the topic (which concluded that "there is no evidence to justify recent emphasis on the presumed advantage of observations . . . in canines"), the FDA did not cancel the requirement until 1988. By that time, several steroid contraceptives had been withdrawn from the market or dropped, at an advanced clinical stage, from further consideration, solely because of ambiguous results in beagles. I believe that at least four large pharmaceutical companies withdrew totally from the contraceptive field as a result of the FDA's inflexibility. Yet from the agency's perspective, was it totally unreasonable? The criticism to which the FDA had been exposed during the 1960s had taught the regulators one key lesson: kudos are never tendered for expediting approval of a new drug, whereas failure to anticipate every possible side effect can lead to crucifixion. No wonder hypercaution won and contraceptive research lost.

Women's concern, politicians politicizing the subject, the FDA's response, ten-year toxicology in primates—all these were issues I could understand and, with all but one, even sympathize—at least in the abstract. But their combination in a real-life context struck me as extremely counterproductive: ultimately, they only penalized the very constituency that most stood to benefit from continued and even expedited research in contraception. My impatience ("How come they don't see what I see?") was the predictable response of a scientist who wanted to get on with his job—in this instance, with the development of new and better agents for birth control. My frustration caused me in 1973 to write an editorial in *Science* entitled "Research Impact Statements." The impact—direct as well as indirect—of regulatory agencies, notably the Food and Drug Administration and the Environmental Protection Agency, on research is now so enormous that the agencies should bear some responsibility for *prospective* research planning—especially if the effect can be felt on a national scale. Given the general acceptance and utility, in other areas of public concern, of "environmental impact statements," would it not be reasonable to ask that research impact statements be prepared by regulatory agencies? A typical one should include a cost-benefit determination: for example, a new regulatory requirement might achieve a relatively minor gain in safety information at the expense of a societally important line of research. If so, what alternatives might provide such safety information without paying the price of considerable delay or total abandonment of a given research area?

Unfortunately, my research impact trial balloon never made it beyond the launching pad. Around the twentieth anniversary of the Pill's chemical birth, I opened a fortune cookie in a San Francisco Chinatown restaurant. Its message, "Your problems are too complicated for fortune cookies," may have been the reason that—as I record in chapter 15—during the ensuing years I changed much more than did the field of contraception.

CHAPTER 10

Condoms for the Teacher

MY ASPIRATION FOR AN ACADEMIC CAREER, I am now certain as I cast my mind back to my late twenties, was predicated largely on my yen to conduct research on my personal intellectual turf without apparent outside interference or control. Such a view of life in academe, especially nowadays, is naïve, because the search for monetary support for one's research is so tough, time-consuming, and even demeaning that it constitutes a form of control frequently more oppressive than that always assumed to exist in industry. While this presumed freedom for research, coupled with academe's nebulous aura of prestige, was the chief attraction, the prospect of teaching also appealed to me.

In 1976, a reporter, sitting in on a few of my lectures at Stanford, was impressed by a gift two students brought me. "Not exactly an apple for the teacher," the reporter wrote in *People*, "it was a box of pink condoms. Djerassi was delighted." She was right, but such details give a skewed impression of my teaching methods and career. Condoms were never a topic of my chemistry lectures, although they could have served as a catchy starting point to a lecture on the chemistry of latex or of lubricants. Nevertheless, it's the catchy aspects of my teaching that stick most in my memory.

Until I arrived at Wayne University in 1952 as a tenured associate professor, I had never taught—not even as a teaching assistant in graduate school. But like a baby seal entering water, I felt at home the day I faced my first class. Some of that self-assurance came from the fact that in the deeper sense of the word, I had already served as a highly successful teacher: I had taught my laboratory colleagues in Mexico City, primarily by precept and example, how to do chemical research. Thus, classroom instruction to graduate students in a subject with which I felt highly comfortable did not seem that different from laboratory mentoring. (My lack of nervousness in front of an audience may even have had its root in my late teenage public appearances on the Corn Belt church circuit.) But I have to admit, even several decades later, that in chemistry I have never had to prove my mettle as a teacher on the most difficult terrain, that of large undergraduate classes.

I did not teach undergraduate chemistry because Wayne and later Stanford hired me to upgrade doctoral programs in organic chemistry. When in the late 1950s Stanford's provost, Frederick Terman, decided to buy himself a chemistry department as good as the other science and engineering departments at Stanford, he brought to the university no less than seven new full professors. William Johnson, one of my former organic chemistry professors at Wisconsin, and I arrived in 1960. The following year, Paul Florey came from the Mellon Institute in Pittsburgh; and in 1962, Henry Taube from the University of Chicago. Both subsequently won the Nobel Prize: Florey for his work on the physical chemistry of polymers, and Taube for his many contributions in inorganic chemistry. Harden McConnell, a chemical physicist from Caltech, Eugene van Tamelen, another organic chemist from Wisconsin, and the inorganic chemist James P. Collman from the University of North Carolina completed the initial roster. Aside from directing the research of graduate students and postdoctorate fellows, each of us gave seminars and taught advanced courses in our special subdisciplines. My métier was the chemistry of natural products; at Stanford, I offered courses in the fields that reflected my research interests: steroid synthesis, structure elucidation, and applications of physical methods to organic chemical problems.

These may sound like dry topics—and, indeed, they can be. Students have been known to enroll in a poetry or history class out of curiosity and then get hooked on the subject by a brilliant teacher. Even chemists walk on impulse into poetry classes. But students don't open the doors of chemistry or physics lecture halls unless they have to take the course or have already decided to get some exposure to the subject. This is even truer of graduate students in chemistry: they have already made their career choice;

at that stage, a professor might influence them, by good teaching, to focus on a certain chemical specialty or, by dull or obtuse lectures, push them into another one. I always took my classroom teaching seriously, especially since the formal teaching load at Stanford was never onerous. But I didn't want only to stimulate the students; I also wanted to involve them in a variety of pedagogic experiences—to experiment with variations on the usual one-way flow from lecturing professor to note-taking student.

I

My first pedagogic experiment was also the most ambitious. In the fall of 1962, I offered a graduate course on recent advances in organic chemical synthesis. In order to reduce the subject to manageable proportions, I decided to use steroids as the instructional template, because during the preceding decade the synthesis of natural steroid hormones and their analogs represented the ultimate in complexity and sophistication. Few newly discovered synthetic organic reactions were not immediately applied to the steroid field. It was as if, for purposes of illustrating the state of the art to a budding chef, I limited myself to French *nouvelle cuisine*. I would not touch on Chinese, German, Greek, or Indian cooking; yet the new chef would learn how to prepare all courses in a meal, from soup and salad, to entrée, to dessert, through exposure to a newly introduced methodology. I decided to go a step farther, however; I asked the apprentice chefs to write a cookbook, each student being responsible for one chapter.

My course was obligatory for Ph.D. candidates in organic chemistry, so I knew in the spring who the students would be in my autumn class. Before the summer recess, I convened all sixteen students and offered them a choice of sixteen topics in the field of steroid synthesis for detailed scrutiny. I provided each student with a quick survey of their selected subject and with leading references. I then asked them—in lieu of any examinations at the end of the course—to spend the summer going through every issue of sixteen international chemical journals (American, British, German, French, Swiss, Japanese, Canadian, and Czechoslovakian) covering the last ten years and to look for every article relevant to their topic. In culinary terms, one student would search all recipes for soups, another for sauces, a third for fish, and so on. At the beginning of the fall quarter, the students presented me with the first drafts of sixteen chapters—mostly a series of staccato phrases, with much of the information presented in terms of chemical structures—which we then studied together over the course of the quarter.

About a hundred copies of this text were distributed to steroid chemists throughout the world, soliciting their comments and criticism. The response was so enthusiastic that the following quarter, the sixteen authors polished their chapters, and two of the students redrew the chemical structures in a form suitable for commercial publication. The book appeared in 1963 under the title *Steroid Reactions: An Outline for Organic Chemists*, "prepared by sixteen graduate students at Stanford University under the editorship of Carl Djerassi." The name of each chapter's author appeared at the end of that chapter; for most of the students, it was their very first professional publication. Eight of these authors are now full professors in various universities; and I like to think that this experience contributed to their career choice. The book was an instant success, and we all agreed to assign the significant royalties to the university to use in the construction and furnishing of a small seminar building, which on all Stanford University maps is now identified as the "Chemistry Gazebo."

II

Not all my courses were devoid of examinations, though I favored open-book or take-home exams over the standard true-or-false or multiple-choice questions; I was not interested in promoting rote learning or rewarding a capacity for memorization. I wanted students to face real-world facts: that time is the most expensive commodity, and that to solve difficult problems as quickly as possible, one needs to know *where* to look for the answers. This thinking eventually brought me to the most time-consuming examination of them all—at least for myself. I even gave it a name: the maximum-leverage test.

I used this exam in the early 1960s in a course dealing with contemporary methods of structure elucidation of complex natural products. At the time, this activity required a fair amount of chemical experimentation and intuition; the use of physical methods was not yet well developed or all-pervasive. In terms of the "dark room" analogy I introduced in chapter 7, our flashlights were not yet powerful, and the modus operandi was still "Twenty Questions." The aim of my course was to teach students chemical *Fingerspitzengefühl*—the intellectual fingertip sensitivity that, for instance, distinguished the real medical diagnosticians from the hacks during the days when diagnostic medicine was still dependent more on "Twenty Questions" than on laboratory analyses and sophisticated scanning techniques. For examinations, I gave students chemical puzzles to solve at home or in the library. Creating such puzzles is not easy, and one day, while starting to think about the midterm exam, it occurred to me to give myself a break. Why not teach the students how to ask questions rather than simply how to answer them? When the midterm day of judgment arrived, I appeared empty-handed. As the nervous group looked anxiously around the room for the examination questions, I informed them that for our next scheduled meeting I wanted from each student a set of questions that could be used for an open-book, take-home exam and would cover the contents of the first half of the course. I would grade them on the appropriateness and the pedagogic value of their questions. The students were at once jubilant and disturbed. It seemed all so easy, but was there a catch? Indeed, there were two.

First, as the students soon found out at home, it isn't easy to pose test questions to someone who has access to every type of reference book; it is harder even than generating a crossword puzzle for people with a good dictionary and a thesaurus. As I expected, many of the questions the students asked were much more difficult than the ones I would have raised; many students confused trickiness, even deviousness, with subtlety. Second, when the students handed in the questions, they learned a new definition of *leverage*. I proceeded to hand the questions out to different students, being careful that no pair of students got each other's questions. I now asked them to *answer* these colleague-produced questions. When they had, I asked the original questioner to grade the answers, and the respondent to grade the quality of the questions. Finally, I graded each of the answers as well as the fairness of the grading the students applied to each other. Anyone patient enough to penetrate this thicket of grades and countergrades will appreciate how time-consuming the process was for me—each student had a different examination—but also how many different grades I generated out of one such examination. The vast majority of students agreed that in the process they had learned not just chemistry but also pedagogy.

When the time of the next examination approached, the end-of-term test, I told the students that I wanted them again to present me with a set of questions, which were this time to cover the material of the entire course and to be answered within two hours in class. When the day of the final examination arrived, I collected the questions and then handed them out to the various students. I had presented the first set to one student, the second to the next, and was about to offer a set to the third student, when the first called out. "Professor Djerassi, these are my own questions!" I ignored the interruption and proceeded with the distribution. "Professor Djerassi," the second student then complained, "you made the same mistake with me!" "And with me!" chimed the third. It gradually dawned on the class that this had been my intention all along. Most of the students were delighted, but a significant few were horrified. They had never worried about the answers—after all, this was not an open-book examination; they thought they would demonstrate their virtuosity by the complexity of the questions they had asked. Hoist with their own chemical petards!

III

By the 1970s, structure elucidation had largely been transformed into an exercise in the judicious use of physical methods, the various flashlights; and most of my chemical lectures focused then on that exercise. This was also the time when our research on computer-aided structure elucidation, conducted jointly with the research groups of Joshua Lederberg and Edward Feigenbaum, was at its most intense. I thought that it was time to expose a diverse group of chemists, rather than just my own research co-workers, to the power and limitations of knowledge engineering, otherwise known as "artificial intelligence." Instead of lecturing about the various spectroscopic methods and their applications, I told the students that I would take for granted their working knowledge of the various physical methods. If their knowledge was deficient, they could repair it on their own, using the standard texts. What I wanted to do was to demonstrate how diverse information—the various portions of the dark room illuminated by different flashlights—is put together to make a whole picture, and how one ensures that only *that* combination corresponds to the correct spatial arrangement of the room's contents. The computer programs our AI group had developed were designed to accomplish a task for which the computer is best qualified, and that is, at the same time, most difficult to perform manually: the *exhaustive* generation of all possible structural candidates consistent with the *isolated* bits of information collected with the different flashlights. Once all of these structural straw men have been assembled through intuition and knowledge, the chemist can usually design a few key experiments or measurements that will demolish experimentally all but one of these alternatives, leaving only the correct structure behind.

Our software programs were written in user-friendly English and thus immediately accessible to the students. I asked each student to search the chemical literature for a publication in which the structure elucidation of some natural product was based on conclusions derived from a variety of physical methods (flashlights), but not confirmed by the unambiguous method of X-ray crystallography (equivalent to a color photograph in my dark-room analogy). After each student had selected such a paper, I asked that they subject the literature data to scrutiny by our computer program.

Did the computer agree with the chemist's conclusion that no other structural alternative was consistent with the published data? Or was some straw man lurking in the background which had not yet been eliminated by the evidence at hand? Had a straw man possibly been overlooked by the chemist? This hands-on approach to real-life problems would, I hoped, effectively illustrate the power of computer-aided checks and at the same time offer the class a view of the wide variety of structure-elucidation problems that were being studied all over the world.

The results of this pedagogic experiment were even more dramatic than I had anticipated. Without exception, each student discovered that the evidence cited in the published literature was consistent with at least one structural alternative that the authors had not considered. In one instance, the computer generated over two dozen structural straw men that had not been eliminated by the experimental evidence in the literature! I wrote to each author—in Japan, Italy, Spain, England, and North America—describing the student's (really the computer's) conclusions and asking whether the author had any comments about the ambiguity of his or her published results. Most authors gave the expected, "Ah well, but . . . " response and then cited some additional spectroscopic or other experimental data that were not contained in the publication, but that the outraged author had dug up in order to demolish one of the computer-generated alternatives. My answer was, of course, that these data should have been in the paper in the first place; and I suggested, only partly tongue in cheek, to one of the journal editors that our computer program could become a completely automated and totally unbiased journal referee for any manuscript dealing with structure determination. I even made this proposal in one of our review articles; but to my knowledge, no journal has so far had the courage to try such an experiment. Some authors, however, never replied—possibly out of shock or chagrin; and I used those examples for a further educational experience for the students. I asked them to come up with the most time- and material-saving experiments that would differentiate among these remaining structural alternatives. A third group of respondents pleased me most: they wanted to know how they could get a copy of the program.

IV

It was also in the early 1970s—a watershed in chemistry's approach to structure elucidation and in my own attitude about classroom teaching—that I finally started to lecture to undergraduates. Why is it that as a young teacher I concentrated solely on graduate students, often older than I, whereas in the twilight of my professorial career, my principal educational constituency has turned into undergraduates? As I have begun to realize in the course of writing about the teaching component of my life, my gradual conversion from "hard" scientist to one with softer overtones occurred largely in the classroom.

In 1969, I had published my first "public policy" articles forecasting the decline in contraception research and the associated costs to society. I soon realized that the only way to reverse this decline would be to create a better-informed citizenry, and that the media, notably television, would never accomplish this through their present mode of spending a minute or two of precious broadcast time on complicated issues requiring extended discussion and critical thought. Precisely at that period, as it happened, an innovative new undergraduate program was established at Stanford with financial support from the Ford Foundation. The Program in Human Biology was designed to combat the increasing scientific illiteracy of our population during a time when most public policy issues had acquired technological or scientific aspects. Much of that illiteracy can be traced to the poor quality of our high school education in mathematics and the hard sciences, which still manifests itself as a fear of such subjects among undergraduates at even the most prestigious universities.

One way to offset this tendency is to emphasize the less physically oriented sectors of science, notably the biological ones, and to do so on the most anthropocentric and thus most persuasive front: the study of man. Not surprisingly, considering the composition of university faculties at that time, all the founders of Stanford's Human Biology Program were men: the geneticist Joshua Lederberg, the pediatrician Norman Kretchmer, the population biologist Paul Ehrlich, the neurobiologist Donald Kennedy (later to become commissioner of the FDA in Washington, and then president of Stanford University), the sociologist Sanford Dornbush, the psychologist (and later Stanford's provost) Albert Hastorf, and the psychiatrist David Hamburg, now president of the Carnegie Foundation. They devised a two-year core curriculum, that would both enable students with minimal exposure to the physical sciences to become proficient in biological and social science areas, and be followed by two years of advanced courses in more specialized fields—all this to be superimposed on the regular liberal arts requirements of the university. These senior professors also served as the principal lecturers in the courses.

The response of the students was remarkable: classes, which were scheduled in lecture halls accommodating some fifty students, had to be transferred to auditoriums for four hundred. Within a few years, Human

Biology became one of the most popular undergraduate majors at Stanford, selected by students whose goals were medicine, public health, law, environmental sciences, and politics—precisely the constituency I wanted to address in terms of contraception and population issues. Since no chemistry professors were participating in the Human Biology Program, which by then had attracted a highly interdisciplinary faculty, I volunteered to offer a course for advanced undergraduates under the rubric "Biosocial Aspects of Birth Control"—a course that eventually led to a total change in my life as a classroom teacher. I chose that topic because I felt that birth control affects nearly everybody: people have used it, will use it, or are, at the very least, against it.

Of my several aims, the most important was to encourage students to think seriously about public policy and with real problems in mind. At a time when Stanford offered no formal undergraduate public policy courses, I felt that at least my professional background, bridging academia and an industry highly concerned with risk-benefit considerations, would qualify me for such teaching. I did not want to limit myself to prospective scientists; the future legislators and formulators of public policy are unlikely to come from that guild. By using the modifier *biosocial*, I hoped to make it plain that I was emphasizing the "softer" and broader aspects of birth control, and thus to attract students from a wider circle. I omitted all course prerequisites other than the requirement that students be seniors and thus competent in at least one relevant discipline: religion, psychology, sociology, anthropology, economics, political science were some of the departments to which I proselytized. I knew that in biology and chemistry I would find the premedical candidates. Never in my career as a chemistry professor had I looked for customers; now I found myself becoming a promoter. I composed a one-page broadsheet in which I outlined the purpose of my course and the manner in which it would be taught. Attached to it was a questionnaire, which every interested student was asked to complete. I was curious not just about their academic qualifications but also about their social and geographic backgrounds, especially their exposure to travel and life abroad. I had a special educational experiment in mind, for which I needed a special group: equally distributed by gender, and with adequate representation from various ethnic, social, and religious backgrounds. I limited enrollment to forty. Since over eighty students completed the questionnaire, I was able to start with a highly select and motivated group.

I like to think that it wasn't only the subject matter that attracted the students, although 1972 was the height of the sexual revolution, and contraception a topic that either interested or antagonized almost everyone. I like to believe it was the unusual structure of the course I described in my blurb.

There would be no examinations, I announced, and my formal lectures would end after two weeks. During that time, the students could pick among a series of population groups, whose birth control options they would then study in depth in groups of six or seven. The emphasis would be on projected improvements in birth control, with each student examining the chosen population group from a particular disciplinary standpoint. A typical task force might include majors in pre-medicine, pre-law, economics, religion, anthropology, chemistry, and psychology. The students would organize their research together, but each task force member would write a separate chapter of the group's report from her or his professional perspective. The main purpose of my course was to demonstrate that the concept of an ideal, universal birth control agent or approach was a chimera—in retrospect, an obvious conclusion, but one I had paid little attention to during my days as a "hard" scientist in the 1950s and early 1960s. Because of the tremendous divergence of different populations, what is appropriate for one group or even one individual may not suit the next. I wanted the students both to see that what the world needs is a kind of contraceptive supermarket, and to propose, through their own research, what some of the components of that supermarket might be. In the event, my first class in Biosocial Aspects of Birth Control picked the following seven population subgroups: white, American college students, typified by the majority of Stanford's affluent student population; Chicanos in San Jose, a politically and economically disenfranchised group of Catholics; Puerto Ricans in Manhattan, a similar group on the East Coast; people in the lower-income strata of Mexico City, a group related to the preceding two in economic status and religion, but living within their own political setting; Egyptian peasants in the Nile Delta, and Indian slum dwellers in Calcutta—two third-world constituencies existing in quite different religious and political settings; and finally, a group representing the "women's liberation" position.

This first class in 1972 turned out to be an important educational experience for me as well as for the students. Both of us worked extremely hard. After the second week, once I had completed my lectures—illustrated with many slides, and each lasting for nearly three hours—I met twice a week separately with each task force. During those sessions, I questioned each student about her or his research progress; I provided students with key contacts and encouraged them, using a modest financial kitty provided by the Human Biology office, to use long-distance phone calls as the most rapid way of extracting information from government bureaucrats here and abroad. Most important, I insisted that the students collaborate. Although all important social and technical advances in real life are the result of interdisciplinary team efforts, we tend not to incorporate that concept formally in our undergraduate curriculum. Our entire grading and evaluation system emphasizes individual performance and competition; collaboration among students is explicitly or implicitly considered cheating. In the student evaluations of my course, this task-force approach was voted the most original and worthwhile learning experience. (Even nineteen years later, a student from that first class, now equipped with both M.D. and Ph.D. degrees, wrote what every teacher adores to read:" 'Biosocial Aspects of Birth Control' was *the* most important course I have ever taken in my career as a student. . . . You taught me how to fish instead of simply giving me a fish to eat when I was hungry.") I had no difficulty in evaluating the individual accomplishments, since everyone wrote a separate chapter, but these contributions had to be integrated within the entire group's report; each student had to know what every other member of the group was writing.

The climax of the course was the presentation of each task force's conclusion to the rest of the class and some invited guests. Each group had available three hours—half for the formal presentation, the other half for questions and answers. This was another time when I could evaluate each student's performance: by the manner of the presentation, by the incisiveness of the questions, and by the perspicacity of the response. It was during these presentations that the students really surprised me. I had given them carte blanche in presenting their conclusions, provided every member of the group participated in some fashion and thus had the opportunity also to be questioned. The first task force used a *laterna magica* format, similar to what Czech filmmakers employed with notable success at one of the world's fairs—a device that pushed some thespian button in the other groups. From then on, students used everything from skits to full-fledged dramas. Even though I taught this course only every two years during the 1970s, word spread among the students about these presentations, and subsequent classes tried to outperform each other.

Two of the most memorable presentations in the mid-1970s were given by task forces dealing with birth control problems among black Americans. On each occasion, all but one of the members of these task forces were black. One of these events was organized by Brenda Jo Young, now a practicing psychiatrist, who, in those days of unisex student garb marked by blue jeans and hiking boots, stood out in her high-heeled shoes and fashionable dresses. Her group took over the main chemistry lecture room to stage an imitation mini-rock concert with strobe lights, raucous music, and clever skits illuminating the attitudinal differences between blacks and whites. As usual, I sat in a corner seat in front, so that I could also observe the audience by making just a half-turn. Just as one of the students was wildly dancing on top of the lecture demonstrating table, I noticed the partially open rear door and the horrified face of our departmental vice chairman. Somebody having reported to him that something close to bedlam was going on in the auditorium, he had rushed down. Only my cheerful wave from the front row made him withdraw.

The second black group wrote and performed a tragic-comic drama, which effectively demonstrated several basic factors that they felt determined birth control alternatives chosen by an American black, urban population: the high teenage pregnancy rate; the nonjudgmental and generally supportive attitude of black parents and grandparents in respect to teenage pregnancy; young black males' general lack of interest in effective birth control; and white social workers' relative ignorance of black family interactions. The role of the white social worker was played by a light-skinned black student, who took it for granted that the young teenage woman would have an abortion—only to find upon coming to visit the family to arrange for the procedure, the boyfriend, the girl's parents, and a grandparent all sitting in a modest living room and planning the birth of the baby. The woman, who had assumed in the play the role of the pregnant teenager, subsequently became pregnant herself, shortly before entering medical school. I was both pleased and proud when I learned later that as a single mother she had successfully graduated as an M.D.

The most ambitious projects were conducted by my third class in the fall of 1975 and the spring of 1976. By then I had received feedback from two classes who, having taken Biosocial Aspects of Birth Control as a one-quarter course, had complained about its extreme time pressure and work load. Most of these students claimed that it demanded more work than any other class in their undergraduate experience, and I certainly found the same to be true of my professorial life. Since each student worked on a different project, and the bulk of the quarter involved one-on-one meetings, I had to be prepared to cover an extraordinarily wide range of subjects. At the end I had to read, criticize, and grade the final reports from each group, which were usually at least one hundred pages long and frequently included several hundred references. This was a process that I could not delegate to others, and I found myself spending solid days when I did nothing but read and jot down marginal comments on these volumes—an experience that could not help but sensitize me further to the numerous sociopolitical and cultural issues associated with birth control. Additionally, these class papers—many of them quite sophisticated—also contributed to my knowledge of diverse population groups, as illustrated by a comparative study of the birth control problems of three Chinese populations: in San Francisco's Chinatown, in Taiwan, and in the People's Republic of China. I learned most from this third class, when the course was spread over two quarters, with some of the students using the Christmas break for a type of field research not often available to undergraduates.

I had contacted the Rockefeller Foundation to ask whether it would fund, as a one-time experiment, the travel expenses of my human biology class for some exploratory research in more distant locations. Until now, my students' research was limited not only by time pressure but also by the financial resources at their disposal. These consisted of reimbursement for telephone calls and local travel within a hundred-mile radius of San Francisco. Students who had chosen Egyptian, Indian, or other distant population groups had to depend on library resources or past foreign travel experiences. The Rockefeller Foundation, being especially devoted to supporting research in developing countries, agreed to fund this educational experiment because of an interest in birth control in general and its application to poorer populations in particular. As a result, I was able to organize the largest class of all—with ten task forces—and to offer each group the opportunity to send at least two, and sometimes all, members to sites irrespective of distance. Geographically, the three most ambitious projects involved populations in Kenya, Java, and rural Mexico, but the American-oriented projects were also interesting. For instance, the Chicano task force, consisting of four students named Martinez, Ramos, Renteria, and Rios, decided to conduct a comparative study of three Chicano communities in Denver (second and even third-generation Mexican-Americans), El Paso (a floating population on either side of the border), and Los Angeles (a site of numerous illegal immigrants who spoke no English). Several members of another group, which chose native Americans, spent a couple of weeks in New Mexico with an Indian tribe with which one of the anthropology students had established contact. A third group picked a rural setting in the South—Cherokee County, North Carolina, the home of one student—and provided a generally unfamiliar view of the educational and public health restrictions operating there.

Two particularly interesting choices had no geographical, but rather a functional definition: one dealt with the birth control problems of carriers of genetic diseases; the other, with those of developmentally disabled persons. Reading all of these reports was a monstrous task, and to address it, I secluded myself one drizzly weekend during California's rainy season at my ranch home. Soon wearying, on the spur of the moment I picked up my umbrella and took to my outdoor hot tub, where I floated naked without dropping a single page into the water. Of course, the steam was not without effect, but I never confessed to the students why the pages of their reports came back slightly curled.

The oral presentations of these groups were on the whole impressive—luckily, for so was the composition of the invited audience. The medical director of the Rockefeller Foundation flew out from New York for several presentations, and the chairperson of the California State Assembly's subcommittee on health came to those on genetic disorders and developmentally disabled persons—in view of then-pending hearings on these topics in Sacramento. The report of the Indonesia task force, which dealt with market and social incentives for contraceptives in Java, got one of the students a job with the Agency for International Development in Washington; the World Health Organization hired a member of the Kenya group, on the basis of his field report, for a summer internship in Geneva before he entered medical school. Sharon Rockefeller, the wife of the present senator from West Virginia, attended the presentation of the Kenya task force, since she was also a trustee of Stanford University and acquainted with one of the student members of that group—the one who presented me with the pink condoms that had drawn the attention of the *People* magazine reporter. The group graphically demonstrated to the audience the gulf in attitudinal differences between *us* and *them* by passing around fried termites, a Kenyan delicacy, and challenging everyone to taste them. I seem to recall that Mrs. Rockefeller was one of the few to take up the offer.

When I started teaching the birth control class, the distribution of the students by gender was approximately equal. By the late 1970s, fewer and fewer men were choosing to enroll; and by the early 1980s, at most 20 percent of the students were males. This lack of male interest in the subject was even more pronounced in an offshoot course I first sponsored in 1983. I had observed that the one task-force topic always selected by each class dealt with what I called at that time "women's liberation position." Aside from its obvious timeliness, there was another reason it was such a popular choice. I always drew attention to a quotation by Margaret Mead that to me is a distillation of all the misconceptions carried by modern American women:

> [The pill] is entirely the invention of men. And why did they do it? . . .
> Because they are extraordinarily unwilling to experiment with their own
> bodies . . . and they're extremely willing to experiment with women's
> bodies . . . it would be much safer to monkey with men than monkey with
> women . . . Now the ideal contraceptive undoubtedly would be a pill that
> a man and a woman would have to take simultaneously.

I invariably asked the students to start out with Mead's position and then to present evidence either for or against it. The students who considered Mead's thesis justified were asked to develop a realistic proposal for ameliorating the perceived male dominance in birth control research. As the years passed, and especially when Stanford introduced a special Feminist Studies Program, I decided to create a specific course under the title "Feminist Perspectives on Birth Control." I have now given it five times, once at Bard College in New York, because I was interested in contrasting the perspective of some students in a small eastern college with that of their western counterparts in a large university. With a solitary exception, all the students in those classes were women.

Have men suddenly stopped believing in birth control? Has "yuppification," the present student generation's preoccupation with material goods and professional advancement, made the men relegate birth control to a low priority? I believe that the real reason is that the students of the 1980s are all children of the Pill generation of mothers. The Pill has made many important social contributions, not the least of them that birth control became an accepted topic of dinner conversation. But, concomitantly, it has also created a social atmosphere in which one more responsibility—this time that of contraception—has fallen on the shoulders of women. Many women, of course, accepted it eagerly as an important sign of emancipation and freedom from male dominance, but one of the consequences of that achievement has been a collective shrug of male shoulders, an outcome I regret deeply.

I find it both disheartening and amusing that it was the women in my class who played the biggest role in making condoms available at Stanford University. In view of the fact that approximately 40 percent of all condom purchasers are now women, I thought it only appropriate to encourage some of the students in "Feminist Perspectives" to focus on that form of contraception. At a time when AIDS was still considered a misspelling for the dietary pill AYDS, I wrote in an article dealing with teenage pregnancy in the United States that if high schools and colleges were to make condoms readily available to students, they would not only be contributing to public health but also helping to teach young men at the most impressionable stage of life to accept some responsibility for contraception. Among the papers women in my class wrote were critical feminist evaluations of condom advertising and promotion. For instance, instead of a phallocentric terminology like Sheik or Ramses or Trojan—or, for that matter, the spear-throwing Masai on the box of Kenyan condoms the *People* writer reported—why not call a brand of condoms Cleopatra? And instead of blue and green and orange, one of my feminist warriors in class asked, why not color the Cleopatras gold?

In 1980, two women task-force members examined what it would take to introduce condom dispensers at Stanford University—and received a first-class lesson in academic bureaucratism. The dean of student affairs sent them to the acting deputy vice president for administrative services and facilities, who suggested they see first one of the university's legal counsels, and then the athletic director since they were thinking of gyms as a possible location. Even the university's ombudsperson was of no help when the students reported the horrified response of one librarian after they had suggested the library's toilets as a suitable site. "Just imagine all the high school students who would come to the library to get condoms?" he exclaimed. I could hardly think of a better use for condoms: reducing teenage pregnancy while increasing literacy, even at the price of finding a used condom or two on the floor among the stacks. Not until 1987 did a feminist Gang of Five, dealing with over-the-counter contraceptives and led by my students Shirley Wang and Jennifer Yu, succeed in wearing down Stanford's administration and getting the first condom dispensers into some of the toilets. Were it not for the fact that I practice what I preach by having had a vasectomy many years ago, I would have been one of the first customers. Thus, the box from Kenya still rests unused in my huge collection of condoms into which I dip for class demonstration purposes. I am probably one of the few persons who could claim the cost of condoms as an income tax deduction for my professional activities as a teacher.

CHAPTER 11

"How Do You Get a Cockroach to Take the Pill?"

I N 1972, I SURPRISED EVERYONE, including myself, by resigning as president of Syntex Research in order to dedicate the industrial portion of my workday to insects. "Why insects?" I have often been asked. Until the mid-1960s, preoccupation with insects required a minute portion of my neural network. My formal knowledge of entomology was minimal, my attitude essentially entomophobic: when I encountered a spider or beetle, I was likely to step on it or zap it with an aerosol spray. Yet within just a few years, I became deeply involved with insects through an apparently disjointed course of my industrial life that jumped from steroids to super-conductors and then to drugs of abuse, to end among mosquitoes, fleas, and cockroaches.

Ordinarily, one thinks of science as a rational and orderly process, with discoveries following one upon another in a vertical progression. But a scientist's life also features serendipity and a version of Jung's *synchronicity*—seemingly haphazard timing and disparate circumstances all falling into place so as to produce what in the end seems inevitable. Such coincidences apply particularly to the opposite extremes of a research project: the initial choice of topic and its ultimate practical application. My twenty-year-long affair with insects is a case in point.

Around 1970, coincidental with my increasing concern about the societal ramifications of my industrial life, I had also come to realize the depth of my belief that small is more beautiful than big. My metamorphosis into super administrator seemed inevitable, given the track my life was then on. But how had my corporate life become so complicated and consuming? It had become obvious to me that there were not enough hours in a day to continue, in addition to my Stanford professorship, as president of Syntex Research as well as the CEO and chairman, respectively, of two other industrial ventures, whose genesis I am about to describe. Syntex was then growing so rapidly that everyone expected me to relinquish my other corporate interests and to concentrate on it. But I chose the youngest company for my nonacademic hours. I fantasized about duplicating the Syntex experiment once more—converting a small, innovative research enterprise into an integrated operation involving research and development, manufacture and sales—and to do this in a field of high societal benefit. On 31 December 1972, I left Syntex, and quickly learned how short corporate memories are. Occasionally when I telephone one of my ex-students still working in the upper echelons of Syntex management, I have to spell my name.

I

Shortly after my arrival in Palo Alto from Mexico City in the early autumn of 1960, I persuaded my fellow Syntex directors that the time was ripe for diversification beyond steroids. My first Stanford friend, Joshua Lederberg, had been awarded the Nobel Prize in Medicine in 1958 for the discovery of bacterial genetics; Arthur Kornberg, chairman of Stanford's new biochemistry department, had won it the following year for his enzymatic synthesis of DNA: almost overnight, Stanford had become a world center in the new field of molecular biology. Since no pharmaceutical company had as yet made a significant commitment to that area, I suggested that we be among the first. Within a year, we established the Syntex Institute for Molecular Biology in a new one-story building on the Stanford Industrial Park—with me its head as a part-time Syntex vice president, and Joshua Lederberg as its advisory research director. He was chiefly responsible for setting our scientific priorities and hiring the research group leaders. (Fred Terman, who, as provost, had brought me to Stanford, proudly participated in the 1962 inauguration of our institute because he saw his dream of attracting biomedical industry to the Stanford Industrial Park realized in record time. The opening was a star-studded affair, quite out of proportion to the actual size of our operation, and included Stanford's president, J. Wallace Sterling; David Packard, then CEO of our closest industrial neighbor, the Hewlett-Packard Company; and Charles Allen, Jr., the legendary New York investment banker who had been responsible for launching Syntex's Wall Street success.)

In early 1963, when Syntex felt ready to enter the American pharmaceutical market under its own name with some of the drugs we had invented in the late 1950s in Mexico, I urged that the company establish its U.S. headquarters next to Stanford—where we already had our Institute of Molecular Biology, and would be next door to a major medical school and only thirty minutes away from an international airport with direct flights to Mexico, Japan, and Europe. The clincher was my argument that, since virtually all American pharmaceutical companies were east of the Mississippi, we would have no competition in attracting top scientists to the San Francisco Bay area. Alex Zaffaroni was persuaded to move to California as head of Syntex's American commercial entity and president of Syntex Research in the beautiful new complex, to which most of the Mexico City research staff was soon transferred. I took on the part-time position of executive vice president of Syntex Research, while continuing as a professor of chemistry at Stanford—a combination Provost Terman approved with gusto. Before the end of that decade, Syntex's move to the campus had spawned three additional, research-intensive companies—ALZA, Syva, and Zoecon—in close proximity to each other.

Within a couple of years, the molecular biology group also shifted to the new Syntex research complex, fortuitously vacating the one-story laboratory building that had been its first home. Timing could not have been better. William Little, a Stanford physics professor, who had just published a controversial theory of superconductivity, had approached me with a challenge. Until then, superconductivity had been displayed only by some carefully purified metals near absolute zero, which required the use of expensive liquid helium. (A theory to explain that phenomenon eventually won John Bardeen, Leon N. Cooper, and John R. Schrieffer the Nobel Prize in physics in 1972.) Little proposed that certain hypothetical *organic* polymers should also be capable of superconductivity—and at near room temperatures. If correct, the implications were mind-boggling: for a start, it would revolutionize power transmission. But to prove Little's hypothesis, one would have to synthesize a polymer that had never been seen before: a linear, conductive, polymeric backbone, with branching dye molecules bearing electric charges. Such work needed participation by industrial experts conversant with organic synthesis and with practical applications in electronics and possessing deep pockets. After discussing the matter with my friend and colleague Elliott Levinthal (Varian's first research director, but since 1961 a faculty member of the Stanford Medical School), I recommended to the ever-adventurous Syntex board that we undertake the backing for Little's superconductivity gamble by forming a joint venture with Varian Associates (along with Hewlett-Packard, one of the first tenants of the Stanford Industrial Park).

In just a few months, Synvar Associates, as the new partnership was christened, was housed in the newly vacated Institute of Molecular Biology building. Since the building was ten minutes walking distance from the headquarters of the two corporate parents, Syntex and Varian, it was easy for the board of governors to meet almost daily at lunchtime. I served as chairman; Zaffaroni, Edward Ginzton (Varian's CEO and former physics professor at Stanford), and Martin Packard (a Varian vice president of the scientific instrument division) were the other members. We agreed that all important decisions had to be unanimous—an apparent recipe for disaster, which actually worked beautifully. The physicists Ginzton and Packard didn't second-guess the Syntex chemists on matters chemical, but neither did they serve as rubber stamps. I took the responsibility for locating and hiring the key staff members, starting with Edwin Ullman, a Harvard Ph.D. then in charge of a basic research group in photochemistry at American Cyanamid, as scientific director.

Though skeptical about the possibility of actually synthesizing Little's designer molecule for organic superconductivity, Ullman was willing to give it a try. He would, after all, have as a consultant my Stanford colleague Harden McConnell, a chemical physicist, who himself had a theory of superconductivity (based on certain types of metal sandwiches). In addition, McConnell was also studying the biophysical properties of "free radicals" (electron-deficient chemical species) whose electron deficiency made it possible to detect them in complex mixtures by a technique called "electron-spin resonance" (ESR), for which Varian was the principal supplier of instruments. Chemical free radicals are usually capable only of very short lifetimes, but McConnell was focusing on a group of organic free radicals that were essentially immortal. We offered Ullman the opportunity of hedging our research bet by pursuing McConnell's idea in parallel with Little's project, and to see whether such stable free radicals might actually have practical utility. And we agreed to fund a third group working on new applications of photochemistry, an area dear to Ullman's heart. The project was a search for colorless molecules that, upon irradiation with light rays of skin-burning wavelength, would be transformed gradually into mole-

155

cules opaque to such rays. The idea was to create a pre-timed sunscreen by synthesizing molecules whose conversion time from transmissive to opaque spanned a wide range.

Consciously or not, any enterprise subsidizing a group of bright and adventurous researchers becomes a proponent of serendipity, because such a venture is likely to pay off sooner or later, even if not in the area originally envisioned. In 1971, Synvar abandoned the attempt to synthesize Little's dream polymer, which proved too difficult. We had also shelved Ullman's photochemical program—although that research had very nearly paid off. Our photochemists had synthesized and patented a group of compounds that had all the requisite properties of a timed sunscreen, and we had gone so far as to secure FDA approval for limited human trials (which we conducted in our sunny parking lot). I approached Charles Revson, the founder of Revlon, as a possible marketing partner. Visiting Revson in his Manhattan penthouse lair, I discovered that he passionately believed in sunscreens, because of his skin oncophobia; though an oddly crude man (as I judged from the vulgar mottoes embroidered on his sofa pillows), he immediately saw both the potential of our product and the cost of the educational campaign it would demand. But we decided to reject Revson's offer to fund this project, in return for one-third Revlon ownership in Synvar, mostly because we had begun, in the early 1970s, to strike gold with our third research topic: the search for practical applications of organic free radicals.

A decade later, the company's revenue from diagnostic products arising from the original stable free-radical work had passed the $100-million mark. The seminal idea had been provided by Avram Goldstein, then head of the department of pharmacology at the Stanford Medical School and a consultant to Synvar on possible biological applications of the unique ESR properties of stable free radicals. A neuropharmacologist of international repute, Goldstein was particularly interested in opiate addiction and called to our attention the need, in methadone treatment centers, for a fast and sensitive method to screen patients who might be taking heroin surreptitiously. He also contributed to the Synvar team's invention in 1970 of the FRAT (Free Radical Assay Technique) approach to the detection in urine of traces of morphine, a metabolite of heroin. Varian made a couple of prototype modifications of their research ESR machine to provide clinical laboratories with a simple "black box" which would convert the free radical's ESR signals into a graphic output indicating the presence and amount of morphine in urine. From this point on, developments proceeded at a stunning rate.

One Sunday in early 1971, while working on the roof of his house, Bill

McGlashan—an extraordinarily bright Stanford MBA whom Syntex had seconded to Synvar, and who became our commercial vice president while still in his twenties—was called to the phone. Dr. Jerome Jaffe, then the head of the Illinois methadone treatment program, where some of the earliest field demonstrations of our FRAT procedure were performed, was calling from the White House to ask about the whereabouts of the two FRAT prototype instruments. When told that they were about to be shipped to Seattle for another field trial, Jaffe told McGlashan that he had a general from the Pentagon on the line. The general's message was curt: "You can't ship them. I'm now informing you that they're U.S. government property. They're going to 'Nam' and someone from your place will take them there to teach the army how to use them." Two days later, McGlashan, Richard Leute (the Synvar chemist with the most FRAT experience), and a Varian engineer got their cholera, typhoid, and other shots at Moffett Field in San Jose; and the next morning, the three aching men, the two machines, and enough reagents for tens of thousands of opiate assays took off from Travis Air Base on a C-141 transport for Saigon. The Synvar team set up the instruments at Cam Rahn Bay and at Long Binh—two of the biggest American bases in Vietnam—and trained army personnel to perform FRAT assays. A week later on TV, President Nixon announced Jaffe's appointment as the national drug czar and the initiation of a compulsory urine analysis program designed to detect opiate drug abuse among servicemen in Vietnam. The true extent of such abuse was unknown, but there was great worry that we would be spreading the epidemic at home if we returned soldiers who were actively addicted and physically dependent on opiates. The plan, therefore, was to test all the troops in Vietnam in order to collect reliable data on heroin use, and to hold and detoxify anyone with a positive urine test before permitting that person to return to the United States.

Our first reagent order from the army amounted to nearly $2 million, which transformed us overnight from a research venture into a business. It also made us think about trade names. In the process, we discovered that SYNVAR was the registered name of a synthetic varnish company in Delaware. So we decided to retain only the first two letters of the two corporate parents and became Syva. This designation became a household word in clinical laboratories when Ullman's team developed a second method, termed EMIT for Enzyme Multiplied Immunoassay Technique, which eventually superseded FRAT as the preferred method for detecting drugs of abuse, as well as many other therapeutically significant medicines. The rationale for this second application is easily appreciated: since in the treatment of many chronic diseases—for instance epilepsy, asthma, heart problems—it is important to tailor the dosage to the individual patient, rapid and simple assays are required for these particular medicines. EMIT (*Time* spelled backward) proved to be ideal for such purposes.

Syva's scientific and commercial success is a first-class example of the synergy generated when the interplay between academia and industry is allowed to proceed in an enlightened environment—especially when the academics serve not just as consultants, but also as initiators of research projects. (Generally, this works best in small entrepreneurial settings and not in large establishments, where Parkinson's Law is inexorably operating on a grand scale.) Like most research universities, Stanford allows its professors the equivalent of one day per week for outside, personal activities. Little, McConnell, and Goldstein divided that "free" day into four or five lunch periods at Syva, which offered them almost daily opportunities with Syva scientists. These highly focused contacts, undiluted by administrative trivia or telephone interruptions, produced intellectual sparks that benefited both constituencies. But there is no question in my mind that the professorial participation was the indispensable component to Syva's success: Little's superconductivity theory had been the raison d'être for the enterprise; McConnell's free radicals had provided the diversification; and Goldstein had pointed the way to the first practical, biomedical applications.

II

Meanwhile, a quite different sort of project, which was to become my future, had begun. The year 1968, which saw the assassinations of Martin Luther King and Robert Kennedy, the demise of Lyndon Johnson's continuing presidential dreams, and the height of student unrest, anticipated also the death knell of DDT (initiated by the Environmental Defense Fund suit that year in Wisconsin) and the birth pangs of the National Environmental Protection Act (leading to the creation of the Environmental Protection Agency)—both partly prompted by the publication of Rachel Carson's *Silent Spring*. In that year, we founded the first company dedicated solely to the development of new approaches to insect control. We were bullish enough to believe that our new baby would make obsolete DDT and other persistent pesticides, as well as the neurotoxic organophosphates. We wanted to name this company Biocon, an abbreviation for *biological* (or *biochemical*) *control* that would be subliminally obvious without raising anyone's hackles. But since that name was already in use, according to the U.S. Trademark Office, we came up with Zoecon (from the Greek *zoe*, "life"). Zoecon's research history mirrors the fundamental breakthroughs in invertebrate endocrinology that occurred in the 1960s. Its research approach made the company the invertebrate counterpart of Syntex, from whose corporate and managerial entrepreneurship it sprang.

In the 1930s and 1940s, the various steroid hormones associated with sexual and adrenal function had begun to be isolated and their chemical structures established. The 1950s saw the creation of more powerful synthetic analogs—anti-inflammatory corticosteroids, oral contraceptives, and other "biorational" drugs modeled on natural hormones—and their introduction into human medicine. Corresponding advances in invertebrate biology were delayed by thirty years. Only with the advent of sensitive modern analytical and separation techniques like mass spectrometry and gas chromatography was it possible to isolate and characterize the minute quantities of naturally occurring insect hormones and to gain some insight into the endocrinology of the arthropods, which in complexity rivals that of vertebrate animals.

Syntex's interest in insects dated from the mid-1960s, when a group of German biochemists led by Peter Karlson discovered that molting—the periodic shedding of the outer shell of insects and other arthropods—is governed by the hormone ecdysone, which they showed to be a steroid. Though structurally related to cholesterol, ecdysone bore several oxygen substituents, which made its synthesis exceedingly complicated. Only minute amounts of the hormone could be obtained, through laborious isolation from hundreds of thousands of dissected insects; for its mode of action to be studied in any detail, larger amounts would have to become available. Despite its total irrelevance to the corporate business objectives of Syntex, we were fascinated by the challenge to synthetic chemistry posed by the complexity of ecdysone. We assigned this project to a small group of chemists, among them John Siddall, a British postdoctorate research fellow who eventually became Zoecon's director of research.

The synthesis of ecdysone was so complex, and its biological function so exciting, that a number of academic and industrial groups competed to be the first to prepare adequate quantities of it. The Syntex group was the first to publish a successful ecdysone synthesis (a second method developed by a cooperative group from the Swiss pharmaceutical company Hoffmann-La Roche and the German drug house Schering, A.G., followed shortly thereafter); but we were no longer satisfied with demonstrating intellectual prowess and synthetic skill. We were tempted by the biological properties of ecdysone, which prompted us to establish a consulting relationship with Carroll M. Williams, the Harvard insect biologist. The discovery of ecdysone seemed to promise a completely new approach to insect control: instead of poisoning the bug, one might interfere with a natural process necessary for survival—such as molting—which was peculiar to arthropods and absent in vertebrates. Using ecdysone itself seemed economically hopeless—steroids are much too expensive to be used in lieu of pesticides; but if we could learn more about ecdysone's biological function, and especially about its biosynthesis within the insect's body, we might synthesize a cheaper chemical that could interfere with the periodic shedding of the outer skin.

Just as we started to gain some knowledge of insect physiology, a second endocrinological bombshell exploded. Herbert Röller, a German-born and trained insect physiologist, then teaching at my alma mater, the University of Wisconsin, announced the successful isolation, structure elucidation, and synthesis of an insect hormone that governs certain processes peculiar to the early developmental stages of insects, notably, the larval phase. Only when production of this hormone stops can the insect mature and reproduce. Carroll Williams, himself active in this field, had called attention to the potential of this hormone as a new method of insect control. What was so exciting about Röller's announcement was that his "juvenile hormone" (eventually abbreviated as JH) was a sesquiterpenoid—a substance with only seventeen carbon atoms (in contrast to the twenty-seven in ecdysone or cholesterol) and closely related to the well-known sesquiterpenes, a class of naturally occurring essential oils based on a fifteen-carbon skeleton. The structure of JH was so much simpler than that of ecdysone that one could conceive of devising a sufficiently economic synthesis of it for use in agrichemical applications. Siddall's group at Syntex completed such a synthesis in 1967. Right timing is everything—be it in love, politics, or science. Syntex's involvement with insects in the second half of the 1960s had started out of pure intellectual curiosity, flavored with chemical machismo: "Let's show them how good we really are in steroid chemistry." But Rachel Carson's *Silent Spring* had sensitized the public to the need for a different look at insect pests. As far as we at Syntex were concerned, the new science of insect hormones seemed just the key to an environmentally more benign approach, and we decided to find it.

The year 1968 was also the time when my own corporate activities really exploded. Alex Zaffaroni had decided to leave Syntex and form his own company, ALZA, dedicated to developing not more potent or specific drugs but methods of delivery. As executive vice president of Syntex Research, I was the second in command—a position I had held, however, only by utilizing efficiently the one day per week allowed full-time university professors for consulting and other outside commitments. Since my Stanford office was five minutes from Syntex's headquarters, I cannibalized that nonacademic time allowance by taking long daily lunches at Syntex. With Zaffaroni's departure, this had to change. I assumed the post of president and formally went on a half-time academic schedule. The operative term is *formally*, because in actual fact I reduced neither my academic research load nor the size of my research group. Even my teaching schedule at that time was not much lower than that of my full-time colleagues.

One of the first steps I took as president was to escalate our efforts in the insect field. I realized, as did the rest of the Syntex board and management, that this would cost real money. Even if the science went right, we estimated it would take at least $10 million for such a research effort, and we would not know for at least five years whether it was successful. In 1968, Syntex was still too small for such a gamble: the company's entire annual research and development budget was on the order of $10 million. But this was in the heyday of the go-go stock market, out of which many speculative new companies were being funded. We decided to put all of our patents, know-how, and key research personnel from our insect research into a separate company, in which Syntex would retain 49-percent ownership. The remaining 51 percent would be spun off to Syntex stockholders as a stock-rights offering for $10 million. By comparison with some of the other ventures being launched in that frenzied Wall Street climate, Zoecon seemed almost positively safe, especially since it had the virtues of scientific glamour and responsiveness to a social need.

As if I didn't have enough to do at Syntex, Syva, and Stanford, I now also became president and chairman of the board of Zoecon. We housed the company in a new building—whose parking lot backed onto the lot of Alex Zaffaroni's ALZA, enabling us to meet easily for lunch. (We had both continued a Syntex tradition, which was a luxury but also a time saver: a corporate dining room run by a first-class cook, where we could conduct our business in style and total privacy.) The initial staff of Zoecon was lean, but what we lacked in numbers, we made up in dedication and commitment. As they were in the graduate student laboratories at Stanford, the lights at Zoecon were on until all hours. Herbert Röller, who had just moved from the University of Wisconsin to a professorship at Texas A & M, served as a part-time vice president in charge of research. His principal functions were attracting the key scientists for our biological laboratories, establishing a top-notch insectary, and supervising by long distance and periodic short visits the progress of the biological program. John Siddall, who had been the key Syntex chemist on the ecdysone and juvenile hormone projects, together with a former Syntex postdoctorate fellow from Australia, Clive Henrick, headed the chemical program. Administrative and financial functions were grouped under one vice president, Dan Lazare, who had been in charge of research administration at Syntex. Two other young scientists who eventually filled key functions at Zoecon were my former Stanford Ph.D. students, John Diekman, who joined Zoecon's budding development and registration department and eventually ended up as president of the company; and David Schooley, who became the head of the insect biochemistry division and is now a professor of biochemistry at the University of Nevada.

Although most of us were agricultural greenhorns, it didn't take us long to learn why insects have managed to survive for millions of years. All one has to do to control a particular insect population, we reasoned, is expose the insect continuously to its own juvenile hormone, so that it can never mature and replicate. The farmer would have to tolerate only one generation of juvenile insects and his problems would be over. But even if that gross oversimplification were true, we discovered, the approach involved a major economic cost. The insect eats most voraciously and causes most of its economic damage during its juvenile, larval stage. It then changes into the nonfeeding pupal form before turning into a reproducing adult, after another hormone (now identified as allatostatin) shuts off the insect's production of JH by its *corpora allata*. The human counterpart to such a form of birth control would be the administration to infants of a chemical preventing the onset of puberty: although the children would never become parents, they might well survive beyond the usual time of puberty and thus certainly be costly in economic and social terms. Even this scenario, moreover, was hypothetical, because the natural JH, when administered by conventional methods such as spraying, was quite unstable. Both bacterial enzymes and sunlight decompose the natural hormone so quickly that its half-life under field conditions probably does not exceed a day or two. Administration would have to be repeated so frequently as to be prohibitively costly. We had to hope that chemical alteration of the insect juvenile hormone might create a more active variant that might be more stable under field conditions—not unlike what we had accomplished in the field of oral contraception by synthesizing a more effective congener of the natural female hormone progesterone. Finally, there are nearly one million different species of insect: How do we know that the JH Röller isolated in 1967 from the *Cecropia* moth is the same juvenile hormone in all other insect species? A group in Ohio had isolated a structurally similar substance, called JH-II, from another insect. Clearly, we could not isolate the natural juvenile hormone from every economically important insect pest. Rather, we had to settle on a few scientifically and economically relevant insect targets, which could be raised easily in an insectary and upon which we could then assay any synthetic molecules.

We decided to focus on those insect pests that cause their damage as adults. We thereby eliminated most serious agricultural pests, all of which cause havoc in their juvenile larval stage, when they feed on a particular agricultural crop. It is the public health pests—flies, mosquitoes, fleas, fire ants—that are harmless as juveniles and become dangerous or annoying as biting, stinging, or blood-sucking adults. In the 1960s and early 1970s, malaria was still the biggest killer worldwide; and the responsible vectors— the various mosquito species—were then primarily controlled by DDT. Now that DDT was being banned in many parts of the world, and some mosquito species had started to develop resistance to it and other conventional insecticides, it seemed to us that the world was ready for a new approach to mosquito control. Various mosquito *Aedes* and *Anopheles* species headed our list of target insects, followed by flies and certain beetles.

Initially, our research went well—perhaps too well. Siddall's chemistry group systematically modified the structure of Röller's JH, in the process greatly augmenting its potency. The availability of a sensitive bioassay was an essential ingredient of that research, and much of Zoecon's initial success could be attributed to the methods set up by Gerardus Staal, a Dutch entomologist, who had completed his postdoctoral studies in Carroll Williams's lab at Harvard. Until then, industrial researchers on new pesticides had simply screened new chemical candidates for their ability to kill. But we were not really searching for new insecti*cides*: a juvenile hormone mimic would not kill an insect; it would only prevent its maturation. Staal's methods had to be much more sophisticated since they had to monitor the insect's entire life span. In less than eighteen months, our chemists synthesized several hundred variants of the natural juvenile hormone and finally arrived at a structural analog 2,430 times more active than the natural hormone in Staal's *Aedes egypti* mosquito assay and much less prone to bacterial or photochemical decomposition in outdoor, aquatic environments. We christened the new compound ALTOSID (Palo Alto + John Siddall).

At our first stockholders' meeting—unlike most start-up companies, we had thousands of stockholders from the very start, because Zoecon stock had been floated through a rights offering to owners of Syntex shares—the meeting room was packed with investors who were insect novices and wanted to know what they had bought. In addition, a scoop of security analysts was there to look over the company. I knew many of them by sight from Syntex sessions, where I was usually one of the two representatives of top management reporting on Syntex's progress. Thus, we were no slouches when it came to stockholders' or analysts' meetings, and we put on quite a show. After my own presentation, Herbert Röller waxed enthusiastic—

his polished, though somewhat convoluted sentences, delivered in a German accent, making him a scientist's version of Thomas Mann—about the exciting potential of our insect growth regulators (IGRs)—the new term we had introduced to differentiate our products from conventional insecticides. He finished by showing color slides of the insect freaks resulting from exposure to minute amounts of JH—the few flies that managed to emerge from their pupae without wings, the Colorado beetles looking like arthropod lepers, and the cream-colored corn leafhopper suddenly turned pitch-black. When he asked, triumphantly, "Any questions?" the proverbial old lady stockholder in tennis shoes raised her hand. "But Dr. Roller," she exclaimed indignantly, blithely ignoring the carefully cultivated umlaut in his name, "aren't you *sorry* for the little beasts? Just look what you've done to them!" Röller stared at the woman, his mouth agape. For fifteen pregnant seconds, the room so still that one could have heard a buzzing insect. "No!" he bellowed suddenly, and brought down the house.

But we, who were used to designing drugs for humans, had to take a sudden cold shower as we confronted the realities of the pest-control marketplace. Cost and price are never total blockades of a truly important new drug in humans—one that alleviates suffering or prevents death in the affluent world upon which most pharmaceutical companies focus. The situation is different for the prevention of disease or of deterioration in agricultural commodities. The marketplace completely controls what a grower can pay to prevent the spoilage of apples, the destruction of cotton, the rusting of wheat. It makes no difference how environmentally harmless or how biodegradable the new insect control agent is: if it exceeds the amount allowable in the farmer's highly constrained budget, the apple is allowed to rot, the field plowed over. This we knew; but it took us some time to realize how little people are willing to pay for the wholesale control of public health pests at the breeding places; how little premium is placed upon preventive rather than acute control. Most people are willing to do something about mosquitoes that are biting them; fewer are willing to take seriously future generations of mosquitoes that may never appear. IGRs also have an inherent disadvantage: while they can occasionally be administered even to mature insects (their growth-regulating effect is transmittable in some species to the next generation through a "venereal" mechanism), the exposure time is usually limited to a window of opportunity during the larval stage. Our highly biodegradable product has to be administered at the correct time, as a persistent pesticide, like DDT, does not. Furthermore, for mosquito control by means of ALTOSID to be effective, it must be carried out on a large scale, typically by mosquito-abatement districts or other public agencies. There would be little purpose in applying the material to a pond in one's backyard if the neighboring swamp is not treated.

To gain public attention, we concluded, we had to focus on an operationally convenient problem, rather than on the largest possible market; and we looked to a problem in California's most important industry. Most agriculture in California is performed in irrigated areas and involves intense pesticide use. By the early 1970s, mosquitoes in floodwater-irrigated fields had become resistant to DDT and other insecticides. Only spraying with oil worked, but this control procedure did not seem sensible during the height of the OPEC-induced petroleum shortage. In addition, outbreaks of equine encephalitis—spread by a mosquito vector—had been reported in the delta region of northern California. Therefore, we decided to home in on floodwater-mosquito control, since the IGR-vulnerable larvae accumulated only during the irrigation period—a short enough time for ALTOSID (formulated in microencapsulated form) to survive unchanged.

Before conducting field trials, we had to determine the potential toxicity of ALTOSID. We first had to establish its LD_{50} acute toxicity—the lethal dose when 50 percent of the animals fail to survive—so as to settle on a sublethal dose to be fed to rodents and dogs for periods long enough to uncover carcinogenicity or other serious problems. Our first tests were spectacular: we could not determine the LD_{50} of ALTOSID because we could not administer enough of it to kill *any* rats. We had to stop administering when we reached the enormous, though apparently harmless, level of 35 grams per kilogram of body weight, because excretion outstripped administration. Our exultation at this spectacular demonstration of harmlessness must have provoked the gods. Instead of complimenting us, the EPA chided us for not having found a lethal dose, and asked us to try again in other animals. The agency, accustomed to dealing with toxic pesticides, did not know how to handle Zoecon's innocuous ALTOSID. Other delays were more complimentary in a backhanded sort of way. In view of the novelty of our approach—soon anointed by the media as "third-generation pesticides"—our application was passed around to officials in the EPA who ordinarily would not have had anything to do with the registration of a new insecticide; they were simply curious. The longest delays occurred because ALTOSID, since it would be sprayed on floodwater, had to be shown innocuous to other aquatic, nontarget organisms. The requested list seemed Sisyphean: by the time we finally received EPA approval for field applications, ALTOSID's lack of toxicity had been demonstrated in water fleas, protozoa, copepods, sideswimmers, aquatic earthworms, mudworms, leeches, tadpoles, and snails; in mosquito fish, bluegill, trout, channel catfish, coho salmon, carp, and stickleback; in crustaceans like seashore crabs, blue crabs, mud crabs, crayfish, acorn barnacles, and various species of shrimp. By that time we didn't have to be asked about oysters; we threw them in voluntarily.

All this, of course, made sense from the standpoint of a cautious regulatory agency facing a completely new type of pesticide registration. They, or the public, couldn't have cared less if we had pointed out that blockbuster drugs for humans, commanding annual sales in the many hundreds of million dollars, required only a fraction of such toxicological scrutiny. A hard-nosed businessman would have thrown in the towel long before this—especially if he had known that our eventual annual IGR sales for California floodwater mosquito control would barely reach $1 million. But we were stubborn: we felt that we had to demonstrate the practicality of IGR-promoted insect control with some concrete example; and that if we could accomplish this in an aquatic environment, all future applications would have an easier passage through the bureaucratic maze of the EPA. In fact, one of the most persuasive indications of ALTOSID's safety margin was the World Health Organization's eventual recommendation that our IGR could be added to human drinking water—a feature that proved useful for malaria control in countries like Thailand, where drinking water is frequently stored in open vessels that are potential mosquito breeding grounds.

III

It might be asked how we managed to sustain such expensive and time-consuming development efforts, and how we thought we could compete with the industrial Goliaths—Shell, DuPont, Dow—that were our competitors. We did have one thing going for us: they had huge markets of conventional pesticides to defend, while we could focus on something brand-new. Still, we could not have made it if we had depended solely on our original new venture dowry; but while I am quite willing to gamble in research, I am a fiscal conservative. Within a year of Zoecon's creation—with our share price holding up well in the stock market based on future expectations—we hired a consultant to identify for us a corporate acquisition candidate with certain criteria: experience in some market niche of the pesticide field; profitable, but weak in research and development; not publicly traded and hence attracted by a company listed on the stock exchange; and small enough so that we would remain the controlling entity.

We found just such a willing corporate bride in Thuron Industries, a $5-million company founded in Dallas by two chemist brothers, Thurman and Byron Williamson. Thuron concentrated on the animal health market, with emphasis on fleas, ticks, and other ectoparasites. They had no research and were marketing conventional pesticides in novel formulations they manufactured themselves, such as the plastic flea collar for dogs and cats, which they were about to bring on the market when we acquired Thuron. Within a couple of years of our merger, Zoecon's Dallas subsidiary became the largest manufacturer of pet flea collars in the world. In the crude terms of high finance, Thuron became our cash cow. Three years after we had launched Zoecon with a $10-million stock offering, we still had that much money in the bank and were already approaching the $10-million annual sales level. Those figures caused no ripple of concern in the boardrooms of our billion-dollar competitors, several of whom had predicted our prompt demise; but they gave us sufficient financial muscle to pursue an ambitious goal: to be the first company to receive EPA approval for commercial use of an insect-growth regulator in lieu of conventional insecticides.

Concurrently with our insect hormone research, we undertook a second R&D program in insect pheromones, and especially sex attractants, many of which had only recently been isolated and identified. Clive Henrick's group undertook the synthesis of attractants specific to some of the major economic pests; and by the early 1970s, we had become the largest and most diverse supplier of pheromones in the world. We were able to enter this market very quickly, because it did not require approval by the EPA. At that time, pheromones were simply used as monitoring devices. Rubber stoppers containing minute quantities of the pure chemical were placed in sticky traps that were hung on trees or bushes. Periodic canvassing of these traps by entomologists provided a qualitative and quantitative indication of insect infestation. Since this monitor market was, of course, quite small, large pesticide companies had paid no attention to it. We, however, were then so small that even boutique markets seemed attractive, especially if they also carried a socially beneficial message. We considered pheromones to be an effective way of spreading our name among professional entomologists and the lay public.

One way of doing this was through our annual reports to stockholders. In contrast to the glossy, multicolored but frequently somniferous corporate reports, Zoecon's was produced in the format of a newsmagazine, with the requisite financial information in an appendix. Each year, we featured a major article on a topic of technical and social interest, with some relevance to Zoecon's corporate objectives. These articles were so timely and well written that college teachers frequently asked us for multiple copies. The annual report for 1971 contained an article entitled "The Language of Scent" by Morton Grosser. To this brilliant piece on pheromones, we added olfactory garnish by printing the entire annual report in odoriferous ink—a woodsy, pine odor, commensurate with our perceived corporate image. Having, however, neglected to inform our transfer agent, the Wells Fargo Bank, of this tongue-in-cheek PR ploy, we soon received a panicky call from a bank officer—"Your report smells!"—when the cartons containing fifteen thousand copies arrived from the printer. The report was quite a success, even getting a comment from the *San Francisco Chronicle*'s star columnist, Herb Caen, to the effect that ours was the first truly, rather than just figuratively, odoriferous annual report in American corporate history. The fame of our annual reports spread even into literature in Arthur Herzog's 1974 novel, *The Swarm*, which describes the invasion of the African killer bee and the resulting virtual immobilization of New York City. A state of emergency is declared by the President, and the Defense Department selects Zoecon's ALTOSID as one means of combating the invasion: "The insect growth regulator (IGR) was manufactured by Zoecon, a California company that specialized in insecticide alternatives. To produce IGR on the scale necessary demanded a thousand-gallon capacity, which Zoecon had." (I hope Herzog will not consider me ungrateful if I note that in 1974 we, in fact, had a 2,000-gallon reactor in our small chemical plant in East Palo Alto.) Herzog's book, which became the basis of a Hollywood film script, acknowledged Zoecon's 1970 annual report as the inspiration for some of the scenes.

Literary panache and perfumed reports are not necessarily signs of financial success; in fact, Zoecon would never have emerged from its pupal shell if the company had depended solely on marketing IGRs for mosquito control and pheromones for insect monitoring. Our early field trials, however, had taught us a lot, and so had our market-savvy Texan associates at Thuron (soon thereafter renamed Zoccon Industries). I was so convinced that Zoecon would become a viable adult company that I decided at the end of 1972 to stake my industrial career on this conviction and to resign from Syntex.

The synergy with our Texas marketing group manifested itself in various ways. One of the products Thuron Industries had sold for a number of years was Golden Malrin, a conventional organophosphate neurotoxin mixed with a sugar bait to attract flies, which would then be killed instantaneously. When Thuron became part of Zoecon, we used Golden Malrin as one of the first practical demonstrations of how pheromones can improve the efficacy of a conventional pesticide. We synthesized muscalure, the natural pheromone attractant of the house fly (*Musca domestica*) and added it to Golden Malrin, thus bringing many more flies to the bait. A second, and more innovative, method of fly control was also developed as a result of our Thuron acquisition—this time by taking advantage of our insect hormone work.

Flies are, like mosquitoes, prime candidates for IGR control of insects, because they are bothersome only as adults. Biting flies like the horn fly so irritate cattle as to affect their feeding habits and cause weight loss. The cradle and the nursery of the horn fly is cattle manure. With range cattle, therefore, entire fields would have to be sprayed periodically with conventional insecticides to cover all of the old and new fecal droppings. Gerardus Staal had found ALTOSID to be highly effective in inhibiting the maturation of horn fly pupae into adult flies, but the question was how to administer the active agent. This is where Thuron's experience with animal pests came to the rescue. The company introduced us to MoorMan's, one of the country's largest suppliers of mineral blocks, which the cattle lick freely to supplement their salt and mineral consumption. In collaboration with MoorMan's staff, we formulated ALTOSID into one of their salt blocks and discovered that enough of our IGR, so ingested by the animal, would pass in undecomposed form through its alimentary canal, that every time the beast defecated, it deposited with its feces a small amount of ALTOSID, which completely inhibited any maturation of horn flies. We had planted a highly efficient and totally nontoxic insect-control agent, which decomposes into natural, innocuous chemicals like water, carbon dioxide, and acetic acid, into every fecal dropping—by converting the animal itself into the delivery system. Reducing the chemical load in the environment is clearly one of the main objectives of future pest control, and our salt blocks certainly accomplished that aim. This method of horn fly control was approved by the EPA in 1975, the same year in which we received government approval for our IGR mosquito product. Economically, the former proved to be much more important to Zoecon.

A juvenile hormone mimic, like ALTOSID, cannot be used in the control of agricultural pests since the IGR increases the life span and even the size of the damage-producing larvae, giving rise at times to monster-sized ones. We discovered, however, an interesting economic use of this apparent shortcoming. In Japan, China, India, and a few other countries with a natural silk industry, silkworm larvae are carefully grown on trays and fed mulberry leaves in order to spin their larval cocoons. At the end of that growth period, the cocoons are unwound to yield the precious silk fiber. We discovered that administration of small amounts of our IGR to young silkworm larvae increased their lifetime and size to such an extent that from 15 percent to 40 percent more silk was produced by such hormonally stimulated insects. In 1976, we received approval by the Japanese government for marketing our IGR, under the trade name MANTA, as a "silkworm production enhancer."

IV

By 1976, Zoecon's position in the insect field mirrored that of Syntex twenty years earlier in pharmaceuticals: we were hardly known by farmers or the public; but in scientific circles, we had become known internationally for the quality and quantity of our publications on insect hormones and pheromones. Even some of the snickering Goliaths among our industrial competition had begun to think of us as a David; especially since we had now decided that we needed to get our fingers wet in the larger area of agricultural crop protection. Our financial resources were still so modest that we could afford to focus only on a single, new, major research topic. I challenged our synthetic chemistry group, under Clive Henrick, to come up within two years with a patentable and more cost-effective analog of the natural insecticide found in pyrethrum flowers. It was then believed that such "synthetic pyrethroids" would replace many of the more conventional insecticides used by the cotton industry (then the most insecticide-consuming crop in the United States) and by fruit growers. Only three of the largest agrichemical companies—Shell, Imperial Chemical Industries (ICI), and FMC Corporation—were then in the market, all of them with products developed abroad in Great Britain and Japan. If we were successful in creating such a proprietary pyrethroid, we could probably entice a large company to fund much of our research in return for co-marketing rights, as Syntex had enticed Lilly in the 1950s. My decision to try to repeat this scoop with Zoecon ultimately resulted in the company being swallowed up—not once, but twice.

For the first seven years of Zoecon's existence until 1975, Syntex had remained the largest stockholder. This had complicated some commercial negotiations with other companies, who were never sure whether they were dealing with Zoecon—a small, insignificant competitor in the insect field—or with a surrogate of Syntex, potentially a much larger rival. It became clear that we would have to be totally independent before we could undertake the type of commercial initiative I had in mind. The Syntex board agreed to distribute to Syntex shareholders its remaining shares of Zoecon as a stock dividend. As a consequence, we suddenly became a totally independent company and at the same time had gained a large number of new stockholders: the recipients of Syntex's largesse.

I first approached the Monsanto Corporation about funding our new program on synthetic pyrethroids. A number of years earlier, this chemical giant had dropped insecticide research to concentrate on herbicides, a field in which they became one of America's leaders. Monsanto agreed that a new synthetic pyrethrum analog would be very attractive for them, but they were not sure we would be successful in our ambitious time schedule. "Come see us when you are closer to your goal" was the message of their president. In other words, they wanted us to fund all of the research by ourselves and talk about commercial arrangements only when the risk was negligible. Then an unexpected partner appeared in the form of the Occidental Petroleum Corporation, or Oxy, headed by Dr. Armand Hammer, Lenin's first capitalist friend after the Bolsheviks took over.

At a Stanford dinner in late 1976, I represented our chemistry department's Industrial Affiliate Program, which sought to raise unrestricted funds from a group of corporations in return for their attendance at technical symposia and for their sending research staff on sabbatical leave to Stanford. One of my dinner partners was Donald Baeder, a former research executive from Exxon, who had just accepted a position as vice president in charge of research of Oxy. The company had a large agrichemical division that did little research and sold primarily commodity agrichemicals, including fertilizers. Baeder knew about Zoecon and our research success with IGRs. When he heard about our synthetic pyrethroid plans, he became our most effective advocate in Oxy's management. Soon after, Zoecon signed a virtual duplicate of the Syntex-Lilly agreement with the Hooker Chemical Corporation, the billion-dollar division of Oxy responsible for marketing pesticides. (Hooker's notoriety and association with the chemical contamination of Love Canal in Niagara Falls surfaced only later.) By early 1977, we had narrowed down our choice of pyrethroid to four promising compounds, which merited more preliminary field trials. I showed my pride in our group's success with an I-told-you-so swagger, which Baeder, who had just been promoted to president of the Hooker Chemical Division, amplified within Oxy by his own pleasure with our research performance. By then, our sales of IGRs, pheromones, dog and cat flea collars, and other Thuron products had reached $30 million; this success, combined with our research prospects, convinced us that we could raise additional capital on Wall Street through a secondary stock offering.

The sale of the additional shares of stock was scheduled for a Wednesday morning. On Monday, I received a telephone call from Don Baeder asking whether I could meet on Tuesday with Dr. Hammer ("the Doctor," in Oxy parlance) in Los Angeles; he was due that morning from Moscow and wanted to discuss some matter of mutual interest. I had never met Hammer, but had heard plenty about him. I even suspected what was on his mind. At an earlier meeting with some Hooker executives, I had overheard the question "Why buy just the milk? Why not the cow?" I had the feeling that I, for once, was going to be the propositioned rather than the propositioner. I decided to be cool. "I can't," I said. "Not Tuesday morning. I teach a class in the morning, and I have a seminar in the afternoon." I did, in fact, have those academic commitments, and as a matter of principle, I never canceled them. I offered to fly to Los Angeles on Wednesday (after our stock sale had gone through), but Baeder refused to take no for an answer. Could I meet the Doctor and Oxy's president on Tuesday at six P.M.? "Impossible," I replied. "I can't leave the campus until four fifteen, and by the time I get to the San Francisco airport, fly to L.A. and then take a cab—" That's when I learned about Dr. Hammer's style of traveling. "If you can get to the San Jose airport by four forty-five P.M.," they assured me to my amazement, "we'll get you to the Doctor's office on Wilshire Boulevard by six."

I had barely entered the San Jose terminal when a young man in coat and tie approached me. "Dr. Djerassi," he said, as if I'd had a label on my forehead, "this way, please." On the tarmac, among the many single-engined private planes, was a sleek jet, its engines humming. I ascended the steps, the door closed behind me, and off we went. I was presented with the *Wall Street Journal* and a shrimp cocktail. I refused the former, having brought with me a thin anthology of imagist poetry which I browsed in as I nibbled on the shrimp. The moment I deplaned in Los Angeles, another young man led me to a nearby helicopter, its rotor blade whirling impatiently; ten minutes later, I was deposited on the roof of the office building housing the corporate headquarters of the Occidental Petroleum Corporation.

Dr. Hammer's office at that time was small and unpretentious, unlike the palatial quarters he occupied a few years later. But I couldn't help stare at the battalion of photographs lined up on the table behind his desk, featuring inscribed pictures of all the American presidents since Franklin Roosevelt and of various heads of state, notably of the Soviet Union. I doubt whether any other capitalist tycoon can boast of having an autographed photo with the handwritten legend "To comrade Armand Hammer from V. I. Ulyanov (Lenin) 10.XI.1921." Although nearly eighty and having returned only that morning from Moscow, Dr. Hammer was wide-awake and charming. While Don Baeder and Joe Baird, the president of the company, listened respectfully, Hammer told me stories of his early medical education, before he took off for the Soviet Union shortly after the Russian Revolution as a budding capitalist entrepreneur. He knew a great deal about Syntex and especially about Charles Allen, whose firm was Syntex's as well as Zoecon's investment banker. I had heard rumors about Hammer's legal battles with Allen & Company concerning Oxy's initial development of the Libyan oil fields, but the Doctor gave them a bygones-be-bygones shrug, though not before informing me that he *had* won the suit. The conversation then shifted to cattle—I had just divorced my second wife and was living at my ranch—and then to art, since we were both collectors (although I was hardly in Hammer's class).

When it got to be seven o'clock, and I was getting hungry and wondering how long our social chitchat would go on, Dr. Hammer suddenly leaned forward and, shifting without warning into his tycoon mode, said he would offer a 30-percent premium to Zoecon's stockholders to acquire our company. Responding like a coy maiden to the marriage proposal of a rich old suitor, I asked, "What's in it for us in the long run?" and pointed out that the real assets of Zoecon were its research aims and the people working on them. Before discussing any stock premium, we had to be assured of operating independence, that increased funding for our ambitious research plans would be forthcoming, and that our views about the future of insect control would continue to be supported. Only after Hammer and his two colleagues had convinced me that their vigorous nodding on these topics was indeed serious, did we return to the *mano a mano* bargaining the Doctor enjoyed most. I had two aces in my hand: in less than twelve hours, we would be selling several million dollars' worth of Zoecon shares, which, if we did not reach an agreement that very evening, Oxy would have to buy in addition to the outstanding stock. Yet an unfriendly, direct stock tender by Oxy to our stockholders could well turn into a Pyrrhic victory, if Zoecon's key scientists and management did not remain with the company. Oxy might end up with a cow producing thin, sour milk.

By eight o'clock, we had reached a handshake agreement on an 80-percent premium to be paid Zoecon stockholders—an offer our board of directors would certainly have to consider seriously. The problem was that only a few hours were left for aborting Zoecon's stock sale on Wednesday. I telephoned our corporate secretary to arrange for a special meeting of our directors for 10:00 P.M. and to ask our two nonresident members, one in New York and the other in St. Louis, to participate by speaker telephone. Iron in constitution, Hammer assured me that I could call him even after midnight about the decision of the board. I went back on the roof, climbed into the waiting helicopter, and repeated in reverse the trip of a few hours before. With no more shrimp on board the company jet, I had to assuage the gnawing in my stomach with more imagist poems. At least, Wallace Stevens's lines, "I do not know which to prefer,/ The beauty of inflections/

173

Or the beauty of innuendoes," offered food for thought about how to approach the Zoecon board.

The lights were blazing in the corporate office wing of Zoecon as I drove up, shortly before 10:00 P.M. We had a full attendance—in person or by telephone; and by midnight, the directors had agreed unanimously to accept the Oxy proposal and to cancel the Wednesday stock offering. The investment bankers handling that sale were deeply disappointed. I suspect that to this day they refuse to believe that we had no advance notice of the Hammer proposal.

Oxy's ownership of Zoecon lasted five years—the managerial lifetime of three Occidental Petroleum Corporation presidents. But if it was not easy to be president of the parent company under the Doctor's chairmanship, it was neither difficult nor unpleasant to serve as president of the Zoecon division of Occidental Petroleum. Hammer and his itinerant presidents stuck to their bargain: they never second-guessed us in our research priorities and afforded us, the smallest of all of Oxy's divisions, a degree of autonomy that none of the others enjoyed. Our research budget more than tripled during those five years; Oxy even provided us with the funds to purchase a small seed company, headquartered in Alabama, which undertook pioneering research with the aim of introducing hybrid cotton and rice into the United States. In the penultimate year of our corporate union, Oxy went along with still another incremental financial and operational expansion: the creation of Zoecon's molecular biology division, one of the first industrial laboratories to focus on agricultural applications of genetic engineering.

One feature of Zoecon's earlier life, our innovative annual reports, did bite the dust when we became part of Occidental Petroleum; but even here, we contributed to the uniqueness of one of Occidental's annual reports—if in microscopic fashion and in a way carefully kept from Dr. Hammer and all other members of Oxy's top management. These reports had a standard format: first, a letter to stockholders, adorned by a large picture of the Doctor with the then-reigning president, exuding optimism and "appreciation for the dedicated efforts of Occidental's men and women." Then came the more detailed operational results of the three main groups—Oil and Gas, Coal, and Chemicals—with smaller photographs of the various group and division presidents. Zoecon's report was included with the Chemical Division (Hooker), and I appeared in the group photograph of the six Hooker divisional presidents taken during one of my monthly visits to the Hooker headquarters in Houston. In the photo taken for the 1979 report, Corporate Relations in Los Angeles noticed just in time that one of the six presidents—contrary to firm company policy—was smiling. When first told of my faux pas, I took it as a premature April Fool's Day joke, but inspection of the last few annual reports confirmed that, except for a faint suspicion of a smile on the Doctor's face, everybody looked grimly serious. Moreover, this president was shown wearing a turtleneck sweater instead of a tie. My protest that I always wear turtlenecks in the winter was met with a snort over the phone and a request to fly to Houston for another presidential group picture, this time wearing a tie and a serious look. I categorically refused, pointing out that my smile and turtleneck would not have the slightest effect on Oxy's corporate image or the value of its stock. A crisis of major proportions in my corporate life was defused only when the telephone voice compromised by asking that I contribute a snapshot showing me with serious mien. I obliged, and a new group photo was shot in Houston. My tie-wearing stand-in was photographically decapitated, my nonsmiling head substituted, and the new tableau submitted to Los Angeles, where it passed scrutiny. I wonder how many readers of the 1979 Occidental Petroleum Corporation Annual Report noticed that one of the Chemical Division's group presidents lacked a neck. The day after my neckless picture appeared, a member of Oxy's publicity department sent me another photograph with the legend, "We just caught this in time!" It showed the same group picture, except that in it my head had been grafted onto a woman's torso.

V

After five years under Oxy's wings, Zoecon's sales had crossed the $100-million mark, the bulk of the profits coming from the sale of IGRs for insects *other* than mosquitoes and flies. One of these pests I would have thought especially improbable, since I am, and always have been, an undisguised tobaccophobe. But when an entomologist from the Philip Morris Company contacted Zoecon about ALTOSID's effectiveness against the cigarette beetle, which feeds on stored tobacco leaves, we were intrigued. When the wooden hogsheads, each containing one thousand pounds of tobacco, are opened, after many months of storage, their contents are on occasion useless for cigarette manufacture owing to the ravages of hungry beetles. In spite of the health hazards of cigarettes, the tobacco companies are loath to use new chemical agents—in part, because they do not wish to be accused of adding more potential toxins; in part, because of possible effects on taste. But since our ALTOSID had been shown to be both harmless and active in extremely low dosages, the Philip Morris entomologist convinced his company that once its laboratory efficacy on the cigarette beetle and another pest, the tobacco moth, had been demonstrated, larger-scale trials should be initiated. His management agreed to underwrite some warehouse experiments, putting at risk $2 million worth of tobacco. The experiment worked, and a series of taste tests demonstrated that ALTOSID-treated tobacco could not be distinguished from untreated material. When in 1979 we celebrated receipt of the EPA registration, I made the rash promise to be photographed with a cigar once we reached the first $1-million sales of KABAT (*tabac* spelled backward), our special IGR formulation for protection of stored tobacco. (More than one colleague pointed out that I had thereby established the price at which my principles were for sale.) It took some time before my bluff was called, because Philip Morris was not prepared to use KABAT until their competitors joined in. Philip Morris was afraid that rumors would be spread about "hormone-treated" tobacco. If KABAT prevented beetles from maturing, couldn't someone claim that it might do the same to smokers of Marlboro or Lucky Strike? But eventually KABAT became the first significant crop-protection application of an insect juvenile hormone mimic. (IGR-mediated protection from attack by beetles of other stored commodities, such as peanuts, followed later.) When the time finally came, I weaseled out of my promise by claiming to have agreed only to be photographed *with* a cigar. The phallic object pressed into my hand for the photo was never lit, nor did it even cross my lips.

But in the end, the real payback for the years of research and multispecies toxicology came from fleas and cockroaches. These pests are usually thought of as the bane of the poor, who can hardly afford the cheapest of conventional insecticides, let alone a relatively expensive insect-growth regulator. In the United States, however, fleas are largely a sign of affluence: carpets, upholstery, and drapes are ideal breeding grounds for fleas, which the family pet introduces continually into the suburban home. (On both an absolute and a per-capita basis, Americans lead the world in dog and cat ownership.) Few people are aware of the flea's proclivity for survival: the insect is difficult to kill and reproduces prolifically all year long, its development time from egg to adult spanning a period of two weeks to several months. Once fed, adult fleas can be kept alive for fifty to a hundred days without further nourishment, while unfed ones can survive as long as two years; thus, fleas can suddenly appear in a home that has not seen a cat or a dog for weeks or even months. Nor are fleas only itch- and scratch-producing nuisances; they spread serious diseases such as bubonic plague. This type of horror scenario can convert even the most apathetic of affluent pet owners into a potential customer. Our Texas colleagues, with years of experience in flea control by means of conventional insecticides, knew how to formulate our IGR, christened PRECOR, in aerosol and fogger forms, which were the usual means for household application. Tests on flea-infested carpets treated with PRECOR demonstrated almost total inhibition of adult flea emergence for as long as three months; and when the EPA gave us marketing approval in 1980, we thought that Zoecon and PRECOR would soon become household words. It didn't take us long to learn the facts of life in the commercial jungle of consumer pest-control products.

Although niche markets, such as veterinarians and professional pest-control operators, were not difficult to penetrate, the projected multi-million-dollar bonanza required that we appear on supermarket shelves. We couldn't compete with billion-dollar colossi like S. C. Johnson, which controls nearly half the domestic insecticide market and whose annual advertising budgets exceed Zoecon's total corporate sales. Instead, we started out with a micro-Johnsonian advertising campaign in a few test markets in the South—Miami, New Orleans, and Houston—helped by a small public relations firm whose function it was to secure us affordable TV exposure. "Affordable" in our case meant "free," and this is how my brief career as a media pitchman first blossomed.

On the face of it, choosing me to represent Zoecon to the public, in the manner in which Chrysler's chief executive officer Lee Iacocca promoted his company's automobiles on TV, seemed to me preposterous. I was thinking not just of the quantitative difference, which in magnitude corresponded to that existing between a bus and a flea, but also of the fact that Chrysler was prepared to shell out millions, while we didn't offer one cent. Our PR advisor, however, decided that we should take advantage of my accent, my bearded professorial appearance, and my scientific reputation. We filmed a brief interview in the Zoecon laboratories, during which I explained how our Zoecon approach to flea birth control did not differ much, philosophically, from our Syntex research on the human birth control pill. This was followed, in the commercial, by a film clip of our insectary, where, in his heavy Dutch accent, Gerardus Staal gave a deadpan account of the flea's sex life. The videocassettes were sent to the TV stations in our test markets; and with hardly an exception, the bait—"Father of the Pill announces new birth control for fleas"—was swallowed. Many of the stations supplemented this prepackaged promotional material, camouflaged as science news, with personal appearances by me, in which talk of oral contraceptives in humans frequently overshadowed that of fleas. But this was not the end of free media coverage. For a few weeks after a brief article in *USA Today* on our solution to the domestic flea problem generated an avalanche of phone calls from radio talk shows all over the country, fleas became the center and bane of my daily life. I didn't have any fleas in my home, but I scratched in my dreams.

This flurry of publicity gained us entrée into important supermarket chains, but the real success depended on getting adequate shelf space, so that the customer saw the product before buying. Since we had only a single product, the supermarkets offered us precious small space, but even that was too much for our competitors, the big boys. Their roving employees or surrogates periodically patrolled supermarket aisles and moved our black and orange containers out of sight behind a screen of their own packages. Unable to beat them, we decided to join them: we offered marketing rights to some of our largest competitors, who had to purchase the patented active ingredient, PRECOR, from Zoecon, but then packaged and sold it under their own label and trademark. Customers equipped with magnifying glasses and sufficient curiosity can find our credit line near the bottom of the can.

VI

Toward the end of Zoecon's fifth year in Oxy-land, the Doctor made the biggest acquisition of his long collector's career: he bought the much larger Cities Service Company and, in the process, shouldered a multibillion-dollar debt. The acquisition made perfect business sense for Oxy's largest and most profitable division (Oil and Gas), but it also meant that Oxy would have to divest itself of many ancillary businesses to reduce its massive debt. We were a logical candidate: even though we had crossed the $100-million sales level, we were still small potatoes in the huge Oxy patch. Our value had increased greatly over what Hammer had paid five years earlier, however, and Oxy stood to make a handsome profit. The Doctor realized that we would be our own best salesmen; and in contrast to some of the other divestiture candidates, whose future was decided for them in Los Angeles, we were given the responsibility of selling ourselves. I acted as Zoecon's chief spokesperson in that endeavor—a role that, had I not taken care, might have reduced me to the level of used-car salesman. Instead, I emphasized in every presentation to potential purchasers that they were dealing with a unique racing car, small but powerful, that was designed to win the Le Mans races of the future, rather than just next year's competition. But first I consulted Zoecon's key managers to help me construct a priority list of some three dozen companies from the chemical, petroleum, pesticide, and pharmaceutical sectors. Since our emphasis was research on novel approaches to pest control in the 1990s and beyond, we felt that only a corporation comfortable with long lead times and experienced with the barriers imposed by government regulatory agencies would make sense for us. We placed foreign pharmaceutical companies on the top of our wish list, on the assumption that a non-American enterprise wishing to break into the U.S. market would be more likely to offer us the autonomy we enjoyed under Oxy ownership. We did manage to attract such an enterprise, but the autonomy did not follow.

After ten months of vigorous presentations to over a dozen candidates, Zoecon was bought in 1983 by Sandoz, Ltd., one of the big three Swiss pharmaceutical companies headquartered in Basel. Unlike Oxy, Sandoz understood our business and research objectives very well; long lead times and government regulatory requirements were nothing new to a company that is invariably among the ten largest drug houses in the world. In the American agrichemical field, however, Sandoz played a relatively small role, their main product being the bacterial pathogen *Bacillus thuringensis*, which is generally considered a "soft" insecticide and environmentally superior to chemical pesticides. (It paralyzes the gut of most lepidopterous larvae, which include some of the most important insect pests in the world.) There seemed considerable synergy, therefore; and as soon as the acquisition of Zoecon was completed, Sandoz's small U.S. agrichemical arm was folded into Zoecon, and we became their American presence in that field. I remained as chairman of the board of directors, which otherwise consisted of Swiss appointees from Basel, and our executive vice president, Dr. Alexander Cross (whom, a few years earlier, I had brought over from Syntex), became the president. Nominally, it appeared that little had changed in Zoecon's management, but in actual fact all important decisions were now made with Swiss thoroughness in Basel. In my experience, the proverbial description of life in Switzerland—"what is not forbidden seems proscribed"—applies with equal force to the corporate sphere.

It was during the first three years of our Swiss corporate existence in the middle 1980s that cockroaches entered my life. More money is spent on cockroaches than any other insect pest in the home: not because they cause more damage, although they can feed on just about everything (fruit, crackers, garbage, marijuana, grease, beer, Coke—which they prefer to Diet Coke); but because people find them more repulsive. Almost invariably, the cockroach can be found at or near the top of every entomophobe's hate list. The distaste carries over into national name calling: the Poles call their cockroaches Russian, the French refer to them as Prussian, and the Germans reciprocate by naming them *Franzosen*. One can even find local nuances: within Germany, the Prussians christen them *Schwaben*.

The huge American cockroach (*Periplaneta americana*) is not very fecund: one female will produce at most 800 annual descendants. By far the most common pest in the United States is the German cockroach (*Blatella germanica*), which, though one third the size of its American cousin, is spectacularly prolific. One female produces a capsule containing 30 to 48 eggs, which mature within 36 days. In theory, in a warm, moist setting, wherever there are cracks, holes, and dirt, a single adult can be responsible for up to 400,000 cockroach descendants in one year! As with fleas, the poor have more need for cockroach control (a government survey of low-income urban housing in central Florida showed the presence of 13,000 to 26,000 cockroaches per apartment), but only the affluent can afford to do something about the problem.

Initial cage experiments in our insectary led us to develop a more powerful analog to ALTOSID (by then also known under the generic term METHOPRENE) generically named HYDROPRENE, which had passed EPA requirements by 1983. The trouble with our birth control approach— using a juvenile hormone to extend the life of the immature "nymphal" stage of the roach so that neither female nor male adults can reproduce—is that people must be willing to put up with live cockroaches for weeks until the current generation has died out from natural causes. While this might be acceptable to the environmentalists—a clear minority among the entomophobes—the real cockroach hater wants to see *dead* roaches or, even better, *no* roaches. Therefore, our cockroach IGR, under the trade name GENCOR, was usually mixed with a pyrethrum insecticide, which is known to kill cockroaches on contact. Our marketing group in Texas wanted to give GENCOR in supermarkets another try under our own label; now we would have two products for the shelves, PRECOR for fleas and GENCOR for cockroaches. More cautious heads in Switzerland prevailed, however; and we licensed the marketing right to our cockroach IGR to American Home Products Corporation, which sells household insecticides under the Black Flag label. Having heard about my mini-Iacocca performances with fleas, their New York public relations firm asked whether I would expand my TV repertoire to cockroaches.

I premiered on the cockroach circuit in Orlando, Florida, where newspapers were at the time full of stories of sightings of the Asian cockroach, *Blattella asahinai* (not to be confused with the Oriental cockroach, *Blattella orientalis*, a common outdoor roach). In contrast to the German cockroach, which it resembles in size and superfecundity, the new Asian immigrant can fly. Its mobility in a solo flight has been tracked over a distance of 120 feet—enough to strike terror into every Florida suburb. I did TV interviews on the same day in four local stations: the mother of Zoecon's newest president, John Diekman, was astonished to see her son's former professor pontificating about cockroaches on her favorite Orlando channel one afternoon, then again on the new channel she switched to, then again on the evening news of a third channel! My professorial spiel started with my early work in the 1950s on steroid oral contraceptives, then noted the conceptual similarity between Zoecon's research and the development of the Pill, and ended by calling GENCOR a fundamentally new prophylactic approach to cockroaches. My references to "cockroach birth control" may have been too clever for our own good, or perhaps I was catering too much to the anthropomorphism of my TV hostesses, because invariably I would hear some version of "But doctor, how do you get a cockroach to take the pill?" My explanation that one had only to spray room corners, baseboards, and other likely paths seemed to disappoint them.

VII

If we wish to think about insect control in the early twenty-first century, then the groundwork needs to be laid now. Zoecon's experience with the pursuit of a biological lead that pointed to an Achilles' heel in insects showed that it takes well over a decade to convert such a finding into a commercial reality. In the early 1980s, Herbert Röller called our attention to the new area of invertebrate neuropeptide hormones—chemical messengers emanating from the midbrain that consist of amino acids strung together (hence, the name "peptide"). The isolation and identification of peptide hormones secreted by the hypothalamus won Roger Guillemin and Andrew Schally the 1977 Nobel Prize in medicine. Since the chemical methods for handling minute amounts of material were all available, the transfer of this knowledge from vertebrates to invertebrates took only a few years, rather than the three decades that had been the case with the earlier work on insect hormones. It was clear from biological assays with crude extracts that neural chemotransmitters were intimately involved in numerous essential functions of insects: water balance seemed to be controlled by a diuretic hormone; heart function and blood pressure by a cardio-accelerating factor; lipid metabolism by an adipokinetic hormone; and biosynthesis of sex attractants by a pheromone-biosynthesis activating hormone (PBAH). Röller suggested that we form a group within Zoecon to isolate and characterize some of these hormones. Then we could examine their biosynthesis within the insect's body and see whether we could synthesize substances to interfere in some manner with the insect's production of this essential factor. Interfering with the diuretic hormone might simply "dry up" the insect; affecting the cardio-accelerating factor might produce "heart attacks"; producing an antagonist to the pheromone-biosynthesis activating hormone might make it impossible for the male to find the female.

Since no one at Zoecon had experience in the chemistry of such peptide hormones, David Schooley offered to take a short sabbatical from his directorship of our biochemistry section to receive the appropriate training in Roger Guillemin's laboratory at the Salk Institute in La Jolla, where the early Nobel Prize-winning work in this field had been conducted. By the time Schooley had returned from his training stint with Guillemin's chief lieutenant, Nicholas Ling (who had received his Ph.D. in my Stanford laboratory around the same period as Schooley), Steven Kramer, Zoecon's most skilled insect physiologist, was already busy dissecting the appropriate insect brain sections. The insect he picked was the cockroach (its heart function being easily monitored, it offers a convenient bioassay for the cardio-accelerating factor)—as King Carl XVI Gustaf of Sweden can testify.

In early 1984, the king led a small group of Swedish industrialists on a study mission to Silicon Valley. (Although he would not have remembered it, I had bowed before him a few years earlier on the occasion of an honorary doctorate conferral at the five hundredth birthday of the University of Uppsala.) Since I was a foreign member of the Royal Swedish Academy of Sciences, I had been asked to organize a royal visit to Zoecon in order to expose His Majesty to insect entrepreneurship. First we visited the insectary—a series of small, humidified chambers maintained at constant temperature—into which we had to squeeze the king, the elegant female consul general of Sweden, and a few members of the king's industrial entourage. The rest of the delegation had to wait outside the humid room. Gerardus Staal proudly pointed to the teeming mob of cockroaches reared inside, and then proceeded to demonstrate the morphological abnormalities, such as malformed wings, in IGR-treated cockroaches. When a cockroach was thrust practically under the royal nose, the king drew back startled; he did not know that the insect was temporarily immobilized, Staal having kept it in the refrigerator for the past hour.

The king's group then moved to the biochemistry laboratory where Kramer had arranged a spectacular display: a live cockroach heart under a dissecting microscope, which had been connected to a TV monitor. For the first—and most likely also the last—time of his reign, the king of Sweden saw an enormously magnified cockroach heart, which resembles a pulsating gut. Kramer then added to the isolated organ a minute amount of the cardio-accelerating factor that Schooley and his colleagues had isolated. The resulting convulsive contraction drew gasps from all of us. When the king asked how imminent the conquest of the cockroach through chemically produced heart attacks really was, Kramer cautiously replied that cockroaches had been around for at least 350 million years; and that, in addition to the main cardiac organ, the cockroach has auxiliary hearts in each of its six legs as well as in its antennae. Schooley's group had just established the chemical structure of this neuropeptide hormone, but we were years away from converting this lead into a practical and economically feasible method of insect control. In fact, subsequent work at Zoecon has shown that other neurohormones are probably better targets than the cardio-accelerating factor of the multihearted cockroach. Still, the king and his colleagues felt instructed. Before departing, His Majesty gave me a diploma testifying that I had been elected a foreign member of another royal academy. I wanted to reciprocate this gesture with some memento of his visit, but I didn't think a cockroach would be appropriate. Instead, I quickly autographed a copy of my book, *The Politics of Contraception*, and presented it to the king. The thirty-eight-year-old monarch looked slightly puzzled as he read the title and then turned a few pages. "Do you really think I need this?" he asked. The general laughter saved me further embarrassment.

Even as one part of Sandoz's Swiss management agreed to an infusion of research money into Zoecon for these new neuropeptide projects and to a substantial expansion of our molecular biology program, the business arm of the agrichemical division in Basel took a step that spelled the end of Zoecon's corporate culture as we knew it. In Sandoz's view, the economic facts of life in the pesticide business meant that only the largest companies were likely to prosper, and it would take too long to reach such a size only through internal growth based on in-house research. Furthermore, the herbicide field was larger and more profitable than insecticides. The Swiss pharmaceutical giants are not great believers in participatory management, and Sandoz was no exception. Thus one day we learned, *post facto*, that our Basel parent had acquired a large traditional pesticide company in Chicago, whose main product was a chemical herbicide that had been developed a quarter-century ago. Zoecon was folded into the Chicago operation; and except for our research staff, virtually everyone was transferred or terminated. The research programs initiated by Zoecon were continued; but by the late 1980s, the entire original management and many of the senior scientists had departed; even the Zoecon name was deleted from the front door. It remains only in the Dallas operation, which continues as a highly profitable, but comparatively small, company marketing insect-growth regulators for the control of fleas, cockroaches, flies, and mosquitoes, but not conducting any new research. Zoecon had acquired, within a relatively short period, an international research reputation surpassing in our field that of companies many times our size; indeed, in 1991, I received from President Bush the National Medal of Technology in recognition of Zoecon's pioneering work on environmentally more benign insect-control agents. But if the measure of success is an independent corporate existence, we didn't make it. If fleas and cockroaches could gloat, they probably would.

CHAPTER 12

Pugwash

I

On 9 July 1955, during the height of the cold war, Bertrand Russell issued in London's Caxton Hall the now famous Russell-Einstein Manifesto, co-signed by seven other Nobel laureates. "In the tragic situation which confronts humanity," it started,

> we feel that scientists should assemble in conference to appraise the perils that have arisen as a result of the development of weapons of mass destruction, and to discuss a resolution in the spirit of the appended draft. We are speaking on this occasion, not as members of this or that nation, continent or creed, but as human beings, members of the species Man, whose continued existence is in doubt. The world is full of conflict; and, overshadowing all minor conflicts, the titanic struggle between Communism and anti-Communism.

Four days later, Cyrus Eaton, the maverick capitalist, then chairman of the board of the Chesapeake & Ohio Railway Company, wrote to Russell:

Your brilliant statement on nuclear warfare has made a dramatic world-wide impact. . . . Could I help toward the realization of your proposal by anonymously financing a meeting of the scientists of your group at Pugwash, Nova Scotia? I have dedicated a comfortably equipped residence there by the sea to scholarly groups. . . . I suggest Pugwash because I believe you could more readily focus the attention of the world on the problems you wish to stress by meeting in such a relatively remote and quiet community than by choosing one of the great metropolises where the gathering would be but one of a number of events competing for public notice.

The first meeting was held in July 1957 in Eaton's family home and attended by twenty-two scientists (mostly physicists, with a sprinkling of chemists and biologists and one lawyer) from ten countries. The three largest delegations came from the United States, the Soviet Union, and Japan. Since there was no hotel in Pugwash, the participants were put up in Eaton's house and in three railway sleeping cars, which Eaton had shipped up from Cleveland, the headquarters of his company. This modest beginning led to the annual Pugwash Conferences on Science and World Affairs, which, though subsequently held around the world in places such as Kitzbühel, Moscow, Stowe, Dubrovnik, Udaipur, and Venice, continued to carry the name of the Nova Scotian village. Insiders refer to themselves as "Pugwashites," many of them persons who subsequently acquired real power in government. (Henry Kissinger, for instance, is a quintuple Pugwashite, as is Georgi Arbatov, for many years the Soviet government's top advisor on American affairs.) The Soviet Academy of Sciences as well as their government (including, right from the beginning, Chairman Khrushchev and Foreign Minister Gromyko) so valued these unofficial contacts that they allowed Soviet scientists to travel abroad when foreign trips were otherwise greatly restricted.

Although little known to the general public, the Pugwash Movement provides testimony that at times scientists are willing to descend from their academic ivory towers to address important policy issues. Whether policymakers are willing to listen is another matter. The U.S. State Department, for instance, has never paid much attention to science and scientists. In the few embassies where we have science attachés, they are far down on the pecking order. (In the mid-1950s, we even closed the science attaché's office in London and other capitals, only to reopen them a few years later when Sputnik shot across the sky.) Nonetheless, during the coldest period of the cold war, when diplomats most distrusted each other, Pugwash managed to establish a climate of confidence among influential scientists from East and West, thus laying much of the groundwork for the success of the Limited Test Ban Treaty signed in 1963 in Geneva.

In 1966, Sweden celebrated one hundred fifty years of unbroken peace, and among the commemorative events was the seventeenth Pugwash Conference, held in 1967 in Ronneby, a lovely resort in southern Sweden. The opening address was given by the Swedish Prime Minister, Tage Erlander. It was by far the largest Pugwash Conference to that date, with nearly two hundred participants from forty-four countries; and it was my first. (That day also represented an important first for the country: the change in Swedish traffic from left to right. To avoid accidents, private automobile traffic was banned for twenty-four hours. Our bus, which I boarded in Malmö after crossing by hydrofoil from Copenhagen, was led and followed on the empty highway by police escorts at a top speed of twenty-five miles per hour. An Israeli scientist, arriving that day at the Stockholm airport without prior knowledge of the monumental caution of the Swedish traffic authorities, assumed from the eerie absence of vehicles that war had broken out.)

Until the mid-1960s, all Pugwash Conferences had focused on questions of warfare—especially nuclear, chemical, and biological—and on disarmament. These were matters of East-West interaction, and the geographic origin of the participants reflected that bias. But in 1964 in Udaipur, India, Pugwash started to address also the North-South axis, the gap between the rich and the poor. The following year in Addis Ababa, the theme of the entire conference was "Science in Aid of Developing Countries"; since then, at least one working group in the annual Pugwash Conferences has concentrated on problems of developing countries. This is why I was invited by the American Pugwash Committee, then dominated by scientists from the northeast (and especially Boston), to attend the Ronneby meeting.

Pugwash participants are encouraged to prepare discussion papers, which are distributed ahead of time to expedite the flow of ideas. My own professional competence was outside the area of arms control, but I had ample experience—from my life in Mexico, from my research in Brazil, and from my travels—in the ever-widening "North-South" gulf, especially as it pertained to science and technology. In the mid-1960s, I had even acquired some titles: I had been chairman of the National Academy's Latin America Science Board and later of the Academy's Board on Science and Technology in International Development. BOSTID conducted bilateral workshops and other programs between the American scientific community and lesser-developed countries, with financial support from the United States Agency for International Development. I took the Pugwash invitation seriously, feeling the time was ripe to generalize before an international audience from my personal experiences of the conduct of scientific research in Mexico and Brazil.

Thus, in a paper entitled "A High Priority? Research Centers in Developing Nations," I suggested that, from the standpoint of scientific development, a "developing" country becomes a "developed" one when original research emanates from it. The eventual consequence of such research is the creation of technological innovations, which may then be used in other countries that have the manpower to accept such innovations but not necessarily the technical ability to create them. The ability to perform such advanced research, be it in a university or other research center, usually appears at the end of the list of priorities for developing countries. The priority items are the widening of the elementary educational base to reduce illiteracy, and the creation of universities and technological institutes whose main purpose is to train technicians. From this pool come the teachers, civil servants, public health personnel, and applied technologists who are indispensable to the operation of any country. But such improvements take many years to have an effect. In the light of the ever-increasing tempo of scientific and technological progress in the advanced countries, the creation of competitive, basic research centers in a developing country through the traditional routes becomes a hopeless proposition. This is particularly true in scientific research, where there exists only one standard of excellence. Saying "this is very good chemical research for Kenya, but rather poor for Sweden," is like saying that poor chemical research is being performed in Kenya.

It is ironic that I should have arbitrarily chosen Kenya as an example of a developing country, for it was there that the proposal made in my paper was actually realized. I suggested, to quote the summary in the *Bulletin of the Atomic Scientists* (the house organ of the American Pugwash Committee), that, even in the absence of the requisite indigenous scientific manpower, a research center could be established featuring:

(1) an international cadre of postdoctorate research fellows; (2) overall scientific direction by a group of part-time directors from major universities in different developed countries; and (3) selection of research areas with a possible ultimate economic pay-off and a maximum multiplication factor.

Surprisingly, my proposal was taken up not by a scientist from one of the affluent countries, but rather by an African entomologist, Professor Thomas Odhiambo of Nairobi University. He wrote to me in 1968:

Can a move be made to develop one such center of excellence in mid-Africa, for example in Nairobi? At the risk of appearing presumptuous, I would like to see such a center—on insect physiology and endocrinology—established in Nairobi. Insects play a most basic role in tropical Africa; insect endocrinology is one of the newer areas in the upsurge of modern biology; and it is waiting to be exploited through interdisciplinary research. Nairobi also happens to be an ideal situation from other criteria (climate, international communications, etc.). Can you suggest how to achieve this? Would you be prepared to help launch such a scheme?

Even in ordinary circumstances I would probably have found it difficult to refuse such a challenge. But 1968 was the year of the insect in my personal Chinese calendar, when I was about to lead the newly founded Zoecon Corporation's exploration for applications of recent advances in insect endocrinology. In addition, I had fallen in love with East Africa during two trips with my children, when we roamed the game parks in Uganda, Tanzania, and Kenya. At the suggestion of another Pugwashite, Victor Rabinowitch, the staff director of BOSTID, I contacted the American Academy of Arts and Sciences in Boston, then also the home of the American Pugwash Committee. Its general secretary, John Voss, managed to persuade the governing council of his academy to fund Odhiambo's travel to Boston. (Eight years later, Voss wrote in the Academy's *Bulletin*, "I will never forget the polite but incredulous reaction of the Council when it was announced that the academy was considering helping found an insect pest control center in, of all places, East Africa.") The purpose of the trip was for Odhiambo to meet a few American insect biologists, notably Harvard's Carroll Williams, then a consultant for Syntex, and several other scientists from the Boston area and from Cornell. Key to the success of my Ronneby proposal was the willingness of scientists from advanced countries to serve as part-time research directors—as I had done in Mexico and Brazil. Only then would it be possible to attract young postdoctorate fellows to some new research center thousands of miles from their home bases, both to help train local scientists and to establish quickly an institution of high visibility. Carroll Williams, one of the pioneers in insect hormones, was a prime candidate for such leadership, and his participation was likely to sway other prima donnas of the insect world. Odhiambo, charismatic and intelligent, immediately seduced Williams and several colleagues into examining the feasibility of my proposal in situ, whereupon Voss and Rabinowitch went into high gear to organize a meeting in Nairobi.

We raised some money from various philanthropic sources to cover the travel expenses of a number of Americans. Once we knew that American involvement was assured, Voss and Rabinowitch contacted the officers of several foreign academies and research institutions—among them the Royal

Society of London, the Dutch Academy, the Max Planck Gesellschaft, and, most important (as it turned out), the Royal Swedish Academy of Sciences—and persuaded them to join. Out of this planning meeting in Nairobi in the fall of 1969 came ICIPE—the International Centre for Insect Physiology and Ecology, a remarkable example of international cooperation by scientific academies. Eventually, a consortium of twenty-one national academies became the sponsor of ICIPE, with the Swedish Academy providing the site and staff for an international secretariat. Until the mid-1970s, I made annual or semiannual trips to Nairobi and other meeting places as the representative of the two American sponsoring academies, the National Academy of Sciences in Washington and the American Academy of Arts and Sciences (the only time in my life when I could legally cast two votes). The first long-distance research directors included two organic chemists: Koji Nakanishi from Columbia and Jerrold Meinwald from Cornell. Among my most vivid recollections of African trips remain two with these friends: Meinwald, a flutist of Boston Symphony caliber from his graduate school days at Harvard, playing Mozart for me on a magical African night in the woods outside Nairobi; and Nakanishi giving one of his performances of legerdemain before a group of skeptical Masai, while we were waiting for clearance on the Tanzanian border. It was the only time that I saw this usually unperturbable magician drop a prop. To this day he does not believe that I heard one of the Masai mumble, "That's the trouble with the Japanese."

In the intervening two decades, ICIPE has become an internationally known center of insect science, still headed by Tom Odhiambo, who now deals with multimillion-dollar budgets. My original prescription for the genesis of an instantaneous oasis in a scientific desert could have turned into benevolent do-goodism, or, even worse, into some sort of scientific neocolonialism. But it did not work out that way: both Odhiambo and ICIPE's governing council understood that the Africanization of the enterprise had to be the ultimate criterion of its success, and it is now largely staffed and directed by African scientists. The 1988 annual report of the Royal Swedish Academy of Sciences states, "ICIPE was created as a center of scientific excellence which would work at a level equal to that of scientific institutions in developed countries and would develop a self-sustaining scientific infrastructure in Africa. . . . without doubt ICIPE is the leading scientific institution in Africa in its field."

II

For the next seven years, I was a regular Pugwashite, at meetings in Nice, Sochi (U.S.S.R.), Fontana (Wisconsin), Sinaia (Romania), Oxford, Aulanko (Finland), and Baden (bringing me back to the area of my childhood hikes in Austria), their tempting locations owing as much to hospitality as to nationalistic one-upmanship: each host Pugwash group wanted to place its best tourist foot forward for the annual conferences. Scientists from the West accepted these visits almost as matters of course; but to participants from Eastern Europe and the Soviet Union, where draconic travel restrictions operated, officially sanctioned attendance at such exotic places represented the ultimate recognition of their *persona gratissima* status back home. Not too surprisingly, many of these scientists converted their Pugwash participation into an annual right they were loath to relinquish. As a result, there was little turnover in Eastern European and Soviet membership during those years of restricted travel.

The eighteenth conference in Nice, in 1968, turned out to be extremely contentious. Many of the discussions—inside the working groups and outside—concerned an item not on the original agenda: the entry of Soviet troops into Czechoslovakia a couple of weeks earlier. The Czechs had been very active in Pugwash, notably the microbiologist Ivan Málek and František Šorm, the president of the Czechoslovak Academy of Sciences and, without doubt, the scientist with the biggest political clout in that country. Everyone in Nice was expecting an up-to-date report from them. Was the Soviet invasion the irrevocable end of the Prague Spring, as Alexander Dubček's liberalization was then called; or could a compromise still be reached? But the two never showed up, and the Soviet participants' stonewalling of this issue and their insistence on watering down the final report outraged many of us. With four other Americans, including Harrison Brown of Caltech, the foreign secretary of the National Academy of Sciences, I signed a bitter dissent. The Vietnam War had been opposed in successive Pugwash Conferences and practically all American participants had joined in the condemnation. We felt that the Soviet invasion of Czechoslovakia should be examined with the same candor. Paul Doty from Harvard, a specialist in arms control negotiations with the Russians and well respected by them, put it succinctly: "There is much to do, the time is late. But first the two super-powers must put their affairs in order. End the Vietnam War. Get out of Czechoslovakia."

The day we composed the document I had persuaded Doty and Brown—along with Bentley Glass, the geneticist from Stony Brook, and

Frank Long, a physical chemist from Cornell and long-time Pugwashite—to join me on a drive to St. Paul. We were to see the exhibition at the Fondation Maeght, which had been established by the Paris art dealer Aimée Maeght, and to lunch at La Colombe d'Or, an inn "decorated" with Giacomettis, Chagalls, and Braques. But all of this was but an apéritif to the main course, the Chapel of the Rosary in Vence, the "Matisse Chapel." It belongs to the local Dominican convent, and an old nun gave us a hushed tour of Matisse's black-and-white murals, starting with the Passion of Christ on the wall by the entrance, and ending with the huge figure of St. Dominic behind the simple, white stone altar. The only color was provided by the sunlight streaming through the stained-glass windows. These had also been designed by Matisse, as had the brilliant raiments of the priests, using only four colors, each corresponding to one of the seasons.

I left Nice after the conference was over to fly by way of Zurich to Prague, where earlier in the year Šorm had invited me to give a lecture. He was not only the president of the Czechoslovak Academy but also an organic chemist whom I had gotten to know well. A group in his laboratory had been working on the chemistry of insect hormones, and we had initiated a collaborative research program between Zoecon and the Czech Academy—the first such formal arrangement between an American corporation and their academy. Šorm and I had exchanged reprints of our respective publications in two fields of common interest: steroids and terpenoids. In 1956, he had invited me to give some lectures in Prague. A few weeks before my scheduled visit, the Russians had invaded Hungary, and the political climate in Eastern Europe had deteriorated dramatically. The American consul in Switzerland strongly urged me not to go, but I was curious to learn first-hand what was going on. Šorm was personally charming and scientifically open, but when it came to Hungarian events, he mouthed the Party line—in keeping with the distracting picture of Stalin (his cunning eyes seemed to follow me whichever way I sat during our conversation) that hung on the wall behind his desk. The skies in Prague were overcast, as was the mood of most of the scientists I met during those few days—except during a marvelous performance at the Prague Opera of Janáček's *Její Pastorkyna*. When we departed on a Soviet version of a DC-3, the plane rumbled down the runway for an excessively long time. "I think there's something wrong with this Russian plane," said my wife, clutching the armrest. "You're getting too paranoid about the Communists," I replied, not wanting to show my own concern. The next day in Zurich, as we devoured the latest newspapers to learn what had happened during the past week in the outside world, we read that the Czechoslovak Airlines plane on which we had arrived had crashed on take-off from Zurich, killing everyone on board, including an entire Chinese opera troupe.

And now in 1968, another major political disruption was under way—this time in Czechoslovakia, where I was due to speak. I decided to go ahead anyway, assuming that my Czech visa, which had been issued before the Russians had moved into Prague, was still valid. Philip Handler, the president of our National Academy of Sciences, asked me to transmit orally to Šorm the American scientific community's deep sympathy and support and to inquire what, if anything, we could do to help. I also took with me all of the Pugwash papers and a copy of our official statement of support for the Czech Pugwashites. At the Swiss Air counter in Zurich, I asked as usual for a seat in the first row, right aisle, to accommodate my fused left knee. But the agent didn't seem to hear me. "You can pick any seat you want, sir," he replied. "But I don't want *any* seat, I want—" "What I'm trying to say, sir," he interrupted, "is that you'll have no problem with your leg. There are only two passengers on this flight. Don't you know," he eyed me curiously, "this is our first flight into Prague since the Russians moved in? Your problem will be on your way out. All flights are jammed."

Later, as the empty Swiss Air plane roared along the Prague runway, I saw the tents and equipment of bivouacking Russian soldiers on each side—so close, in fact, that I thought we would mow them down. A whole group of Czech chemists, led by Šorm, was there to greet me. A sense of bravado and even elation emanated from the younger men, some of whom had been postdoctorate fellows in my laboratory. They still did not believe that the Russians would stay and a Stalinist regime take over. They imagined a slightly more conservative version of Dubček would head their government. Like the Chinese students in Tienanmen Square in 1989, the young Czechs were still too euphoric to believe that an autocratic juggernaut might actually crush them. As we drove into town, my hosts pointed proudly to the graffiti and slogans that had not yet been erased. Stalin's picture was long gone from Šorm's office, having disappeared in 1962, at the time of an international conference held in Prague. Šorm was moved by the expressions of support I had brought, and hopeful that Western pressure would lead to a compromise acceptable to everyone.

When I met him again, less than a year later, he was deeply depressed. It was a strange meeting: in Sofia at the centenary celebration of the Bulgarian Academy of Sciences, a duplicate in miniature, in terms of power and hierarchy, of the Soviet Academy. In the West, and especially in the United States, scientific academies are mostly mutual admiration societies; they have prestige but little real power. Few of them have operating research institutes or laboratories. The academies in the socialist countries, however, invariably top the totem pole of national power and prestige, their huge scientific staffs and laboratories far surpassing those of the universities. In 1969, Bulgaria was the only Eastern European socialist country with whom our National Academy had not yet established formal exchange programs. The time seemed ripe to do so, and our academy's president decided that, as a good-will gesture, the United States should be formally represented at the centenary celebrations. As the only academy member tracing even part of his origin to Bulgaria, I was selected to do the honors. When the "other" academy, the American Academy of Arts and Sciences in Boston, learned of my forthcoming trip, I was asked—again, as its only vicarious Bulgarian connection—also to present a diploma and greetings on its behalf. So when I arrived in Sofia in the autumn of 1969—thirty years almost to the day after I had last been there as a student in the American College in Simeonovo—my wife and I were received royally. Only three other Western academies were represented, and the protocol-conscious Bulgarians repeatedly called attention to our presence among the numerous delegations from the Soviet republics and all the socialist bloc countries, ranging from Cuba to North Korea and Vietnam.

At a tree-planting ceremony, in front of one of the academy institutes, each delegate was provided with a small tree, a hole, and a name plate, the idea being that our trees should serve as living mementos to Bulgaria's scientific relations with our respective countries. I do not know whether it was somebody's sense of political humor or just coincidence that my tree found itself between the ones labeled *Cuba* and *Vietnam*. An event with more serious political overtones was the laying of wreaths at the mausoleum of Georgi Dimitrov, who is Bulgaria's Lenin. The main thoroughfare, Boulevard Russki, was cleared of traffic and all the delegates from the various academies marched solemnly past lines of gaping pedestrians, while our wreaths were carried by Bulgarian attachés. The wreaths had been provided by our hosts; when they had asked for the text to be printed on my ribbon, I called our ambassador. "Something personal and nonpolitical," he recommended—wise advice, as I knew once I saw some of the passionate revolutionary slogans adorning several of the other wreaths. Šorm, still the president of the Czechoslovak Academy and thus the official representative of his country, was marching next to me—probably the only person in the entire procession to be an honorary member of every Eastern European scientific academy as well as of our own. "Watch," he whispered, "when I lay our wreath. They'll kiss me on both cheeks, but when I return home, I'll be a nonperson."

He was right. Shortly after his return from Sofia, he lost his position; and until his death, he was never again permitted to leave his country. Only after the collapse of the Czechoslovak Communist regime was Šorm's name rehabilitated in a special issue of the *Collection of Czechoslovak Chemical Communications*. In homage to him, one of my graduate students, Christopher Silva, and I contributed to this special 1991 number a paper in which we reported the isolation and structure elucidation of a new marine sterol we had named "Šormosterol."

III

The 1969 Pugwash meeting was held in Sochi, a popular resort on the Black Sea. It was my first trip to the Soviet Union, and I spent my first few days in Moscow on personal business. Two of my technical books had been translated into Russian at the instigation of Academician Oleg Reutov, who asked that I prepare a preface for the Russian edition. At that time, the Soviet Union did not subscribe to the international copyright convention and hence did not pay royalties. "No royalties, no preface," I had countered, whereupon I was informed that, if an exception were made, I would have to pick up my rubles in person. My participation in the Sochi conference offered the first opportunity to do so, and my royalties had been languishing for several years at the Moscow publishing house Mir. Therefore, when I applied for my Soviet visa, I refused to prepay any expenses through Intourist, the government tourist agency, intending to use my own rubles for the purpose. "No dollar prepayment to Intourist, no visa" was the message from the embassy in Washington, which arrived only a few days before my departure for a lecture trip to Switzerland from which I intended to continue to Moscow. I cabled the Soviet organizers of the Pugwash Conference that if a visa without Intourist were not waiting for me in Switzerland, I would not come to Sochi. In the end, the visa was produced; and when I landed at Sheremetyevo airport, a friend, the steroid chemist Igor Torgov, was there with a fistful of rubles to tide me over for the first couple of days. At the offices of Mir, the director rummaged through his files, eventually producing a fat envelope containing my royalties in the form of ten-ruble notes. Until then, I had not realized how a checkless society really operates. After signing the proffered receipt for a thousand rubles, I reached for my envelope. "Not yet," the director said, placing his hand over my cash. "First you pay income tax." After making the first cash income tax payment of my life, I started to rise with the envelope in my hand. "No!" the man called out. "You must count the money." "It's O.K.," I said, "I trust you." "Count!" resounded the commissar's voice, and count I did, all eighty-eight ten-ruble notes.

It proved difficult to make even a small dent in my hoard of rubles. The hotel and food expenses were minimal, and the few attractive consumer goods could be purchased only with hard currency at Berioshka stores. In the late 1960s, the lines were even longer and shortages even greater than they are now. Several times my wife and I were accosted on the street and asked whether we wanted to sell some part of our clothing. One such incident could have put me into jail.

Service in the restaurant of our hotel, the Ukraine, was lackadaisical, and the tables always crowded. It was standard procedure to share a table with strangers. One day our lunch partners turned out to be a pleasant young couple (especially the woman, a minor ballerina, whose face was attractively made up, her blonde hair pulled back in a French twist), who entered our conversation the moment they heard my wife and me speak. "Do you like Russian icons?" the man asked in surprisingly fluent English. "Sure," I replied, wishing to be polite even though icons are not really to my taste. "Would you like to buy icons?" he continued. I had heard sufficient horror stories about foreigners being picked up for smuggling Russian art objects out of the country to respond with an instant, panicky "No!" But our lunch partner reassured me: "No dollars, only a trade." He reached over and fingered my shirt. "Nice material," he murmured. As I drew back, he promptly switched to a soft sell. "Just look at the icons," he coaxed me. "Come to our apartment." I lied, "We are busy today," but in the end curiosity won over caution. We made a date for the following afternoon to meet around the corner from the hotel.

This time, the man was the cautious one. Hailing a taxi, he put his index finger over his lips while motioning toward the driver. When we reached his neighborhood, a good half-hour's drive in total silence, he walked ahead of us. Only when we had entered his overcrowded studio apartment did he relax. His wife had laid out a sumptuous table—caviar, sausages, a cake. I was embarrassed, realizing what effort had gone into this repast in terms of money spent and time wasted in store lines. We must have chatted for nearly an hour, during which time I learned that the man restored antiques, before the icons started to materialize: from under the bed, from the top of the old-fashioned wardrobe, out of drawers. A couple were even hidden under the embroidered blanket covering the bed. I could not help but admire the barter system he had worked out, because any bargaining on my part—supposing I were interested in the first place— would have been boorish in the extreme. While still tasting his wife's sausage and caviar, how could I say that the icon of Our Lady of Smolensk was not worth the shirt I was wearing, or that my jacket was too much recompense for that large icon in a shadow box depicting Our Lady of

Tenderness? Especially when the gilt halo around her head sparkled seductively under the light of the desk lamp? Fortunately, he understood that I was not ready to strip right then and there; we made a second date for after our return from Sochi, a date I intended not to keep. I was not prepared to take the risk of being arrested for illegal possession of icons. Furthermore, even though the couple was disarmingly hospitable, how did I know he was not just a clever provocateur? One of my Russian chemical colleagues had warned me of such hazards, and said that our hotel room was probably bugged.

But as I rose to leave, our host pressed on me two icons, so small that they fit into my pocket—a gift for which I could think of no gracious refusal. Was this a device for assuring that I would feel indebted enough to show up for our next date, or was he planting the criminal evidence on me? I was almost sure it was the latter when he informed us that he could not accompany us back to the hotel, nor could a taxi be found in the neighborhood. Instead, he stepped into the middle of the road and hailed the first car passing by. After exchanging a few words, he opened the car door, whispering that the man would drive us to our hotel for four rubles. "But who is he?" I asked, my mouth suddenly so dry that I seemed to be croaking. He shrugged as he held the car door open for us, "I don't know." In the end, it turned out to be a passerby willing to earn a few extra rubles—a small foretaste of the late 1980s *perestroika*.

IV

In late October, the Moscow weather had already turned cool, but in Sochi it was mild and sunny. The beach is separated from the hotels and sanatoriums by the railroad line running parallel to the water. To reach it, one needs to pass through pedestrian tunnels under the tracks. During our first lunch break, I wandered off to inspect the beaches and Russian tourists. As I entered the underpass, I saw a group of young people heading toward me. As they got closer, I could read the legend "Stanford University" on one of the T-shirts. "What are you doing here?" I exclaimed, pointing at the man's chest, only to be greeted by smiling incomprehension. None knew English, but after testing the linguistic waters, I discovered that one of the women spoke broken German. The young man had obtained his trophy by barter in Baku; when he learned that I came from Stanford, he inquired eagerly where that was. My reply, "Northern California," was greeted with a delighted beam. "Ah, Hollywood!" the proud owner exclaimed, and clapped me on the shoulder. "*Mir i druzhba*," they called out as we parted.

I heard these Russian words for peace and friendship many times throughout the conference—even though my own message was not an optimistic one. The paper I prepared for the Sochi meeting, "The Increasingly Dismal Prognosis for the Development of New Chemical Birth Control Agents," represented a watershed in my thinking about the future of birth control. Until the mid-1960s, I had been optimistic. The speed with which steroid oral contraceptives had moved from the laboratory to wide acceptance, and the popular demand for further improvements in contraception, suggested that research in this field would flourish. But by 1968— the year I assumed the presidency of Syntex Research—I saw real storm clouds on the horizon. I wanted to introduce into the Pugwash agenda a discussion of population and birth control topics and felt that a presentation of technical issues before an international audience of scientists might be a good start. I was particularly interested in doing so in the Soviet Union, where the quality of birth control was (and is) abysmal. The paper accomplished two aims: its eventual publication in *Science*, a journal of wide circulation, guaranteed that the issues would reach a wide audience. It also served the purpose of stimulating the Pugwash Council to put similar topics on the agenda of future conferences.

Thus, the following year in Fontana, Wisconsin, the 1970 Pugwash Conference included an entire symposium on "Problems of Population and Economic Growth." I took advantage of that forum to launch another notion that had preoccupied me for some time. I felt that all recent ideas about new approaches to human fertility control had essentially started in the head or in the laboratory of scientists. Once the technical feasibility of a method had been established, these scientists went around peddling their new contraceptive wares. Why not reverse the process and start by canvassing social scientists (sociologists, anthropologists, political scientists, even lawyers and economists) about the perceived need and acceptability of whatever improved fertility control method their population group would particularly favor? Only then should a group of "hard" scientists be brought in to examine the technical feasibility of converting society's wish list into reality. No new contraceptive procedure, however attractive and logical it may appear on scientific grounds, will be used on a massive scale unless it fits within the cultural attitudes and resulting family-planning limitations of a given population group.

In the beginning, it looked as if I had picked the right forum, especially after Hannes Alfvén was elected president of Pugwash. Although a plasma physicist by profession (winner of the 1970 Nobel Prize in physics), he and his wife, Kirsten, had an abiding interest in birth control and population issues. At the 1971 conference in Sinaia, Romania, Alfvén presented a major paper entitled "The Population Problem," which included his recommendation that this issue should get high priority in future Pugwash deliberations. My optimism increased in 1972 in Oxford, when the Pugwash Conference accepted my recommendation that a study center for such interchange between social and natural scientists on population issues be established in Stockholm. My choice of Stockholm was predicated on Sweden's great interest in population programs in developing countries (much of its foreign aid was centered in that field) and on Sweden's highly respected position internationally as a small neutral country. The Swedish Pugwash group, under Hannes Alfvén, endorsed this view and sponsored a special panel discussion on population problems at the 1973 conference in Aulanko, Finland. Helvi Sipilä, the Finnish assistant secretary general of the United Nations, opened the session; she was followed by speakers from Sweden, India, Egypt, Chile, and Kenya. As chairman of the session, I took the opportunity to report on China's massive population-control programs, then essentially unknown abroad.

Just three months earlier in May 1973, I had been one of the first American scientists to visit China after Henry Kissinger's trip in 1971, because the Chinese Academy of Sciences had invited me to lecture in various centers on recent advances in human birth control and on new hormonal approaches to insect control. Americans were then such a novelty in China that I had the opportunity to participate, in Beijing, in an hour-long interview with Premier Chou En-lai. I was allowed to tour pharmaceutical manufacturing facilities and learned of the Chinese efforts in the field of oral contraception and their development of the "Paper Pill." After impregnating water-soluble edible paper strips with the steroid contraceptive we had synthesized at Syntex in Mexico, the Chinese scientists had then perforated the paper into stamp-sized segments, each "stamp" corresponding to one daily "pill." I returned to California with a box full of these Chinese contraceptive stamps, which, upon analysis in our laboratory, were found to be remarkably well formulated.

But the Finnish conference in 1973 turned out to be both the high point and virtual end of Pugwash involvement in population issues. At the instigation of the Swedish scientists and the Royal Swedish Academy of Sciences, I went to Stockholm to outline my proposal to some Swedish sociologists. I had no luck. They did not feel that social scientists were knowledgeable enough to address the issues I had in mind. A similar response faced me in later years when I tried to proselytize among social scientists in the United States and among several philanthropic foundations. I was surprised: I had thought that "soft" scientists would jump at the chance to suggest to their "hard" counterparts what to do in a field with such enormous social implications. As a result of the social scientists' striking lack of enthusiasm, I increasingly focused on the difficult "soft" issues, but outside the Pugwash umbrella.

At the 1974 Pugwash Conference in Baden, near Vienna, the population problem had disappeared from the agenda. It was also in Baden where Alfvén, a driving force on population issues, resigned from the Pugwash presidency. To me, this meeting showed that Pugwash was not yet ready to tackle fundamentally new topics, but that it did continue to fulfill an important forum for the exchange of views between ideological antagonists. At the Baden meeting, I spent two days in a crowded, smoke-filled room, listening to an impassioned debate between three Israelis and a group of Arab scientists, decorum just barely being maintained by the former Yugoslav ambassador to Washington. For once, I didn't mind the smoke. The day after, I saw in an outdoor café one of Israel's most distinguished scientific statesmen sitting at a table in animated conversation with the most vocal Arab opponent of the day before. This was Pugwash at its best. It occurred to me that the Latin saying on the entrance to the Austrian Ministry of Defense, *Si vis pacem, para bellum* ("If you want peace, prepare for war"), might well be reworked into a Pugwash motto: *Si vis pacem, para pacem.*

V

In 1975, nearly eight years after attending my first Pugwash Conference in Sweden, I finally visited Pugwash in Nova Scotia and met Cyrus Eaton, by now in his early nineties and still hale and hearty, though hard of hearing. Besides holding the first meeting at his Pugwash home in 1957, Eaton had paid for the second conference in the Canadian ski resort of Lac Beauport, Quebec. By the mid-1950s, he had acquired not only a well-deserved reputation as one of the Midwest's most successful industrial tycoons—in steel, coal, iron, utilities, and railroads—but also an equally controversial one as a fellow traveler, to use the least pejorative of descriptive terms then hurled at him. A personal friend of Nikita Khrushchev and Deputy Premier Anastas Mikoyan, two of many Russians he had been host to in the United States, Eaton and his wife were in 1958 presented by Khrushchev himself with an extraordinary gift: a Russian troika, consisting of three matched white horses and an open carriage. Even more spectacular, on 3 May 1960—two days after Francis Gary Powers was shot down over the Soviet Union in his U-2 spy plane—the Soviet news agency Tass announced that Eaton had been awarded the Lenin Peace Prize in recognition of his efforts to promote friendlier relations between the Soviet Union and the United States. Among North American capitalist czars, only Armand Hammer, the chairman of the Occidental Petroleum Corporation, with his autographed picture of Lenin and his acquaintance with Soviet heads from Brezhnev to Gorbachev, could match Eaton's acceptance by the Russians. (Strangely, Cyrus Eaton's last biographical entry in *Who's Who*, which treats in extraordinary detail his industrial activities, club memberships, and affiliations with institutions ranging from the American Academy of Arts and Sciences to the American Shorthorn Breeders Association, does not mention Pugwash, the Lenin Peace Prize, or any other recognitions by Eastern European socialist countries, other than his honorary doctorates from Prague and Sofia. Did he not want to be remembered as a Russophile?)

It was precisely this image of a fellow traveler during the McCarthy-Dulles era that had led to the Pugwash Movement's separation from Pugwash's foremost resident. In 1959, shortly after Eaton had offered to fund still another Pugwash Conference, three of the most influential American Pugwashites—Harrison Brown, Bentley Glass, and Eugene Rabinowitch (editor of the *Bulletin of the Atomic Scientists* and father of Victor Rabinowitch)—thanked him for his generosity "without attempting to influence the composition, program, and conclusion of the Conference." But then they turned him down in a letter published in the *Bulletin*:

> However, as Mr. Eaton has come to play an increasingly active and controversial role in political affairs, the scientists felt that the exclusive support of their conferences may place them in the wrong light. . . . We are sorry that an encouraging co-operation between a generous businessman, eager to assist the scientists of the world in their efforts to prevent the misuse of science for the destruction of mankind, and to further its use for constructive purposes, has been made impossible by his reluctance to keep his support of the scientists' conferences clearly separated from his increasing involvement. . . . The Continuing Committee, therefore, solicited and obtained the greater part of funds for the conference in Kitzbühel from other individuals and foundations, and did not ask for support from Mr. Eaton.

Both the caution of the scientists, many of whom were already considered liberal "pinkos" and did not want to be painted red, and Eaton's resentment of this apparent ingratitude are readily understood.

But as the cold war had changed to détente, Eaton let bygones be bygones by inviting in 1975 a small group of American and Canadian Pugwashites for a discussion of Pugwash objectives at his home on the shore of the Northumberland Strait facing Prince Edward Island. We were expected at the Eatons' for cocktails, a rather formal affair, and all of the men wore ties and jackets. Bernard Feld, a physics professor from MIT who had attended more Pugwash Conferences than any American, walked with me and noticed the canoe moored by Eaton's home. "How about it?" he asked. "Sure," I nodded, "but let's ask whether it's O.K." It turned out that we were somewhat early, and that Eaton had not yet made his appearance, so we took to the canoe. As we were about to push off, Antonia Chayes (soon to be appointed by President Carter the first female assistant secretary of the air force) hailed us to ask whether she could join. A slender, handsome woman, dressed in white, she stepped carefully into the canoe while her two academic boatmen, in coats and ties, held it steady. Feld took the bow, and I the stern, and off we pushed into the calm but rapidly flowing water. After rowing with the current for half an hour, we reversed course so as not to be too late for the party. In less than twenty minutes, we could see the crowd on the lawn by the side of Eaton's mansion. A few hands waved in the distance, and Tony Chayes returned the greeting while we rowed steadily. The cool breeze kept me from perspiring, and I felt content and masculine.

We must have rowed for another five minutes when I called to my fellow oarsman, "Bernie, we aren't getting anywhere. I bet the tide is pushing us out." The Nova Scotia tides being famous for their height, my explanation seemed plausible. "Let's go faster," I yelled and stepped up the tempo. Minutes passed, and I started to perspire; but as far as I could tell, we had come no closer to our destination. We seemed just to be keeping up with the outgoing tide. We were easily within shouting distance of the shore, but it would have been embarrassing to yell for help. Precisely at the moment when I started to weigh the cost of embarrassment against increasingly strenuous physical effort, a canoe passed us. In fact, it shot by, the two men paddling with insolent ease. They didn't look like supermen, yet in seconds they were past us while we were still rowing furiously. Then I had a thought. I cautiously pushed my oar vertically into the water to find that only the paddle got wet before I touched bottom. We two scientists, MIT physicist and Stanford chemist, carrying with us a future assistant secretary of the air force, had been doing vigorous stationary paddling exercises without realizing it. It remained for Bernie Feld to take off his shoes and socks, roll up his pants to the knees, and push us off the sandbar on which we had been stuck for the last fifteen minutes.

Although I didn't realize it at the time, the Nova Scotia visit coincided with my gradual withdrawal from Pugwash activities. The topic interesting me most—global population issues—had by then dropped from the Pugwash agenda. Even problems of developing countries played second fiddle to arms control issues. While the latter were of crucial importance, I felt that by the late 1970s, Pugwash had turned into just one more forum for addressing questions of disarmament. The last meeting I attended was the 1982 conference in Warsaw, then in the throes of the Polish government's attempt to repress Solidarity—an occasion that left me deeply disillusioned.

VI

I traveled from San Francisco to Warsaw in a roundabout way. After attending in August 1982 an international conference on the chemistry of natural products in South Africa, I spent a week with my future wife, Diane Middlebrook, and her daughter, Leah, in Namibia, including a memorable side trip to the Gobabeb Desert ecology station. Like a fata morgana, the oasis suddenly appeared in the distance in the shimmering sands of the Namib Desert. The visit had been arranged by radio from Pretoria; and when the director greeted us, she demonstrated in a particularly dramatic way how small the scientific world really is: one of her first questions was about two Zoecon scientists whose work she had followed, and whom she had actually visited once in Palo Alto. As we climbed up a steep dune, the sand finer and cleaner than anything I had ever experienced, she suddenly bent down to point to an insect that, in anthropomorphic terms, seemed to be walking on eight-foot-high stilts, so far was its body from the ground— evolution's way of keeping the body away from the oven heat of the sand surface. Two days later, we were sipping coffee in the Arab quarter of Jerusalem, hotly debating the then-ongoing incursion of the Israeli army into Lebanon; and by the end of the week, we were deplaning in Warsaw, in time for the twenty-fifth Pugwash Conference and the second anniversary of the founding of Solidarity.

For the first time in Pugwash history, the American Pugwash Committee had voted not to participate, since attendance might be construed as a sign of approval for the repressive steps the Polish government was taking against Solidarity. The vote was not meant to be binding; and several Americans, like myself, felt that precisely at such times should we be there to offer support to the repressed. The Poles went to a great deal of trouble to make the guests feel comfortable and unthreatened. All the hospitality accomplished, however, was to emphasize grotesquely the difference between us and the average Poles. We were put up at one of the top luxury hotels, the Victoria Intercontinental, where it was easy to pretend that there were no shortages of meat, fresh fruit, and sweets. The meetings were held in the seventeenth-century Radziwill Palace, known also as the Palace of the Council of Ministers, but the walk of a few blocks between these two conference sites was enough to show us that something was in the air. Police and militia in grayish-green or brown uniforms were everywhere, strutting in groups of four or five, white truncheons hanging from their belts, guns at the ready, face shields pushed up. Churches were one of the principal focuses of popular resistance. The one I passed every day was marked by a huge cross of flowers on the pavement, interspersed with religious messages and photographs of Lech Walesa. The cross grew every day as people added fresh red and white flowers—the colors of the Polish flag. Sporadically, passersby would congregate and sing, their fingers raised to denote victory in the Churchillian manner which Walesa had used in the first Solidarity meetings. Still etched in my mind is the image of a small girl, no older than three, with arms raised, two tiny Vs pointing toward the blue sky, and just past her the Church-inspired posters with their gruesome pictures of fetuses. The anti-abortion message in this country of low-quality contraception and abortion on demand was so crudely obvious that the Polish text seemed superfluous.

Two days later, 31 August 1982, was the second anniversary of the banned Solidarity movement, and serious trouble was anticipated. The Polish Pugwash Committee organized an all-day tour to Torun, the birth place of Copernicus, to get everyone out of Warsaw, and urged all the foreigners to take advantage of the tourist trip. I chose to stay behind to observe events, as did an American physicist, Peter Stein from Cornell. I did not feel that the purpose of a Pugwash meeting was to keep us from seeing the consequences of political oppression. A Polish Pugwashite and open Solidarity sympathizer had shown me a leaflet calling for demonstrations at 4:00 P.M. at four different sites in Warsaw. The biggest demonstration was expected to be in the center of town at Plac Defilad, Warsaw's Parade Square in front of the Palace of Culture and Science, a building in the typical Stalinesque style of the early 1950s, featuring a huge gingerbread tower stacked on top in tiers like a wedding cake, with smaller turrets clustered around it. These architectural monstrosities, seemingly made from one plan, were Russia's gift to its satellites in the 1950s and can be found all over the communist world, from East Berlin to Shanghai. The best the official guidebook has to say about this biggest edifice in Warsaw is that "if a child were born in one of its rooms, and then spent each day in a different room, it would leave the Palace at the age of nine." Stein had discovered that a TV crew from NBC had a room on the twenty-first floor of the Forum Hotel overlooking Parade Square. Though uninvited, we decided to join them; and by 3:30, we were walking along Marszalkowska Street (sometimes called Warsaw's Broadway), which for one long stretch becomes the eastern flank of Parade Square.

The sidewalks were crowded, but people seemed to be going about their own business; the street was full of traffic. One side of the square was packed with military vehicles, mobile water cannon, and several hundred militia and other uniformed men. I couldn't imagine how a demonstration could even be launched, let alone continue, in the face of such armed might. After we had identified ourselves as Americans from the Pugwash Conference, the two Polish cameramen working for NBC admitted us to their room, which had an excellent view of the entire area. The Venetian blinds were drawn, the slats arranged in such a manner that the camera lens could record the proceedings without being easily spotted from the building facing us. The TV men doubted that anything would transpire in view of the heavy military presence; when everything seemed peaceful well after the 4:00 P.M. deadline, Stein and I decided to return to the street and walk along the open, and much less populated, side of Marszalkowska Street.

Suddenly the scene on our side changed: groups of young men appeared apparently from nowhere (in fact, an underground pedestrian tunnel did offer a partially hidden entrance). Sensing trouble, with nothing between us and the waiting water cannon, we started to walk as fast as my stiff leg would permit. But it was too late. A column of men—nearly one thousand according to the subsequent NBC report—had formed, flags had been raised, and the sound of voices yelling in unison reverberated from the buildings across the street. To make matters worse, the demonstrators threw a few firecrackers, causing instantaneous bedlam. Everyone panicked as, within seconds, a column of militiamen moved toward us, their face shields lowered. Then the tear gas canisters started to fall. People scurried across the street for shelter in one of the big stores, and I hobbled behind as fast as possible. By the time we reached the Wars-Sawa department store, the entrance had been locked. All we could do was to pound on the doors and yell at the mass of silent shoppers and store personnel staring at us through the thick plate glass. As we ran along the buildings, pushing at every door, we finally had luck. Someone ahead of us had found one unlocked. Within seconds, more than three dozen people, Stein and I among them, had pushed their way in before someone rushed up to padlock the door. It was not a store but a wide hallway leading to some steps, up which raced our panting mob of street refugees. We ended up in a second-floor reading room, a Polish equivalent of a Christian Science center, startling the attendant and half a dozen newspaper readers. Without a word, each of the invaders grabbed a newspaper or magazine, sat down, and, in total silence, pretended to read. Even Stein and I, illiterate in Polish, held up a newspaper, mine implausibly upside down.

The reading room was lined with windows so that, even peering from behind my paper, I had a full balcony view of the street below. The armored cars bore men with gas masks and face shields, who were loading the tear gas guns and shooting down every side street. A shell hit our window and cracked with a loud sound that froze everybody—except for three young deaf men whose hands and fingers were moving frantically in sign language. Every once in a while, a figure darted from the shelter of a doorway, picked up a tear gas canister, and threw it back before it exploded. At the same time, a curious side spectacle was unfolding, as if two completely different plays were simultaneously being performed on the same stage. On the opposite side of the street, parallel with the charge of armed might down our side, an old stooped man with a cane walked slowly up and down, eyes fixed on the ground, oblivious of the pandemonium and the clouds of gas. Had he already used up his life's supply of tears? A scene as absurd as it was serious, it tempted me to take a picture. But as soon as I raised my small pocket camera, people hid their faces and a man gestured angrily that I was not to take any photographs.

By this time, tear gas was drifting into the room through the cracks in the windows, causing our eyes to smart, and we decided to leave. The German-speaking attendant, who accompanied us downstairs to unlock the door, actually managed to produce a wan smile. When I complimented her in German upon her residual sense of humor, she sighed, *"Humor ist das einzige, was wir noch übrig haben"* ("humor is the only thing still left to us").

We ran down a side street, thick with gas. But once away from the area, we were in another country. Except for a few persons in a doorway here and there, the streets were empty. Only the clatter of the low-flying helicopters showed that something was amiss. The atmosphere around our hotel was equally misleading. The building faced Ogród Saski, the Saxon Gardens, with the Tomb of the Unknown Soldier on the left. Some time earlier, a huge cross made out of flowers had been placed on the grass as another sign of opposition to General Wojciech Jaruzelski's regime. The government had reciprocated by erecting a high wooden fence around the entire area, as a way of preventing crowds from congregating. As a result, there were almost no pedestrians near the hotel. After identifying ourselves to the guard at its only unlocked door, and climbing to the second floor to get a better view across the wooden enclosure, we saw that Senatorska Street and the area in front of the Opera, on the far side of the Saxon Gardens, had become another staging area for the water cannon, armored vehicles, and associated armed personnel.

The second anniversary of Solidarity also coincided with a national holiday in Malaysia, and that country's ambassador had picked our hotel for a diplomatic reception. The Mercedes and Volvos with small diplomatic flags rolled up, followed by the black Chrysler of the U.S. ambassador; and the formal couples entered the hotel: it seemed like an absurd performance from another time. Though made more absurd by the events of the day, it was not unlike our experience the evening before, at the posh reception given by the foreign minister in the "Polish Versailles," as Wilanów Palace is often called. The buffet tables were laden with delicacies, and the Pugwash guests, the Russians leading the pack, descended on them like a swarm of locusts. What must the Polish Pugwashites, who lived with a shortage of meat and of most other staples, have been thinking?

Early in the morning on the day after the tear gas episode, we drove to the airport past the deserted scene of the demonstrations. There were no military vehicles, no police, no gas canisters or other debris on the pavement; it had been swept and freshly hosed down, perhaps with the remnants of the water used to douse the people. The car window was open, and no trace of tear gas was in the air. Yet as I looked at the Parade Square, tears sprang to my eyes. I felt helpless and ashamed. Neither the Pugwash Conference in the Radziwill Palace nor I, fleeing with Solidarity supporters along Marszalkowska Street, had accomplished anything in Warsaw. Even the Polish protests, though brave, seemed utterly quixotic. On 1 September 1982, was any Pole, let alone foreigner, optimistic enough to imagine that seven years later Solidarity would win the first free election? And, even more unlikely, that Walesa would succeed General Jaruzelski as president of Poland?

CHAPTER 13

Perestroika 1970

I T SEEMS TO ME THAT SCIENTISTS are today's counterparts to the seafarers of old. While most scientists range along the East-West axis from Japan through North America to Europe and the Soviet Union, the professional life of some also takes them south to Africa and Latin America. Just try to locate one of your colleagues on your home turf! He or she has just left for Stockholm, or is lecturing at a NATO workshop in Corsica, or is in Kyoto or Munich on a sabbatical. Such intercontinental flitting is, of course, much safer on the whole than seafaring was; perhaps the major hazard today is that one becomes jaded, as well as unusually demanding, about airlines.

I have long passed the stage of having any favorites among carriers, but I always have a couple at the bottom of my preference list. Alitalia and Iberia have been there several times because their tendency to have sudden strikes can leave passengers stranded, as it were, in midair; but one airline has always hovered near the bottom: Aeroflot, with whom I flew on many occasions in the 1960s and 1970s. All kinds of reasons for this low opinion vie for priority in my mind. Is it mostly because I never saw a smiling stewardess on Aeroflot? Or because the air-conditioning on the Soviet planes—the piston-powered Ilyushin 12, the turbo-prop Antonovs, or even the Tupolev jets—never functioned until they were up in the air? (Anyone who has sat, in July, on the runway in Tashkent or Cairo in a hermetically sealed Aeroflot plane will know that this is not the complaint of a perfectionist.) Then again, it may be because on flights within the Soviet Union the standard fare for breakfast, lunch, and dinner was boiled, stringy chicken. (I am probably exaggerating, but this is the message my still-irritated palate sends my brain.) Or because lines at ticket counters were chaotic, the agents ferocious or sullen, the antediluvian reservation system totally dependent on overloaded telephones and abacuses?

I offer this litany of complaints not to undermine the spirit of *glasnost*, but rather as background to a small victory over the Soviet bureaucracy at Domodedovo airport in Moscow in the summer of 1970—my own experimental demonstration that Russia was indeed ready for *perestroika*.

Two Russians—one, Alena, the striking, bilingual daughter of Academician Vladimir Aleksandrovich Engelhardt, then the director of the Soviet Academy's Institute of Molecular Biology; the other, a young chemist, Boris Zaslavsky, who also spoke fluent English—had been assigned by the Soviet Academy of Sciences to escort me to Central Asia, together with my wife, my two children, and my friend Koji Nakanishi, who had just accepted a professorship at Columbia University. We had spent a week in Riga on the Baltic, attending a scientific conference, and then headed for Uzbekistan to see the ruins of the Mongol empire. Tashkent, the capital of Uzbekistan, rebuilt in post-Stalinist architecture after the huge earthquake of 1966, wasn't much to see; our goals were the medieval mosques and madrasahs of Samarkand, Bukhara, and Khiva. The one daily flight to Khiva was booked for days in advance by *Intourist*. As a private party who had refused to go through the Soviet tourist bureaucracy (which was interested only in hard-currency clients), we found ourselves waiting in the Tashkent airport for the departure of a long-delayed flight to Samarkand. Here, however, we turned this temporary defeat into success, one of two such incidents that led up to the victory of Domodedovo.

While I conversed with one of our Russian companions, Nakanishi idly inspected the sole tourist gift counter, over which presided a rosy-cheeked Uzbek maiden. She hadn't a single customer and didn't appear interested in attracting any. The goods behind the dirty glass were standard junk—cheap Uzbek skullcaps, some embroidered handkerchiefs, the typical nested *Matrioshka* dolls. Koji bent down and tapped on the glass. "How much?" he asked, receiving a blank stare in reply. "Alena, can you help me?" he called out to our friend. "I'd like to buy those cards."

We walked to the counter to discover that Koji was interested not in postcards, but in a deck of playing cards costing two rubles. There was nothing unusual about them. "Why do you want to buy those cheap cards?" I asked. There wasn't much to buy, but this seemed to be scraping the bottom of an already pitiful souvenir barrel. "I forgot to bring mine along," he murmured, as he bent over the glass, tapping it again.

Nakanishi is not only a world-famous scientist. Among organic chemists, he is equally well known as a magician and manipulator of cards. His card tricks border on the extrasensory. Once, in San Francisco, he offered my wife a stack of cards, asked her to select one, and, after she had slipped it back into the stack, stared into her eyes and asked in a faintly mocking voice, "Why don't you or Carl call my wife. She'll tell you which card you picked." So I dialed the Tokyo number he gave me, as if this were the most natural thing to do, and asked his wife whether she knew which card had just been selected in San Francisco. "Ah so!" she inhaled, and then named it, the six of hearts.

This trick was obviously too complicated for the Tashkent airport. In 1970, I doubt that one could have dialed Moscow directly, let alone Tokyo. As soon as Koji had handed over his two rubles and taken possession of the Uzbek cards, he shuffled them with a loud rattle, Las Vegas style, and tried "something simple." He made the woman behind the counter pick a card; after she inserted it back into the stack, he shuffled the cards and then spread them, face down, over the glass surface of the counter. "Just separate them into two halves," he asked via Alena. Too shy or too dense, she refused to follow his directions even after he had gone through the entire process by pantomime. I have marveled at this trick of Koji's many times. All you do is separate the cards into two approximately equal piles. Koji selects one and then asks you to repeat the process. This goes on until only two cards remain on the table, both of them face down. He points to one, daring you to turn it over. When you finally do, you find the card you selected at the very beginning. I never get bored watching this performance, so I was sorry when the girl did not go along with his challenge, and glad when she finally did.

Originally, only the three of us—Koji Nakanishi, Alena Engelhardt, and I—were standing by the gift counter. My seventeen-year-old son, Dale, soon joined us. In the Soviet Union of the 1960s or early 1970s, the appearance of four people at any sales counter—be it meat, jewelry, or shoes—was like a magnet: it attracted other people curious to know whether, in fact, anything was available for purchase. Koji, the magician, could not resist the temptation of an instant audience. Before the Uzbek maiden behind the counter realized it, she became the center of attention. She picked a card, clumsily showed it to some spectators, and then stuffed it back into the pack. Giving it a quick, resounding shuffle, Koji then reached over the counter and pulled a card out of the pocket of her blouse. "Isn't that the one you just picked?" he asked. No translation was needed; the girl covered her blushing face with her hands and giggled.

We were all sorry when the departure of our plane for Samarkand was finally announced. The audience loved the free card show and I loved watching the audience. In Samarkand, however, the cards would bring another kind of benefit. Our sightseeing there was done mostly on foot in oven-dry heat reminiscent of Arizona in August. The buildings were spectacular: the group of Shah-i-Zindeh mausoleums, ribbed cupolas like giant cacti, with the chain of mountains as a scenic backdrop; the spectacular Gur-Amir mausoleum of 1404, circled by enormous Arabic inscriptions, with its multicolored dome of glazed tile; the gigantic stone quadrant of the observatory of Ulugh Beg (Tamerlane's grandson), carved in a rock. But as we walked and gaped in the shimmering heat, we became dehydrated. Finally we found a tea garden, where one sat on elevated wooden platforms shaded by tall trees. Under ordinary circumstances, hot tea would not have been my first choice in such heat, but at least it was wet. A group of men lounged on a neighboring platform, their embroidered skullcaps the Uzbek equivalent of yarmulkes. As they inspected the women in our group, my mouth watered at the sight of the juicy melons they were eating. "Koji," I asked, "why don't you offer to show them one of your card tricks and see what happens."

Initially, the men were suspicious when Alena explained in Russian that this Oriental man could perform magic with his cards. After a few warmup exercises, which had most of the men giggling like our Tashkent airport maiden, Koji's performance became progressively more magical. One observer, who had watched the performance suspiciously from the back, pushed through the crowd and pounded his chest. Alena translated his growls, which implied that these were tricks for children. Would Koji dare try him? Koji did dare: he pulled cards out of the man's shirt pocket, his hip pocket, his sleeves—he even found one under the stupefied man's skullcap. Suddenly the man grabbed Koji's hand and whispered urgently to Alena. "He wants to buy your magic cards," she translated. "He's sure he'll win all card games with them." Koji looked worried. "Tell him the cards come from Tashkent. There's nothing magic about them. I'm the magician." But I stopped him: "Forget your pride and offer him the cards in exchange for some melons." Although I hope the man didn't gamble too much with his cards, I still relish the taste of the juiciest melon of my life.

Domodedovo was then the Moscow terminal for long-distance flights from Soviet Asia—that land mass extending over eight time zones all the way to

Vladivostok. The passengers pouring through the gates at all hours of the night, or sleeping on or under the benches in waiting rooms—Uzbeks, Tatars, Tadzhiks, Kirghizis, Mongols, Kazakhs—are descended from the people united by Genghis Khan and Tamerlane who had populated Samarkand and Bukhara in the Middle Ages. We had deplaned after a long and tiring turbo-prop flight from Tashkent, where, before taking off, we had baked half an hour in standard Aeroflot fashion in a sealed plane in 100-degree heat and a high humidity of reeking sweat. When we arrived in Moscow, shortly after midnight, we could think only of reaching our hotel and collapsing into bed. But first, we had to wait for our luggage.

Waiting at Domodedovo, even at midnight, is not dull. The kaleidoscope of features and dress and the babble of languages not only woke me up but brought home to me the extraordinary diversity of the Soviet Union. Still, after twenty minutes or more, I got impatient. "Where is our damn baggage?" I began to mutter to the Academy official who had met us. "You must wait," he said, his voice resigned from a lifetime of waiting, "until your flight number appears." He pointed to the electric signs above the carousels which showed no signs of stirring to receive their usual avalanche of bags. "I won't!" I replied in some annoyance. "This is preposterous!" My two children grinned, while my wife threw a suffering look heavenward—all knowing, from years of experience, that this word meant I was ready to take matters into my own hands.

It seemed obvious to me that our luggage had to have been taken off the plane and deposited in some subterranean pit, probably below the hall in which we were then waiting. At Domodedovo—at least in 1970—the planes stopped out on the tarmac, and passengers were transported by bus to the terminal. One then had to ascend a broad set of steps through doors guarded by armed soldiers before reaching the huge arrival hall with the baggage carousels. I decided to reverse the process: when the next horde of Asian passengers poured through one of the doors, I lowered my head like a *toro* at a bullfight, and charged in the opposite direction. The soldiers shouted after me but were prevented from reaching me by the rushing stream of Genghis Khan's descendants. I headed for the steps and found my way into the cavern that I supposed fed the baggage carousels. But our bags were nowhere in sight.

Having broken through the Soviet security system with unexpected ease—as did the young German, seventeen years later, who landed his single-engine plane in front of the Kremlin—I thought that I might as well continue my exploration. I headed out on the runway to look for our plane among the various Ilyushins and Antonovs lined up in military fashion. With relatively little effort, I found it sitting in the darkness, illuminated by a single bulb attached to a goosenecked lamppost, like the street lamps of my Vienna childhood. I was wondering how to extract our luggage from the abandoned plane when I heard a gruff voice behind me. Though I don't speak Russian, I could well guess from the tone and the expression on the man's face, when I turned, what he was asking.

"Do you speak English?" I asked politely.

"*Nyet.*"

"*Sprechen Sie Deutsch?*"

"*Nyet.*"

"*Parlez-vous français?*"

"*Nyet.*"

"*¿Habla usted español?*"

He did not, and I had exhausted the languages of my childhood, high school, and early career in Mexico. The man must have been impressed, however, because he offered me an encouraging grin.

"Look!" I exclaimed. "Tashkent!" I thrust my right hand in what I assumed was the direction of pitch-dark Central Asia. "Moscow!" I pointed with my left index finger to the brightly lit terminal building. "*Bagage!*" I thundered, using the French word I thought would be closest to Russian. "My *bagage!*" I repeated, pounding my chest and pointing at the dark plane. "Ah!" exclaimed my new friend and then propelled me, his arm across my shoulder, to an empty bus standing nearby. "Intourist," he said. "Intourist," he repeated as he pushed me into the bus, started it, and moved off.

Within minutes we'd driven to the opposite end of the terminal, to the local office of the government tourist bureau where he expected to find someone speaking one of the languages I'd thrust at him. At 1:00 A.M., however, no one was expecting foreign tourists. The two men he woke up were as gregarious as my friend, just as curious as he at encountering a non-Asian foreigner, but just as monolingual. However, I discerned a flash of understanding in the eyes of one of the men when I repeated my hand-waving "Tashkent-Moscow" pantomime, followed by my chest-pounding "*Bagage.*"

"*Vámonos al autobus!*" I exclaimed and clapped my arm over my new Russian friend's shoulder, the way the bus driver had when he moved me to the bus. To this day I can't fathom what made me address the man in Spanish as if we were in Mexico City. I suppose I felt that *Vámonos* somehow sounded more persuasive than "Let's go." In any case, it worked. My newest friend and my private chauffeur returned with me to what I now considered *my* bus, and as soon as I pointed to *my* plane dimly illuminated on the distant runway, we took off. When the three of us disembarked below my plane, I emitted my second multilingual command, *"Vámonos with the bagage!"* and a miracle happened. The two men, having located a ladder on wheels, moved it to the baggage compartment door and managed to open it! I followed, even a fused knee no impediment when the adrenals secrete in triumph. My comrades started to unload the plane. When they reached our bags, I yelled *"Stoi!"* suddenly remembering the Bulgarian word for "Hold it!" (There are probably no more than two dozen Bulgarian words that I remember from my youth, including the words for *matches*, *love*, and *watermelon*, and one useful four-letter curse.) My *"Stoi!"* must have sounded sufficiently Slavic because the unloading promptly stopped.

I grabbed two of our bags and started in the direction of the terminal. *"Stoi!"* I heard what seemed the echo of my earlier exclamation, but with a Russian ring. *"Kvitantzia,"* the man added, his tone no longer the soft one of pure comradeship but the harsh one of Soviet bureaucratese. Seeing my look of incomprehension, he switched to his form of Esperanto. *"Bilet,"* he said, mouthing the word carefully, and put his heavy hand on my bags.

"Stoi!" I repeated, this time in desperation, and pointed first to him, then to our bags, and finally to the spot where he stood. *"Stoi!"* I croaked. I was not going to let this triumph over Aeroflot dissolve into last-minute failure because of some miserable claim checks.

Although unable to run with my stiff leg, I can hobble. And this time I moved—skipping stiff-legged, the way kids do, propelling myself quicker than I'd moved in years. I skipped straight for the doors where the same two soldiers were still standing with their guns (I concluded that Russian soldiers only chase and shoot on TV), and skipped right past them into the main hall. My son yelled, "There's Papa!" I was immediately surrounded by my family, my Japanese friend, and my Russian colleagues, all of them bursting with frantic questions about my disappearance. "Never mind!" I panted. "I found them! Quick, who's got the claim checks?"

My Russian companions wanted to accompany me, but I firmly said, *"Nyet!"* This was going to be an American victory over Soviet bureaucracy. Eventually I yielded to the young chemist. "O.K., Boris, you can help with the bags, but you mustn't speak a word of Russian. Remember, you're a foreigner."

Out we ran, past the two soldiers who by now must have thought I owned the airport, down the steps, and along the familiar stretch to the plane where my two Russian comrades were still standing, surrounded by our luggage.

"Thanks, *spasibo*," I yelled, adding one of the few Russian words I'd picked up, and thrust the *Kvitantzia* into their hands. A few minutes later, the three of us arrived triumphantly with our luggage in front of the still-inert carousel.

My Soviet friends from the Academy were jubilant at my triumph, and the chauffeur so much so that he roared the wrong way down the exit road from Domodedovo. As for me, I was so excited I didn't fall asleep for hours.

In September 1989, almost two decades after my triumph over Aeroflot's baggage delivery system at Domodedovo airport, I arrive there again—this time from Vladivostok with luggage in hand—to be met by an old friend and retired member of the Soviet Academy of Sciences. We drive through a lovely fall landscape full of birch, oak, and fir, with hardly a house in sight. One would never think that we have landed at one of the main airports of the largest city in the Soviet Union, so bucolic is the initial impression when coming in from Domodedovo. Moscow starts to announce itself by the abrupt appearance of a group of huge white apartment blocks, which increase in frequency until we are suddenly on one of the distinctive wide, uncrowded boulevards. The spaciousness distracts one in a car from the mediocrity of the recently constructed buildings and the poor maintenance of the older ones. The gold of the early evening sun is the perfect light for the brick façades. My old friend also serves as my local savings account, because Russian currency cannot be taken out of the country. I have never been able to spend all the rubles I receive here, either from earlier book royalties or from the per-diem allowances the Soviet Academy of Sciences pays its official guests, so he greets me with some banknotes which I always treat as funny money.

This is also the occasion when, after an interval of nineteen years, I meet again one of my companions from our 1970 excursion to Uzbekistan. On my last night in Moscow, I dine at the home of Boris Zaslavsky, who greets me with a big grin, "Do you remember when we arrived at Domodedovo?" and then proceeds to tell the tale to his wife and son. But then he turns serious. Now in his late forties and a distinguished physical chemist working in an esoteric field not well represented in the Soviet Union, Boris craves scientific collegiality and a future for his son. He has decided to chuck everything for a new life in America—if they have not waited too long to make the decision. Just as Soviet emigration rules have been relaxed dramatically, American barriers to Russian immigration have risen.

I try to be upbeat. When during dinner Boris recalls how a couple of decades ago, he and six friends borrowed for exactly one night a *samizdat* version of Solzhenitsyn's *Gulag Archipelago* and read it aloud all night in shifts in the kitchen, but still were unable to finish it before having to hand it over to the next group of hungry readers, I say, "But things *are* changing now. You can buy Solzhenitsyn in the bookshops. And look at your apartment."

By Russian standards, they are well off, but Boris says it is all too late. His father was a fairly high-placed scientist, who worked for years in a defense-oriented field. In spite of the father's eligibility for special housing benefits, Boris, his parents, and his grandmother lived for twenty years in a two-room flat with access to a bathroom and kitchen shared with several families. "Do you know there is no Russian word for *privacy*?" Boris says, shaking his index finger at me. "Can you imagine sleeping the first twenty years of your life in the same room with your grandmother?"

Upon my arrival, it had still been light. But now, as Boris takes me downstairs to catch a taxi, the corridor outside his apartment is barely lit and, when we step into the elevator and close the door, it is pitch-dark. He lights a match to find the right button to press. "Is it always this dark?" I ask. "No," he mutters, "the bulb must have burned out. God only knows when they'll replace it." I observe half seriously, "This country offers a great opportunity to flashlight manufacturers." "But where," the sardonic voice asks in the stygian blackness, "would you find any batteries?" By the time we reach bottom, I conclude that *missing batteries* may well be an apt epitaph for *perestroika*.

CHAPTER 14

Pygmy Chimps

I

In 1971, the country was still the Democratic Republic of the Congo and just emerging from the disruption and instability that followed the departure of the Belgians in 1960. The first prime minister, Patrice Lumumba, had been killed; the republic's first president, Joseph Kasavubu, had died; the Katanga secession led by Moise Tshombe had been put down; and Mobutu SeSe Seko had emerged, through a combination of cunning and corruption, as the new power. The Congolese, eager to demonstrate their independence from their former colonial masters in every way possible, invited the National Academy of Sciences in Washington to hold a workshop in Kinshasa to advise on research priorities for their nation. The U.S. response illustrates the enthusiasm as well as the naïveté of well-meaning scientists from a highly developed country trying to address some of the needs of people facing basic problems of survival.

During the late 1960s and early 1970s, I was active in BOSTID, the academy's Board on Science and Technology for International Development, the last few years as its chairman. The question raised by the Congolese was much like the one I had considered four years earlier in a Pugwash Conference paper in Sweden. Since it had already been realized in Kenya, I wondered whether my model might not be applicable also to the Congo. That I knew little about that country didn't bother me; the Congolese were looking not for experts on their country (for that they could have depended on the Belgians), but for unbiased advice by professionals in certain technical areas and in science policy. Harrison Brown, a geochemist from Caltech and then the academy's foreign secretary, asked me to serve as chairman of a small American task force. Besides Brown, some of the other members were John McKelvey, head of the agricultural development program at the Rockefeller Foundation; Carl Eicher, an agricultural economist from Michigan State; Ernst Pariser, an MIT nutritionist; and James Carter, a black pediatrician from Vanderbilt. BOSTID's staff officer for our group was Julien Engel, an Africanist who spoke faultless French. We were scheduled to assemble in Kinshasa for a briefing by our hosts, headed by Joseph Ileo, a savvy Congolese politician, who had been a leading figure in the independence movement and editor of a newspaper. Though a scientific layman, he had been appointed president of the Congolese National Research and Development Council by President Mobutu, partly in recognition of his services as interim prime minister after Lumumba and as cabinet minister in succeeding governments during the 1960s. The appointment testified to Ileo's talent for survival in a notoriously unstable country: he was one of the few politicians who had managed to retain continuous membership in the Bureau Politique of the country's single party. After the briefing, Ileo and his staff planned to take us on a week-long survey of the eastern Congo before holding formal discussions in Kinshasa, all of this to culminate in a report to the Congolese government.

The American group flew into Kinshasa from Washington, but since I was spending a week in Nairobi on ICIPE affairs, I planned to arrive on one of the biweekly flights of East African Airways. I knew that most air travel in Africa proceeded on a north-south axis, with the final destination usually being Johannesburg, whatever the intermediate stops in Anglophone East Africa or in the Francophone ex-colonies in the west. Still, I did not appreciate just how haphazard travel could be across the wide middle of the continent. Three days before my departure, East African Airways had canceled its biweekly flight without notifying me—a fact I learned only through my compulsive suspicion of airline schedules. There was no other way of getting to Kinshasa in time for the meeting. Even long-distance telephone calls between Nairobi and Kinshasa (along the east-west axis) were limited to a few hours during the middle of the day, when most

Congolese government offices were likely to be closed. Eventually an officer from the Agency for International Development at the American embassy in Nairobi came up with a plan that would permit me to participate in most of the U.S.-Congo workshop: I was to take an Air Zaire flight to Bujumbura, the capital of Burundi, where further instructions would await me.

When I deplaned in Burundi, a staff member of the four-person American embassy informed me that the rest of the Americans and the Congolese participants would arrive in two days in nearby Bukavu, a Congolese town on Lake Kivu which, prior to independence, was one of the favorite vacation spots of the Belgian colonials. Ambassador Thomas Melady offered me the hospitality of his residence, a welcome gesture that made my exploration of Bujumbura and surroundings much more convenient. Although I knew that Burundi was one of the most densely populated countries in the world, I was still taken aback by the surging masses of children and young people I encountered—a graphic demonstration of the African population problem. Late in the morning of the second day, the ambassador's chauffeur drove me across the borders of Burundi and Rwanda to the Congo. My destination was the U.S. "consulate" in Bukavu, where a further message from Kinshasa was supposed to await me. All I found were two young men in shirt sleeves hunched over a telex machine. They looked like CIA types: why else have an American consulate in a place to which hardly any tourists or businessmen had come for years in view of the periodic uprisings and general instability? They were clearly anxious to get rid of me. "Your party will meet you tomorrow," was the message, but they didn't know where. "Try IRSAC at Lwiro," one of them said shortly.

It was plausible. IRSAC was the Institut pour la Recherche Scientifique en Afrique Centrale—the leading Belgian research institute in the former colony and a scheduled stop on our professional itinerary. Unfortunately, the Burundian driver, though claiming to know where Lwiro was, drove some seventy miles over rutted roads before admitting that we were lost. Both of us started to be concerned: he because the border posts would be closed before he could make it back to Bujumbura, and I because I was wondering where I would spend the night. Eventually he deposited me at a peeling, fungal-gray hotel with tightly shuttered windows, which had clearly seen better days under the Belgians. The seedy-looking, aged chameleon lounging behind the desk—concierge, bellhop, and cashier wrapped into one—looked startled to see a paying customer; later I learned that there was one other guest in the four-story building. When I asked about a restaurant, I was directed down the street to a bistro owned and operated by one of the few Belgians who had remained behind after the mercenary-led revolt of 1967. The single entrée turned out to be fish doused in golden mayonnaise, the ideal culture medium for every known pathogen as well as many unknown ones. Still, I had not eaten since breakfast, and so, risking stomach cramps and diarrhea, dug in—though not without first making some attempt to scrape off the biggest blobs of the golden poison.

Back at the hotel, I felt so sorry for myself that I decided to console myself with a hot bath. The enormous hotel bathroom had an old-fashioned tub on four legs in one corner, and I turned on the water. It had a brownish hue, but was hot; and, once in, I started to relax. For some moments, I even closed my eyes. When I opened them, looking up at the stained ceiling some ten feet above me, I thought I saw one of the largest dark blotches move. I first ascribed it to some optical effect of the steam and the low illumination from the single bare bulb. But no, it was moving. I stood up in the tub and looked again. The blotch was alive, and it was a giant scorpion. Although I was reasonably sure that the man downstairs would understand if I complained "*Il y a un scorpion*," there was no phone, and I certainly was not going to leave the creature, which seemed to be growing bigger, unobserved. Instead, I threw my slipper at the ceiling. Missing its intended object, it splashed into the bathwater. I pulled out the plug, keeping my eyes on my arachnid nemesis while waiting for the water to stop gurgling. I grabbed the soaked slipper, then the dry one, and started a bombardment which caused the scorpion to drop from the ceiling. As the monster stalked across the floor, I raced after it and smashed it with the mightiest wet whack I could muster. Leaving the messy evidence of my entomophobia on the floor, I got into bed, and averted my eyes from the bedroom ceiling until I could switch off the light. I didn't want to find something else above me moving.

Bushed, I slept past 10:00 A.M., when the persistent honking of an automobile awoke me. From the window of my second-floor room I caught a welcome sight: several beige Mercedeses were parked in front of the hotel, and an odd mix of men were getting out of them. The Congolese, dressed in dark business suits, with vests and ties, were perspiring heavily. The Americans were in shirtsleeves and open collars, except for McKelvey, who wore a tie, and Engel, who looked like a continental dandy in his ascot. "*Monsieur le Président*," he called up as he saw my wave, "come on down to meet your delegation." "*Monsieur le Président de la Délégation Américaine*" is what the Congolese thereafter called me on all formal occasions. I got to like it.

Traveling with the entourage of President Ileo, we got plenty of attention and the best treatment in the circumstances. The next few days in Kivu Province were spent on a variety of inspections and some tourism. Bukavu had a rundown look. The mansions and suburban houses of the Belgian colonials, undoubtedly pampered by poorly paid servants, must have once had lush, well-cared-for gardens, but now they were full of weeds. Many of the windows were broken, the paint or stucco peeling, the houses themselves deserted or taken over by squatters, obviously concerned more with matters of survival rather than with real estate maintenance.

IRSAC proved to be a monument to short-sighted colonial rule, which had never taken into account its inevitable end. A huge institution, and at one time reputedly the best research institute in central Africa, IRSAC had been abandoned by the Belgians at independence. They had trained virtually no native scientists; and except for a handful of Congolese technicians and a German primatologist serving as interim director, the institute was a sorry spectacle. Although primatology had been one of IRSAC's specialities, now only a couple of shabby-looking gorillas were lolling in a large sunken enclosure. The library was absurdly grand, with the heavy dark wood paneling of an old Central European university. Journal subscriptions and book purchases had ceased, of course, but the library had remained undisturbed, and apparently unused. As I browsed through a table of unbound publications, I picked up, to my astonishment, the transactions of the Albanian Academy of Sciences. I didn't know of such a journal's existence; even the Library of Congress in Washington, I discovered upon my return to the States, didn't carry it. Yet here in Central Africa a complete set lay unread, waiting for the inevitable arrival of termites. When I expressed my astonishment at this and other, only slightly less esoteric and (in view of the Congo's crying priorities) useless journals, I was informed that they had been obtained on a reciprocal basis when the Proceedings of IRSAC had been sent, during its Belgian heyday, to professional societies and institutes all over the world. If I ever get to Tirana, I will ask the Albanians about their Congolese connection.

I made a slightly more reassuring visit to the still-operating National Institute of Mines, where the European director offered me his left hand; his right was, I noticed, missing below the wrist. "*Monsieur le Président*," one of our Congolese hosts said to me, "let me present the director, Monsieur Alexandre Prigogine." "Prigogine?" I echoed in surprise. "There's a chemist by that name, an Ilya Prigogine." (In 1977, this Belgian physical chemist won the Nobel Prize.) "He's my brother," came the answer, and I thought no more of it.

Two days later, we crossed Lake Kivu to Goma, starting point of our single touristic detour: two days of game viewing in Parc Albert, the huge animal preserve in the northeastern Congo, with a side trip to view the recently erupted Nyamuragira volcano. I never grow tired of watching wild animals in their natural habitat, but what remains indelible in my memory from this trip are the white pelicans at one of the fishing villages near Goma. There were hundreds of them, so close together that their bodies obscured the water and they seemed to be walking on solid ground. Close up, their whiteness emphasized the impeccably straight, thin blue line along and below their long beaks and the sharply defined yellow bib on their necks. This living mass of white was broken every once in a while by dark-feathered pelicans, which, with their sausagelike, flesh-colored crops, were in striking contrast to their elegant, swanlike cousins.

The organizer of our venture was a dashing black version of the hand-some game hunter. His Australian bush hat went with the role. "Call me Albert," he told us. His humor, however, was more sophomoric than dashing. On the way to Rwindi, our overnight destination, he stopped the jeep by the side of a stream across which we could see some hippos and water buffalo. As we watched them, he suddenly yelled, "*Attention! Un crocodile!*" and started to run. Everyone scattered, most rapidly our Congolese hosts, who had still not changed from their business suits. "Where is it?" I panted as I finally caught up with Albert. "Just a joke," he laughed. In spite of my admonition that if he kept that up people would ignore any real warnings of his, his cavalier attitude was infectious. When we encountered a magnificent herd of elephants, he encouraged me to leave the jeep and approach them on foot with him. In South Africa's Kruger National Park, where years before I had seen my first elephants in the wild, any ranger making such a suggestion would be fired on the spot, and any tourist sent packing. Even in the East African game preserves, such bravado would have been discouraged. But with Albert somehow, I threw caution to the wind.

At the end of our trip, just before we boarded our Fokker Friendship plane for Kinshasa, he told me, "Come back alone and I'll arrange a real trip for you." He organized game trips professionally and owned the vehicles we had used. "Give me your address," I said (and my son did, in fact, take up Albert's offer a few years later). "Just write to me—Albert in Goma—you don't need a post office box." "But what is your last name?" I persisted. "Prigogine," he replied. I repeated my sentence of a couple of days before, "There's a chemist. . . ." Albert shrugged his shoulders. "My uncle in Brussels." "And the director of the Institute of Mines?" "My father," he said, and then told me about his native mother and about the leopard that had bitten off his father's hand before he was able to kill the beast.

II

The serious part of the trip started in Kinshasa. My colleagues dwelt on research areas related to many of the Congo's burning problems. Harrison Brown discussed the need for training native geologists if the rich mineral resources of the Congo were ever to be exploited properly. Addressing the sad state of the children we had seen near Bukavu, whose potbellies and reddish hair indicated that they suffered from kwashiorkor because they ate primarily bananas and hardly any protein, James Carter and Ernst Pariser proposed making available fish proteins among other solutions. McKelvey and Eicher addressed themselves to projects in agriculture. And I suggested a new area of research, based on a special natural resource of the Congo.

Back in the States when I started to read up on the area, I had been struck by its being the natural habitat of the largest number of gorillas and chimpanzees in the world. I was also preoccupied at the time with the lack of suitable animal models for contraceptive research. Reproduction is the most species-specific property of living organisms; and the higher primates, notably chimpanzees, were thought to be best suited for the purpose. They are not easily handled, however, because of their size, strength, and ungovernable temper; furthermore, chimpanzee-breeding colonies in the United States produced only a limited supply of animals at precisely the time when the Food and Drug Administration introduced the requirement of ten-year-long toxicology in monkeys for steroid contraceptives. For these reasons, and also because of cost, the less suitable lower primates had to be employed. I knew that *Pan paniscus*, usually called the pygmy chimpanzee (or *bonobo* in the African vernacular), was somewhat smaller than the common chimp (*Pan troglydotes*), and that it had been placed on the endangered list. I wondered whether we could consider using *Pan paniscus* as a biomedical animal model and at the same time do something about its endangered status. Wouldn't everyone be pleased, I thought, scientists concerned with birth control, and conservationists committed to the preservation of a shrinking animal species? In retrospect, I doubt whether I would have made this seemingly innocuous proposal had I anticipated some of its highly politicized consequences.

At the Kinshasa meeting, I proposed a multistage project: capturing of a few animals of both sexes, examining their health status, and, finally, releasing them on an island near their natural habitat to see whether they would easily reproduce in such quasi freedom. Kakowet, the prized male pygmy chimp of the San Diego Zoo, had fathered four offspring in captivity. A smallish island would have the advantage of preventing their escape without requiring any enclosure; at the same time, adequate food supplies could be assured by planting fruit trees, such as oranges, papaya, and guava, in addition to providing supplemental staples. An island would also make it easier to prevent poaching, which was common in inhabited areas. Concomitantly, detailed biochemical analytical work would have to be performed on a couple of male and female animals to determine whether *Pan paniscus* resembles humans in endocrinological terms, in blood chemistry, and in metabolism. If the supposition of a close evolutionary relationship were borne out, then the pygmy chimp might well become an important addition to the small group of animal species that pharmacologists and toxicologists use in human drug development. Whether we like it or not, animals are indispensable components of much preclinical research; furthermore, in certain fields, primates are the only suitable animal models. Reproductive biology is a case in point, where government regulations *require* the use of primates.

The pygmy chimp's smaller size would simplify handling in the laboratory, and so would its much more tractable nature and relative absence of aggression, as observed in zoos and in the wild. Its typical "Hi, hi, hi" cry—in marked contrast to the shrill, loud "Hou, hou, hou" of the common chimpanzee—typifies that difference in temperament. I felt that if preliminary studies justified it, a multidisciplinary institute could be established in the Congo, on the model of the International Center for Insect Physiology and Ecology in Nairobi. Congolese nationals could be trained in a variety of scientific disciplines related to reproductive biology and toxicology, as well as in primate behavior and large-scale breeding of *Pan paniscus*. It might even stimulate interest in birth control, an issue that was not even broached in that country, whose present lack of birth control was a ticking time bomb.

My proposal was accepted with enthusiasm by Ileo and officials from other institutions in Kinshasa, such as the Institut National pour la Conservation de la Nature, which, in view of its grossly inadequate resources, saw this as a welcome infusion of funds and sophisticated manpower for furthering its aim of preserving endangered species. This latter aim became one of the features of our formal written recommendations to the Congolese government. I knew, from more than one occasion at past BOSTID workshops in Latin America and Asia, that recommendations could be filed and not necessarily acted upon. Within a few months, however, the Congolese National Research Council formally asked our National Academy of Sciences to convene a small task force to get the pygmy chimp project under way. Even though I had made the suggestion, I was surprised when the National Academy selected me, an organic chemist without any expertise in primatology, to serve as chairman of the American group. The appointment made me an instant *persona summa grata* among ape specialists. An outsider with no desire to trespass on their professional turf, I was proposing an international research project under the auspices of America's most august scientific body, in a country that was heaven to primatologists but, at that time of political turmoil, hellish to work in.

The other Americans selected by the academy were the Harvard endocrinologist Roy Greep, Richard Thorington of the Division of Mammals at the Smithsonian Institution, and Geoffrey Bourne, director of the Yerkes Regional Primate Research Center at Emory University and editor of a six-volume treatise on chimpanzees. Prior to our departure, Bourne spent an entire weekend showing me through the Yerkes facilities; many a human baby would be considered pampered if it were treated the way Yerkes housed and handled its baby orangutans. Bourne was an enthusiastic supporter of the pygmy chimp project, *Pan paniscus* being the only higher ape species not then represented at Yerkes. Not in his wildest dreams did he anticipate the trouble the first pygmy chimps would cause there.

My former wife Norma, who usually joined me in my professional foreign travels, was the only woman in our African group. It also included Julien Engel, who had carried the brunt of all administrative details during our first Congo trip and had, as it turned out, to use all of his considerable diplomatic skills on this one. During the eleven months since my earlier visit, major changes had occurred. President Mobutu had consolidated his political supremacy after being elected in 1970. As part of his attempt to convert the many tribes of the former Belgian colony into a single constituency with a national identification, he had changed the name of the country and its currency. When we arrived in Kinshasa in April 1972, both were now called Zaire. Even the Congo River became the Zaire (the native word for "river"). Instead of business suits, most government officials now copied Mobutu's African version of the Mao suit, except with short sleeves and open collar. Popularly known as *abacost* (*à bas le costume*, "down with the suit"), it certainly made more sense in the hot, humid equatorial climate. Everyone was now called *citoyen*, and it was "citizen" Ileo who now received our delegation. However, the key member of the Zaire group was Joseph Ghesquiere, a Belgian expatriate and physiology professor at the University of Kinshasa. His knowledge of past and current political affairs, coupled with his brutal but also humorous realism, proved invaluable. Even more important, he had recently been appointed associate director of IRSAC in charge of its Mabali Experiment Station in the Equateur Province, where most of the pygmy chimps were thought to live. He had sent us great news: the government of Zaire would make available one or more small islands on Lake Tumba for the pygmy chimp breeding colony and was putting otherwise hard-to-obtain travel facilities at the disposal of our group.

III

Early one morning in 1972, we left our Kinshasa hotel for a military airport, where we boarded our private plane, an ancient white DC-3 with a bright red band around the windows. Our flight to Mbandaka, an important trading center on the Zaire River, took over two hours, much of it less than a thousand feet above the dense canopy of the tropical forest, a blurred mosaic in shades of green. We had a superb view of the varied tropical flora, streams, and occasional habitations, but since the plane had no functioning air conditioning, it was hot and muggy. Since the best way to cool off was to stand by the door, which could not be closed completely, and enjoy the rush of fresh air that came through the crack, I spent most of the flight standing up. When we reached Mbandaka, we circled the airport, which seemed virtually abandoned except for an airplane sitting upright on its nose and blocking the only runway. The Belgian pilot informed us that this accident had happened that very morning, and that since he could not land until the wreck was removed, we would have to land elsewhere—and promptly.

That alternate airport also seemed deserted. But as we buzzed the town, circling it a couple of times, people appeared from all over, on foot, by bicycle, and in a few motorized vehicles. By the time we got out of the plane on the hard dirt strip, a reception committee had formed and a band was striking its first notes. I can still see the chest-high drums, adorned in red and white on the sides, and the singing, swaying women. Most wore bandannas arranged like turbans, but the real knockouts were the ones without head covers. The variety of coiffures was surely beyond the imagination of most Western hairdressers: corn rows of tiny, woven pigtails constituted the tidiest and most symmetrical arrangement; the more substantial stumplike plaits made the women look like voodoo heads with nails stuck into them. The most imaginative designs were abstract sculptures of hair, strung like wire, that emanated from either side of the head and joined high up in the air. These resembled complicated cages into which a small pet might fit.

In town we were promptly served a feast. We later discovered how this nearly instantaneous reception and midday repast had materialized out of the hot, humid air. A minister of the central government in Kinshasa had been expected around that time, plus or minus a day, and the populace had simply assumed that we were he. They went ahead even after discovering the error: the cork of civic hospitality had been pulled. Except for some milky, fermented brew produced from coconut sap, which I refused, I ate most of what I was served out of a sense of noblesse oblige. Because I was being observed and coaxed, there was no way to nibble. Ever since my research days at Syntex in Mexico—where my daughter caught typhoid, my wife a brutal case of amoebic dysentery, and I uncontrolled diarrhea (at least three times per month)—I had taken the usual precautions when traveling in countries requiring an iron stomach and impenetrable intestines: don't eat anything raw that can't be peeled, and always ascertain what is being put on your plate. But now I violated every precaution. Only later did I learn from my wife that the unknown goo on my plate consisted of manioc dumplings drowned in goat stew. I prayed to all the pagan gods of hospitality to spare my intestines—and they heard me. I survived this culinary hurdle unscathed.

A couple of hours later, our pilot learned by radio that the runway in Mbandaka had been cleared, and we took off for our original destination. The car trip over terrible dirt roads to the IRSAC station at Mabali on Lake Tumba took nearly four hours, by which time we were exhausted. Everyone traveled by canvas-covered Toyota jeeps, except for my wife and me. Protocol demanded that we ride in the only automobile, a white Volkswagen beetle, which proved to be the worst possible vehicle for the red mud and deep puddles we had to traverse during a tropical downpour and for the fine red dust that later penetrated every crack and opening. We were as red as the VW by the time we arrived at the guest cottage. It had a huge bed—specially constructed, I was told, to accommodate the extremely tall King Leopold III, who visited here when Zaire was still the Belgian Congo. I and my consort were assigned the royal couch.

The next few days were spent inspecting the future island home of the pygmy chimps, examining the caged enclosure at the station which was intended for the initial quarantine and checks for tuberculosis and parasites, and going over logistic details: Should a Yerkes veterinarian be seconded to IRSAC, or should a Zairois be sent to Atlanta for training in accepted practices of careful and humane treatment of apes? Miraculously, the IRSAC station had been spared the depredations common in the Congo during the early 1960s. In addition to several substantial structures housing the research and supporting facilities, there were eight residences for senior staff, our guest house, and two native hamlets for the station's work force. The construction of the European-style residencies was simple: brick support columns, white stucco walls, and thatched roofs. What distinguished the structures were the primitive murals of native flora, fauna, and humans—all in a style reminiscent of cave paintings and remarkably well preserved. The station and hamlets were situated in a tropical forest, but each house or hut was surrounded by a clearing of dirt which was frequently raked or swept. One purpose of these clearings was to facilitate the recognition of poisonous snakes. Their camouflage was extraordinary. I took a series of color slides of a chicken-wire enclosure partially entwined by a long, brownish, leafless twig. Only when I saw its flitting red tongue did I realize what risks the naked village children took each day, and why their parents carefully cleared the areas surrounding the huts where they played.

We agreed that the Lake Tumba site was adequate for our purposes and the island large enough to offer its future inhabitants an acceptable facsimile of their natural forest habitat. The only thing missing were the chimps. The year before, a troop had been sighted in the neighborhood of the IRSAC station, but now only abandoned nests were left in the trees. Were the chimps killed by hunters, or did they simply disappear into a natural refuge like the newly established and virtually inaccessible Salonga National Park? (Within a few months of our departure, independently of our project, an American field primatologist, Arthur Horn from the Peabody Museum at Yale, came to Mabali and spent over a year with minimal success on a population survey of *Pan paniscus*.) To bring a breeding colony to the island, we concluded, an expedition using nets and tranquilizers would have to be launched.

I did encounter pygmies, if not chimps. One day, on a side trip with Ghesquiere, we followed some animal tracks until suddenly our jeep began to tilt at a precarious angle. Unbeknown to us, we had entered a swampy area; our left wheels were in the oozing ground up to the running boards. I visualized us walking for hours back to the station, even after Ghesquiere took off to see whether he could find any help in the neighborhood. But after a barely worrisome interval, I heard voices in the distance and saw Ghesquiere running toward me with a group of boisterous pygmies in tow. I am not tall, barely five foot seven, but I towered above all twenty of them. With conceit generated by my unexpected elevation to the hitherto unfamiliar status of a giant, I whispered to Ghesquiere, "How are *they* going to get us out of here?" as if the pygmies would have understood even if I had shouted. At a command from their headman, they moved to the tilting side of the jeep, grabbed whatever part of the vehicle was closest, and started to yell the pygmy equivalent of "One, two, three, hup! One, two, three. . . ." In practically no time the muddy jeep was back on terra firma.

"Now what?" I asked, surrounded by our cheery pygmy saviors. "Better pay them," Ghesquiere advised, whereupon I distributed one zaire to each. My expense voucher to the National Academy went all the way to the president's office and back to Engel for verification before the twenty-dollar item marked "tip to twenty pygmies for lifting jeep out of swamp" was authorized.

Even the return flight to Kinshasa could hardly be termed uneventful. An hour after take-off, my wife grabbed my arm and pointed out the window. One of the propellers was not turning. I do not know how long this had been going on, but moments later, the plane made a wide turn and the pilot appeared in the cabin. "We are returning to Mbandaka," he announced with a notable lack of assurance in his voice, "before we reach *le point de non retour.*" None of us spoke as we watched the green canopy of forest, a few hundred feet below, rush by our eyes. After one low pass over the town to alert somebody to come to the airport, we landed close to the damaged plane, which was still on the grass where it had been pushed a few days earlier. I was not surprised to learn that we would have to stay overnight to wait for a replacement plane because nobody would be able to repair our engine. It was scorchingly hot as we sat on the steps of the closed airport building, hoping that somebody in Mbandaka would be curious enough to drive out. Deciding to use the time productively, I stripped to my waist and washed my dirty, sweaty shirt under a spigot by the side of the building. I had barely draped my shirt over a low brick wall when we heard vehicles in the distance. Soon a Mercedes and a pickup could be seen heading for us. The former contained the local governor, who had seen us off just a few hours earlier and come to see what had happened. As *Monsieur le Président*, I could not possibly appear in dishabille before this official in his crisp brown *abacost*. I quickly put on the shirt, trusting that he would either not notice that it was soaking, or ascribe the dampness to white man's sweat. As I should have guessed, I was asked to ride in the Mercedes, and did so sitting ramrod straight without touching the back of the seat lest I leave a blotch. As we drove, natural capillary action drove rivulets of water down my shirt. I hoped that we would get to the town hall before the flow reached my groin and buttocks. Fortunately, the trip ended before I had to use the clumsily formal explanation I had prepared: *Je n'ais souffre pas d'incontinence.*

Protocol continued to plague me. There was no hotel in town, and three of the Americans were put up in the guest quarters of the Mbandaka brewery. I would not have minded staying there: although no beer drinker, on this trip along the equator I had consumed what to me seemed barrels of this brewery's product, which I considered the only safe beverage in the entire Equateur Province. But my wife and I, along with the oldest member of our group, Roy Greep, were put into stuffy, dusty rooms in the local bank, devoid of maid or even teller, since it was long past closing hours. The bank was considered the very top in the local pecking order.

We spent hours during our forced stay in Mbandaka walking through the market, which, in terms of diversity of color, people, and goods, was a sight to behold. There was a remarkable variety of pottery—white, brown, black, ochre; and the decanters had elegant long necks, many incised with graceful abstract designs. One stand displayed a charmingly bizarre combination of bright-colored plastic suitcases and, unexpected in this country of extraordinary hairdos, a selection of curly black wigs. Afterward, we headed for the banks of the Zaire River, the main artery of the country, to observe the loading and unloading of goods and packages, many of which women balanced on their heads with agile grace. I was almost sorry to learn of the arrival of a replacement DC-3 from Kinshasa to take us back to our first hot bath in a week.

Back in Kinshasa, before our departure for the United States, the Zairois and Americans agreed upon the appointment of Ghesquiere as local expediter of the project. His assigned task was to look into the shipment of a few pygmy chimpanzees to Yerkes for preliminary biochemical, immunological, and genetic studies before moving to the next and more expensive phases of my proposal. Yerkes would raise the funds for a Zairois veterinarian to accompany the animals and to be trained for a year at Emory. While I was disappointed not to have encountered in the wild a single pygmy chimp (every morning at Lake Tumba, I woke up thinking, "This will be the day"), I felt that everything was on a track quite as fast as the one that led to the establishment of ICIPE in Nairobi within two years. As it turned out, it took three years before the first pygmy chimps arrived at Yerkes; and like all major and even minor decisions in Zaire, even this one required President Mobutu's intervention.

IV

As one of those statistical implausibilities that turn up in life, I find myself writing this account of the dénouement of the *Pan paniscus* affair on a Sabena plane, flying again from Africa to Brussels. It is seventeen years later, the middle of July 1989, and I am on my way back to Stanford after a week-long scientific conference on marine chemistry in Senegal. On the way down, the movie shown was none other than *Gorillas in the Mist*, the story of Dian Fossey, the American woman who spent years in Rwanda studying the mountain gorillas before she was murdered. For once, I asked the stewardess for the earphones. I had followed Fossey's work for some time and knew that, having started in Zaire, she had been driven across the border to Rwanda only by the political turmoil in the former. Waiting for the film to begin, I reflected on the gorilla connection in my family.

An undergraduate at Stanford in the early 1970s, my son, Dale, got to know Francine Patterson, a graduate student in psychology whose doctoral dissertation dealt with her attempt to establish sign-language communication with Koko, a young gorilla living with her in a trailer on campus. Dale was interested in her project, and they soon became friends. I once slowed down on narrow Bear Gulch Road to let an oncoming car pass, only to see a gorilla sitting upright in the passenger seat next to the driver. It was Patterson and Koko on their way to Dale's house. I followed them and soon learned how truly social an animal young Koko was. Firmly, but friendly, she put one arm around my shoulder and then attempted with index finger and thumb of the other hand to remove a mole on my forehead, evidently assuming it to be an insect. (Shortly thereafter, I had it removed surgically.) On another occasion, while hiking over my son's side of the ranch, I was startled to see two gorillas running toward me. I did not know that Koko had acquired a male companion named Michael, and, for a crazy second, wondered whether I was back in Africa.

Dale made his professional debut as a filmmaker with Koko. With a friend, the French producer and director Barbet Schroeder, he produced a documentary of Patterson's intimate association and interaction with Koko, which was shown both in the States and Europe. This project was the preamble to a much more ambitious, full-length film, featuring the return of Koko, who was born in the San Francisco Zoo, to her ancestral home in Africa. Michael had not yet entered Koko's life; and, until he did, this female gorilla had known only human companionship and established primitive communication through sign language. The feature film was intended to deal with Koko's version of culture shock upon meeting her mountain gorilla cousins in eastern Zaire. Dale and Schroeder commissioned Sam Shepard to write the script; and in December 1976, they flew to Bujumbura to see what it would take to proceed. Adrien Deschryver, a Belgian then living near Bukavu, who had extensively studied the mountain gorillas on the Zaire side, provided them with a small plane to overfly the area. Later, in part through Albert Prigogine's organization, they hiked through the Kahuzi-Biega National Park, a gorilla preserve founded by Deschryver in the mountains between Zaire and Rwanda, and there located their first gorilla troop. Dale's family name even gained him entry to IRSAC's new Zairois director, who promised to offer local support for the film. Unfortunately, the project never got off the ground, and only the documentary was shot. As my jet hurtled toward Dakar, I could not help admiring the professional skill of *Gorillas in the Mist* and the logistical complications the producer and the director had overcome.

At Dakar, my hosts whisked me through the air-conditioned VIP lounge. Only a week later, departing, did I see—my vision only slightly exaggerated by frustration—that the Dakar airport affords passengers a glimpse of what it must have been like for slaves penned at Dakar harbor when that port was one of the main centers of the slave trade to the New World. Inside the dimly lit terminal, the humidity was 100 percent, and even though it was late in the evening, I was drenched in perspiration, working my way through the packed, pushing crowd toward the ticket counter. In spite of a marvelous week in Senegal, my irritation threshold was rapidly dropping as I waited twenty minutes while the passenger ahead of me, a grande dame in a dark suit, negotiated in elegant French the admission of her poodle into the first-class cabin. Three Sabena agents (lackeys, to my jaundiced eyes), two Senegalese, and one Belgian were fully occupied in the transaction with this woman who apparently lacked sweat glands, while I must have shed a pound or two of H_2O, as did most waiting passengers around us. Finally, the poodle was admitted into first class when it was agreed ("*Ça va, Madame, ça va*"), without resorting to scales, that he weighed only 4.5 kilos (the Sabena cut-off for canine cabin passengers is 5 kilos).

I may not like it, but at least I understand when a baby screams in a plane. But must one put up with barking dogs? The plane was about to leave, with the seat next to mine still unoccupied, when my nemesis from the check-in counter and her canine darling arrived. I repressed a snarl in my sympathy for the woolly dog and silently cursed Sabena. I wondered in whispered English to the stewardess standing next to me how they could possibly permit this sort of thing on board. What if he pissed all over me? I certainly wouldn't be able to contain *my* bladder from Dakar all the way to Brussels. She gave me a Gallic shrug, but my future travel companion had overheard me. Coolly, and in impeccable English, she replied that the poodle had taken a pill that guaranteed continence. After a few hours of writing, I finally fell asleep. When I woke up and turned to look out the window, I saw only the dog standing alertly on the seat, his gaze fixed on me. "So what were you bitching about?" the cuddly, quiet poodle seemed to be saying. When his owner returned, I apologized to her. From now on, I'm more than willing to travel with poodles—and will even take them over babies.

V

Would that our pygmy chimps had, once found, been able to travel as pleasantly from Kinshasa to Atlanta. As happens so often in Zaire, there was a complete turnover in the personnel of IRSAC and the National Research and Development Council, which meant that the wheel had to be reinvented before an acceptable agreement dealing with the transfer of the animals to Yerkes could be consummated—a process that caused my office files on the Zaire project to expand exponentially. During that time, Ghesquiere discovered that a Belgian physician and his wife living near Bosondjo in the Equateur Province had purchased four baby pygmy chimps from some hunters and raised them with tender care. They were prepared to lend a pair to Yerkes. But before this offer could be pursued, the couple had emigrated back to Belgium, somehow managing to "export" the chimps without a permit. The animals were eventually placed in first-class facilities at the Stuttgart Zoo, whose director offered to lend two of these animals to Yerkes for biomedical studies. When this possibility fell through because of a legal (and, to me, wise) restriction—animals on the endangered species list cannot be introduced into the United States without a legal permit from the country of origin (in this case Zaire)—we proceeded with the original plan of capturing some animals under IRSAC auspices. By then, President Mobutu's office had entered the picture. He had established his own private zoo and wanted any breeding colony established there rather than at Lake Tumba. The American ambassador, Sheldon Vance, did, however, succeed in persuading Mobutu to authorize under a lend-lease arrangement the shipment of three adult pygmy chimps to Yerkes, whereupon I managed to secure a small research grant from the Commonwealth Fund to cover the expenses of the capture and shipment of the animals.

Ghesquiere wrote in detail how this was accomplished. Citizen Jeje Songo, who, in addition to his native Lingala, spoke fluent French and German but no English, had participated at IRSAC in earlier captures of gorillas and chimpanzees. Geoffrey Bourne had raised funds to bring Jeje to Atlanta for one year's training at Yerkes; Jeje was also appointed to accompany the animals to the United States after their capture. Jeje and Sinclair Dunnett, an Englishman who had come to Zaire with a British expedition to retrace Stanley's route through the Congo ("Mr. Livingstone, I presume?"), headed for the plantation at Bosondjo, where the Belgian couple had purchased and raised their four baby chimps.

Of the manner of capture, Ghesquiere wrote:

The southern route had not been used for years, and it took us five hours (in a 4-wheel drive Toyota pickup) to move some fifteen miles as we had to hack our way through most of the time. We contacted the villagers, who all confirmed that bonobos (*Pan paniscus*) abounded in the forest. Catching young ones would be easy enough—they could deliver them within a day or two—but adults was another story. They agreed, however, that it could be done using their local nets. The basic procedure is the same as that described by *Citoyen* Jeje for the capture operations in Kivu. First, a few scouts will follow the chimps, sometimes for days, until they locate the nesting places in which the animals usually settle about one hour before dark, and which they do not leave until daybreak. The rest of the captors will then be brought to the site where they set up the nets. Early in the morning, one man is sent up into the tree where the chimps are nesting to scare them out. The pygmy chimps drop to the ground, where they are chased by the other men toward the nets. Once caught in the net, the captor standing closest keeps the chimp immobilized with a long stick until one of us can knock it out with an intramuscular injection of sodium pentothal. The chimp is then transferred to a cage, and some Valium added to the food for the first day to keep it quiet.

In this manner, *Citoyen* Jeje and Sinclair Dunnett captured a pubescent male and female, as well as an older female. At Bosondjo, the villagers offered them two baby chimps, apparently unconsumed leftovers from a hunt for meat. These animals were weak and suffered from intestinal parasites, a common occurrence among animals kept by villagers. All five chimps were flown by the U.S. military attaché in his Beechcraft to Kinshasa and, after transfer to President Mobutu's private zoo for a two-week period for preliminary health checks, were put aboard a Pan American cargo plane for New York. Jeje stayed with them throughout the flight, administering food and water and checking the cabin temperature. On 26 March 1975, shortly before midnight, the five chimps arrived at Kennedy Airport in New York, where they were met by Dr. Grant Kuhn, the chief veterinarian from Yerkes, who took them by heated van to the local animal shelter. The following day, the chimps went on a Delta Airlines DC-10 to Atlanta and then by heated van to the quarantine quarters at the Yerkes Center. Within a day, rectal and throat swabs were taken, blood samples collected for various hematological assays, and TB tests performed. It was essential that their health status be established before the initiation of any serious biochemical, immunological, and endocrinological tests.

After ten days, the babies, named Mukili and Masikini, stopped eating because of a severe *Candida* infection. In spite of treatment with penicillin and the fungicide Nystatin, and eventual feeding by stomach tube, the two infants died. Subsequent autopsy showed them to have been suffering from a variety of complications, including trench mouth, necrosis of the liver, and chronic pericarditis; there is little doubt that they would have died from these complications in Zaire. The three chimps captured by Jeje and Dunnett were named Lokolema (a mature female weighing over fifty pounds), Matata (a twenty-pound female), and Bosondjo (a twenty-three-pound male). Except for intestinal parasites, which they had brought with them from Zaire and were easily controlled by deworming, these three animals thrived at Yerkes and eventually provided a wealth of information.

In 1923, Robert Yerkes, then at Yale and later the founder of the primate center named after him, purchased from the Bronx Zoo his first two chimpanzees, which he named Chim and Panzee. Only after the formal description of *Pan paniscus* in 1928 was it recognized that Chim, whom Yerkes called an "intellectual genius" and whose "remarkable alertness and quickness to learn were associated with a cheerful and happy disposition which made him the favorite of all," was a pygmy chimp. Since its scientific description, in fact, *Pan paniscus*, partly because of its size and posture, has been thought to be closer to the suggested ancestors of humans (such as *Ramapithecus* and *Australopithecus*) than any other living anthropoid.

The initial blood chemistry and hematology values of the three pygmy chimps seemed to offer support to this view of an ancestral connection. As one who watches his cholesterol carefully and maintains it around 195 only with heroic dietary measures, I was pleased to learn that Lokolema's cholesterol value was 202, while Matata's and Bosondjo's were 182 and 195, respectively—without sticking to low-fat yogurt and fish. After the initial health checks, the three pygmy chimps were subjected to careful observation, which, in the case of the younger Matata and Lokolema, also involved close physical contact with a human observer. A psychologist, Sue Savage, described the two animals in terms that would have pleased Dr. Yerkes. In addition to their alertness and liveliness, and their responsiveness to social cues, she noted "a shyness, hesitancy, sensitivity, and affection not found among common chimpanzees." While the latter tend to sit apart when not playing or grooming, "pygmy chimpanzees tend to sit together, usually with one arm draped casually across the companion's shoulder." The pygmy chimp's sexual behavior also sounds almost human in Savage's account:

> Copulation may be either ventro-ventral or dorso-ventral and in either position several different postures may be assumed. Face-to-face peering and eye contact precedes almost every copulatory bout. . . . Responsive-

ness to the partner's facial expressions and vocalizations during the copulatory bout appears to be the rule rather than the exception.

These examples testify to the care and attention that the Yerkes staff extended to their temporary primate guests from Zaire. All of us associated with the project were chagrined, therefore, at the sudden eruption of almost hysterical charges and insinuations to the contrary. These were prompted by a page-long feature article in the *New York Times* on 15 May 1975, which described the arrival of the five animals at Yerkes, the death of the two baby chimps, and the scientific rationale for the project. The subsequent vituperation probably stemmed from the article's erroneous claim that all five chimps had been captured with nets under our project's auspices, with the implication that we were responsible for killing two members of an endangered species. The first missives came from a Shirley McGreal, who identified herself as the co-chairwoman of the International Primate Protection League in Bangkok. After writing to Bourne and receiving a lengthy, polite reply, she wrote to Engel asking for precise details of the National Academy's involvement, including the dates of our committee's visit to Zaire, and how much time was spent respectively in Kinshasa and in the field. After Engel replied in a long letter, McGreal wrote to the State Department, to the president of the National Academy of Sciences, and finally to me. Detailed replies from each of us did not satisfy her: she was convinced we had connived in a sinister operation to decimate the pygmy chimpanzee population. While I have a great deal of sympathy and admiration for conservationists working with modest resources and against great odds to promote an important issue, most of my abundant reservoir of good will got drained when I realized that McGreal, rather than being interested in the facts, simply wanted to tar and feather us as brutal animal killers. (I have never permitted the killing of deer or coyotes on our ranch; nor have I ever hunted or even owned a gun.) Thus, Bourne's statement, quoted by the *New York Times*, to the effect that an important goal of the collaboration between Yerkes and IRSAC "was to develop a conservation program for what remains of the wild population of pygmy chimpanzees" carried no weight with her. Nor did the written rebuttals by the chimpanzee specialist and ethologist A. Kortlandt from Amsterdam, and by Jacques Verschuren, the former director general of the Congolese National Institute for the Conservation of Nature, who even disputed the endangered status of *Pan paniscus*. But worse was to come.

Prompted by the same *Times* article, a Dr. W. C. McGrew of Stirling University in Scotland circulated a petition, eventually signed by some forty-three individuals, which opened with the blatant accusation that

Yerkes had illegally imported five chimpanzees that had been trapped for that purpose, two of which had already died. After condemning the Yerkes Center, the resolution "urged the government and people of Zaire to impose a total ban on the capture of pygmy chimpanzees from the wild." Copies were also sent to many scientific and government institutions, including the U.S. Department of the Interior and President Mobuto. That's when all hell broke loose.

The export and trapping of chimpanzees in Zaire was already strictly prohibited except under special dispensation, such as the one we had received. That neither the government of Zaire nor any other African country had been able to prevent all hunting or smuggling was, of course, well known; but it did not help to rub in that fact, least of all to President Mobutu, who was scheduled to deliver the opening address at a meeting in Kinshasa of the International Union for the Conservation of Nature. A hilarious letter from Zaire told me how the new director of IRSAC on his knees, practically kissing the ground, informed the president of the McGreal and McGrew petitions, whereupon Mobuto—formally known as *Citoyen Président Fondateur du Mouvement Populaire et Président de la République*—roared that this was an *"outrage à la souverainité nationale."* According to Ghesquiere, it was lucky that the copy of the petition shown to Mobuto did not include the names of the signatories, who would otherwise have been banned from ever entering Zaire and studying the very species they wished to protect. Mobuto proclaimed that Zaire had no lessons to receive from anybody in regard to conservation of nature; that *Pan paniscus* was Zaire's own and exclusive property and would be treated as the government saw fit; and finally, that plans with the breeding colony should go ahead full blast.

In spite of this presidential edict, the pygmy chimp project never progressed beyond the Yerkes biomedical research—for two reasons. First, there simply was no Zairois influential enough and willing to commit his time and career to the realization of such a project, in the way Thomas Odhiambo had done in Kenya with ICIPE. Ghesquiere, though a Belgian, had all the talents and energy to accomplish the task, but he had returned to Belgium to teach at Louvain. The second reason was that the middle and late 1970s were not good years to raise money for scientific work in developing countries, least of all in Africa; the necessary funds could simply not be obtained from organizations like UNESCO and WHO, to whom proposals had been submitted.

The signatories to the McGrew petition were a motley group which included some distinguished names like Jane Goodall, the chimpanzee ethologist. Almost one fourth of the signers were Stanford undergraduates who had been working with Jane Goodall at the Gombe Stream Research Center in western Tanzania. Three of them had been kidnaped by guerrillas from Zaire, who had held them for several weeks in Kivu Province before ransom was paid to effect their release. This unfortunate affair was largely responsible for Goodall's subsequent "divorce" from Stanford. I invited eight of these students to my office and then found out how little they really knew about *Pan paniscus* as a species and the project itself. Only when I dug through my bulging files to produce some of the actual evidence did it become obvious that they had been fed a garbled and incomplete version; they left, satisfied that ours had not been a venal attempt to decimate Zaire's pygmy chimp population.

The pygmy chimp project had one more outcome. In August 1976, Geoffrey Bourne wrote to the director of IRSAC: "As a token, we wish to seize this opportunity to offer the President [Mobutu] a pair of young orangutans, a great ape species that is not found in Africa. We do so in the hope that their sojourn in Zaire will symbolize even further the friendly and fraternal bonds that already exist so happily between our two countries." Then the diplomatic mill started to grind, slow and fine. The American ambassador, Walter Cutler, suggested that the two orangutans be transported on one of the semimonthly military flights from Charleston, South Carolina, that serviced the U.S. military establishment and the embassy in Zaire. After extensive trilateral cable traffic between the embassy in Kinshasa, the Pentagon, and the State Department, we learned that for the princely sum of $400 the U.S. Air Force would be prepared to undertake what might well be the very first shipment of an orangutan to Africa. And who finally made that generous offer? A colonel named Geraci. I should probably have written asking this phonetic relative of mine whether a dyslexic immigration official at Ellis Island had been responsible for the peculiar spelling of his name, but resisted the temptation. The files in my office and in my head were already stuffed to overflowing with pygmy chimp tidbits. Somehow, I sensed that Geraci's genealogical antecedents might just prove anticlimactic.

VI

It was April 1991. As an experienced skimmer of scientific journals, I quickly turned the pages of the latest issue of *Science*, when a striking color picture restrained my impatient finger. The legend "*Big talker*. Pygmy chimp Kanzi fashions a stone tool" froze the page before my eyes for a microsecond, just long enough for me to catch a portion of a sentence: "Sue

Savage-Rumbaugh of Georgia State University and Patricia Marks Green-field of the University of California at Los Angeles, claim a pygmy chimp named Kanzi can create sentences as grammatical as those of a 2-year-old child—and even invent new syntactical rules." If that were not persuasive enough, the next sentence in *Science*'s news report—"It would seem that the debate whether language is uniquely human is about to be opened again"—did the trick: once more I turned to my bulging pygmy chimp files.

They didn't lead me to Kanzi, but I did find an unhyphenated Sue Savage, the psychologist who had been the first person in the middle 1970s to have prolonged personal contact at Yerkes with two of our Zairean pygmy chimp immigrants, Matata and Lokolema. In response to my inquiry, she wrote that Matata eventually gave birth to four infants—three females and one male—all of them fathered by Bosondjo, the older male immigrant from the 1970s. Our Matata also became the stepmother of Kanzi, whom she had stolen from his natural mother, Lorel (on loan from the San Diego Zoo). Kanzi and two of his stepsisters are now living outside Atlanta in a fifty-five-acre forest, the Language Research Center (a joint enterprise of Yerkes and Georgia State University), as part of a program designed to examine their cognitive skills.

I was much too proud about this lately discovered outcome of our pygmy chimp project to kibitz on the preliminary research results accumulated by Savage-Rumbaugh, even if I were professionally qualified to do so. Why question Kanzi's ability to express a change in meaning by altering the order of words? For instance, when the trainer grabbed Kanzi's stepmother, Matata, Kanzi used symbols in the order, "Grab Matata." Yet when the stepmother bit someone, Kanzi selected "Matata bite." Other displays of pygmy chimp linguistic dexterity are evident in extracts of a letter Sue Savage-Rumbaugh sent me: "This morning he said 'Sue ball' to ask me to get him a ball, 'key open' to ask to go into the adjacent living area with Matata, and 'Hide Matata,' when I told him he could not open the door. He then said, 'colony room bedroom,' to tell me that he wanted to go through the colony room and into the bedroom." As Savage had mentioned in 1976, pygmy chimps differ from the common chimpanzee, *Pan troglodytes*, by their close resemblance to humans in social and sexual behavior. She was now in 1991 suggesting that the language behavior of our pygmy chimpanzee relative may point to language as originating (some five million years ago) in a common apelike ancestor, rather than as emerging solely in humans.

Another investigator, Nicholas Toth of the University of Indiana, has taught Kanzi how to strike flints from a stone and then to use them as tools. Toth is now checking whether Kanzi can teach flint making and tool use to the other pygmy chimps in Georgia and perhaps start a small community of toolmakers resembling early hominids.

The biggest difficulty in extending these provocative studies is the paucity of experimental animals (only seven founder animals in North America). Had our Lake Tumba breeding colony project taken off, that location in Zaire would have been the ideal spot for what could have turned out to be an idyllic bonobo kibbutz, in light of the fact that unlike other apes, the pygmy chimps (bonobo) display kibbutz behavior: all adults, irrespective of gender, participate in the care of offspring and in the collection and distribution of food. Their sexual behavior—as reported recently by the Japanese primatologist Takayoshi Kano—would, though distinct from that of regular chimpanzees, hardly pass muster in a kibbutz.

Kano was able to observe from a secret hiding place a troop of some sixty pygmy chimps which congregated around a feeding place where fresh fruit and sugar cane was provided daily. Like regular chimpanzees, the pygmies first displayed great excitement; but, in contrast to the former, among whom such excitement rapidly turns to aggression and fighting for food, the pygmy chimps' initial agitation was promptly transformed into sexual intercourse in the missionary position. Never did Kano observe any forced copulation or heterosexual rear entry.

If two females encounter each other during the initial excitatory phase when exposed to food, they approach each other belly to belly, rub against each other's genitalia, and then start to eat. A similar meeting by two males of equal rank manifests itself in a back-to-back approach, followed by rapid rubbing against each other's buttocks. Kato interprets such rubbing as a form of greeting, and the heterosexual as well as homosexual activity as a mechanism of excitatory release when coming upon a supply of food. All of these sexual manifestations stop within ten minutes, whereupon the animals cluster together and share the food peacefully. Another fascinating behavioral difference between regular and pygmy chimps, according to Kano, is the hierarchical position of the females. Male dominance is the rule among the ordinary chimpanzee, so that even the lowest-ranking male surpasses the highest-ranking female. Among the bonobos, however, senior females, and especially mothers, often occupy the dominant position. I was rather pleased to see that feminism among primates may have had its origin among the pygmy chimps.

Sue Savage-Rumbaugh, together with a group of Japanese primatologists, is now attempting to establish one or two bonobo conservation centers some two hundred miles west of our original Lake Tumba site. I wish them luck—enough of it so that one day Matata and her American pygmy chimp offspring can return to a safe haven in their ancestral home.

CHAPTER 15

The Pill at Forty: What Now?

M ANY WOMEN—PROMOTERS AS WELL AS CRITICS of steroid oral contraceptives—justifiedly perceive the 1960s as the Decade of the Pill. The 1970s, when the Pill entered adulthood, can equally appropriately be called the Decade of Abortion. The Pill seemed less important, because abortion had become a fundamental right of women, a status the Pill as just another drug, however revolutionary, had never acquired. The 1970s featured vehement arguments among women (and men) whether abortion should become legal or again be made illegal; in the process, a much more important and less divisive issue was largely forgotten: how to make abortion unnecessary.

This is the issue that grasped my attention—not overnight, but gradually. In my own professional life, the Decade of Abortion was full of contradictions. As a "hard" scientist, I was then in charge of all research—from chemistry through clinical studies—at Syntex, a firm that until then had spent a higher proportion of its R&D budget on contraception than had any other pharmaceutical company. In that industrial capacity, I had to take the regrettable, though unavoidable, step of recommending to my fellow directors on Syntex's board that we withdraw from this field of research and spend our stockholder's money on health areas for which there were fewer FDA barriers and shorter development times. At the same time, as both an academic at Stanford University next door and a concerned citizen, I started to speak out more and more about the tougher "soft" issues associated with birth control and population pressures.

I

Publicly, this gradual shift started in 1969 when I published an article in *Science* suggesting that whatever the United States does in contraceptive policy and research will have an overwhelming impact on developing countries; and that, as a matter of fundamental decency and even enlightened self-interest, we ought to take a global view of contraception. From such a perspective, I felt that we should visualize the world as consisting not so much of developed and developing nations, but as rather of geriatric and pediatric entities. In some of the most affluent countries, a fifth of the population will soon be above the age of sixty, whereas in many third-world areas, close to half the population is under the age of fifteen. No wonder that heart disease, cancer, and rheumatoid illnesses are high on the priority list of pharmaceutical companies, which focus mainly on the affluent geriatric consumers and not on the impoverished pediatric ones whose lives could be significantly eased by improved birth control.

The following year, in 1970, I published in the same journal a second article, "Birth Control after 1984," where I emphasized that unless major and largely unpopular changes in public policy were instituted (for instance, providing operational and legal incentives to prevent the pharmaceutical industry from leaving the field), birth control choices in 1984 would not differ much from those of 1970. Our increasing knowledge of human reproduction, along with American society's new preoccupation with safety and risk aversion, now made it necessary to plan on a twelve- to twenty-year development period for any new chemical contraceptive agent. In other words, around the twentieth birthday of the Pill, the rules of the game had changed dramatically.

As I started to move away from laboratory considerations to think more about the global issues associated with birth control, I found myself using a computer metaphor. *Hardware*, for me, meant all the actual methods used by people—steroid contraceptives, abortion, condoms, sterilization, and related topics that I, like other scientists in the field of birth control, understood and addressed. *Software* covered the more difficult political, religious, legal, economic, and sociocultural issues that individuals and, ultimately, governments must resolve before birth control hardware is employed. A deepening conviction that no advances in contraceptive hardware were possible without progress in software led me to shift to this topic much of my university teaching and even some of my outside lecturing. (I stuck to the metaphor, despite the unintended sexual innuendos of *hardware* and *software*, and it is now accepted jargon in the field.)

In the 1960s, the threat of an unmanageably crowded world (the "population bomb") had received so much notoriety in the press and other lay literature that some scientists and naïve technocrats even dared to broach the ultimate solution: a government-imposed contraceptive additive to food or water. I considered such an approach so absurd on technical grounds alone as to deem it pointless to address its ethical consequences. My earlier articles on birth control had always appeared in the scientific literature, but now I felt it was time to address a wider public, largely as a result of the feedback I had received during the early 1970s from my Stanford undergraduates in my new course "Biosocial Aspects of Birth Control." In the fall of 1978, I sat down at my thirty-year-old portable Olivetti to start on my first book addressed to a lay audience: *The Politics of Contraception*. In it, in a chapter entitled "Birth Control à la 1984," I posed a series of hypothetical questions:

What would a birth control czar do about the majority of the world's population who lack access to piped water? How could one set about discovering an agent that is effective only in humans, but not in pets and animals? How would one find a substance whose dosage could not be controlled; whose effectiveness should be limited to a person's fertile life span without affecting sexual development in infants and adolescents; whose effect would have to be offset through another magic chemical bullet?

In preparation for the chapter, I reread George Orwell's *1984* and Aldous Huxley's *Brave New World*, both of which envision government-imposed birth control as an aspect of a nightmarish future society. Just as I was ready to start writing, I found in Huxley's 1958 collection of essays, entitled *Brave New World Revisited*, the origin of the capitalized pill: "Most of us choose birth control—and immediately find ourselves confronted by a problem that is simultaneously a puzzle in physiology, pharmacology, sociology, psychology and even theology. 'The Pill' has not yet been invented." Might my imaginary journalist, to whom I had ascribed authorship of the new meaning of "The Pill," have actually read Huxley?

II

On this threshold of the Pill's entry into middle age, the glamour area of human reproductive biology has become the study of treating infertility rather than of controlling fertility. The lessened prestige of the latter field is reflected by the paucity of new talent entering it. Much less money is dedicated to contraceptive research and development than was twenty years ago; and now that the pharmaceutical industry has firmly turned its back on it, many scientists faced with the lack of material and societal support have switched to other fields.

The withdrawal, starting near the Pill's twentieth birthday, of the large American pharmaceutical companies from contraception research and development has had three major causes, as I indicated in chapter 9. The first was the extremely stringent animal toxicology tests newly demanded by the FDA in response to concerns about the long-term effects of steroid contraceptives. Second, the strident Nelson hearings in Congress had given the contraceptive field an extremely poor image, which was exacerbated by the commentary of certain women's groups and further sensationalized by the press. The third factor, and in the end the most devastating, has been the increasingly litigious character of our society during the past two decades, especially in respect to drugs and medical practice.

Unquestionably, the fear of litigation had a salutary impact on some practitioners and manufacturers in medicine in general, and in birth control in particular. The Dalkon shield IUD is a prime example of a case in which litigation was essential. But it is equally clear that the legal profession has gone overboard and that contemporary tort law with respect to legal liability has altered medical practice for the worse. No other country displays such litigious ferocity on matters medical—in terms of medical malpractice or product liability suits; and some (such as New Zealand) eliminate the need for such legal recourse altogether through a form of no-fault insurance. Is there any evidence that the lack of a pervasive "let's sue the bastard" philosophy makes the Scandinavian, Dutch, or Swiss consumer—to pick only a few examples—worse off in terms of ensuring acceptable medical standards than the average American?

In the case of contraceptives, litigious practices have bordered on the bizarre. In 1986, for instance, the Ortho Pharmaceutical Company lost a $5,151,030 judgment in Georgia because a woman who had used its spermicide, Ortho-Gynol, while unknowingly pregnant, claimed it to be the cause of her baby's birth defects—a possibility overwhelmingly rejected by current epidemiological evidence. And since the victim in most malpractice and product liability cases frequently recovers, after a delay of years, less than one half of the financial judgment, the remainder being consumed by the legal community, such litigation has imposed an enormous financial burden on precisely that segment of the population—the uninjured consumer— whom the legal system was designed to protect. Peter W. Huber, a legal scholar who coined the phrase "Bhopalization of U.S. tort law" (after the huge chemical accident in Bhopal, India, in 1984), summarized the situation in 1985 in one sentence: "For the many somewhat risky—but in the aggregate risk-reducing—products and services that may be deterred by the new tort system, the interests of future consumers are directly opposed to those of unlucky prior consumers who have already been injured by the hazard in question."

The impact of litigation on the Pill is especially instructive. Indisputably, a small percentage of women users has been physically harmed by the Pill. Society believes, as do I, that such victims should be compensated. But American society does not seem to believe, unlike the majority of advanced industrialized countries, that the tax-paying public should foot the bill or that the cost be shared equitably by the millions of beneficiaries of a drug—in this instance, the Pill. Our system simply dumps the problem into the lap of the manufacturers through product liability legislation. Even though few Pill suits brought to trial have been won by the plaintiffs, the legal cost for the drug and insurance companies over approximately ten years, starting in the late 1960s, escalated to such an extent, especially because of liberalized "discovery" rules permitting plaintiffs' attorneys to demand tens of thousands of documents, that settling out of court was often cheaper than defending in court. This fact did not escape the notice of its chief beneficiaries, a group of contingency-fee lawyers specializing in such litigation, who often share huge computer data bases built up from masses of documents.

The congressional Office of Technology Assessment reported in 1982 that during the preceding decade liability costs in the oral contraceptive field had been higher than for any other drug category. Who pays for these legal costs? The millions of women who benefit from the Pill and who would object greatly if they were returned to the narrow contraceptive options available before the Second World War. The cost of a monthly regimen of the Pill has increased tenfold during the past dozen years, even though most Pills currently on the U.S. market have been off patent for many years. Fear of litigation and unavailability of insurance has eliminated market competition: until 1988, no generic versions were available, and even the ones that have subsequently appeared cover only a fraction of the market (they are, in any event, manufactured by the producers of the original formulations). During the height of these Pill litigations, starting in the mid-1960s and tapering off in the late 1970s, drug companies were unwilling to publicize the number of suits and the collective legal costs associated with defending them, ostensibly because such publicity would stimulate further frivolous litigation. Yet true ambulance chasers would never shy from the latter; in reality, such secrecy only prevents the public from knowing the real financial burden Pill users ultimately have to assume. Only in the vaccine field has the public, or at least Congress, begun to learn the facts of life in the medical litigation jungle.

Vaccines and contraceptives are obvious targets for superlitigation, because they are not curative drugs to be taken by people already ill; they are administered to healthy people to prevent a condition that may never occur. Even though a no-fault insurance system (structured around self-funding) for certain medications, which have passed FDA scrutiny, would be the single most important incentive for the gradual re-entry of the pharmaceutical industry into the field of contraceptive innovation, certain differences in the public's perception of vaccines versus contraceptives operate against the extension of special incentives to the latter class.

The National Childhood Vaccine Injury Act of 1986 had been introduced by Congressman Henry A. Waxman, a Democrat from California, to provide a form of no-fault insurance against possible injuries from the seven pediatric vaccines. The rationale for this limitation was that all children must receive such vaccinations to attend school, and that a few children are bound to be harmed by such compulsory vaccination (an implicit acknowledgment that "safe" is not "absolutely safe"). Manufacturers of these vaccines were threatening to withdraw from the field because of ever-increasing liability suits, and the Waxman bill was designed to stem such a crisis in vaccine production. Revenues come from a special tax imposed on any childhood vaccine. Like any insurance system, the beneficiaries are expected to pay the premium for risk protection. The Childhood Vaccine Injury Act became a model for a subsequent California State Assembly bill that exempts prospective AIDS vaccines from such product-liability barriers. In my opinion, both of these legislative actions are appropriate precedents for similar initiatives in the contraceptive field.

A substantial portion of the public does not, however, equate the societal and personal costs of an unwanted pregnancy and of an unwanted child with the immediately evident health consequences of a disease, be it measles or AIDS. Among some groups in the United States, notably in congressional and administrative circles, contraception is inherently suspect because of its actual or perceived effect on sexual mores. But most important, American society is likely to look askance at incentives that, directly or indirectly, may benefit pharmaceutical companies, when such firms are generally among the most profitable sectors of U.S. industry. Although we live in the most capitalist country of them all, we are sufficiently suspicious of corporate profits, especially those associated with health care, to prefer penalizing our own purses rather than appear to be filling corporate coffers.

III

According to a 1990 survey by the Population Council, the cost ($216) for a year's supply of Pills in the United States is the highest in the world. To cite just a few comparisons: German women, with an annual expenditure of $105, come closest, followed by Dutch ($96), Swedish ($58), British ($43), French ($30), and Singaporean ($7) consumers. Even more damning is the observation that our cost of Pills as a percentage of GNP per capita is also the highest: four times that in Sweden and ten times that in Singapore.

To add insult to injury, no new active progestational ingredients have been added to the Pills of American women since the 1960s. (In fact, as far as the Pill is concerned, America is now a "banana republic": *none* of the active steroid ingredients of the Pill is manufactured in the United States; they are imported from Germany, France, or Japan.) By contrast, no fewer than three new ones were introduced in Europe in the 1980s. The leading manufacturer of the most widely prescribed Pill in Europe has still not introduced its product (desogestrel) in the United States—in part because of potential liability exposures. Yet this product has one of the lowest dosages of all Pills and, moreover, an improved metabolic profile compared with the other progestational steroids currently available to American women.

In some respects, the situation has improved since the scare of the Nelson hearings, partly because Pill dosages have continued to be reduced since the mid-1970s, and with them the incidence of serious side effects. Although the number of American users dropped by over 20 percent to about eight million women in the 1970s (though continuing to increase in third-world countries), it has, since 1981, risen precipitately to the current all-time high of over sixteen million. The consensus now is that for healthy young women, the Pill is certainly the most effective contraceptive method and probably one of the safest. Women in their middle thirties and older were thought to be at greater risk in terms of cardiovascular complications, and the current use pattern among such women in the United States still reflects these beliefs, although the most recent epidemiological evidence with low-dose Pills suggests that such risk applies only to heavy smokers.

Dosage reduction has not only been achieved by further lowering of the progestational and estrogenic components of the Pill; in addition, phasic regimens have been introduced in which the hormonal content of the Pills does not remain fixed but fluctuates in order to mimic more closely the fluctuations of the natural hormones during a woman's monthly cycle. This effect has even led many physicians to recommend the use of such triphasic Pills (with their reduced influence on lipids and lack of deleterious effect on glucose tolerance) for young insulin-dependent diabetic women—a group for whom the Pill was previously strongly counterindicated.

Still, it would be naïve to assume that most women have now dropped all of their misgivings about the Pill's possible dangers. The legacy of the early 1970s is still with many; as a consequence of these concerns, of cultural changes such as the marked increase in working women, and of the lack of other acceptable alternatives, the incidence of sterilization has risen so sharply that this essentially irreversible method now surpasses Pill use among American married couples. Here we see again a peculiar American phenomenon in comparison with Western Europe: according to a survey conducted in the mid-1980s, 1 percent, 5 percent, and 7 percent, respectively, of Italian, French, and West German women used sterilization for birth control, compared with over 30 percent of Americans.

The attitude of feminist activists toward the Pill has also changed. Sarcastic pronouncements like "Get high on our latest special, the power-penis-potency complex's Pill," found in some of the radical press of the late 1960s and early 1970s, are rarely seen any more. Germaine Greer, author of *The Female Eunuch*—an influential book of the 1960s—is one of the few feminists who remains implacably opposed to the Pill. Had Greer's more recent, weighty opus, *Sex & Destiny: The Politics of Human Fertility*, not carried her name on the cover, I would not have guessed the author to be the same sharp and witty woman I had once seen on a Dick Cavett TV talk show. The date of Greer's *Sex & Destiny* (1984 of all years) seems to be off by about a century. Her born-again contraceptive fundamentalism still has no use for the Pill and even denigrates the diaphragm in favor of the classic nineteenth-century combination of cervical cap, condoms, and her cosset, coitus interruptus. Greer pays homage to Italian men, who—according to her admittedly "impressionistic evidence"—hone their proficiency at coitus interruptus out of regard for the sexual pleasure of their women. I cannot help but interpret Greer's Mozartian description of such Italian competence as a discreetly public tribute to the source of her impressionistic evidence for, generally speaking, the state of birth control for women in Italy is deplorable: studies published in 1987 show that the quality of contraception in Italy is the worst in Western Europe. No wonder that abortion was legalized in the middle 1970s, and that the Vatican's objections were over-ridden in two plebiscites.

The current position of the majority of informed and influential feminist spokeswomen toward contraception in general, and the Pill in particular, reflects the realities of the 1980s. Like most American women, they want for themselves and for their partners more choices, to suit the personal and professional lives of women working outside the home. They want up-to-date information on each method, which, in the case of the Pill, includes discussion of potential negative side effects as well as of the more recently discovered noncontraceptive benefits, such as the reduction in pelvic inflammatory disease, ectopic pregnancy, benign breast disease, ovarian cysts, endometrial and ovarian carcinomas, dysmenorrhea, and premenstrual syndrome. The press started to publicize these only during the last few years, and the FDA has now followed suit by adding the list of benefits to that of the side effects in package inserts of oral contraceptives.

Largely as a result of their activism, moreover, women are now represented in substantial numbers in decision-making bodies dealing with contraception, such as the advisory committees of the FDA, the National Academy of Sciences, the National Institutes of Health, and the World Health Organization. Many of the scientists and section heads of the CDC (Centers for Disease Control) in Atlanta—the U.S. government's main monitoring center for epidemiological studies on contraceptives—are women, and so is the current director of the NIH's Center for Population Research, which funds all NIH-supported work on contraceptives. And whereas in the 1960s the overwhelming majority of American obstetricians and gynecologists were men, more than half of the medical residents and young practitioners in that subdiscipline are now women. For the first time in the history of my own university's medical school, the chair of the Stanford Gynecology and Obstetrics department is a woman, Dr. Mary Lake Polan, who manages to combine active research, clinical practice, and administration with raising three small children.

Yet just as women have finally entered every aspect of contraceptive development—from research and testing all the way to delivery of the product—their choices are becoming fewer. This is primarily a consequence, again, of public, governmental, and media response to the complaints in the 1960s and 1970s of women who dreamed of a perfectly "safe" Pill or other contraceptive without accepting the caveat that "safe" simply means "generally not unsafe." Few of these women would then have predicted that their understandable outcries during those teenage years of the Pill would also significantly discourage any prospect of a male Pill. If a woman objects to wishy-washy answers to the question, "What happens if

I take the Pill for twenty years?" how would she feel if the period of time were escalated—as it would be with men—to forty or more years? With women, the question usually reflects their fear of cancer, whereas men are even more afraid of possible interference with sexual potency. Just consider the resulting legal exposure to potential liability suits: impotence or prostatic cancer are two conditions commonly associated with aging in males, but is it not likely that many a man on *his* Pill might then blame one or the other condition on the contraceptive he had been taken during the preceding decades of his reproductive life?

In 1979, in *The Politics of Contraception*, I dedicated a long chapter to the topic "Future Prospects in Male Contraception," in which I pointed out that "it is not unreasonable to ask the man to carry more than an equal share of the contraceptive burden since the woman bears all of the reproductive load" (this is why years ago I underwent a vasectomy). Yet in spite of interesting laboratory leads, I felt that I had to make the brutal, but also realistic, prediction "that every postpubescent American female reading this chapter in 1979 will be past the menopause before she can depend on her male sexual partner to use his Pill." If pharmaceutical companies are not willing to confront the myriad questions and problems associated with the development of a new contraceptive to be taken by healthy women for a decade or two, are they likely to change their minds in the face of the even more complicated issue of male contraception?

When Sunday's *New York Times Book Review* carried a long critique of my book, its author, a male political scientist, categorized that sentence as "nasty," and my attitude toward women as "depressing." His conclusion—that I seemed "most sympathetic to men who object to contraceptives"—promptly led me to see his name, A. Hacker, as a job description. But even a hacker's gut response of simply damning the messenger without bothering to understand the message demonstrates that the public simply does not want to hear about the ever-decreasing chances for a male Pill.

IV

Another reason scientific attention has moved away from contraceptive research is that, since the late 1960s, country after country in the developing world has recognized the threat of uncontrolled population growth and started to implement birth control programs—in some cases, such as China's, on a huge scale. Health professionals in these countries are concentrating on the *delivery* rather than the *creation* of contraceptive methods and, thus, are promoting—in my opinion, correctly—education, the creation of the appropriate infrastructure, the integration of contraception with maternal and child health care, and the optimum utilization of *existing* methods (the Pill, IUD, condom, injectable steroids, and sterilization), rather than searching for new contraceptive methods. In other words, the emphasis is now on contraceptive software coupled with the hardware in hand, rather than on the development of major changes in the latter, because time has become vital if population growth is to be contained.

On the fortieth birthday of the Pill, the world's rate of natural population increase is estimated at 1.8 percent per annum—a significant improvement over the situation a decade earlier and to a considerable extent ascribable to the effectiveness of the birth control program in China, which contains one fifth of the world's population. Although 1.8 percent may constitute a poor return for one's bank account, such an annually sustained rate of population growth still has the staggering consequence of doubling within thirty-nine years the number of potential future parents—that is, an increase of today's 5.3 billion people to over 10 billion before the year 2030. But even a cursory analysis will show that the situation is much grimmer than these figures indicate, because people are spread across the world no more evenly than are economic or natural resources.

Two thirds of the world's inhabitants are centered in only twelve countries ranked here in respect to population size: China, India, the Soviet Union, the United States, Indonesia, Brazil, Japan, Nigeria, Bangladesh, Pakistan, Mexico, and Germany. Assuming 1990 natural growth rates, what will the numbers be twenty-four years from now, an insignificant time interval on the scale of human existence? (If I should live as long as my father, I will still be able to see the numbers rolling in.)

Long before 2015 (when the Pill will be sixty-four years old—ancient for a drug, but still sprightly for many a woman), Europe's sole representative, Germany, will have disappeared from that list, for its population doubling time is seven thousand years! Newcomers to the list, such as Egypt, whose present population of 55 million will double in twenty-four years, will replace Europe's only representative. But instead of newcomers, let us focus on Africa's representative, Nigeria, currently the world's eighth largest country. Like Egypt, its doubling time is only twenty-four years, which means that, unless dramatic steps are instituted soon, Nigeria's population by 2015 will be essentially equal to that of today's United States (now the fourth most populated country in the world and also ranked fourth in terms of land surface). Nigeria is not only incomparably poorer, but it occupies the thirty-first position in terms of area. I could cite other horror scenarios, such as Bangladesh's: given its current doubling time, it could also approach the United States's current population by the year 2015. Yet Bangladesh, frequently called an economic basket case, is not even among the top fifty countries in terms of land surface.

The availability of contraceptives alone will, of course, not stem this population growth. Many "software" issues of a political, economic, cultural, and religious nature play a key role. Nevertheless, the actual contraceptive hardware available and acceptable in these countries is also important; it is here that the differing perspective of women in America compared with that of their counterparts in poor countries is particularly striking. With us, IUDs have practically become a dirty word; yet in China, 45 million women are estimated to be wearing an IUD developed in the 1960s, so that it is the most prevalent contraceptive in that country. In Mexico, similarly, where the government switched in 1974 from a laissez-faire, pronatalist policy to one of increasingly aggressive population control, of which IUDs and steroid contraceptives are the key components, followed by abortion. But then Mexico faces other problems that hardly permit product-liability litigation or other luxuries of a rich society. In 1951, when our group synthesized the Pill in a Mexican laboratory, Mexico had 28 million inhabitants; in 1991, as I write these words, its 86 million makes it the eleventh most populous country. Its capital has become the biggest and most polluted city in the world; by the turn of this century, Mexico City's population will probably equal that of the entire country in the year of the Pill's birth. In other Latin American countries, such as Brazil, IUDs are hardly used, and the Pill continues to be the method of choice. Finally, many Asian women prefer steroid injectables, which certain women's health groups in America continue to oppose ferociously.

As for the United States, Japan, and the Soviet Union—two of these superpowers that might be expected to be taking the technological lead in extending the range and quality of human birth control—the situation is distinctly stagnant. No meaningful research is performed in this field in the Soviet Union, the country with the highest per-capita abortion rate in the world; the quality of its birth control is miserable, and the Pill essentially unavailable. Japan's contribution has been limited to condom improvements; and the United States, as a result of White House pressure, has essentially prohibited government support for any research in methods that interfere with reproduction once an egg is fertilized—precisely the area where advances are most likely. Yet until now, the governments of these three countries have been dangerously oblivious of the stark fact that *the incidence of abortion reflects the quality of contraception*. The Pill is still not approved in Japan; indeed, Japan, though racing into the twenty-first century in most technological and economic respects, still depends on two prewar methods of birth control: condoms and abortion. Although not officially acknowledged, its abortion rate is one of the highest in the world.

V

Because it teaches important lessons about "software" issues, I often discuss in my public lectures the little-known background responsible for the anachronistic situation in Japan. Why, on the Pill's fortieth birthday, should its use for contraception still be illegal in a technological superpower? The story starts in early 1958, when Dr. Edward Tyler of the Los Angeles Planned Parenthood Center, Alejandro Zaffaroni, my Syntex colleague, and I flew to Japan under the auspices of the Japanese Pharmaceutical Society to present lectures on the chemistry, biochemistry, and clinical results in regard to Syntex's norethindrone as an orally effective progestational agent for menstrual regulation and for contraception. Our purpose was to arrange for commercial distribution of that drug in Japan. In a remarkably short time, Shionogi & Company, the large drug firm located in Osaka, became Syntex's Japanese distributor and soon thereafter received Japanese government permission to market norethindrone for the treatment of menstrual disorders. I was convinced that Japan would be one of the first countries after the United States to sanction the use of steroid oral contraceptives. There were no religious or moral obstacles to its use. After the end of the war, the Japanese government had instituted a strong antinatalist policy, which was implemented primarily through readily available abortion provided by the *private medical sector*. My prediction was about to be realized, since in the early 1960s *Kosei-sho*, Japan's FDA, was on the verge of recommending approval of the Pill for oral contraception. The thalidomide episode and several other related drug-toxicity issues, however, caused *Kosei-sho* to become extraordinarily cautious. Ever since, safety rather than efficacy has been the watchword for the Japanese drug-regulatory authorities. No wonder Japan now boasts of more "useless" but otherwise harmless drugs than any other modern country (including a supposed anticancer remedy, selling at the rate of over half a billion dollars per annum, which no other country has approved).

Two other grounds—associated, ironically, with the unsurpassed efficacy of oral contraceptives—kept the Pill from the Japanese market, although officially the delay was solely attributed to a concern for side effects. The first was the opposition of a segment of the Japanese medical profession that provided abortion services and feared the loss of substantial income if the Pill were to be used widely in Japan. The size of this income can be judged from the fact that most Japanese physicians charge for abortions outside the national health insurance system, and do so at rates that are comparable or even higher than American ones. By the late 1980s, I estimate that such annual income easily exceeded half a billion dollars, money that is frequently not reported to the tax authorities. In addition, the government feared that approval of the Pill would also make it more readily available to the unmarried young and increase premarital sex. Such a concern is consistent with the Japanese social setting; its youth supposedly exhibits one of the industrialized world's lowest rates of premarital sexual activity.

Given this background, why has the Japanese government suddenly decided—after thirty years of clinical experience in the United States and Western Europe—to join the rest of the world in terms of modern birth control and approve the Pill for contraception in 1992? *Kosei-sho* decided to follow the recommendations of a specially appointed advisory group of twelve men. (The absence of female members prompted the following comment in the *Asahi Evening News*: "All 12 members of the Pill research group of the Health and Welfare Ministry were men. We do not know why the team was dominated by males, but this strikes us as strange.") These dozen wise men presented the following convincing arguments:

1. The introduction during the past fifteen years in the West of low-dosage oral contraceptive formulations that reduced or even eliminated a number of deleterious side effects.
2. The publication, during the 1980s, of major studies in Britain and the United States reporting the occurrence of several important, beneficial, noncontraceptive effects associated with the use of the Pill.
3. Consideration of the *true* (rather than *officially* reported) incidence of abortion in Japan. Reduction of that incidence through wider use of oral contraceptives is now considered a significant benefit, which was not taken into consideration earlier.
4. Perhaps most important, recognition of the current use pattern by nearly a million Japanese women of the high-dosage progestin-estrogen combination that *Kosei-sho* had approved over thirty years ago. Officially, such a regimen is only to be applied therapeutically for the treatment of gynecological disorders, but as many as 80 percent of these users actually employ them solely for contraceptive purposes. This means that hundreds of thousands of Japanese

women may be consuming a contraceptive Pill at least ten times stronger than any used elsewhere, without having recourse to the lower dosages with their well-documented, marked advantages for long-term administration. Even more important, since such use for contraception was not officially sanctioned, none of the presently available Japanese steroid preparations can contain any package inserts or other descriptive information warning a woman about the consequences of long-term consumption of such high-dosage Pills.

The Soviet Union and Japan strikingly illustrate the close relation between abortion and contraception. But in these countries the abortion issue is not politicized. What about the United States, which has a comparatively much lower abortion incidence ("only" 1.6 million per annum), but the highest teenage pregnancy and teenage abortion rate of any industrialized nation? It is here that in the 1970s and 1980s, we have, in allowing abortion to become a matter of single-issue politics, lost any hope of enlightened policy in respect to birth control. Therefore, before I can address the Pill's future beyond its fortieth birthday, I need to examine the policy issues associated with abortion in America. This topic has preoccupied my thoughts and lectures for nearly two decades.

VI

For most women who have an abortion, it is a choice of last resort. But like it or not, of the various means of birth control, abortion is, worldwide, one of the most frequently practiced methods: approximately 50 million are performed each year. Only the Pill and sterilization are used more widely. Except in China, most abortions are the result of individual women's decisions, rather than government-imposed.

Nearly 40 percent of the world's people live in countries where there are virtually no restrictions on first-trimester abortion. These range from the United States and Holland, to Catholic countries like Italy and France, Muslim countries like Tunisia, and officially atheist countries like China and the Soviet Union. In another 25 percent of the world—in nations as diverse as India, Great Britain, Japan, and most East European countries (including firmly Catholic Poland)—permission for abortion is granted almost as liberally, since social factors such as inadequate income and unmarried status are taken into consideration. Among another 10 percent of the world's population, narrower grounds (fetal damage, rape, and incest) are accepted as reasons for abortion.

Therefore, only a quarter of the world's population lives in countries where abortion is still either totally illegal or permitted only to save the life of a pregnant woman. These include most of the Muslim nations of Asia, the majority of Africa, four West European countries (Ireland, Spain, Portugal, and Belgium), and two thirds of Latin American countries. In these Latin American states occur the largest number of illegal abortions (and deaths associated with them). Although today in the United States abortion is legal, and has been since the 1973 Supreme court decision of *Roe* v. *Wade*, presidents Reagan and Bush's attempts to pack the Court with strict anti-abortionists may well turn the clock back to the days when hundreds of thousands of women had illegal abortions, many self-induced or performed under dangerous and life-threatening conditions. Before we allow this to happen, we ought to learn from the experience of other countries that have tried to outlaw abortion—Romania, for instance.

In 1965, abortion was legal and virtually free in Romania, whereas contraception was essentially unavailable; abortion, therefore, became the main vehicle for fertility control. The Romanian government was concerned not so much about the number of abortions as about its falling birth rate at a time of relatively rapid economic growth. Overnight, the government instituted a very restrictive abortion law, with the result, unprecedented anywhere in the world, that Romania's birth rate skyrocketed in one year from 13 to 34 per 1,000. How jubilantly the men in Bucharest—and I use the word *men* with intention—must have congratulated themselves on the spectacular success of their anti-abortion policy.

Admittedly, this was policy, not politics, but the results were an almost unmitigated disaster. By 1968, the birth rate underwent an equally dramatic drop—from 34 back to 19 per 1,000—because it took less than two years for the abortion system to move underground. What the men in Bucharest had not taken into consideration, but could easily have predicted, was the increase in deaths associated with illegal abortions. By the time a decade had passed, this death rate had increased by a factor of 10; but the birth rate has not changed since 1972.

Now, if the Bush and Reagan appointees to the Supreme Court illegalize abortion, there will unquestionably be a similar rise in the maternal death rate. This increase would, however, occur among the poorest women and would otherwise not be as widespread as many people predict. The reason is that, having had access to safe abortions for nearly two decades, American women will hardly permit themselves to resort once again to bent coat hangers. Initially, well over a million women would look for illegal but relatively safe abortions—which organized crime would take the opportunity of providing for a substantial fee. All but the most naïve will concur that criminalizing abortion inevitably will draw more criminals to the scene. Surely the lesson of Prohibition days should not be lost, nor that of the present drug abuse problem. Unless we address ourselves to the underlying causes of such social problems, declaring them illegal is almost pointless, however virtuous we may feel in doing so.

Much as laws against alcohol and drug abuse, however, are designed to protect the users, no anti-abortion law has ever been introduced anywhere for the protection of women. On occasion, as in Romania, the rationale has been blatantly demographic. Most countries, including the United States, have used these laws to enforce a standard of sexual morality; even today, the common objection that removing a few-weeks-old embryo is "killing a baby" frequently reflects puritanical attitudes toward sex that the objector, whether sincere or not, feels should be imposed on others. Why do the vast majority of anti-abortionists make exceptions in cases of incest or rape? The answer is that the anti-abortionists consider a raped woman innocent and hence eligible for an abortion, while a woman who indulges in voluntary intercourse is judged guilty and hence doomed to an unwanted pregnancy.

The pointlessness of legal sanctions is most obvious in the shockingly high teenage abortion rate in the United States. To the pious, who cite Sodom and Gomorrah, this bespeaks lax sexual morality, greatly increased sexual activity at an increasingly early age, the breakdown of the American family. Of course, the reasons behind the breakdown of the American family are well documented, and making abortion illegal is hardly likely to bring it together again. And the argument about the cause of American teenage abortions is at least partly specious. A study of teenage sexual conduct and abortion in the United States, as compared with other affluent countries such as Sweden, Holland, and France, showed that their teenage abortion rates are just a fraction of our own. Holland's, for instance, is almost one tenth of ours. Yet by age seventeen, just about as high a proportion of Dutch or French girls have become sexually active as have American ones. In Sweden, every age group shows a considerably higher percentage of sexually experienced females than in the United States, yet the Swedish abortion rate is less than half of ours.

Of the many reasons for our extremely poor showing in terms of teenage pregnancies, three stand out. Instead of providing early and realistic sex education focusing on human sexuality, as Sweden does, with birth control then following as a logical appendix, the American decentralized educational system does a terrible disservice to many youngsters who attend schools where such curricula can be vetoed by a few vociferous parents. Similarly, until recently, no American high school was prepared to provide contraceptive counseling or services to its students, even though in many of these schools more than half the students were known to be sexually active. Finally, we provide strikingly mixed signals to our youth: on the one hand, sex is displayed graphically in magazines and films at its most prurient, while simultaneously we proclaim a sexual morality reminiscent of the Puritans. For instance, in the late 1980s when sexually transmitted diseases and AIDS had become rampant, all three national TV networks refused to air a two-minute public service announcement prepared and paid for by the American College of Obstetricians and Gynecologists. What were the contents of that dangerous message? A brief discussion of various contraceptive options and a toll-free number that teenagers could call to obtain a free pamphlet on birth control. A CBS executive even had the temerity to state that "contraception is an unacceptable subject for public service announcements." That network had no difficulty rationalizing a daily TV fare for teenagers replete with brutality, killing, and overt sexual behavior. But condoms? Never!

VII

The Pill, condoms, IUDs, and diaphragms are all precoital methods of birth control and would, if used consistently, render abortion rarely necessary. For most women, an unwanted pregnancy is the outcome of unavailable contraceptives or of inadequate contraception and/or information. If we are to achieve the social objective of making every pregnancy deliberate, and every newborn a wanted child, I believe that the means may well lie in interfering in the earliest stages of fertilization—that is, in postcoital contraception.

At present, abortion is the sole, available postcoital means, since the "morning-after pill"—a high dosage of orally effective progestins or estrogens that a woman ingests within a few days of intercourse—is employed only as an occasional emergency step, because of the otherwise grossly excessive cumulative exposure to potent hormones. For the individual who believes that any interference with a fertilized egg—however recent the fertilization—constitutes abortion, postcoital contraception would be acceptable for only the briefest of intervals: that during which the sperm travels toward the ovum. There are, however, millions of women who could accept as contraception interference with a fertilized egg for a few days or even three or four weeks following conception. This huge group, including the vast majority of pregnant American teenagers, would clearly benefit from research into postcoital contraception thus broadly defined.

Unfortunately, the administration since 1980, first under President Reagan and now under President Bush, adheres to the narrowest definition of *postcoital*. The American administration's obsession with abortion is reflected in its cancellation, since 1986, of all financial contributions to the U.N. Population Fund because of the latter's support of China's family-planning program, which is reported to include forced abortion among many other options. Instead of supporting a United Nations initiative that clearly reduces global abortion rates by promoting better contraception, the White House insists on boycotting this worldwide effort in order to demonstrate its displeasure with one component of one country's birth control program.

If I were restricted to choosing a single new contraceptive, it would be a once-a-month pill effective as a menses inducer. Instead of the current oral contraceptive, which a woman takes daily for most of the month twelve months a year, she would ingest a menses inducer, a single pill (containing a short-lived and rapidly metabolized drug), once a month to induce menstrual flow at the expected time; or only during those months when she had unprotected intercourse, instead of waiting to see whether she had missed her period. While not acceptable or suitable to every woman, such a regimen would represent an enormous improvement for many: a woman would take, at most, 12 pills annually, rather than the present 250 or more, and would not know in any month whether her egg had been fertilized. The crucial feature of such a method is that one decides on contraception after intercourse.

I first presented the case for a hypothetical once-a-month pill in my 1970 *Science* paper "Birth Control after 1984," where I estimated that it would take approximately fourteen years to convert such a discovery into a practical method of birth control. *Mirabile dictu*, in the early 1980s, a group of French investigators (Georges Teutsch, Daniel Philibert, and André Ulmann of Roussel-Uclaf, and Etienne-Emile Baulieu of INSERM in Paris) reported that a synthetic steroid progesterone antagonist, named RU-486, possessed such menses-inducing properties. While not suitable for regular, monthly menses induction of the type I postulated, RU-486 has, nevertheless, turned out to be the single most important new development in birth control of the past two decades as an important alternative to surgical abortion. A single oral ingestion of RU-486 (after confirmed pregnancy, but not later than seven weeks after the last menstruation), followed two days later by a single (intramuscular, intravaginal, or oral) administration of a prostaglandin, resulted in heavy bleeding with complete expulsion of the embryo in 96 percent of the women tested. By now, at least one third of all abortions performed in France are based on this RU-486 regimen. In addition to eliminating the cost and burden of surgical intervention and anesthesia, this method also puts a premium on early abortion—precisely as recommended on safety grounds to any woman choosing abortion.

Since 1983, the World Health Organization has sponsored clinical trials with RU-486 in a variety of countries (China, India, Singapore, Cuba, Italy, Hungary, Yugoslavia, and others) to examine its performance in women of different ethnic backgrounds. Great Britain has already officially approved the use of RU-486 for early abortions, an action that will probably be followed soon by some of the Scandinavian countries, Holland, and China. Yet in the United States, where abortion is legal and used annually by 1.6 million women (at least one fourth of them teenagers), no pharmaceutical company has dared to apply for government approval in the face of a virulent anti-abortion campaign centered on RU-486 and supported vigorously by the last two administrations. The American government has not confined its opposition to its national borders. Even though the United States does not contribute to the World Health Organization's Special Programme of Research, Development and Research Training in Human Reproduction—an international effort heavily supported by the Scandinavian countries, Great Britain, Germany, Canada, and many other governments—the State Department in 1991 saw fit to question whether the WHO used World Bank funds for some of its clinical research on RU-486, the implication being that the United States might reconsider its continued funding of World Bank activities.

I cite these details to illustrate the enormous politicization of birth control in my country: the field has become an issue rather than a neutral area of research for truly revolutionary methods of contraception. I am thinking, for example, of a menses-inducer progesterone antagonist for women, of an antifertility vaccine, or a male Pill, to cite only three novel and scientifically feasible approaches to birth control (all of which have been investigated in animals and humans under the umbrella of the WHO program and other agencies, but which, for all practical purposes, are not pursued clinically in the United States). Some developments continue, of course; but a new delivery system for steroid contraceptives, which replaces the daily ingestion of a tablet by steroid-loaded vaginal rings or subcutaneous implants (such as the recent FDA-approved NORPLANT), though clearly useful in a public health and demographic context, is no consolation to women looking for new nonhormonal methods of birth control. Even more discouraging is the fact that such improved steroid delivery systems have been in the works for over two decades, however much they are foisted on both gullible media and hopeful public as "new" or "revolutionary." The experts all know that "new" may not be truly new, that "safe" is never totally safe, that "a few years" will almost certainly take much longer. But the public little realizes how sparsely stocked will be the shelves of an American contraceptive supermarket by the turn of the century.

VIII

Now, instead of ending on this discouraging note, let me—who have been intimately involved with "high-tech" contraception—turn to what may be the lowest of "low-tech" methods: that is, "natural family planning" (NFP), the "rhythm method," "periodic abstinence," "Vatican roulette," or whatever euphemistic or pejorative term one may use to describe the determination of the "safe" period. Even though this is one of the oldest and, in many respects, least reliable methods of birth control, determination of the "safe" period is one of the few areas of contraception where current scientific advances—that is, high technology—may actually serve to overcome some of the political obstacles, and to do so with extra bonuses outside the specific realm of birth control.

Aside from the inconvenience of daily record keeping, the "sympto-thermal" method of NFP (keeping track of changes in basal body temperature as well as in the viscosity of cervical mucus) requires an average of seventeen days of abstinence from intravaginal intercourse. In principle, accurate determination of the onset of ovulation could reduce this period of abstinence by over 50 percent and thus improve significantly NFP's poor acceptability and efficacy. Since the fertile period of an egg is approximately one day, precise knowledge of the conclusion of ovulation would provide a "green light": unprotected coitus is now safe. This moment can be established by a rise, following ovulation (that is, in the *post*ovulatory phase of the menstrual cycle), of the female sex hormone progesterone (or its metabolites) in blood, saliva, or urine.

In order to cover the first half (or *pre*ovulatory phase) of the month, one must be able to *predict* ovulation by three or four days: an advance warning ("red light") is needed, because sperm can remain viable in a woman's fertile mucus for approximately three days. Ovulation is preceded by a rise of the female sex hormone estradiol in a woman's body fluids; and during the 1970s and 1980s, advances in analytical biochemistry (notably radioimmunoassays) have led to accurate determinations of these hormonal changes in the laboratory. More recently, monoclonal antibody techniques in ingenious formulations have made it possible to detect visually—by the appearance of a colored spot in one drop of urine—the rise in progesterone metabolites in less than one minute. In other words, one can now have a convenient "green light" in the home by performing two or, at most, three such tests during the postovulatory phase.

While the absolute concentrations of estrogenic hormones and metabolites are considerably lower than those of progesterone, there is no question in my mind that a similar "red light" home test based on detecting the preovulatory rise in estrogens can be developed for urine or saliva within two to three years. Is the effort worthwhile?

As a means of birth control in third-world countries, such a high-tech method would be useless on financial and operational grounds alone. Given the poor image of NFP, even in advanced countries, such as the United States, the initial impact in terms of improved birth control is likely to be low, although any addition to the contraceptive supermarket (metaphorically speaking) is desirable. Since a combined "red light–green light" test, involving approximately five assays per month, would cost no more than a monthly supply of oral contraceptives, it would be acceptable to a segment of those women who already practice NFP or do not tolerate the Pill.

However, I would focus on a potentially much wider customer base under the banner of "fertility awareness." I am not referring to women with known infertility problems—a somewhat limited, though highly committed group, through whose cooperation many advances in hormonal detection of ovulation have first been accomplished, and for whom neither cost nor inconvenience are disincentives. Rather, I am thinking of the many women who now feel strongly about health awareness and about making more health-related decisions by themselves: for instance, the rapidly increasing number of professional women in America, who postpone childbearing until their late thirties; or the serious female joggers and athletes. For many a woman in our affluent society, knowing whether and when she is ovulating should be a routine item of personal health information, which could have advantages quite separate from birth control.

Two large surveys conducted during 1989 and 1991 by Stanford University students in my course "Feminist Perspectives on Birth Control" have shown that the majority of these women would be interested in purchasing and using such a biochemical ovulation kit (named "The Wizard of Ov" by one medical student), irrespective of sexual activity. Many physicians, especially epidemiologists, studying the incidence of cancer in female reproductive organs might find a long-time record of ovulatory behavior extremely useful. Evidence for excessive calcium loss in women who menstruate regularly, yet do not ovulate, is another example where such knowledge might offer useful information. And finally, why not employ such hormonal methods of ovulation detection and prediction as routine teaching tools in high schools? Emphasis on fertility awareness rather than on birth control

My daughter, Pamela, age twenty-five.

Dale and Pamela at SMIP Ranch, 1977—one year before her suicide.

Four generations of Djerassi males—myself; my son, Dale; my grandson, Alexander; my father, Samuel (age ninety-two)—each separated by thirty-one years; SMIP Ranch, 1984.

Myself with my first wife, Virginia, while studying for my doctorate at the University of Wisconsin, 1943.

With my second wife, Norma Lundholm, in Hidalgo, Mexico, 1951.

Myself and third wife, Diane Middlebrook, at wedding party at SMIP Ranch,
22 June 1985.

A literary booksigning shortly after the publication of *Cantor's Dilemma*, November 1989, in the presence of my stepdaughter, Leah Middlebrook.

Myself and the British playwright Tom Stoppard at SMIP Ranch, mid-1970s.

might be an effective strategy to fight the continuing politicization of sex education in American high schools. Who knows? It might even lead to a reduction in unwanted pregnancies.

Finally, precise and convenient determination of ovulation might be much more than a jet-age rhythm method. It might even lead to a jet-age contraceptive method that could substantially reduce abortions. In the fortieth year of the Pill's life, Dr. Marc Bygdeman of the Karolinska Institute in Stockholm, the first clinician to introduce the use of prostaglandin in conjunction with RU-486, made the intriguing observation that the administration of a single pill of RU-486 two days after ovulation prevented implantation of a fertilized egg without disrupting the next menstrual flow. Presumably any progesterone antagonist, not just RU-486, would have the same effect. While much more extensive clinical work is required, there is in prospect a major advance in postcoital contraception, provided it is combined with a convenient and affordable home test for ovulation detection.

For comparatively affluent, educated, and motivated couples, the prognosis for significant advances in birth control is dim, though not completely hopeless. But the rest of the world will have to depend for a long time on existing methods or minor modifications thereof. However bitter this may sound, to me the ultimate bitter pill is the fact that the United States is the only country other than Iran to have set back the birth control clock during the past decade, and even Iran is now changing. Not only will the current quality of birth control in this country, and thus the 1.6 million annual abortions, not change significantly by the year 2000; but it is quite possible that the contraceptive choices at the turn of this century will be even more limited than they are now. Having answered at some length the "What now?" of this chapter's title, I end with another brief question: "What then?" To it I have no answer.

CHAPTER 16

Interlude: Peacockery

I DIDN'T OWN LONG PANTS until my fifteenth birthday, when I enrolled in the American College of Sofia. In Vienna, prior to the Anschluss, we wore *Lederhosen* or other shorts from spring to autumn, and knickerbockers in the winter. In Bulgaria, all students in the public schools had to wear uniforms, which for boys meant black jackets, black trousers, and a black cap covering a shaven head. In the more prestigious private high schools, the children of the bourgeois learned one or both of the *linguae francae* (German and French) of the Balkans. Only the most adventurous or cosmopolitan families sent their offspring to the American College in the outskirts of Sofia. Unlike the students in other private schools, who slept at home, we lived in dormitories and had to wear uniforms only when we spent weekends in Sofia. Even more important, we were permitted to grow our hair *ad libitum*; in addition, the obligatory weekend suit was not a real uniform but only a blue ensemble consisting of a double-breasted jacket and long pants, with a white shirt and black shoes. Only the cap bore the insignia of our school.

Instead of being grateful for such minimal sartorial rules, I refused to wear blue clothes or black shoes from the day of my arrival in New York

Harbor in December of 1939. For two decades, I remained in my pre-peacock plumage: my clothes were store-bought, never tailor-made, the suits either brown or gray, all my shoes brown, my ties woolen, my shirts white or on occasion modest shades of pink. But, finally, I spread my tail.

I

In February 1958, I flew with Alex Zaffaroni, then executive vice president of Syntex, from Mexico City to Tokyo to find a Japanese distributor for Syntex's Pill. It was a long trip, but we did it in luxury: we took a Canadian Pacific DC-6 equipped with Pullman-style berths in the rear of the plane. Sleeping undisturbed in pajamas, receiving morning tea in bed, and sampling delicacies high over the Pacific was a painless entry into the Orient.

In contrast to today's transpacific flitting about by American scientists, few American chemists had visited Japanese universities in the 1950s. We were treated royally, as were our wives, who went shopping and sightseeing while we lectured. One morning, we all went together to a fine silk merchant in Kyoto. In my "ready-to-wear" manner, I picked for myself a red kimono with a hexagon design that looked like a chemist's logo-dream of black benzene rings on a red background. That's when Zaffaroni led me down a never-ending garden path.

"Look at this gray raw silk," he murmured. "Just feel it."

"It's different," I volunteered, my right thumb and index finger massaging the sensuous material. Most of the silk I had touched before was worn by women; caressing a cool sheet of silk felt somehow different from sensing bodily warmth through it.

"Buy it," Alex said.

"Buy it? But look how much Norma has already picked."

"Buy it for yourself. Remember, we are going to Hong Kong. They'll make you a shirt overnight."

A tall Uruguayan with a thin, Cesar Romero–style mustache, Alex looked like a Latin diplomat or banker, impeccably dressed and groomed, all his suits made to order. Our projected three-day stopover in Hong Kong would be sufficient for Alex to get an entire wardrobe. When in Mexico City he had first broached the idea of the Hong Kong detour, my hand lightly brushing the sleeve of Alex's cashmere jacket had made me wonder how it would feel to run my hands over my own cashmere jacket. A gray raw silk shirt would go well with gray cashmere. I was thirty-five years old, and I'd never owned a silk shirt. Why not? I reflected, and bought enough of the sinfully elegant gray silk for two shirts.

Alex was right; in Hong Kong they could do anything in twenty-four hours and at prices that were then veritable bagatelles. Alex picked a tailor and selected his material: he was to be measured that afternoon, and return the next morning for a fitting; his clothes would be ready that evening. When I asked to see the cashmere samples, the tailor looked pleased. "Ah yes," he exhaled, and disappeared, returning promptly with two bolts of soft cashmere—one blue, the other gray. Thirty years later, I still wear the gray cashmere jacket that Hong Kong tailor made for me. It has a new lining and black elbow patches, but wears like a thirty-year-old Rolls-Royce.

We were about to leave to pick up our wives when Alex reminded me about the silk. "By the way," I asked the tailor with new-found confidence, "do you make shirts to order?"

"Ah yes, let me show—"

"Don't bother about the material," I stopped him. "I've brought some silk." Immediately the man's ingratiating posture stiffened. "Why, yes," he almost hissed the word, "but it will take some time. It is difficult—"

"Of course, I know," I said quickly, although I had no reason to know. I'd never had a custom-made shirt. In the 1950s, a five-dollar shirt was of superior quality, as many an advertisement featuring the man with the black eye patch in a Hathaway shirt proclaimed. I could well imagine that it might be more difficult to construct a silk shirt than a cashmere jacket. "Three days," I offered. "We won't leave until Thursday." I figured that a 200-percent time concession would do the trick.

"Two weeks," he announced in an inexorable tone that better fit a British colonial magistrate than a Chinese haberdasher. "Never mind," Alex interrupted, before I could argue further. "Have it made in Mexico. My tailor doesn't make shirts, but I'm sure George's does."

George Rosenkranz, the other member of the Syntex troika back in Mexico City, was short and stocky, more like an affluent continental businessman—as befitted his Hungarian background and Swiss education—than a South American diplomat who was likely to tango your wife away. But I knew that George's clothes were also tailor-made: he didn't believe in zippers and had four-button trouser fronts. Had some zipper disaster converted him into a button-fly aficionado? In spite of our friendship, I never asked.

This time, Alex was wrong. George's tailor didn't make shirts to order. Moreover, George didn't know any tailor in Mexico City who did. So for months my Japanese gray silk rested untouched in my bureau drawer, until one day, while reading the *New Yorker*, I saw an ad by A. Sulka & Company: "Shirts to order. Paris, London, New York, San Francisco."

I'd been to San Francisco only once, in 1946, on my first postwar vacation when Gilbert Stork, my oldest friend from graduate school days at the University of Wisconsin, and I had decided to drive west with our wives to see a part of the country we Central European immigrants had never visited. As we approached the Mount Rushmore National Memorial in the Black Hills of South Dakota, driving our 1944 Nash, we looked forward to seeing the huge forms of Washington, Jefferson, Lincoln, and Roosevelt. Talking over my shoulder to our two WASP wives, I remarked that my early Viennese and Bulgarian education had not included American history. The same was true of Gilbert in France. But, we both bragged, we'd picked it up on the sly. "I can tell you the most obscure American presidents," I proclaimed. "Pierce, Fillmore—" "Bewkahnón," Gilbert interrupted proudly, accenting the last syllable, as Charles Boyer or Maurice Chevalier might have done. "Bewkahnón," I repeated scornfully. "That's not how you pronounce his name. It's Bookanan. The emphasis is on the first syllable. Just say it after me—Bookanan."

Now, a dozen years later, I knew how to pronounce the last name of America's fifteenth president—and was about to head west again, this time by plane from Mexico City, to receive the American Chemical Society's Award in Pure Chemistry at the convention in San Francisco. I tore the Sulka ad out of the *New Yorker* and stuck it and the raw silk into my bag.

It was a glorious spring morning in San Francisco: blue sky, cool, windy. I called Sulka's from the hotel. "Do you make shirts to order?" They did. "Even if a customer brings his own material?" Of course. "Even silk?" The tone of the affirmative on the other end of the line intimated that I'd asked an insulting question.

To avoid paying duty, I'd wrapped the silk in my underwear; now I put it in a hotel laundry bag for the ten-minute walk to Post Street. At first I couldn't find the place, but finally I saw a discreet metal plaque: "A. Sulka, second floor." I climbed the stairs, laundry bag in hand. I pushed open the smallish glass door of Sulka's second-floor showroom, to find it empty— except for two impeccably dressed middle-aged gentlemen. With their meticulously brushed hair, they looked, at first glance, like investment bankers; but as soon as they saw me, they started to move, one approaching from the left, the other circling in from the right. The first to reach me focused his X-ray eyes on the laundry bag tucked under my left arm. "So you're the gentleman who called about the silk shirt." Not posed as a question, it was a simple preamble to his "May I?" as he reached for the bag and placed it on the glass shelf below which plush silk ties were arranged with precision. Carefully but quickly, he extricated the silk and with one experienced snap spread it over the glass. A slight nod of his head led his colleague to join him in inspecting my silk. After a moment of silence, the older of my two bankers touched the silk. Not as I had done at the shop in Kyoto, rubbing the fabric between thumb and forefinger like a bazaar merchant, but as art dealers handle a rare print or watercolor.

"First class," he finally murmured. "Would you mind removing your coat?" he asked, his tone as deferential as if I were being admitted to an exclusive club. "My colleague and I will measure you."

They subjected me to a quantitative anatomical analysis I'd never experienced before and haven't since. It's probably imagination that makes me recall their measuring my dimensions down to the second decimal point, but *se non é vero, é ben trovato*. I am certain, however, about a compliment, paid me in a voice of undisguised admiration: "Your arms are the same length, sir. Quite unusual."

I was still absorbing this unexpected news when I was invited to participate in weightier matters: the location of the monogram, the style of the letters, the choice of collar and cuff. After some deliberation I settled on French cuffs. "Very wise, sir," my youngest banker whispered. "When French cuffs are too worn, they can be turned." I thought of Fitzgerald's remark, "The very rich are different from you or me"—and of Hemingway's riposte, "Yes, they have more money"—to which I could now add, "And they can have their worn French cuffs turned at Sulka's."

The news that Sulka's San Francisco outpost had to ship my raw silk to their New York headquarters for metamorphosis didn't faze me. I planned to be in New York City in a couple of months and could easily pick up the finished masterpiece. They further comforted me with the news that henceforth I could order any shirt by mail or telephone, since my symmetrical arm measurements and the distance from my armpit to the inside of my elbow would be retained on permanent file. "Should I pay now?" I asked, "or when I pick them up?" "As you wish, sir," replied the younger man to the accompanying slight frown of his companion; it seemed as if I'd pained him by such a crass inquiry. "I might as well pay now," I said, whereupon both men went to the rear of the emporium and remained there for some time.

They returned to me not in their original double-flanked approach, but in single file and with measured step, their eyes focused on some imaginary spot behind my right ear. Have they noticed my only birthmark, I wondered, my right earlobe, which is much smaller than its left counterpart? The grayer-haired of my bankers presented me with a folded piece of paper—in precisely the manner with which my orthopedic surgeon had a year earlier presented me with the most expensive medical bill of my life. As I unfolded the starched piece of paper, my two bankers became fascinated by the view of Post Street from Sulka's second-story window again, just like Dr. Farill who, after giving me his folded bill, had turned sideways toward his desk as if suddenly remembering some urgent unfinished business.

Only when staring at the haberdasher's bill—positively monstrous in those days of three- to five-dollar Hathaway shirts—did I make the connection between my surgeon's sudden focus on his desk and my two bankers' behavior. But a bill for a fused knee, however preposterous, could somehow be tolerated; I was prepared to amortize Dr. Farill's fee over a period of forty pain-free years, which, taking account of inflation, didn't seem so exorbitant after all. But two shirts were clearly a different investment, in terms of time and fragility. One inexperienced Mexican laundress could convert such a shirt into the sark equivalent of Russian imperial bonds.

Of course, I could have just grabbed the silk and run, except that my fused knee permitted at best a clumsy hop. Or I could have asked for the men's room and then escaped, cutting my losses and leaving the silk behind. But a few additional microseconds of financial analysis convinced me that I had no one to blame but myself. I'd spent at least forty minutes at Sulka's as the exclusive object of the attention of two extremely well-dressed men, who were surely not working there solely for pleasure. Not a single customer had disturbed this establishment's elegant silence. I should have realized that somebody, or something—such as my two silk shirts—would have to carry the overhead of this fancy haberdashery. In the brutal light of such realities, I concluded that the absurd sum was almost fair. "You do take a check?" I asked in a shaky voice; a cash payment (in those pre-credit card days) would have required me to make an immediate move to the YMCA for the balance of my San Francisco sojourn.

In spite of extraordinary care, the two gray silk shirts didn't make it past a dog's lifetime. I never did turn the French cuffs. When they started to wear, I had them cut above the elbows; but somehow a short-sleeved gray silk shirt, with hand-stitched monogram and longish, button-down collar, doesn't retain the panache of the Sulka original.

II

By then I was living in the San Francisco Bay area, and my tail was unfolding in earnest—a process furthered by my new companion (now my wife), the most elegant woman I'd ever lived with. In the summer of 1981, she suggested a visit to the annual Pacific Arts and Crafts Show, held that year at one of the piers off Fort Mason. We were walking down the stalls, looking at the range of jewelry, leather goods, hand-blown glass, finely crafted furniture, and painted silk garments, when I stopped at a stand belonging to a tall freckled woman, whose curly reddish hair spilled around her open smiling face and down her shoulders. "Power coats by Tegen Greene, Pt. Reyes," the sign said. "Why do you call them power coats?" I asked, pointing to the cloaklike vestments with attached hoods made in a quiltlike pattern out of corduroy, velour, whipcord, leather, and heavy cotton. "Try one and see," she said, grinning. "But they aren't for men, are they?" I asked warily. She shrugged her shoulders. "Try one."

I picked a bluish one that seemed my size and stepped over to the mirror. Not bad, I concluded, as I put the hood over my hair so that only my silver beard and face showed. I rather fancied the medieval abbot looking at me through the looking glass. A young man appeared by my side. "That's neat!" he exclaimed. "You ought to lead a cult."

So I ordered one, a patchwork of green and ocher, but without a hood. I wasn't quite ready for that much power. "Don't you want to measure me?" I asked Tegen Greene as she filled out the order. "I don't need to," she said, with a disarming smile. "I can see your size."

It didn't matter that my power coat wouldn't be ready for a couple of months. I'd bought it as a birthday present for myself. That was the end of August, and I didn't want it until 29 October, after my return from a trek through northwestern Bhutan in the Himalayas. While there, I bought some of the multicolored, woven, and embroidered material that Bhutanese women use in their festive dresses. When I returned to San Francisco and picked up my power coat, which hung loosely, but just right, from my shoulders almost down to my knees, I decided that Tegen Greene had the taste and temperament to convert the Bhutanese embroidery into a unique blue coatlike gown for the woman who had brought out the peacock in me.

The finished gown was so sensational that when Tegen mentioned that some swatches of the Bhutanese material were still left, I asked her to incorporate them into a blue velvet jacket for me. It would take a fashion vocabulary I do not possess to describe the garment she produced—but we two Bhutanized showoffs were a sensation at the San Francisco Opera. For a dozen years, my father and his wife had had their subscription tickets on the same night as I, and I usually paid my filial respects in the grand entrance hall before the opera and during intermission. Although eighty-nine years old, my father was as dapper and worldly as ever; but that night, as he took in the vivid embroidery against the blue background of my sleeves and down the length of the jacket, his astonishment was obvious. "Carli!" he exclaimed (he was the only person still to use that Viennese diminutive). "How could you?" "How could I what?" I replied, a fifty-eight-year-old juvenile, knowing full well what would follow and enjoying every second of it.

Since the Bhutanese version, Tegen made six more jackets, each of increasing complexity and sophistication. One was the purplish-silver silk coat I wore when Diane Middlebrook, dressed in an Italian red silk suit, married me in 1985. Tegen even made me a wedding shirt with an Indo-Russian-style collar that required no tie. Another was an all-black velvet jacket, adorned with a subtle design of black, thin leather strips, and slightly puffed and slit Shakespearean sleeves, which I always wear with tuxedo trousers to black-tie events. The most complicated of all—a jacket consisting of over six hundred individual cloth tesserae of every conceivable variation on the color brown—proved to be, literally, my royal mosaic pièce de résistance.

When, in 1984, King Carl XVI Gustaf of Sweden visited Zoecon (see chapter 11), I, as its chief executive officer and the king's official host, greeted him in another Tegen Greene creation, this time in champagne. It contrasted strikingly with the conservative dark business suits of the king's entourage, even though it was Tegen's most restrained design. Once on the slippery slope of sartorial exhibitionism, however, I kept on sliding. The following day, I attended a reception at the Swedish consulate, where I passed through the royal reception line in a bluish-gray Tegen Greene power coat. On the third day, when the king held a farewell buffet dinner for his local hosts, I came in Tegen's brown mosaic coat. As we shook hands and I bowed before the king, a handsome young man and dapper dresser, His Majesty leaned forward and whispered, "And who makes your coats, Professor Djerassi?"

I paid Tegen in more than money and loyalty. In 1983, during the most feverish period of her coat artistry, the famous Italian men's fashion magazine, *L'Uomo Vogue*, decided to dedicate one entire glossy issue to Italian fashions modeled by American scientists, primarily from MIT, Stanford, Berkeley, and Harvard. My son knew one of the *Vogue* photographers from his filmmaking activity and alerted me the night before that they'd picked me as one of their models. I decided to out-vogue *Vogue* by just "happening" to wear one of Tegen's more spectacular jackets as if it were an everyday lab coat. The *Vogue* crew photographed me in my laboratory, wearing Tegen's blue-gray masterpiece. Her jacket got a full-page color spread in *L'Uomo Vogue* with the description "*Casacca di velluto patchwork, pezzo unico.*" I had reached full plumage.

III

On a lecture trip to Korea in 1984, while shopping for presents, I suddenly found myself reliving my 1958 Kyoto experience. I'd bought some exquisite green silk, embroidered with gold thread, with which I wanted to surprise Diane. "Silk for you?" the saleswoman had asked and promptly seduced me with a champagne-colored sample of silk woven in a pattern of orange and blue lines. I was certain Tegen would come up with something special out of this Korean silk. But I was wrong. When I called her upon my return, I learned that she had stopped her needle-and-thread artistry to become a Toyota saleswoman in Berkeley. In an indirect way, the six-hundred-piece brown mosaic that had impressed the king of Sweden had been responsible for this tragic transformation. Even though I'd paid a high price, it had taken her over three months to construct that masterpiece, and she reckoned that it had earned her the subminimum hourly wage of $2.50. She concluded that a fair recompense, commensurate with her talent and experience, would require prices only the Getty Museum could afford if it had a section of contemporary clothing designs. Selling Toyotas was easier and more lucrative.

Well, I consoled myself, there's always A. Sulka & Co. I hadn't been there for thirty years, but a glance at the Yellow Pages confirmed that they were still on Post Street.

"A. Sulka, Bob speaking." The informality of the voice on the telephone took me aback. The Sulka quasi-bankers from the 1950s surely would have used their last names.

"Do you make silk shirts to order?" I asked cautiously.

"Y-e-e-e-s, we could do that."

"If one were to bring one's own silk?" I asked in my most ingratiating tone.

"No, we don't fool with anything like that!" came the brusque reply from Sulka's Bob. *Sic transit gloria Sulka!*

A couple of years later, while packing for a trip to London, I came across the long-forgotten Korean silk in one of my drawers. On the spur of the moment, I stuck it into my suitcase. What Savile Row is to tailor-made suits, I knew, Jermyn Street is to custom-made shirts. I stopped at four exclusive stores that proclaimed expertise in custom-fitted shirts, only to encounter snootiness and outright prevarication. None of them showed the slightest interest in a customer with his own material, the last one insisting, "We can't guarantee the job, sir, if it's not with our own material." "This is preposterous!" I retorted. "There *must* be a place in London that makes shirts with a man's own silk." Maybe the desperation in my voice touched the clerk, or perhaps he just wanted to be rid of me. "Try Brewer Street in Soho," he said. He couldn't give me a name, just told me to look at the signs on upper-floor windows. My search in Soho took me finally up some narrow stairs to a gruff Greek hunched over his sewing machine. "Do you make shirts?" I asked, knowing the likely answer. But, unlike the Jermyn Street snobs who hadn't deigned to inspect my material, this tailor pointed to the package under my arm. After I had unwrapped the silk, he regarded it respectfully in the way of my Sulka bankers. "I know who can help you," he said, and directed me to a fellow Greek on Lexington Street just a few blocks away. "Tell him Andy sent you."

The rest is a modern fairy tale with only one character: a magician dressed as a tailor. His sign was unpretentious; the reception area was a small space on the ground floor, the length of one showroom window, clean, and—except for bolt after bolt of material—furnished only with two chairs and a table. The smiling middle-aged man who came out of a back room to greet me took one look at my material and said, "Yes." Although he clucked his tongue and looked distressed when I informed him that I'd be returning to California in three days, he said, "I'll try." I left him my card with my Stanford Chemistry Department address, whereupon he volunteered that his son was about to enter a university to study chemistry. I left on cloud nine, not even asking what he would charge. After my Sulka experience three decades earlier, I was prepared to call anything below 150 pounds a bargain.

Three days later, on the way to the Theatre Royal at the Haymarket to see *Orpheus Descending*, I stopped at the tailor's shop. After we shook hands, he told me that he had been responsible for all of the shirts in *The Phantom of the Opera* and *Les Liaisons Dangereuses*, two hits of the London theater season, but that my material had sufficed for only one shirt, not the two I had arranged for. He held that one out to me as tenderly as if he were handing a new baby to its father. The shirt was beautiful, and I braced myself for the bill. "You do take credit cards?" I asked, suddenly realizing that I was probably carrying no more than fifty or sixty pounds in cash. "Every card," he assured me, his manner in no way recalling that of my Mexican surgeon or my two Sulka bankers. "How much?" I asked, hoping that the tremor in my voice wasn't noticeable. Neither looking down at the table by his side nor suddenly becoming enamored with the evening traffic, he looked me straight in the eye and said, "Thirty-five." For a moment I was stunned. Thirty-five what? Of course, he couldn't want 35 pounds for this hand-fashioned, Korean silk creation which he had produced in three days flat while all the stars at the West End were clamoring

273

for their blouses. But even with inflation, $350 for one shirt seemed very stiff, and 350 pounds completely outrageous, especially in January 1989, when the exchange rate was $1.81 to the pound. "Thirty-five?" I croaked. "Thirty-five pounds," he said evenly, taking the credit card from my limp hand. "Now that I have your measurements, you can order your shirts by mail. I can even send you swatches."

We all know how self-defeating it would be to discover a superb restaurant in France that's reasonably priced and known to few, and then to pass its name on to the *Guide Michelin*. The same pure selfishness keeps me from making my tailor hero's name public. It is simply too good a name to bandy about, but for the sake of accuracy, I shall offer one nugget of information: he isn't Greek, he's a Cypriot from way back. I haven't written him yet, but if that chemist son of his wants to work in my lab, he's got a job.

CHAPTER 17

Degas' Horse

DEFYING STATISTICAL PROBABILITY, my suitcase is always one of the last ones out of the chute. By the time it appeared, the lines in front of the customs inspectors were discouragingly long. Having flown into Washington to attend a National Academy of Sciences meeting, however, I had no pressing connection to make. Moreover, I needed time to choose a customs agent who was either totally naïve or very sophisticated. Anyone in between was likely to cause trouble, not to speak of the several thousand dollars I might be asked to pay as import duty. I decided to pick the oldest of the harassed agents. He didn't look like one of the brash, steely-eyed types who make you feel like a smuggler even if you have bought, and dutifully declared, only an embroidered handkerchief. And I thought that the oldest of the lot might be sufficiently tired by the time I appeared in front of him as to just wave me on.

The line of passengers was moving so slowly that I had time to think once more of the customs form that I was clutching in my moist hand, and on which I had indicated that I had nothing to declare. And, indeed, I had bought nothing on my brief lecture trip to London that March 1972. Still, in my airline shoulderbag, not even wrapped in paper, I was carrying Edgar

275

Degas' bronze horse, *Cheval au Trot*, which three months earlier a friend had bid for on my behalf at Sotheby's and, to my surprised delight, actually succeeded in purchasing at less than my top limit. Since I was scheduled to visit London anyway, I decided to bring the horse back myself rather than having it shipped. If possible, I wanted to avoid paying import duty, which would not have been trivial considering what I had paid even in 1971 for Degas' nine-inch-high horse.

I pondered how I was going to deal with the customs inspector whose line I was in. If I had bought a Degas painting, drawing, monotype, or even the plaster cast of the horse, the question of duty would not have arisen. But all of the seventy-three known bronzes of horses and dancers were cast after Degas' death, each in editions of twenty-two. United States Customs considers the first ten casts of any sculpture duty-free; any subsequent ones are subject to a hefty duty. I had Sotheby's bill with me, which showed that the sculpture was by Degas. Many an agent would surely have let it pass, not knowing that the actual number of a Degas cast is always indicated by a single letter, starting with *A*, etched in an inconspicuous spot of the sculpture. But, in addition to the twenty bronzes marked *A* to *T* and intended for sale, two additional casts were always produced: one for the Hébrard foundry, and the other for Degas' heirs, which—as in my case—was marked *HER*. During my wait in the slowly moving line, I rehearsed once more the argument I had developed on the plane: Surely, one's heirs would precede any potential customers. Any reasonable person would have to agree that the letters *HER* come before the letter *A* rather than after *T*. The question was, Would the agent be reasonable?

The agent was not as old as he appeared from the distance—at best, a couple of years older than I. If I had bumped into him at some party, I would probably have taken him for a teacher or perhaps a lawyer—not a corporate attorney, but a labor lawyer or arbitrator. I handed over my passport and declaration. He glanced at the latter and asked, his eyes on mine, "Nothing to declare? How long were you in London?" I hesitated a couple of seconds before answering. "Nothing?" he repeated. "You didn't buy anything?" My airline bag was sitting next to my suitcase on the low platform between us. I put my hand on my bag, a protective gesture. "Buy anything?" I echoed. "Oh, I did buy something, but nothing to declare. It's just an art object," I added, silently apologizing to Degas in his grave.

"I see." The agent nodded as if he had expected just this answer. "And what did you pay for it?" Realizing that the time for offhandedness had passed, I mentioned the nontrivial five-digit sum I had paid, and mumbled, "guineas." His face showed no surprise, nor did he pursue the question of currency. He didn't even ask the nature of the "art object." He stroked his

chin, "Are you an art dealer?" "No," I replied quickly, "I'm only a collector." Impassive, he pursued, "And what do you collect?" My left index
finger slowly traced the outline of the bronze horse in the thin airline bag.
I felt like the defendant who knows that each answer will lead to further
questions. "Art," I said. "I understood that," replied the inspector, with
limitless patience. "Whose?"

Whose art? He was, after all, no simpleton, but what did he know
about art? I considered murmuring, "Picasso's"—although I owned only
one of his sculptures, and a rather minor one at that. With our two children,
my second wife and I had visited the Tate Gallery's great Picasso sculpture
retrospective in 1967; and as we stood overwhelmed and euphoric in front
of a glass vitrine containing small bronze female figures from 1945, Norma
had exclaimed, "Look at that one! You can see the outline of Picasso's
thumb on her belly." It was true; a Scotland Yard detective probably could
have lifted Picasso's fingerprint from that cast. Noticing in the catalogue
that most of the figures were owned by the Paris art dealer Heinz Berggruen,
I called Paris information for his telephone number. I knew nothing about
the going prices for Picasso sculptures and was surprised to learn from
Berggruen (once I had persuaded him that I was not an impostor) that he
was prepared to sell that small figure for a sum I considered within my
means. The following week, in a game park in Uganda, as we watched
hippos frolic below Murchison Falls, I gave my wife a birthday card with
the somewhat corny inscription: "What every woman needs for her birthday: a Picasso sculpture from the Tate." Instead of embracing me, she gave
me a skeptical glance I still remember, years after our divorce. "You didn't
buy the Picasso for me," she said. "You bought it for yourself."

I did not tell any of this to the customs inspector. I decided to test rather
than impress him. "Klee," I said, pronouncing it the correct German way
as "clay," figuring that would separate the potters among the inspectors
from the cognoscenti. "Paul Klee!" he exclaimed, a smile stealing over his
face. "My favorite! Have you been to the Phillips Collection here in D.C.?"
he continued. "If you haven't, you should see their Klees." It turned out
that I had picked the principal art specialist among the Washington customs
inspectors. His primary function was the evaluation of important art im-
ports, especially to local dealers and collectors whom he mentioned and
some of whom I knew; he was serving temporarily as backup to some
regular inspectors at Washington's Dulles Airport. For several minutes, we
exchanged Klee lore. "The most intellectual painter of them all, and the
most verbal," I proclaimed, oblivious of the passengers waiting behind me.
"Can you think of anyone else who'd use a title like *Two Men Meet, Each
Thinking the Other of Higher Rank*?" I mentioned that I had bought

several Klees from Berggruen's gallery in Paris; and, when the inspector nodded understandingly, I pointed to my bag. "Don't you want to see this?" "Don't bother," he smiled. "I'd better take care of these passengers. Enjoy D.C.," he waved me on, "and don't forget to stop at the Phillips."

II

I was almost sorry that he had sent me on my way. I would have enjoyed showing him the Degas—and regaling him with the beginnings of my Klee collection, a story I have rarely told to anyone. Klee was clearly the artist who got me interested in serious collecting, which the appreciation of Syntex stock (acquired in the late 1950s and early 1960s) had made possible. In my college days, I had seen reproductions—on postcards, calendars, posters, catalogues, art books—of Paul Klee's most famous works, like the *Twittering Machine* or *Ad Parnassum*. Subsequently I saw many of his oils, drawings, and watercolors in museums in Europe as well as in this country. In the mid-1960s, I went to my first Klee show in a gallery in London, where all of the works were for sale. I kept returning to two magnificent watercolors from his Bauhaus years in the 1920s—rather large ones for an artist who usually worked on a small scale. "Should I? Can I?" I asked myself, and realized for the first time that I actually could own one of them. Finally, I approached one of the gallery employees and asked about the price. "The 1925 *Horse and Man*?" he asked, looking me up and down. "Sixteen," he finally said.

"Sixteen what?" I wanted to ask, but didn't. I knew it could not be 1,600, and was unlikely to be 160,000, so it had to be 16,000. But sixteen thousand what? Dollars, pounds, or even guineas? "And the other one, the 1927 *Heldenmutter*?" I asked hesitantly.

"Eighteen."

"Hm," I replied and went back to look at the pictures. A few minutes later, the man appeared by my side. "Which one do you prefer?" he asked in a slightly warmer tone.

"I can't make up my mind. Both are superb."

"Buy them both," he said matter-of-factly, "and maybe we can arrange a better price."

Bargaining, whether in a marketplace in Mexico or a bazaar in Cairo, always makes me uncomfortable; but this time I haggled by default. Every retreat of mine, every inspection and re-inspection of first one and then the other Klee caused the price to drop. They were not big reductions, but given the overall sums—far above anything I had ever spent before on art—they were not insignificant. Finally, I said, "I'll have to think about it." A couple of days later, I was the owner of not one but two Klees. By now I own nearly one hundred of his works in various media, but these two are still among the *crème de la crème*.

My purchase of these watercolors was probably not very different from the experience of other novice collectors—in contrast to the acquisition of my third. I saw it on the walls of the Guggenheim Museum with the notation "Collection Galerie Rosengart." It did not take me long to secure the address of that gallery in Lucerne, or to consummate by mail the purchase of that small gem—a description Klee would have agreed with, although I did not know it at the time. Galerie Rosengart was owned by a father-daughter pair, Siegfried and Angela Rosengart, who were among the most important Klee dealers and collectors. Eventually I got to know them well and made frequent pilgrimages to their gallery. A couple of years after I bought the watercolor off the Guggenheim walls, Rosengart *père* told me the significance of the small notation "S Cl" which Klee had marked in pencil in the lower left-hand corner of that watercolor. An abbreviation for *Sonderclasse*, "special class," it denoted his own favorites among over nine thousand works. I later learned that Klee had marked earlier works "S Kl," until someone told him that spelling *Classe* with a C had, so to speak, more class.

A few years later, I started to collect also Klee graphics, of which there exist only about one hundred. The early graphics done between 1901 to 1905 are Klee's first truly original creations and also among his rarest. In the middle 1970s, there was a major auction of Klee graphics in Bern, where Klee spent his last years, where his son Felix lived until his recent death, and where, within the walls of the *Kunstmuseum*, the Klee Foundation is situated. By that time I knew most of the important Klee dealers as a customer and, in a couple of instances, as a friend. I had studied the auction catalogue and carefully examined the lots prior to the start of the auction. I had a mental art budget for the year, which promised—with luck—to suffice for the purchase of two of the early graphics. At an auction, of course, one never knows. All it takes is for two people to become enamored with the same lot, and the price heads for the stratosphere.

I informed two of the dealers I saw in the audience that I was going for these two etchings; although I could not ask them openly not to bid in competition with me, I was reasonably sure that they would not drive the price up once they knew of my plans. But then my heart sank. In the distance, I saw Heinz Berggruen, who, I knew, not only had a magnificent personal Klee collection but bid actively at auctions. I approached him and, after exchanging the usual pleasantries, mentioned the lot numbers I planned to bid on. "They're very good impressions," he acknowledged. "I was thinking of buying these for the gallery." There was no question about Berggruen's ability to outbid me any time, but he must have read the disappointment in my face, for he offered to bid for me, saying he would just charge me a commission for any successful bids. I accepted immediately, thinking that such a commission was a bargain insurance premium in return for not having the art dealer as a competitor. I left the auction in shock. I had bought not two, but seven Klees, blowing in just a few minutes my art budget for five years. Yet I have never regretted following Berggruen's advice. Several of the prints I bought have never again appeared at sales; and although I bought the prints purely for delight, my pleasure is not tainted by the fact that they have increased greatly in value. At the auction, Berggruen pointed out to me a man sitting behind us, whom we had outbid, as Felix Klee, the painter's son. A few years later, I visited him in his flat in Bern and saw his extraordinary collection, which included puppets his father had made for him—a genre of Klee until then unknown to me. He also showed me his mother's guest book. The first entry was Wassily Kandinsky, who did not just inscribe the book but drew a colored picture on that page. Not to be outdone, many of the other guests—Lyonel Feininger, George Grosz, and others I do not remember—did likewise. It is one of the most intimate and exquisite documents of European art of the 1920s and 1930s.

It was also at the Bern auction that I met, albeit indirectly, another art dealer who has since become a friend. One of the prints I did not get at that auction was offered to me a few months later by a Robert Light of Santa Barbara. Having heard that I collected works by Klee, but not knowing that I had been the underbidder for that particular work at that auction, he wrote to ask whether I was interested in it. I felt that I could not afford his asking price and turned him down. The following year, at another Klee auction in Bern, a friend bid unsuccessfully on my behalf for another rare Klee print. Two months later, I again received a letter from Santa Barbara, inquiring whether I wanted to buy that item. This time, I confessed that on both occasions I had been the underbidder, whereupon Light and I agreed that the time had come for us to meet and work out a more sensible strategy à la Berggruen. On many occasions since then, Light has been my alter ego at Klee sales.

III

It was indirectly owing to Paul Klee that my first poem was published. In 1983, the Avery Center for the Arts at Bard College organized a major Klee exhibition, producing one of the best and most elegantly printed catalogues of Klee graphics in recent years. Even the Museum of Modern Art in New York has it on permanent display in its graphic section. Since I had lent a majority of the prints in that exhibition, the curator asked whether I would write an introduction, to be followed by essays from various experts and Felix Klee himself. After I had accepted, it occurred to me that preparing the introduction in free verse would have more panache than just trying to emulate the usual exhibition catalogue. I am sure the organizers were surprised, and probably a bit dismayed—after all, I was not exactly John Ashbery or James Merrill; but they published the poem with good grace and without changes. It is not often that a novice poet gets two full pages on glossy paper and with color illustrations by Paul Klee.

Since the Bard College exhibition, I have written and published numerous other poems—many of them confessional, some humorous, but only one other dealing with Paul Klee. After starting to read Wallace Stevens, largely at the instigation of my present wife who teaches Stevens and has written a book about him, I learned that this poet's poet was born in 1878, the same year as Paul Klee, a painter's painter. I have long been fascinated by Klee's infatuation with words (he was himself a poet). Many of his titles are descriptive, but equally many are complicated, ambiguous, at first sight incomprehensible in their relation to the pictorial representation. Readers of Stevens will recognize the similarity, but how many know that Klee was Stevens's favorite artist? I know on impeccable authority (from Klee's son), that Klee never read anything by Wallace Stevens, yet feel sure that "in some august imagination" they knew each other. It was out of this perception that I wrote, on Super Bowl Sunday in 1985, a poem entitled "The Twins," an imaginary dialogue between the two artists in which their statements and responses consist largely of the titles generated in a particular year. For instance:

1919

Stevens writes, "Life is Motion."
Klee agrees. He paints, "Up, Away, and Out."

1922
Stevens complains: "Such 'A High-toned Old Christian Woman!' "
Klee nods: "I'll paint her a 'Morality Wagon.' "

1938
"Poetry is a Destructive Force," warns Stevens.
"Not if you paint 'A Light and Dry Poem,' " grins Klee.

IV

I had said, "I'm only a collector," in response to the inspector's question in Washington. Yet by that time, I had already turned into a serious collector. My own definition of "serious collecting" is rather narrow: I am not referring to the haphazard purchase of occasional pieces of art, or to collecting primarily as an investment. Rather, I consider that a serious collector is one who concentrates on a specific artist or art movement or applies some other self-imposed criterion; and who renders an intellectual judgment and, to that extent, places a personal signature on the collection. Assembling five Picassos at random is very different from deliberately selecting five Picassos to make a specific aesthetic, pedagogic, historic, or personal point about the artist.

The 1960s and through the time of my second divorce in 1976 was the period of my earnest collecting. Aside from Klee, I was particularly enamored by modern (though not contemporary) artists who were both expert painters and sculptors—like, for instance, Alberto Giacometti and Marino Marini. My divorce, however, became a watershed event in more than just my marital life. That is when I shifted, rather abruptly, from collector to art patron. Collecting the works of dead artists, such as Paul Klee, becomes a form of patronage only when it serves the public. In many respects, the serious collector is an artist's interpreter. When such an interpretative collection is made available to the public, the social benefit is clear and the collector has started to turn into a patron.

Around the time I wrote "The Twins," I promised my Klee collection to the San Francisco Museum of Modern Art. My reasons for doing so were complicated, of course, but chief among them was my belief that when a significant portion of an artist's output is concentrated in one collection, eventually it ought to be made available to the public.

But for me, a more important form of patronage is the commissioning of art. When I moved to my ranch in the Santa Cruz Mountains after my 1976 divorce, the wide, open space stimulated me to commission outdoor and frequently site-specific sculpture—an activity that became my first entry into that form of art patronage. My interaction with these artists convinced me that a patron of the arts can be most effective by supporting living rather than dead artists. Even so, the most avant-gardist and daring artists are likely to be the least patronized, primarily because they are exploring unfamiliar aesthetic or intellectual territory. The death in 1978 of my daughter, Pamela, a promising artist in various media, taught me that the ultimate form of art patronage largely separates evaluation of an artist's *product* from that of her or his *creativity*, thus reducing, if not totally eliminating, the effects of subjectivity and unfamiliarity. Why did it take my daughter's death to teach me that?

CHAPTER 18

A Scattering of Ashes

I

I always dread the question, "Do you have any children?" or, as phrased in the Orient, "How many children do you have?" Should I answer, "A son," and let it go at that? Or should I say that once I also had a daughter? If I do, one out of two inquisitors will pursue the topic, usually after an embarrassed look of pity. "How did she die?" is almost bound to follow.

Should I tell them the whole story? How on 5 July 1978, I came home from the lab to the ranch, where I was living alone, to hear my son-in-law's panicky voice tell me my daughter, Pamela, had left a note that morning. It read:

> After all my talking with myself, with you, and with others, I have come
> to the conclusion that today is the day to be my last one alive. I can't go
> on being useless—I've been paralyzed and inactive with my art for too
> long and cannot get started again. . . . I've been chronically depressed for
> years and it's only been getting worse. I just don't want to feel it anymore,
> or my own guilt at being useless, or my loneliness and isolation. . . . I'm

leaving the premises to do my own dying in the woods somewhere because I don't want you to find me. Let someone else do that job. . . .

Ultimately, that job fell to me.

Pami's letter was headed "11 A.M." If she had decided on painkillers or sedatives—she had a large supply because of her chronic back pain—then it was crucial to locate her quickly: pumping out her stomach might still save her life. Steve reported that her green 1972 Opel station wagon was missing. I called the sheriff's office, where a sympathetic voice tried to calm me: "In the end, we almost always locate missing cars." "But when?" I wanted to shout. I tried to contact local radio stations to request that they broadcast a description of the missing car and announce a reward for finding it. But by then, it was past 6:00 P.M., and every station I phoned had only recorded messages detailing programs and regular office hours. In my panic, it didn't occur to me to call Directory Assistance for alternative numbers. Instead, Steve and I used the remaining daylight hours to search for the Opel.

Thirteen years earlier, when Pami was fifteen and Dale twelve, we had agreed to spend most of our money on some spectacularly beautiful land in the Santa Cruz Mountains, before developers discovered and ruined it. There were redwood forests, deep canyons, sweeping views of the Pacific, deer, coyotes, bobcats—even the occasional mountain lion; and it was only a few miles from Stanford University and a metropolitan area inhabited by several million people. In less than an hour, one could drive from the San Francisco Opera House into the magic solitude we had named SMIP for *Syntex Made It Possible*—and later renamed *Sic Manebimus in Pace* ("Thus We'll Remain in Peace"). The first ninety-five acres we purchased were deep in the forest; over the next few years, we acquired additional parcels that extended from the redwoods, through clumps of madrone and oak trees, to the undulating meadows pushing toward the coast. By 1970, SMIP had become a 1,200-acre spread—three quarters of it held in the names of my children—on either side of Bear Gulch Road, a winding country road ending at the property of our neighbor, the rock musician Neil Young. On the eastern half of the property, which rises to over 2,000 feet and drops to 800 feet within our own confines, we erected a twelve-sided barn and a ranch manager's residence, centered on open grazing land, which became the site of a pure-bred, polled shorthorn cattle operation. On the edge of the redwood forest, we built a small second home, exquisitely designed by Gerald McCue, then chairman of the architecture department at the University of California. The setting was so private that one could reach it only by descending, through a screen of bay laurel, live oak, and fir, some seventy-five irregular steps made from railroad ties. Around the same time, my son, not yet twenty, was the beneficiary of a trust fund based on an early gift in Syntex shares, which had multiplied many times in value. He requested that the bulk of the fund be used to construct his own hawk-shaped home near a small lake on the western portion of the ranch, an hour's hike from his parent's ranch abode. In 1974, my daughter—then living in La Jolla while her husband was finishing medical school—followed suit. Her home and studio went up on the west side of Bear Gulch Road, half an hour's walk from her brother's home. Sometimes, when she sat on one of her hills overlooking the wide expanse of the Pacific, and the ocean wind blew the right way, she could faintly hear Neil Young rehearse.

Pami and Steve had moved into their ranch home when the latter started his radiology residency at Stanford, where they had met as undergraduates. In July 1978, I'd been divorced for nearly two years and was also living at SMIP in the redwood house. For well over a decade, we had hiked weekends, and frequently on weekday evenings, all over the property. Still, there were many areas we'd never explored; some sections were simply too rugged or otherwise inaccessible. When, in 1983, I badly fractured my stiff leg while climbing over some fallen logs in a creek bed, it took seven hours for the paramedics and state foresters to transfer me to the Stanford Hospital, during which time I received enough morphine to sedate a couple of adult elephants. If some of my students had not been with me, I would not have been found for days or weeks and surely would have died.

This was the area Steve and I had to cover on 5 July in the remaining two to three hours of daylight—he on the west and I on the east side of Bear Gulch Road. I drove along that road and out to Skyline Boulevard, the main north-south access along the ridge of the Santa Cruz Mountains. No green Opel was parked there. Ever more frantic, I covered the interior ranch forest road, which—though unpaved—was accessible to automobiles except in the winter rainy season. When night fell, and we had found nothing, Steve and I realized that the situation was hopeless.

Since my former wife was then not on speaking terms with me, I phoned her attorney, who had impressed me during our bitter divorce as a warm human being. He discovered that Norma was in Hawaii and promised to locate her. My father was traveling in Europe, and I simply didn't have the heart to notify him. Dale was in Argentina, shooting footage for a documentary on South American soccer. Although I had the home telephone number of his film colleague in the provincial town of San Juan, I decided not to call him until we were more certain of Pami's fate. In the event, Dale's mother cabled him when she heard, and he flew back immediately.

Years later, he told me about some startling coincidences. On 5 July, he was filming in the small town of Balcarce, the site of Argentina's first earth satellite station established to broadcast the soccer world cup events. That night, he read Georg Büchner's novella *Lenz*, based on the sad life and likely suicide of Goethe's friend Jakob Lenz and considered by some the first piece of "modern" prose in German. Büchner, who himself died at age twenty-three, summarizes Lenz's depression in the last sentences of his story. "He did everything that the others did; still there was a dreadful void inside him, he no longer felt any anxiety, nor any desire. His existence was an inevitable burden. And so his life went on. . . ." Dale recalled the terrible nightmare from which he awoke the following morning, the sheets twisted, his body soaking wet. When he returned to Buenos Aires and found his mother's cable announcing a family emergency, he made plane reservations for the first flight out. A torrential rainstorm, the worst in years, nearly prevented him from reaching the airport. Two years later, when he met his future wife, he discovered that she had been at the Buenos Aires airport on the same stormy day, sitting at the same time in that departure lounge, before flying home from a visit to her brother in Argentina.

During the next four days, my terror and loneliness were so concentrated that I could not begin to face the deeper tragedy of Pami's decision. Early on the morning of 6 July, I notified the few ranchers living in the neighborhood as well as Robin Toews, my son's former grade-school teacher who had been living with her daughter as a tenant in my former ranch manager's home since the end of the cattle operation in the year of my divorce. All agreed to search; by the end of the day, all had concluded that the green Opel was not on the ranch. In spite of the miles of trails and canyons and untracked areas where a body could be hidden, only a limited number of sites were accessible to a car. Pami must have driven elsewhere "to do my own dying in the woods." Her mother clung to the hope, reinforced by the advice of some of her friends, that she was just holed up somewhere, perhaps in a motel. Norma had even located a clairvoyant who had promised to use her powers to find Pami. But Steve and I were convinced that Pami had killed herself. But where? What if her car had been stolen after she had left it on the side of some forest road, and the infallible sheriff recovered it, only days or weeks later, at another site, hundreds of miles away? How would we even know where to start the search?

My greatest fear was that I would never know what had happened to my daughter, who, during the past four years, had become my closest friend and only confidante. "In the woods somewhere" didn't have to mean *our* woods. The Santa Cruz Mountains encompassed miles and miles of uninhabited woods. And what about the Sierras? We used to backpack in Desolation Valley near Lake Tahoe and in the Tuolumne Meadows of Yosemite. Only two winters earlier, we had gone cross-country skiing for a long weekend near Donner Pass. We were blessed by one of the most magical winter settings of our experience: blue sky, newly fallen snow covering all but the most recent tracks, the temperature just cold enough to keep us from overheating even after hours of fast skiing. During hours of intimate conversation, in the wood-burning sauna or the hot tub out in the snow under the redwoods, my daughter had turned into a peer—indeed, my confessor and advisor. What if she had driven into those mountain woods, two hundred miles north of us?

On the evening of 9 July, after four desperate days, I was standing at the sink in the galley kitchen of my house when I suddenly felt that I was not alone. The sun had not yet sunk, but dusk was sufficiently far along among the redwoods surrounding my house that inside it was dark except for the kitchen light. As I turned toward the glass door, I caught the outline of three persons. I couldn't make out the figures, and their total stillness made my heart miss a beat. Walking toward them, I finally recognized my tenant, her young daughter, and Bob Mann, the manager of the ranch bordering on Pami's side of our property. As I stood before them, the width of the glass separating us, I saw tears in Bob's eyes.

That evening, Bob related, as the falling sun shone horizontally across the Pacific on an area he had already passed twice during his searches, he noted in the grass the faint outline of car tracks that had escaped him earlier. Following the tracks down to the edge of the forest, he saw the green Opel partly hidden among some bushes. He then headed straight for my home on the other side of Bear Gulch Road. I immediately called the sheriff and then my son-in-law. Steve asked whether I would do what had to be done.

As a physician, Steve Bush had seen many a corpse, but I had led a remarkably sheltered life in that respect. Although I had escaped Nazi Austria and traveled all over the globe, I had never seen a person killed by a gun or any other form of violence; until then, in fact, I'd never seen a dead body. Except for the barely remembered death of my grandmother during my childhood, and my mother's passing at age ninety-one in a nursing home three thousand miles away, I'd hardly ever *thought* of death.

I followed Bob's jeep to the spot where the faint tracks were barely visible in the dusk. He refused to accompany me further, so I walked alone down the golden-brown meadow. Through the Opel's windshield I saw my daughter's lovely face terribly misshapen and bloated; I fled, without opening the car door. Fighting my stiff left leg, I hobbled as quickly as possible to my car and drove off. Interminable minutes later, I saw in the distance the flashing lights of the police car and of the ambulance behind.

Until then, I'd hardly ever cried as an adult. But that night, I cried for hours. Even now, over a decade after the event, I weep uncontrollably when I think back to that night, to the horror of that first sight, to the rush of relief that the gnawing uncertainty was over, to the dawning despair that Pami's suicide was now irrevocable fact.

We agreed that, after the autopsy, Pami's body should be cremated and the ashes spread over the site she loved most—even though I had to lie to accomplish it. A peculiar California law prohibits the open scattering of human ashes anywhere but in the ocean, the progress of "ashes to ashes and dust to dust" being illegal in the Golden State. We picked a spot that years earlier Pami and I had declared the most beautiful one at SMIP: a small waterfall, where Harrington Creek runs past many moss-covered rocks and onto a smooth glistening one, shaped like the orifice of a tilted amphora, whence the water shoots into a clear pool. Since Harrington Creek eventually enters San Gregorio Creek, which terminates in the Pacific, our act was perhaps not wholly outside the law. The spot looks Hawaiian, with huge lush ferns on the sides of the pool and the trees forming a natural dome through which sunlight flickers. Years earlier, on one of our hikes, Pami and I had come upon it. I had decided that this was the place for the eventual disposition of my own ashes, never dreaming that I would pass through the bitterest experience of any parent: to be the survivor, to pick up at the crematorium the cardboard box of my child's ashes.

Diane Middlebrook, who, though not yet my wife, had become one of Pami's few intimates, was present when, to the sound of some fifteenth-century Sephardic songs, Steve scattered the ashes onto the shaped rock at the mouth of the waterfall, while we dropped flower petals into the rapidly clearing pool. Dale and I held each other—one of the first times since his adolescence; and I begged in a whisper, "Please don't leave me, Dalito." Later Diane wrote "At the Scattering of Ashes":

This cloud runs in my dreams,
Part of my bloodstream now:
Cloudy, then clear, the pool at the foot of the falls—
A uniform gray: you . . .
Let it be. But this pure image haunts me,
Of water receiving your death;
Being changed; flowing on.

II

Many a death—especially when caused by accident or sudden disease—is met by the bitter question "Why?" Invariably it is addressed to God or against God, meaning "Why did You let that happen?" But there is another "Why?" after a suicide that must be addressed to the person who is now dead. I was too depressed to ask at the time, nor was I ready to ask myself whether I could have done something to prevent it. On 4 July, the day before she killed herself, Pami had hiked over to my home to spend a few hours with me in the sun, talking about her future. Nothing in her tone or conversation had given me any inkling that she was teetering on the edge of the precipice.

My immediate response to Pami's death was typical of how I coped at that period of my life with personal disaster: I drowned myself in work. Seventeen-hour workdays ensured that when I finally dropped into bed I fell immediately asleep. In addition, there was the legal and accounting work involved in being the executor of Pami's estate, which, like Dale's, had multiplied manifold with the rise of Syntex stock. But after eleven weeks of such work-induced anesthesia, I suddenly decided to travel, and invited Diane Middlebrook to join me. In all my trips to Italy, I'd deliberately avoided visiting Venice and Florence: I felt that these two jewels should not be visited as part of a tourist itinerary in which sites are strung together and no individual component means much. Especially in Florence, I wanted to focus on the art and do it with the right companion.

Three evenings in a row, Diane and I sat in an outdoor café on the Piazza della Signoria facing the Palazzo Vecchio, to relive the day's impressions—and to talk about Pami's decision. Was it an inevitable consequence of a person suffering from depression who had been unwilling to consider therapy? Was it the chronic physical pain that prevented her during the past two years of her life from doing any of the garden and animal work she loved? She could barely feed the horses that had meant so much to her, let alone ride them. Was it her disillusionment with the commercial art scene, with the humiliating compromises a young artist is called upon to make? Or was it the lack of professional peers resulting from her self-imposed isolation in the majestic but also overpowering setting of SMIP? Her husband, surrounded every day by a multitude of people in the hospital, had hardly a minute free for contemplation. Like me, he felt calmed upon returning in the evening to the solitude of the coastal mountains, often shrouded in the veil of the ocean fog pouring in through the canyons. The extraordinary silence, the absence of man-made sounds except for the occasional start of the refrigerator motor, was a soothing contrast to the cacophony of the workplace. But what about the person who remained behind all day? Does beauty in nature, when experienced in solitude, always calm and please, or does it also terrify? Some of Pami's bitterest poetry (published posthumously by her mother) was written during that period of her life.

Pami always read, and during those last few years, she read a great deal. Much of it was women's writings and feminist literature, which provided fertile background to her ideas about the place of women in art. All her artistic role models, all her former teachers at the San Francisco Art Institute and at Stanford University, had been men. Indeed, until the time of her death, Stanford's art department had not a single woman faculty member among its studio art faculty. Diane, then head of Stanford's Center for Research on Women (CROW) in addition to her professorship in English, taught me a great deal about the daily affronts women sense in a male-oriented culture. I am sure that my own quasipatriarchal style contributed to Pami's sensitivity. These, and many other issues, were the subjects of our evening talks in the Piazza della Signoria, practically at the feet of the prancing bronze horse on which Cosimo de' Medici surveyed the splendor his family had sponsored. "It's hard to think what Florence would've been like without the Medicis," I mused, pointing to the Giambologna bronze. "But imagine what it would be today if their patronage had extended to women," said Diane.

In that hour, my own response to Pami's suicide finally took shape. Suicide is a message to the survivors, but the text must be read by each individual—parent, sibling, spouse, friend—in the light of his or her past relationship with the deceased. An answer to the question "why?" can be provided only by the survivor; on that September evening in Florence, I decided that my answer, or at least my response, would be patronage of the type that would have benefited Pami. Diane became my partner—intellectual and operational—in this endeavor. In the 1960s, when we acquired the land that became SMIP, my children agreed with me that it should be kept in an unspoiled state for the ultimate benefit of the public. Though we were not certain of the details, the decision contributed to the legal establishment of the Djerassi Foundation, a nonprofit entity that we envisaged as the eventual beneficiary of our respective testaments. Whatever philanthropic donations I made during the late 1960s and 1970s were funneled through that foundation, but any substantial activities were meant to await my death. In 1978, Pamela and Dale were the two trustees empowered to decide how my own estate—land, art, and remaining assets—would be distributed by the foundation; but none of us were then thinking of death, and the full operation of the foundation still seemed many years away.

This changed on 5 July, 1978, when a bottle of pills transformed the concept of the foundation into a real entity with a substantial financial equity and title to a significant portion of SMIP ranch land, as well as to Pamela's house and studio. Shortly after Diane and I returned from Italy, Steve joined a radiology research unit in Los Alamos, New Mexico, to take advantage of a new radiation source for cancer treatment. The resulting availability of Pamela's house and studio led us to decide to offer to Stanford University's art department the use of these facilities, as well as an annual stipend to underwrite one-year residencies at SMIP for women artists of accomplishment. The incumbent would have no formal teaching duties, but should be prepared for some open-studio events and for interaction with art students and faculty. Toward the end of her stay, an exhibition of the past year's work would be presented at the Art Museum of Stanford University. The foundation offered an initial commitment of four years to test the project's validity. We felt that this would accomplish at least two objectives dear to Pamela's heart: patronage through a public exhibition in a museum, free from commercial considerations; and exposure of mature women artists to the Stanford art community. But while the museum director agreed to the stipulation for an exhibition, and some art history professors, notably Albert Elsen, were supportive, the studio art faculty was not prepared for any obligations that would make such a visiting artist feel welcome. In the end, CROW became the Stanford sponsor, and members of CROW, the art department, and some outside art professionals and museum directors formed a selection committee that began to canvass nominators all over the world.

Out of some forty candidates, four were selected. In 1979 came Tamara Rikman, a graphic artist from Jerusalem, who was accompanied by her husband, the poet T. Carmi. She was followed by Barbara Greenberg, a New York fiber artist and sculptor, who had been nominated by her teacher, the renowned Polish fiber-artist Magdalena Abakanowicz. Greenberg gave birth to her first child in Pami's house and also built a fifteen-foot-high "bird nest" out of twigs, branches, and sisal. Since the nest was too big to be transported by truck along narrow Bear Gulch Road, a helicopter picked up the nest in a sling and deposited it in front of the Stanford Museum, where it gradually decomposed over the next six months. A great believer in ephemeral art, Barbara Greenberg also created a remarkable three-day installation on one of the SMIP hills involving several hundred red highway posts (rented). The third artist, the Maine painter Kathryn Porter, had a commission from the City of San Francisco for a memorial of the recently assassinated mayor, George Moscone. While at SMIP, Porter changed the approved design by including references to Che Guevara, Rosa Luxemburg, George Jackson, Malcolm X, and other revolutionaries. As a result, the commission was canceled, whereupon Porter, claiming censorship, departed in a huff. To fill the unexpected vacancy, the CROW staff proposed as an interim appointment a black writer and poet from Berkeley, Joyce Carol Thomas, who was in the final stages of completing her first novel, *Marked by Fire*. Pami's house provided the undisturbed concentration Thomas needed; and during her Djerassi Foundation residency, she completed also a substantial portion of her second novel. *Marked by Fire* won Thomas the National Book Award in the adolescent literature category on the same occasion that her friend Alice Walker won it in the adult category for *The Color Purple*.

The fourth woman artist was Sue Gussow, a professor of painting at New York's Cooper Union, whose artistic output proved qualitatively and quantitatively outstanding, but who found herself too isolated from the Stanford art community. We finally concluded that, although the driving distance from Pami's studio to Stanford University was only a few miles, the attitudinal gulf was simply too wide. The women artists got a lot done under close to ideal physical conditions, but their presence had only a minimal effect on the Stanford art scene. Barbara Greenberg had suggested during her stay that the buildings owned by me on my side of SMIP ranch—the ranch manager's residence and the twelve-sided barn—would lend themselves to conversion into a small artist's colony, which would overcome the sense of isolation and lack of peer interaction (also Pami's problem) encountered by the artists who had come alone for an entire year. I began to realize that free creative time without conditions may be the ultimate gift for an artist, but it is an incomplete gift if it denies the crucial human need: companionship.

Diane, in her capacity as a foundation trustee, visited the two oldest artist's colonies in the East, Yaddo and McDowell, as well as two smaller ones, the Edna St. Vincent Millay Colony and Hand Hollow—the latter founded by a friend of mine, the kinetic sculptor George Rickey, on his farm in East Chatham, New York. Diane's report and Rickey's counsel persuaded me to convert the four-bedroom former manager's residence into an eight-bedroom, five-bath house and to create two studios in the barn. Leigh Hyams, a San Francisco painter, was appointed interim director; and by late 1982, the Djerassi Foundation artist's colony was born. The gender requirement was dropped as the community expanded; and to make our program available to a larger number of artists, residencies were limited to periods of one to three months. Since all the bedrooms would be large and, with one exception, have balconies or direct access to the surrounding garden, they could easily double as workrooms for the writers. The two studios in the barn would be used by visual artists and composers. Rickey considered good food to be indispensable to the success of an artist's colony—advice we followed by hiring his chef, who had cooked at Hand Hollow with *cordon bleu* elegance.

By the end of that first year, we had housed and fed fifty-two artists, twenty-eight of them women. The friendships and collaborations formed at SMIP extended beyond the professional: two sculptors, Patricia Leighton from Scotland and Del Geist from New York, and the Houston painter Josefa Vaughan and the San Francisco composer Charles Boone, got married after meeting at SMIP. Our first composer, John Adams, who later gained international recognition for his opera *Nixon in China*, spent three months at the foundation, where he composed the music to *Available Light*, a work commissioned for the opening of the Museum of Contemporary Art in Los Angeles. On several occasions, Adams remarked to me how difficult it was to collaborate with his choreographer, Lucinda Childs, three thousand miles away. Adams's comments convinced me that we should encourage interdisciplinary collaboration by creating additional studio spaces within the twelve-sided barn.

By then, the cost of the program had started to exceed the endowment income of the foundation and my personal resources. Not only had my divorce reduced my assets by half, but much of these were tied up in real estate at SMIP and in art. Most of my SMIP property and the artists's residence and studio barn were gifted by me to the foundation, but the bulk of my art collection—the works of Paul Klee—had already been promised to the San Francisco Museum of Art and was thus unavailable to the foundation. I began selling much of my other art, mostly the work of dead artists, in order to support the work of living ones. But even that was not sufficient: in addition to the chef, we had acquired a full-time director (who lived in my daughter's house), a resident manager, and a grounds manager. Several local foundations—notably the Hewlett, the Irvine, and the San Francisco—and later the MacArthur Foundation and the National Endowment for the Arts made generous grants, which, together with contributions from individuals and corporations, enabled us to complete additional studios dedicated to choreography and performing arts, to music, to photography, and to ceramics. The barn renovation included three sleeping lofts, which increased our housing capacity to eleven artists. It has proved to be an ideal size: still small enough for everyone to sit around one table for dinner, yet large enough for real collegiality.

At the end of our seventh year—under the successive directorships of Leigh Hyams, Susan Learned-Driscoll, Sally M. Stillman, and now Charles Boone (a former composer-in-residence)—the program has grown to such an extent that, with over five hundred artists from thirty-four states and twenty-two foreign countries, it has become the largest artist's colony west of the Mississippi. The artists have included a Nobel Prize laureate, a MacArthur Fellow, numerous Guggenheim fellowship holders, and winners of literary and visual art awards, as well as many artists who had not yet received wide public recognition but were considered worthy of support by our selection panels. At one time or another, I have met most of the artists at dinner—occasions that are usually followed by readings, slide presentations, music or dance performances, or just good conversation. As I listen to music just composed, or face a canvas, still moist on a studio wall; as I hear a poet read lines that could only have been born here; as I look with a sculptor for a site in the forest where once I searched for Pami's body; I catch myself wondering what she would have thought of all this.

Five years after Pami's death, I received another panicky phone call, this time from the artist then occupying her former home and studio, saying she had found a note, deep in back of a drawer. She was shaking when she handed me the piece of paper with my daughter's handwriting on it, a ghost's message. That night I recorded this in my journal:

> *My only daughter,*
> *I find this note:*
>
> *"I have nothing left to say,*
> *So I don't talk.*
> *I have nothing left to do,*
> *So I close up shop."*
>
> *No date*
> *No address*
> *No signature*
> *Your handwriting.*
>
> *Written for whom?*
> *Yourself?*
> *To whom it may concern?*

Written when?
Days,
Weeks,
Perhaps months
Before you walked into the woods?

If only you'd said these words to me.

If only, I add in retrospect, your death had not been necessary before I took seriously the patronage of the living.

CODA

Thanksgiving Day 1989. We have already been hiking for four hours in search for some felled redwood trunks at least five feet in diameter. It's the minimum size David Nash requires for the three-part sculpture he intends to site around some of the burned-out giant redwood stumps that can still be found, here or there, on our property from nineteenth-century logging. Nash is one of the most distinguished artists we have had in residence at the foundation. A British sculptor, now working in Wales, he first came to the foundation in 1987 at the time of his retrospective exhibition at the San Francisco Museum of Modern Art. While wood ("King of the Vegetables," he calls it) is his sole medium, and chain saw or ax his principal tools, he had never before handled redwood or madrone, the two most prevalent species in our forest. During his first stay, he had created a group of madrone sculptures for a highly successful show in Los Angeles; in addition, out of a huge redwood trunk that had lain for decades in Harrington Creek, Nash had fashioned *Sylvan Steps*—a Jacob's ladder rising at a steep angle out of the water into the sky. When he first selected that site—accessible only along the creek bed by clambering over rocks and fallen timber—he had had no inkling that a few hundred feet upstream we had, in 1978, scattered my daughter's ashes. Within a minute, some flecks of them must have floated past the spot where Nash's steps now rise into the air. *Sylvan Steps* is a magically simple sculpture which many subsequent artists have drawn, photographed, or written about.

But now, two years later, during his second residency, we cannot find the massive log he needs. During our morning hike, we have located four sites in the forest where blackened trunks rise out of the bracken—just the right backdrop for the scorched pyramid, cube, and ball Nash plans to shape, but still missing is the right arboreal progenitor for these forms. Of course, we cross the shadow of many a living redwood giant, but cutting one is out of the question. Then I recall that some selective logging has just been completed on our neighbor's land across Bear Gulch Road; only a few days ago, I had followed impatiently a slow-moving truck stacked high with redwood logs. Perhaps *our* piece had not yet been removed.

I don't expect anyone to be working there on Thanksgiving Day. But, after climbing over the locked gate and walking down the forest road, inches deep in dust (it had not rained for weeks), we hear in the distance the grinding of gears. Soon we come upon a mammoth tractor setting up erosion breaks to preserve the road bed during the winter rainy season.

"Have you moved out all the logs?" I shout up to the bearded driver after he has shut off the thundering engine. "We need . . . ," I say, and then explain who David Nash is, and why we are searching for a special fallen redwood rather than a turkey for Thanksgiving.

"All gone," he says, then remembers. "A big one fell across the fence near the property line. Probably years ago . . . in some storm." According to him, it was partly rotten—sufficiently so that it had not been worthwhile to haul it to the mill. Nash is dubious that it will do, but I say, "Let's look anyway."

We follow the man's directions to the fence a half-mile down the logging road. When we finally come upon it, I am dumbfounded. Eleven years ago, I had hobbled here as fast as my stiff leg would carry me—but from the opposite direction, down the meadow from our side of the property, toward this fence across which the massive trunk now lies, broken into three enormous pieces. It is the spot where my daughter killed herself, where I have never dared to return. We find the rot to be only superficial; the wood is precisely what David Nash has been seeking all Thanksgiving long.

CHAPTER 19

Return to Vienna:
"Wien, Wien, nur du allein . . ."

I AM ON MY WAY FROM SAN FRANCISCO to the Maldives to board a Soviet research vessel, the *Akademik Oparin*, in the Indian Ocean. Curiously, the best connection is through Vienna, from where Singapore Airlines flies twice weekly nonstop to Male, the capital of the Maldives. My son and I have a few hours to kill between planes, which we decide to spend walking around the inner city. Our taxi passes the apartment house where I lived fifty-one years ago, and from whose balcony I saw the Nazi brownshirts cross over the Aspernbrücke on the way to the predominantly Jewish quarter of Vienna. We get off near St. Stephen's cathedral and head along Kärntnerstrasse—Vienna's most elegant shopping street which leads to the Opera and is now closed to all vehicular traffic.

The weather is balmy this late October 1989, and many people sit in outdoor cafés or stroll in typical late Saturday afternoon fashion. Suddenly we come upon two musicians, a violinist and a cellist, who are surrounded by quiet, almost reverential onlookers. With a flourish of his bow, the violinist starts a highly professional rendition of Mozart's *Eine kleine Nachtmusik*. The choice is so typically Viennese as to defy an attribution of kitschy or banal. As we slow down to listen, I sing into Dale's ear in an undertone, *"Wien, Wien, nur du allein."*

298

"You sound like Grandpa at the opera," my son whispers. I know what he means: at intermission on the way to the foyer, my father used to hum his favorite aria from the last act with a beatific smile. "But what does it mean?" Dale asks, not knowing any German.

" 'Vienna, Vienna, only you alone.' Every Viennese knows this from birth."

Dale squeezes my arm to let me know he understands this sudden outburst of Vienna-bred sentimentality. But then I see three tall policemen—young and not yet potbellied—strut toward the circle of listeners, and my emotional house of cards collapses. "Watch it!" I warn my son with typical Waldheim-induced suspicion. "They'll stop them." "No way," whispers my American son, who is not burdened by a Viennese childhood dating from the 1930s, which includes chases by the grandfathers of these young cops, in identical green uniforms, when we played soccer in the park.

"Break up Mozart in Vienna?" Dale adds incredulously, reaching into his pocket to produce one of Vienna's favorite chocolates, bearing Mozart's portrait on the wrapper.

But I'm right: The trio of police walk straight through the listeners' cordon, which opens like a cell being penetrated by an invading virus. The tallest of the cops stalks toward the violinist, getting so close to him as to force him to glance up from the music stand. Mozart dies instantly. The young violinist looks crestfallen as the policeman addresses him with an arrogant smirk; the only detail missing from the picture forming in my mind is the tapping of a swagger stick. The other player quickly grabs his open cello case and starts to pack his instrument. Only then does one of the silent spectators rush up to slip a twenty-schilling note into the case just as its cover drops—the sole sign of sympathy or protest among the entire crowd. The officious trio move on, perhaps for ten meters, beyond the sullen group; now they stop, turn around in slow motion, and stare to be sure that Mozart is not revived. Past overfed *Loden*-clad burgers gorging themselves with *Schlag*-covered cakes and coffee, my son and I walk on, each in his own way struck dumb.

There is no music anywhere on *Kärntnerstrasse* as we continue to the Opera. The only vestige of *Kultur* are some poems stuck, like Japanese prayers at a shrine, on a tree.

CHAPTER 20

Mind the Gaps

EVERYTHING THAT CAN BE SAID about the self-indulgence, the deviousness, the deliberate or subliminal image massaging, of autobiographical writing has doubtless been said many times; nor is it original, I suspect, to compare autobiography and Swiss cheese. The holes in a life account may be planned or inadvertent, but they are there; self-reflection and disclosure must pass through one's particular psychic filters. Depending on the filter's mesh, all kinds of facts and interpretations are withheld: microscopic or macroscopic blemishes, tragedies, infirmities, faux pas, or worse: sins, hidden lies, treachery. . . . When the Swiss cheese analogy for autobiography first occurred to me, I considered it apt, though a bit corny. But now, as I seek closure for my own account, and a title, all I see are the holes, the innumerable little incidents kept out that, though often mundane, may tell something unexpected.

Filling the gaps in an autobiography serves no more purpose than filling the holes in Swiss cheese. My memory, my sense of shame, and whatever residual discretion is left me guarantee that the fillers I provide are false. To paraphrase a line of Anne Sexton's, I am likely to construct a tree out of used furniture. The gaps, large as they may be, are thus more honest, a truer

reflection of my nature. Freud's insight applies with full force: the unconscious speaks through the gaps in ordinary language. Readers will gather
from my prose intelligence about me of which I remain unaware.

I

Of two lacunae in my life's account I want explicitly to recognize and
acknowledge, one is my son, who has appeared here fleetingly in a few
scenes as if he were a minor character in a complicated play. Nothing
could be further from the truth. I am an only child; my parents are dead,
and so are their siblings; Dale and my grandchild, Alexander, are my sole
direct chromosomal connections. Our father-son relationship has always
been one of the most complicated components of both our lives, even
though at times we may not have recognized it. Our relationship is still
vulnerable enough to demand gentle caution. We are still moving toward
a mutual understanding I cannot write about, nor would even if I understood it completely. This gap is bound to shrink after the dialogue we
have not quite yet held but surely will hold (unless one of us says
"*mañana*" once too often). All I shall offer here is the usual preamble of
the scientific paper, the abstract in the form of a poem I wrote on my
sixtieth birthday.

GODFATHER

To describe one's character is difficult and not necessarily illuminating.
                                                                —Iris Murdoch

   "Quod licet iovi non licet bovi"
   I told my children
   Laughingly.
   Years later,
   I learned they took me seriously.

   "What is allowed to God is not permitted to the oxen."

   Was this said as god—
   Hence seriously, though laughing—
   Or as godfather?

   Can a father be a god?

Why burden my American children
With detritus of my Latin drills?

Forgive me both:
Surviving son.
Dead daughter.

II

The other giant gap refers to the women in my life. I have written of four women: my mother, who died when we were most estranged; my daughter, Pamela, who killed herself when we were closest; and my first two wives, now worlds away in terms of psychic distance. But there are two other inamoratas I must acknowledge.

One is really a generic persona. During the past twenty years of great personal change, of my gradual dismantling of a thick wall of self-imposed, even compulsive, privacy, I have made no new close men friends, but many new women ones. Why only women? It would be disingenuous to deny that the mystery of sexual attraction, or at least its imagined potential, played a role. But if this were all, the dismantling of my wall—a brick here, a larger opening there, an occasional lowering of the drawbridge across the moat in front of the wall—would not have waited until my middle forties, when I should surely have been set in my ways and was most involved in my scientific research and entrepreneurial activities, seemingly without a spare moment for such psychic loosening.

An oversimplified diagnosis is that most male friendships have their origins in early competition: school, sports, establishing of pecking orders, sexual conquest. At that early stage, the border between intimacy and friendly boasting is nebulous. In science, friendship and collaboration often overlap; competition is more circumscribed but nevertheless tacitly acknowledged and accepted. In my own male universe, competition and ambition were especially pronounced, so I was unlikely to search for more of the same as I matured. I have never warmed to the all-American bonding experience of watching football, baseball, and basketball (perhaps because my European childhood totally imprinted me with soccer); and my current active sports, skiing and swimming, are not team activities. Golf may be one fresh ground for new male friendships, but I only sneer at golf as an old man's exercise or a young man's folly, out of a combination of ignorance and inverted snobbery. No wonder that the emotional, psychic, and even social strengths of women, lacking the abrasive male tendency toward competitive jockeying for position, became powerful pheromones for my middle and later years.

Until my middle thirties, all women close to me, including my first two wives, were considerably older than I. Only later did the pendulum swing in the opposite direction. Was I first looking for a mother and then a daughter? The simple fact was that during the later years of emotional solitude and eventual legal unencumbrance, the most likely place for me to meet new friends was not in the usual social setting of suburban dinner parties, attended by middle-aged or older guests. I didn't hold such parties and was rarely invited to any. Rather, I met new acquaintances and friends in the intellectual hustle and bustle of a prestigious university. In those days of major social ferment—feminist and black activism, sexual revolution, antiwar sentiments, recreational drugs—all but the last had an impact on me, primarily through the female generation of the 1970s, the women who became my social peers.

With one exception—an episode in 1955 with mescaline, which I have recounted earlier—recreational drugs have never tempted me. Aldous Huxley took the title for his *The Doors of Perception*, which had prompted that single excursion of mine into chemically induced hallucination, from a line in William Blake's *The Marriage of Heaven and Hell*: "If the doors of perception were cleansed every thing would appear to man as it is, infinite"—an aphorism Blake categorized as "A Memorable Fancy." Though my one attempt at Huxlean cleansing was indeed memorable, it was also mostly a fancy. It points me to a conclusion different from Huxley's: I require a more abrasive cleansing agent than mescaline to be able to look through my doors of perception. Changing his metaphor, Blake goes on: "For man has closed himself up, till he sees all things thro' narrow chinks of his cavern." Years passed before my chinks started to widen perceptibly, as gradually I discovered that it takes more than chemistry to change a man's persona. Women—especially one woman—were the agents of my change.

III

Diane Wood Middlebrook eventually turned into the mentor I never had, and the muse I never dreamed of. As a rule, scientists do not look for muses, and their need for mentors occurs early on, before they pull around themselves the academic security blanket of tenure. When I met her, I was solidly tenured in my academic setting, recently divorced in my private life, and certainly not looking for a mentoring muse. Or was I?

One Sunday in early 1977, I was glancing through the winter issue of the *Stanford Observer*, an alumni quarterly, when my roving eye halted at a picture. It wasn't just the image of the woman that arrested my gaze, but also her name. I had never before met Diane Middlebrook nor did I know what she looked like. Yet her name had stayed in my memory because, on two separate occasions, two women of very different age—one, my former wife; the other, one of my favorite students—had described her to me in subtly sexually charged terms. I started reading the article about the poet Middlebrook and then found myself doing something I don't recall ever having done before: dialing the number of a total stranger for a rendezvous. What would I have said had she picked up the receiver? "Professor Middlebrook, will you have dinner with me?" And how would I have continued had she said, "May I bring my husband, my daughter, my . . . ?"

She wasn't in that Sunday afternoon; and the following day, my impulse seemed sufficiently sophomoric that I didn't try again. But within weeks, a more elegant opportunity arose: a friend from the 1960s, Miriam Stoppard, at that time medical director of Syntex in England, wrote that she and her husband, the British playwright Tom Stoppard, would be visiting San Francisco. We had once had a joyous picnic at my ranch, and I was thinking about a repetition when my plans were changed for me. Another common friend, Alex Cross from Syntex and Zoecon days, had also heard from the Stoppards; realizing that I would be inviting them, he suggested that a dinner be held instead at his home, but with me responsible for the composition of the guests. I accepted and in due course provided Cross with a list of people unknown to him which would, I guaranteed, make stimulating company. Featured were two scientists—the Nobel laureates Don Glaser and Paul Berg—and, for diversity, a poet named Diane Middlebrook. The rest of the story is partly second-hand as told to me by Diane.

"My name is Dr. Cross," a British voice said to her over the telephone. "You do not know me, but my wife and I would like to invite you to dinner with the playwright Tom Stoppard."

"Why me?" she asked.

"I know you're a poet," Cross improvised. "I thought Stoppard would be interested in meeting you."

"Why not?" Diane supposedly replied. "What English professor doesn't want to meet Tom Stoppard?"

A few weeks later, Diane, wearing a full-length, body-hugging, red silk dress and little else, was the first guest to be greeted by Alex Cross's Hungarian wife, Tony, whose Zsa Zsa Gabor–like figure was enhanced by an outfit as daring as Diane's. Shortly thereafter, the rest of the guests arrived and, finally, the glamorous Stoppards. As introductions were made all around, Diane began to realize that, except for the Stoppards, the hosts knew none of their guests. At that point, I arrived with my companion, a Greek sculptor, and—except for Diane—greeted everyone as old friends. Only then did it dawn on her that I was the person responsible for her invitation.

Tony Cross is a spectacularly elegant woman, an equally spectacular Hungarian cook, and as a hostess the possessor of a third sense about who should sit next to whom. Except for the first course—a Hungarian cherry soup—all I can recall of that evening is the impression my dinner companion on my right made on me. Two days later, I made her an offer she did not refuse: "Come live with me, and I'll do the laundry and cook for you while you write."

IV

For six years, I was so confident of my relationship with this young literature professor—strikingly elegant in voice, appearance, and intellect—that I took it for granted. When she announced one day, while on sabbatical leave at Harvard, that she had decided to live with another man, my response was simultaneously expected and strange.

The expected was the brew of resentment, self-pity, felt violation, and desired revenge. The emotional and physical consolation provided by old and new women friends should have extinguished that fire, but didn't. Strange as it seems, this ugly mood was the impetus for a new intellectual life. I, who had never composed a poem or written a word of fiction, decided to revenge myself on that polished poet and literature professor on her own turf. (Was this just another unacknowledged manifestation of male competitiveness?) Out of my typewriter streamed a flood of bitter and self-pitying poems, some even accepted by reputable literary journals. Having emptied that reservoir of bile, I turned on a second faucet, this time one of confessional poetry—a modest poetic, as well as emotional, improvement. But these poems were only a detour. The unconscious *pièce de revanche* was a roman á clef, transparently entitled "Middles." The title's epigraph, taken from Nora Ephron's *Heartburn*, was supposed to hide its real origin: "I insist on happy endings; I would insist on happy beginnings, too, but that's not necessary because all beginnings are intrinsically happy . . . middles are a problem. Middles are perhaps the major problem of contemporary society."

We had not seen each other for a year when I received flowers and a message from Diane about a possible rapprochement. I reciprocated in a typically macho manner: instead of roses, I presented her with the manuscript of my "novel." Fortunately, she persuaded me to bury that manuscript. Nora Ephron's revenge novel about her former husband worked for two reasons: it was the work of a real professional and sprinkled with bittersweet humor. My "Middles" was amateurish, bitter, and bare of humor. Still, it had gotten me into the discipline of nonscientific writing. Much more important, the manuscript brought Diane and me together again; and a year later, the two of us—both twice married before and ostensibly permanently disillusioned with the institution of matrimony—got married. While "Middles" was unpublishable, my appetite for writing only increased.

A second novel, though never more than half finished, contained a story within a story; at my wife's suggestion, to acquire the discipline of repeated revision—something I never do in my scientific writing—I converted that material into my first successful short story, which appeared in the *Hudson Review*. This was followed by a summer at Oxford in 1986, a novel experience as a faculty spouse, where my wife taught while I bought the groceries and wrote short stories during the day. *The Futurist and Other Stories*, my first book of fiction, appropriately enough was first published in 1988 in England, where most of the stories were set on paper. One of these short stories became the nucleus of my first novel to appear in the States, *Cantor's Dilemma,* most of which I wrote in the summers of 1987 and 1988 in London, a setting I needed to separate me in both geography and time from my Stanford laboratory and office. Each evening I passed that day's output to my two most loyal and toughest critics, Diane Middlebrook and her daughter, Leah, who has all the makings of another Vocalissima.

In spite of the extraordinary opportunities chemistry made possible for me, and the intense flashes of pleasure I have experienced over the years in my life as a chemist, my ambition is not completely satisfied. In American academic circles, I have remained mostly an outsider. During three decades as a chemistry professor at Stanford University, I published hundreds of papers on our research in organic mass spectrometry, started and finished all of our methodological research in optical and magnetic circular dichroism and computer artificial intelligence, and completed a great deal of structural and biosynthetic work on marine natural products—enough accomplishments for several full-fledged academic careers. I have won many awards and honors—several of them sponsored by the American Chemical Society; but except for that society's Priestley Medal in 1992, all of them have been in recognition of my industrial work or "public service." That this should have bothered me is an example of how a split research career does not necessarily lead to a split personality. An academic scientist's competitive urge and egocentrism usually demand external, public kudos: awards, honorary degrees, lecture invitations—all offered to reward individual achievement. Industrial scientists, on the other hand, largely expect internal rewards from within the corporate family in the form of financial rewards, perks, and promotions. When it came to drive and personal ambition, I seem to have worn mostly my academic cap and gown. Is that why I became hypersensitive to the fact that, during the decades of my Stanford academic tenure, most of my academic recognitions in my adopted country—in contrast to those received from abroad—appeared to me to have been awarded for my industrial contributions?

By the time I reached the ripe age of sixty, I realized that this perceived slight (if, in fact, it was one) irked me. In my personal watershed year of 1985, when a hospital stay enforced on me an unprecedented period of self-reflection, I decided that this worm of dissatisfaction would have to be extirpated if it were not to cheapen and demean what research should be all about. It was impossible for one who worked on the scale and with the intensity to which I had been accustomed to stop abruptly—without affecting the lives of graduate students, postdoctorate fellows, and research associates. But late in 1989, I put on the brakes and let attrition go to work, at precisely the time when I discovered the existence of my own literary reservoir and noted that it was starting to fill.

Writers are hardly ambitionless, but feeling ambitious at the beginning of a new profession, even if late in life, is very different from trying to fill a bottomless cup near the end of a career. I have been reminded, often enough, that writers have problems of their own: the infamous block, when the amphora is dry, not a ping of inspiration resounding; the fear that once the masterpiece is published, no one will read it. But just as I discarded during the first quarter of my life all caution about the professional risk of moving to Mexico, so in my last quarter I am ignoring the well-founded fear of writer's block and the easily imagined humiliation caused by dismissive readers. I did indeed stop playing poker around the time of my bar mitzvah, but at heart I'm still a gambler. It is in this gambling spirit that I intend to pursue one more life—that of a writer working mostly, though not entirely, in a special and, for me, apposite genre: science-*in*-fiction. I feel elated to be embarking on a new intellectual career in my sixties—in one of the few professions where age is an advantage because of the pool of untapped plots a younger author has not yet experienced but can only imagine. None of it would have happened if the love of my life had not broken off with me for a year. Of course, virtually everything worth saying about this topic remains unwritten. But the gap has narrowed.

Index

Index

China, 199, 251

Cholesterol, 34, 104

Chromatography, gas, 90, 159; paper, 61

CIBA, 24–25, 26, 38, 89

Cigarette beetles, 175

Circular dichroism, 102

Clinical trials: effectiveness of, 122–23, 124–26, 129; ethics of, 61–62, 123–24; purpose of, 123–24. *See also* Pill, the

Cockroaches, 179–81

Coffee, chemistry of, 89–91

Cole, Wayne, 25

Collman, James P., 137

Color Purple, The, 293

Colton, Frank D., 58

Columbia University, 73

Congo, Democratic Republic of the, 217–23. *See also* Zaire

Contraception: abortion and, 258; condoms and, 150–51; male, 249–50; menstrual regulation and, 61, 253; progesterone and, 50–51; public health and, 120–21; public perceptions of, 246–47; research and development of, 118–19, 132–34, 241–47, 250, 258, 259–60, 262

Contraceptives, oral: clinical trials of, 61–62; estradiol and, 56–57; ethics of, 61–62; history of, 59–63, 120–21, 132; norsteroids and, 106–7; sexual revolution and, 116; synthesis of, 54, 56–58, 97. *See also* Pill, the; RU-486

Coolidge, Walter H., 23

Cooper, Leon N., 154

Cortisone: publication process and, 41–44, 45–48; structure of, 35–36; synthesis of, 26, 27, 33–34, 36–38, 39–41, 45–46, 89

Creamer, E. M., 115

Crick, Francis, 84

Cross, Alexander, 179, 304

Cross, Tony, 304, 305

Crotty, J. J., 129

Cutler, Walter, 238

Czechoslovakia, 192, 193, 194–95

Dakar, 232

Dalkon shield, 130–31, 244

Davis, Hugh J., 130–31

DDT, 163

de Beauvoir, Simone, 124

Degas, Edgar, 275–78

de Kruif, Paul, 24

Deoxyribonucleic acid (DNA), 84

Deschryver, Adrien, 231

Diabetes, 248

Diekman, John, 162, 181

Diosgenin, 37, 40, 48

Djerassi, Alexander, 301

Djerassi, Alice, 10, 12–13, 68, 302

Djerassi, Carl: art interests of, 275–83, 294; awards, 2, 23, 72, 73, 94, 182, 184, 267, 306; chemistry interests of, 89–95, 97, 100–107; chimpanzees, pygmy, and, 223–26, 227–28, 230, 233–40; clothing of, 264–74; early years, 5–21, 23–24, 264; education of, 16–18, 22–26; family of, 10–11, 12–13, 15, 16, 68–71, 270–71; friends of, 302–3 (*see also individuals by name*); home of, 98–100, 285–6, 292, 293–95; Jewish origins of, 28–32; knee fusion of, 110; marriages of, 66–68, 71, 73–74, 75, 88, 282, 306; mescaline and, 84–88; movie experiences of, 110–17; National Medal of Science and, 72–73; National Medal of Technology and, 184; oral contraception and, 63–65; politics/public policies of, 72, 144, 147, 150, 151, 203, 242–43; professional development of, 24–28, 53–54, 79–81, 91–92, 107, 152–53, 160–61, 241–42, 306–7; Pugwash Conferences and, 187–90, 191, 198–99, 200–207; teaching of, 136–51; travels of (*see individual countries by name*); writings of, 97–98, 107, 195,

311

Thorington, Richard, 225
Thuron Industries, 166–67, 168. *See also* Zoecon Industries
Tishler, Max, 44
Toews, Robin, 287
Toth, Nicholas, 239–40
Tshombe, Moise, 217
Tursch, Ben, 103
Tyler, Edward, 58, 253

Ullman, Edwin, 155
Ulmann, André, 259
United States, and birth control, 260, 263. *See also* Bush, George; Reagan, Ronald
Universidad Nacional Autónoma de México, 92
University of Michigan, 25
University of Rochester, 42, 43
University of Wisconsin, 25
Upjohn Company, 48
Urine analysis, 156–58

Vaccines, 246
Vance, Sheldon, 233
van Tamelen, Eugene, 137
Varian Associates, 155
Vaughan, Josefa, 294
Verhulst, Henry L., 128
Verschuren, Jacques, 236
Vietnam, 157
Villotti, Riccardo, 91
Voss, John, 189

Walesa, Lech, 204, 207
Walker, Alice, 293
Wang, Shirley, 151
Washton, Nathan, 17
Watson, James, 84
Wayne (State) University, 60, 79–81, 89, 91–93, 137

Waxman, Henry A., 246
Wilds, Alfred L., 25
Williams, Carroll M., 159, 160, 189
Williamson, Byron, 166
Williamson, Thurman, 166
Wittgenstein, Ludwig, 7–8
Women: Pill and, 124–26, 132, 248–49; students, as, 150–51
Woodward, Robert Burns, 41, 43, 44, 46
Worcester Foundation for Experimental Biology, 49, 58–59
World Health Organization, 62, 134, 149, 166, 237, 260

X-ray crystallography, 103–4, 141
X-ray diffraction, 84

Yams. *See* Cortisone, synthesis of
Yerkes, Robert, 235
Yerkes Regional Primate Research Center, 225, 230, 233, 234–37, 239
Young, Brenda Jo, 146–47
Young, Neil, 285, 286
Yu, Jennifer, 151

Zaffaroni, Alejandro: ALZA and, 160; movie-making and, 111, 114, 117; norethindrone and, 63; Syntex and, 61, 154, 161, 253; Synvar Associates and, 155; wardrobe of, 265–66
Zaire, 225–30, 231, 233, 237, 238. *See also* Chimpanzees, pygmy; Congo, Democratic Republic of the
Zaslavsky, Boris, 209, 215
Zionism, 93
Zoecon, 154, 158–59, 160–62, 166–68, 170, 173–79, 183–84
Zoecon Industries, 168. *See also* Thuron Industries